OCTAVIA HILL

A Biography

OCTAVIA HILL IN 1902.

(*From a Photograph by Fredk. Hollyer*).

OCTAVIA HILL

A Biography by

E. MOBERLY BELL

With a Foreword
by
SIR REGINALD ROWE
President of the National Federation
of Housing Societies
and
Eight Illustrations

CONSTABLE & CO LTD
LONDON

PUBLISHED BY
Constable and Company Ltd.
LONDON
.
The Macmillan Company
of Canada, Limited
TORONTO

First Published September 1942
Second Impression (corrected) March 1943

PRINTED IN GREAT BRITAIN BY ROBERT MACLEHOSE AND CO. LTD.
THE UNIVERSITY PRESS, GLASGOW

CONTENTS

v

CONTENTS

ILLUSTRATIONS

FOREWORD

by

SIR REGINALD ROWE

HITHERTO Octavia Hill has been known to this generation chiefly through selections which have been made from her letters and put into print. It is high time and the right time for the full story of her life to be published. It is now almost thirty years since her death and just over a century since her birth, and we are reaping more and more of the rich and varied harvest that has sprung from her labours. After long association with housing activities in this country, I am fully convinced that the best of all that is now being done for the better housing of the poor has had for its origin and inspiration the life-work of this remarkable Englishwoman. I doubt if in the fields of human service there has been any other woman who has sown seeds from which so much has grown and is still growing. In a sense she was never more alive than to-day.

The remarkable change in the last three quarters of a century in the nation's attitude towards the housing problem has not been due to the foresight and benevolent intentions of those in authority, but to the drive of public opinion which has forced Parliament and Local Authorities to recognize and pay attention to conditions to which for very long they were blind. It was Octavia Hill more than anyone else who, little by little, fighting not only inertia but obstruction at almost every step, stirred public opinion to life and at last made it effectively alive in demanding that a disgraceful state of things should be remedied. By precept, by pointing again and again at a true picture, she forced people to realize that the poorer sections of the community lived in conditions of which all should be ashamed; and by degrees more and more thoughtful persons became ashamed. By example, she showed in the most practical ways how the evils which she exposed could be cured.

Octavia Hill's life was in the ordinary sense of the word unspectacular (she would have hated it to be spectacular, hating above all things to attract notice to herself), but both her work and her character were so remarkable that all that is known about them should be of interest to very many. I feel that Chapter VI, 'Beginning of Housing', is in a category by itself and should be of *universal* interest, because it tells what seems to me the beginning of an epic, and most excitingly to those eager to make a better world and anxious to learn how anyone by persistent effort may change 'the shape of things to come'. The unprecedented feat of buying three slum houses, with the slummiest of tenants, and by sheer business ability and greatness of heart turning them, without any monetary loss, into decent dwellings, and their pig-like occupants into decent folk, refuted for ever the lie of the slum-landlord, heard even to-day, that it is useless to give better homes to the poorest because were they palaces their inhabitants would turn them into pig-sties. It should be borne in mind that it was an essential aim of Octavia Hill to make not only the houses of the poor better but by friendly contact to better the lives of their inmates, to give these humiliated men and women self-respect, a feeling of independence, and a pride in good homes that would make them anxious to preserve them. This contact, she maintained, must be a friendship on level terms, with no hint of superiority in the relation of manager to tenant. She condemned the adoption by the charitable not only of a patronising attitude but of all patronising thought, and disapproved of what she regarded as the contemptuous generosity of promiscuous almsgiving. She stoutly denied that the duty of the rich to the poor can be commuted for cash. In fact she valued money hardly at all (though for many years she lived personally in sore need of it) except in so far as it served her beneficent purposes.

The small successful experiment which she made in 1864, when she bought in Paradise Place her first three houses, led to the saving from degradation of the large areas in London which were under her management before her death. It also led during her lifetime to similar work in other cities both in this country and abroad, and by example it has led to all the better housing that is so widely approved and proudly advertised to-day. But Octavia Hill not only revolutionized housing policy, she was a pioneer in the cause of general betterment in many other, and most important, ways, as is told in the later chapters of this book. To take a single instance, the National Trust, which now plays so notable a part in saving from the building speculator and preserving in perpetuity for the common use and benefit beautiful stretches of country, owes its origin largely to her efforts and her passion for 'the healing gift of space'.

I met Octavia Hill in 1899, in connection with the inauguration of the Improved Tenements Association. We had asked for her advice and help. I was struck especially by that notable feature of hers, her brown, and somehow bird-like, eyes, which looked straight at you and quietly into you, and was impressed as much by her quite unassuming though decisive manner as by her compelling knowledge and good sense. She set our scheme on its feet, and allowed us the use of one of her rent-collecting managers to look after the four houses we first bought. Since then the Association has gone expandingly ahead and now owns some hundreds of houses in the poorest parts of North Kensington. There is much work of this kind which, though inspired by her, is beyond the scope of any record of her direct achievements.

In character Octavia Hill was both simple and complex, as will be obvious to anyone who has studied her published letters. Her guiding principle was perfectly simple: it was to do what she believed to be right, judged searchingly by the highest standard. Her mentality was complex. She was quaintly Victorian to present thinking in some ways, more advanced than we are to-day in others. 'In many things,' Miss Moberly Bell truly writes, 'Octavia was not only ahead of her own generation but ahead of ours.' The finer points of her character are skilfully portrayed and examined in the chapters that follow. What strikes me most forcibly as very exceptional in her make-up is that such profound humility should have accompanied such powers of leadership and command. She managed everybody, but, being incapable of self-admiration, was genuinely surprised that people should think so highly of her. 'I wish someone would explode me,' she wrote to a sister at a time when the value of her work was being widely recognized. At an earlier date she had amusedly assured Ruskin that her family considered her 'good only to do a sum, carry a weight, go a long walk in the rain, or decide any difficult question about tangible things'. Two other of her qualities cannot escape the most casual reader's notice. She was completely unselfseeking, and had indomitable courage, both physical and moral. The former quality is revealed in every action of her life, the latter whenever occasion called for it. She walked fearlessly and unscathed in 'Courts' dreaded by the police, and was never daunted by failure. ('It is on defeats,' she wrote, 'that victories are built.') One more point. To any reader who may imagine that isolated from her achievements Octavia Hill was just an ordinarily good woman I commend for consideration her attitude towards Ruskin after their quarrel, in which his behaviour towards her was to my mind inexcusable on the ground of his ill-health or any other.

I maintain that the story of Octavia Hill should be known to the rising generation in every school, and that it should be studied, and thoughtfully studied, by all those who believe, as I do, that to the greatness of our country the lives of its noblest men and women are the essential contributory leaven.

INTRODUCTION

OCTAVIA HILL died in 1912. A Biography by her brother-in-law, C. Edmund Maurice, was published in 1913. It was perhaps too soon to make an estimate of her work, and the deep reserve of her character had made so strong an impression on her family and friends that her biographer undertook his task reluctantly, and was unwilling to reveal her personality in any fullness. He took the course therefore of compiling a book of extracts from her letters, arranged chronologically, and linking them by a very brief narrative with explanatory notes. As most of the letters which he used were subsequently destroyed, this book must of necessity be the quarry from which any life of Octavia Hill is derived, and I have quoted from it very freely.

The Centenary Celebration of Octavia Hill's birth (December, 1938) gave rise to a demand for some fuller account of her life, some more complete presentation of her personality and some estimate of her contribution to the national life. This demand, at the request of her surviving relations, I have endeavoured to meet.

Other books to which I owe valuable help are:

Octavia Hill—Early Ideals. A series of letters edited by her sister E. S. Maurice (1928).

Life of Sophia Jex-Blake by Margaret Todd;

and Octavia's own writings:

'Letters to my Fellow Workers', published privately annually from 1871–1911.

'Homes of the London Poor', 1875; 'Our Common Land', 1877; magazine articles reprinted by Mac-Millan.

These are now out of print.

I have further made use of and carefully studied Octavia's evidence given to the Royal Commission on Housing, 1884, and the Report of the Royal Commission on the Poor Law, 1908.

I would express my thanks to all who have helped me, and first of all to *Mrs. Ouvry*, who has not only put at my disposal many hitherto unpublished letters and memoranda, but has also given me her own recollections of her aunt, with whom for many years she worked in the closest intimacy, and introduced me to other of Octavia's friends and fellow workers, and to some of the pupils of the Nottingham Place School. Finally she has read all that I have written, and I may therefore hope to have avoided inaccuracy and misunderstanding. Among the papers Mrs. Ouvry has given me are:

An account of Octavia's life up to 1870 by Miranda Hill.
A MS. entitled 'Early Life and Influences on the Training of Octavia Hill', by her mother, C. S. Hill.
'Memories of Octavia', by Margaret Howitt.
'A Remembrance of Octavia Hill', by Mary Vidal Stone.

Others to whom I am greatly indebted for the loan of unpublished letters are:

Sir Sydney Cockerell for a matchless series of letters addressed to his father, to his sister, and to himself, dating from 1873–1912.

Mrs. Lee for a most valuable series of letters to Mary Harrison, covering the years 1855-63, with a few of a later date.

Mrs. Macdonell for two series of letters. One from Octavia to Mary Harris, chiefly between 1870–75, though a few are later; and one from Miranda to Mary Harris, 1881–89.

Lady Troup for a series of letters to her father George MacDonald, 1873–1904, and to members of his family.

Sister Mary Christobel for a series of letters to her mother Mrs. Stone, 1876–83.

Single letters for which I am very grateful were lent by Major H. R. Yorke, M.C., Mrs. Bowen, and Miss Tabor.

At the time of the Centenary celebrations, an Exhibition to illustrate Octavia's life and activities was shown at the Housing Centre, Suffolk Street, S.W.1. All the material then collected has been at my disposal, and I would thank Miss Lupton, who made the Exhibition, the Housing Centre, and all who contributed to it.

E. MOBERLY BELL

Midhurst, May, 1941

NOTE TO SECOND IMPRESSION

Sir Sidney Cockerell has pointed out to me that Miranda, in her letter to Mary Harris quoted on p. 244 below, was mistaken in saying that Ruskin read aloud "the next unpublished number of *Fors*." *Fors Clavigera* had come to an end and it must have been *Praeterita* from which Ruskin read. Rather than alter the text of Miranda's letter, I record her slip in this prefatory note.

E.M.B.

December, 1942

Chapter I

VICTORIAN CHILDHOOD

'I am so happy, you don't know how happy':
OCTAVIA TO HER MOTHER, June, 1849

THERE are signs that the Victorian age, so long regarded as a period fit only for derision and contempt, is coming into its own. It has found historians who affirm that a belief in its complacency cannot survive more than a very superficial and cursory study of the period; that, on the contrary, its most marked characteristic was a concentration of intelligence on the maladies of the age which resulted in the foundations being laid of the immense fabric of social legislature in which we are living.

There remains, however, a very general belief that for the Victorian family there is nothing to be said. The Barrett family is taken as the norm, and thence is derived a picture of family life without dignity, freedom or affection, in which hypocritical and tyrannical parents repressed and bullied large families of resentful but subservient children. Since, however, Elizabeth Barrett was thirty-one in the year in which Queen Victoria ascended the throne, it would perhaps be more reasonable not to found an indictment against the Victorian family on her unfortunate circumstances. Actually there is plenty of evidence for the defence, and an age like our own, given to the study of psychology, and insisting perpetually on the fatal effects of repression and unhappiness in childhood, should at least pause in its condemnation to ask how it came to pass that families so deplorably wrong actually produced so many remarkable men and women.

It may be that the popular conception of Victorian domesticity is also superficial. It is certain, if one may judge from biographies and volumes of reminiscences, that many Victorians positively enjoyed their childhood and believed that they had gained something very precious from the calm, well-regulated days which, within an iron framework of punctual meals, duties and bed-times, yet left plenty of leisure, untroubled by grown-ups, for absurd adventures and pretences and for the cheerful rough and tumble of brothers and sisters. It may be that all the advantages are not with the child of to-day, so often an only one, conscientiously understood by a highly trained nurse, and living always 'with light upon him from his father's eyes'.

Be that as it may, for better or worse, the Victorian family was a very closely knit unit; its members accepted a common tradition and mutual responsibilities. They might, as they grew up, abandon both, but they could not altogether escape from the influence of the early days shared together and the experience of their corporate life. There were some who never wished to escape from either, whose gratitude to and sense of responsibility for their families only increased year by year. Octavia Hill was one of these, and this being so, any record of her life must begin with some account of the family from which she sprang.

It was distinguished on both sides for public service. The Hills were long established near Peterborough as farmers and merchants. Octavia's grandfather was a banker, a man of wealth and importance, and her father, James Hill, grew up in affluence. He had, however, no love of luxury; he was methodical and business-like, and having

2

allotted himself a fixed weekly sum for household expenses, he proceeded to live simply enough to save money out of it for buying books.

The early nineteenth century was not an easy time for bankers, and in the panic of 1825 the family bank, like many another, closed its doors. James Hill was not unduly cast down by this misfortune; he set to work to repair it, and established a business in Corn and Wool. He was a very able business man and a very hard worker—possessed indeed of an almost superhuman energy. Not content with building up a new business, he flung himself into every sort of public work. He was a man of large and liberal views and of high principle, and his own interests always came second to those of others. 'Every shower of rain makes me a thousand pounds richer,' he is reported to have said, and then to have added, after a moment's reflection: 'How one hates that it should be by the people's food becoming dearer.' The sincerity of this regret is shown by the fact that he worked wholeheartedly with Cobden and Bright for the repeal of the Corn Laws. He braved considerable unpopularity in Wisbech by his struggles against corruption in the local government, but he lived down the opposition, and his efforts were so successful that when the Municipal Reform Bill came into operation, Wisbech was honourably distinguished by the fact that it needed practically no reform.

He had many irons in the fire. He was interested in education and had some conception that it meant more than merely teaching children laboriously to spell out words and add up figures. He realized that small children need teaching methods widely different from those appropriate to their elders, and therefore he built one of the first

3

Infants' schools in England, that these methods might be applied. He founded a penny paper in order to have some organ in which to advocate social reforms, and at one time he bought a theatre and invited good companies to play in it. He secured Macready among others, and entertained him. Like his daughter after him, he was indefatigable to serve any individual in need, and it is recorded that the last man who was condemned to death for sheep stealing owed his life to James Hill, who rode fifty miles to secure his pardon.

In 1832 James Hill's second wife died. Being left with a son and five daughters, it became necessary for him to find someone to educate and care for these children. He had been greatly interested in some articles on education by Caroline Southwood Smith; now he sought her out and persuaded her to become the governess to his girls. A most happy relationship ensued. When in 1835 she became his wife, her pupils felt nothing but happiness at becoming her step-daughters. There followed five years of happy activity. Caroline Hill shared all her husband's interests. She bore him three daughters: Miranda in 1836, Gertrude in 1837 and Octavia in 1838.

Soon after Octavia's birth, the clouds began to gather again on the horizon. For two years James Hill made the most strenuous efforts, by economizing at home, by working late and early, to save his business, but it was all in vain. In 1840 he became bankrupt and having built up his fortunes from nothing, he saw himself once more without resources, unable even to pay his debts. He may have derived some comfort from the sympathy of his neighbours —the Commissioners sent Mrs. Hill a message of 'respecful recognition of the economy of the household expendi-

4

ture in all the past years'—but nothing could avert the break-up of the home, which had been so happy. The children of the earlier marriages went to their maternal grandfathers. Dr. Southwood Smith adopted Gertrude, the second little girl, and settled the rest of the family in a cottage at Epping, where the fourth daughter, Emily, was born.

For some years James Hill and his wife managed to keep the rest of the family together. It was an anxious time. They moved from Epping to Hampstead, to Gloucester and then to Leeds, where a fifth daughter, Florence, was born in 1843. In all these places Mr. Hill tried to mend his broken fortunes and his wife with extraordinary courage seconded his efforts and kept their children untouched by misfortune. It is related that a friend, coming to call on them in Hampstead and being uncertain of the address, identified the house by the sight of three little girls dancing round a rose-bush.

Octavia was already a remarkable little creature. She had inherited something of her father's energy; she wished for a field 'so large that I could run in it for ever'. She was so gay and vital that, her mother writes: 'She can scarcely walk, she goes leaping as if she were a little Kangaroo.' She was obviously intelligent. Not only did she spend a great deal of time every day reading to herself before she was five (a feat not so unusual a hundred years ago as it is today), but she was writing fluent letters: 'We have a box full of silks; I gave Miranda a beautiful piece; it was velvet and the colours were black, purple, yellow, white and green. Miranda gave me a beautiful piece of crimson plush.' She had also a grasp of words and energy of expression not very common in so young a child. Something she did not like

5

was 'ugly as coal', she was 'as hot as if I were on fire', and being bothered with the fastening of her shoes she declared she could not accomplish it 'if I tried till the world was knocked down'. More remarkable still is a pun recorded of her before she was five. When her father said to her: 'Take care or you will have a downfall,' she replied: 'That I should not mind, if the down was there when I fell.' This nimbleness of wit and mastery of words are so unexpected in so young a child that were it not recorded in a letter of her mother's dated 1843 one would imagine it to be part of a later legend.

By the time Octavia was five Mr. Hill's increasing ill health and depression made it obvious that he could no longer hope to support his family. Shortly afterwards he had a complete mental and physical breakdown, and though later he made a partial recovery, he lived always very quietly in retirement and was never again able to take any responsibility for his children. Mrs. Hill then was left with five little girls, of whom the eldest was eight—with no means at all of supporting them. Fortunately for all of them, her father, Dr. Southwood Smith, who had already adopted one child, was ready to undertake the responsibility for the whole family. He now became a very important person in the lives of the Hills.

He was indeed a person of no small importance in the world of his day. For some twenty years he had been working with single-hearted devotion at various social problems. He had taken part in the agitation for improving factory conditions, and in particular had been concerned about the employment of children in mines. But his principal achievement was in the matter of sanitary reform. As a doctor attached to the fever hospital with a large practice

DR. SOUTHWOOD SMITH
(GRANDFATHER OF OCTAVIA HILL).

in the East End, he was early convinced that the fever epidemics which so constantly swept over the poorer parts of London were due to the insanitary conditions in which the poor lived. This proposition, to us so self-evident, aroused storms of protest. Those who were making money out of bad houses, those in authority in local government who feared they might be forced to *do* something, all became vocal in their belief that fever epidemics were the Act of God, and that, in any case, the poor liked to live in insanitary squalor, and in the name of liberty must be allowed to do so. Dr. Southwood Smith was not the man to be defeated by vested interests and the dead weight of apathy. This is not the place to record his struggle against them; suffice it to say that it was almost entirely due to him that the prevention of insanitary conditions was recognized as a public duty, and that at last the responsibility of the state for public health was accepted. Thence followed the passing of the first Public Health Act in 1848, and the establishment of a General Board of Health—the egg from which the Ministry of Health with its wide powers and responsibilities has in our own day been hatched.

But while the details of the struggle have little bearing on the matter in hand, the personality of the man, Octavia's grandfather and guardian, is of great importance to it. His achievements bear testimony to his public spirit, his pertinacity and his indefatigable energy. These qualities were of less significance to his grandchildren than the 'daily beauty in his life'. He was a man of singularly sweet temperament; he did not allow himself to be embittered by the factiousness of opposition, nor wearied and discouraged by the slow progress of his schemes. The children found in him an evenness of temperament, a serenity, which was very reassuring, and Gertrude has recorded that as a small child she watched the intense concentration with which he worked, recognizing dimly that this work in which he was absorbed was of the greatest importance, and somehow beneficent. When he laid his work aside, he was able to turn with equal zest to his grandchildren, nor did he make the mistake so common to grown-ups of treating them as playthings, to be talked down to and patronized. He knew they were individuals, and that their concerns and problems were as real and important to them as sanitary reform was to him.

But important as their grandfather was to the Hill children, the most potent influence in their lives was no doubt that of their mother, Caroline Southwood Hill. It has been said that her articles on education had first made her known to James Hill. In them is revealed a woman of great intellectual and moral power, very far ahead of her generation in educational theory.

She was, like her husband, a Unitarian, and a deeply religious woman. She rarely spoke of her faith, but all who came in contact with her were conscious of its power. Life had not been easy for her; indeed, it was never to be so. She was sustained by an iron will and a certain austerity which made her unable to conceive the possibility of failing to do what one recognized to be one's duty. So now, in the little cottage at Finchley in which her father had established them, she set to work to make a home for her children. She was not one of those women who delight in running a house, who get real pleasure from seeing how comfortable a home can be made on very little money. Though she was extremely competent, her interests were intellectual rather than practical. But the path of duty was plain;

8

she could not afford servants, she must do all herself, educate her daughters and see to it that in due time they should be qualified to support themselves.

She faced the uncertain future with unruffled serenity. 'Life begins in happiness,' she had written in her Notes on Education, 'and this instructs us how we ought to endeavour that it should continue.' No doubt when Caroline Hill laid down this precept, happiness had seemed easier of attainment, but she was true to it now. She could not give her daughters luxuries, nor indeed much that to most people seem necessities, but she gave them the only things that really matter for children, a sense of security and the power of finding happiness in simple things. She was determined that no material anxiety should cloud their minds; she never talked about food, or dress, or money problems with them, and she hid from them whatever contrivance and care was needed to make ends meet. Being told one day that walking on some heaps of flints by the roadside would wear out her shoes, Octavia answered loftily: 'Do you think I'd be so *mean* as to mind that?'—a childish magnificence embarrassing, no doubt, to the mother who had to pay the bills for shoe-mending—yet perhaps it is only those who have been carefree about money in childhood who can be altogether generous about it when they grow up.

There was no end to the pleasures the children could find. Caroline Hill had touched the essence of the matter when she wrote, in Notes on Education: 'A child should be placed in circumstances where it can neither do harm nor suffer harm; then it should be left to its own devices.' The 'circumstances' were close at hand. Finchley was in those days a pleasant village surrounded by fields and commons; it was here that the sisters could safely be left to their own devices. They were out in all weathers; they were known in Finchley as 'the young ladies who are always up in the hedges'—there was always something to see and to do; the fields were full of flowers and the hedges of one treasure or another.

They had only toys they had devised and made for themselves; they invented their own games; they acted; they wrote and recited poetry. Octavia was the leader; she generally wrote the plays and always wrote the directions for playing the games; the others followed her unquestioningly. On one occasion all her sisters were fastened by a cord tied round her waist, and she ran them violently down the meadow and leapt over the brook at the bottom—forgetting that while she landed on the bank the tail must inevitably land in the brook. But if she led them into danger, it was also she who saved them when a crisis occurred. Before Octavia was six, in the course of a ramble with her sisters, Gertrude jumped into what she thought to be a drift of fallen beech leaves, but the floating leaves covered a deep pond. While Miranda shouted for help, Octavia stepped on to a stone and extended a stick to her sister and succeeded in pulling her out. On another occasion it was Emily who fell head foremost into a water-butt in which she and Octavia were sailing walnut shells, and it was Octavia who, rushing back to get the necessary momentum, flung herself up on the edge of the butt, overbalanced it, and rescued the dripping Emily. The younger sisters regarded her as the fount of all wisdom. 'Ockey, is that dog happy?' Florence asked in complete confidence of her omniscience. The world was full of interest; there were all sorts of things to do. The village carpenter taught her his craft and found her 'wonderfully handy'—gardeners allowed her to help them, everyone was friendly. 'They know every boy and girl, cat, dog and donkey in the village by sight, and a good many of them by name, and for those whose names they do not know they invent one.'

Of formal education the children had none or very little. They were encouraged to read, and all, but especially Octavia, did so voraciously. Mrs. Hill supervised the reading and forbade anything that should teach them of the sin, evil and misery in the world. She believed that by taking this course she would establish within the children's minds the conviction that the principle of the world is good, then when they met evil, they would regard it with abhorrence as something so contrary to the mind of God that it could have no power over them or over the world and thus they would be strong to overcome it. No doubt there is much to be said for this method, and a happy confidence in the goodness of the world is an immensely valuable starting point for a child. But perhaps Mrs. Hill underestimated the severity of the shock which they sustained on their first contact with the uglier side of human nature.

Mrs. Hill read the English classics with her children, and encouraged all their efforts in composition. Apart from this she left them to educate themselves. This they did with a zest for learning that continued all their lives. At one time they instituted a school for their dolls (paper figures, cut out, painted and named by them) and this involved so much real hard work—learning French, History and Geography, and then producing suitable lesson books for the pupils—that Mrs. Hill felt obliged to check the game lest they should over-tire themselves. But happy children are not easily over-tired, and the house rang with the gay laughter of the sisters; Octavia's laugh remained always a joyous memory in the hearts of all that heard it. 'Miranda is . . . full of life and fun and has the same kind of ringing joyous laugh as Ockey, the same in spirit, though not in degree. . . . Ockey's laugh is the happiest and sweetest I ever heard.'

There were pleasures too, to be found farther afield, notably in the expeditions to Hillside, their grandfather's house at Highgate. Here they enjoyed the companionship of their sister, Gertrude, who, at this time, was Octavia's closest friend and companion. The two little girls sometimes helped their grandfather by making copies for him of reports or articles on sanitary reform, and thus at a very early age Octavia became familiar with some of the problems to whose solution her life was to be given. Young as she was, she grasped the significance of the documents she studied. Some twenty years later, she remembered an Order in Council relating to tenement houses which she had learned of in this way, and finding it was still valid, though it had been overlooked by Building Societies, applied it—to the great advantage of her tenants—a striking testimony not only to the retentiveness of her memory, but also to the precocity of her childish mind.

The joys of Hillside were many and various—Highgate was really the country in those days, the house was beautifully situated and looked over Caen Woods, with only Lord Mansfield's Park between the house and the wood. There was a farm, with all that means of happiness for children; a pony, an orchard of wonderful apple-trees, haymaking in the summer, an endless procession of delightful days. When the weather was at all possible they had all their meals out of doors, breakfast in the summer-house, dinner in the garden, dessert in the field where the view was best.

There were generally guests in the house; Dr. Southwood Smith was a most hospitable person, and as his work proceeded and his reputation increased, more and more people sought his advice and became his friends. Thus Hillside became a meeting-place for all who were interested in the social questions of the day, and since inevitably it is the most intelligent people who concern themselves with such things, there was always good company and good talk at Dr. Southwood Smith's table. The Hill children mixed freely in this society; too simple to be shy or awkward, they listened with eager interest to all that was said, and sometimes were even included in the conversation. Browning, who met them there, told Octavia many years later that another guest had said to him: 'Those are wonderful children, you can talk to them about anything.'

To Octavia, the discussions of her elders were of absorbing interest. At an age when most children are immersed in their own childish joys and sorrows, she was filled with compassion for a world that seemed to go so wrong; her vivid imagination and quick sympathy were easily stirred. The potato famine in Ireland moved her to an agony of feeling, and one night the sharer of her bedroom woke up to find her sitting up rigid in bed. 'What are you about, Ockey?' she asked. 'Praying for Poland,' was the fervent reply. All her life she was to feel the sorrows of others with a quite unusual intensity.

Among Dr. Southwood Smith's friends were William and Mary Howitt. They were prolific writers, both jointly and separately, of some reputation in their own day. Mary Howitt, among other things, translated Hans Andersen, and William wrote history and popular science books for boys. They travelled a great deal, but between 1845 and

1850 they were living at Highgate and the Hill children were invited to a party there in 1846. Thence arose a close friendship between the two families. The two youngest Howitt children in particular became Octavia's playmates. Charlton was a little older, and Margaret a little younger than Octavia. The three children shared the delightful fantasies of childhood; it was in their company that Octavia was found looking for fairies, and on being asked if she had seen any replied with conviction: 'No, but I'm *sure* I *shall*.' With them she performed nightly rites of propitiation of goblins whom they had located in the cellar. They passed happy days playing together, and since the friendship was approved and encouraged by the parents on both sides they had many opportunities of developing the intimacy. Mrs. Howitt invited Miranda and Octavia to stay with her children, and Margaret in her turn stayed with the Hills. Mrs. Howitt had a great admiration for Mrs. Hill, and especially for the way she was bringing up her children. 'We find Maggie much improved by Mrs. Hill's kind care of her,' she wrote after a visit, 'and by her intercourse with those dear little children.' For Octavia she developed a very special affection. 'Ockey goes on beautifully,' she wrote to Mrs. Hill. 'We are all charmed with her, and know not how we shall part with her.'

Octavia responded with whole-hearted devotion to this affection. The Howitts had an easier life than her own, they were better off, Mrs. Howitt was less busy than Mrs. Hill, perhaps more demonstrative. Octavia delighted in the peaceful home-like atmosphere and in after years turned again and again in memory to the days spent under the Howitts' roof. 'I shall never forget the atmosphere of love . . . in the long winter evenings with her, I used to sit on a little stool at her feet, she used to take down my hair and I can feel her soft, gentle touch . . . can see the firelight flicker on her face as she worked and Mr. Howitt read.' There were happy summer days too. Mr. Howitt took her for walks, and showed her where to find rare flowers and plants and taught her much about the countryside; she was a delightful companion eager to learn and appreciative of all the beauty around them. There were joyous activities, 'It is so delicious bathing; we stay in so long and try to float and splash and dash and prance and dance—I am so happy: you don't know how happy—they are all so sweet and kind to me, and it's so beautiful here.'

But the shades of the prison house were already closing round the children. In 1849 Miranda, having attained the age of thirteen, was already beginning to earn as a pupil teacher in a private school. Not for much longer might the 'little kangaroo' bound in freedom over fields and commons of Finchley; hard realities must be faced. But she had had her hour of freedom, and she had learned much from it. What were her assets in facing the stern struggle which lay before her? A tremendous fund of healthy energy, an eager curiosity about the world, quick imaginative sympathy, a sensitive appreciation of any sort of beauty, and underlying all, a deep sense of duty, an attitude of mind which Miranda says all her children learned from Caroline Hill, 'an attitude of mind, that if a thing was right it must be done; there ceased to be any question about it.' Octavia, like any happily brought up child, was without any misgivings about the future. She faced it gallantly enough— eager to taste new experiences, ready to meet whatever might come.

Chapter II

LONDON—AGONIES AND EXULTATIONS

'Do you think I ever shall be able to do anything really useful?'
                                    OCTAVIA TO MIRANDA, 14th June, 1852

IT has been left to our own age to discover adolescence, for
though no doubt, earlier generations passed from childhood to manhood through its dizzy rapture and devastating despair, becoming painfully conscious of new emo-
tions dimly understood, of new problems too complex for
dispassionate contemplation, it would seem that no particular attention was paid to the difficulties of that stage of
development, that the child was expected at the appropriate moment to lay aside childish things and to take his
place—albeit a subordinate one—in the affairs of real life.
For many a girl that appropriate moment came only with
matrimony and she passed from the shelter of her father's
house to the control of her husband's.

With the Hill children the case was far otherwise. Mrs.
Hill was naturally anxious that the family should as soon
as possible cease to be dependent on her father; the children, as soon as they were old enough, shared this anxiety.
Miranda began to earn when she was thirteen, and as Octavia approached her 'teens' it was clear that the time had
come to launch her. She for her part was nothing loth. Her
adventurous spirit, full of energy, conscious perhaps of
latent powers, eagerly embraced the prospect of a new way
of life; she was ready for anything. Her half-sister, Margaret, offered to take her as a pupil-teacher in her own

16

school, and start her in that way; a friend of the family, Margaret Gillies, an artist, offered to train her in her studio. Octavia thought either would be delightful. Mrs. Hill hesitated, she wanted very much to keep the family together and either of these openings would have involved parting with the child.

While she hesitated a new idea presented itself. It was not on the face of it a very promising idea, though no doubt it seemed more attractive in 1851 than it would do to-day. It arose from an exhibition of 'consolidated glass'. This appears to have been glass painted and then consolidated by a hard composition put at the back which made it strong enough to bear a weight. The patentee, Miss Wallace, a philanthropist, was concerned to provide employment for poor ladies and offered to train such in the art. Mrs. Hill thought that this might be a suitable opening for Miranda, whose dreamy nature was thought to require some practical training and for Octavia, whose artistic gift was highly thought of by all her family and friends. She consequently applied for a training for both girls; Miss Wallace accepted them but shortly afterwards, finding herself unable to manage the business, she handed over the patent to Mr. Vansittart Neale who had recently joined the Christian Socialists.

The work of the Christian Socialists has been strangely undervalued, perhaps the very success of their movement has contributed to this. The social side of the Gospel is not nowadays likely to be ignored, it seems to-day almost impossible to believe that when the Christian Socialists preached it, they were met with furious abuse and were accused of stirring up revolution, because they maintained that there are rights inherent in humanity and that these

3

must be conceded even to those dangerous people, the Lower Classes. The complete change in the outlook of the Church on social problems is in no small measure due to the heroic work of Frederick Denison Maurice and his followers. In 1851 the Christian Socialists were engaged in founding associations for co-operative production, by means of which they hoped to secure to the workers a fair share of the profits of their labours. Hitherto the associations had been for the working classes, but Maurice was well aware of the needs of others. The problem of the 'distressed Gentlewoman' was a very real one in an age in which matrimony was the only obvious career for a girl, and no steps were taken to make her self-supporting. The patent for consolidated glass seemed to provide an industry which might absorb some of these unfortunate ladies, and a Ladies' Co-operative Guild was formed to produce it.

Caroline Hill was well known both through her father and through her own writings, and when a manager of the Guild was required, the post was offered to her. She of course accepted joyfully. It was exactly what she wanted but had hardly dared to hope for; it offered her a position in which she could support her children without leaving home, as well as a training for her two elder daughters. The Guild was established in Russell Place, Fitzroy Square, and thither the family was transported, full of high hopes for the future. There is always something inspiriting to the young in the idea of being grown up and making a start in the world; there is a certain glamour in London. Octavia stood on the threshold of her new life full of eager anticipation.

The shock of the reality was all the greater. Years afterwards in a letter Octavia refers to this as the time when 'the full weight of London's misery and desolation fell upon me'. The child was only thirteen. She was plunged suddenly into wholly new conditions; from the homely little cottage and garden at Finchley, into a house, tall and rather dark in an unlovely street, large enough for the work of the Guild, and therefore rather too large for comfortable family life; from the freedom of outdoor life and a friendly relationship with all the neighbours to the constraint necessary when streets were ill-lighted and far less adequately policed than they are to-day; from an existence untroubled by knowledge of wealth or want, to one surrounded by evidence of crushing and sordid poverty. She had accepted the world so joyfully, with perfect confidence in the rightness of things; now her faith was shaken, the foundation of her happiness undermined. A worker at the Guild lent her Mayhew's *London Labour and the London Poor*, and this book revealing the intensity and extent of the evils she had already divined, added to her despair. Thirteen years later she revisited the house. 'There,' she wrote, 'the first knowledge of misery and poverty came to me, the first real feeling of poverty for ourselves. . . . There . . . I had sat and watched, through the great windows, the London poor pass in rain and fog. There I sat and cried . . . at the remembrance of Tottenham Court Road on Saturday night, with its haggard faces. There the first awful wonder about why evil was permitted came to me, and I remember well saying "Miranda, I don't believe in a resurrection or that if there were one it would be any blessing, because a little rest for one's brain would be the best thing. It would be very hard to get up and begin questioning and wondering again." '

In this unhappy state the fact that Miranda, three years older and perhaps by nature less passionate, could still laugh and joke as she went about her work seemed intolerable. Octavia could not understand it, it seemed wrong to be able to laugh while people were suffering so bitterly. In vain Miranda tried to coax or tease her out of her misery. She composed an imaginary epitaph on herself, supposed to be written by Octavia which ran:

' Her foibles were many, her virtues were few:
  And the more that she laughed, the more stern
    the world grew.'

Octavia was not amused. The world was black and those who ought to know better could still laugh and pursue frivolous ends. Poor little Octavia!

But fortunately, though suffering at the age of thirteen is as black and devastating as at any other period of life, it is not as a rule very lasting. The friend who had introduced Mayhew to the sisters, had also given them some of the pamphlets and essays by the leaders of the Christian Socialists. These Octavia perused eagerly and since they suggested means of combating the evils which so greatly distressed her, they brought some comfort. Eager to learn more, she attended the lectures at the Hall of Association and presently, with Emily, she acquired the habit of attending Lincoln's Inn Chapel where Maurice regularly preached.

Hitherto she had had no definite religious teaching; her mother had, from principle, been silent on the subject. 'God can only be seen by us through his works,' she had written. 'No system can succeed which shuts out God, which, in fact, does not make Him the centre of all its doings . . . but I must advocate putting off all mention of God, all prayers, as long as possible, provided the teacher feels and lives religion, in which case he will find that the child has unconsciously imbibed it, and has ripened into a fitness to have his impressions put into words.' Octavia was by nature deeply religious; she had, as her mother expected, 'unconsciously imbibed it,' but she had not discovered the support of conscious communion with God, nor the joy of corporate worship. This she now found in the services at Lincoln's Inn Chapel which she and Emily attended daily. Maurice now became the most important influence in Octavia's life. It could not be otherwise. The vision with which he diagnosed the evils from which society was suffering, the magnificent courage with which he attacked them, the noble simplicity of his nature, his sympathy, his utter selflessness, in short, the 'complete drenching of his whole being in Christianity' could not fail to inspire the deepest reverence in all generous beings who came in contact with him. Octavia, aching with pity for the wrongs of humanity, longing to be of service but conscious of her impotence, found herself carried away by his strength and enthusiasm. It became possible to believe that in union with others, following such a leader one might even be able to do something.

Presently he invited the two girls to walk back with him after the service. Octavia could lay her problems before him, ask his advice, listen, entranced, while he expounded this or that doctrine of the Church. In his teaching, she found an answer to her need.'It was Mr. Maurice,' she wrote, 'who showed me a life in the Creeds, the services and the Bible; who interpreted for me much that was dark and puzzling in life; how the belief in a Father, Son and Holy

Ghost might be the most real faith, not a dead notion, that I might believe not only that God was manifesting Himself to each man in the inward consciousness of light and beauty . . . but that a Real Person had come among us, whose will had been brought into harmony with His . . . that He had declared that we might have Life, that Life was knowledge of God.' Her baptism and confirmation were happy experiences to which she looked back again and again with gratitude; thenceforth to the end of her life, she was a devout communicant, one of those happy souls who can say with St. Paul, 'I am persuaded that neither death, nor life, . . . nor powers, nor things present, nor things to come, nor height, nor depth, nor any other creature, shall be able to separate us from the love of God, which is in Christ Jesus our Lord.'

With renewed hope Octavia turned to her work; more than ever she longed to be of service. 'I wish, oh I do so long to do something,' she wrote to Miranda. 'Andy! Do you think I shall ever be able to do anything really useful?' For the moment she had to make herself useful in homely ways. She read to the Guild ladies while they worked, she was made responsible for the stores and had to give them out, and of course she was learning the glass business. She was making new friends too. Chief among them Emma Cons, destined to work with her for many years to come, speedily became her chosen companion and confidante. They discussed all things in Heaven and earth, with the earnestness that belongs to adolescence; they romped and joked, were noisy, and disturbed their elders and were complained of and resented the complaint. Octavia was the leader, now as always, and had the presence of mind for any difficult situation that presented itself. One evening

22

she came out of her room to find a disreputable looking man on the landing at the door of a cupboard in which Guild money was kept, she was alone in the house. 'How did you get here?' she asked sternly and quite calmly, though no doubt her heart was beating uncomfortably. The man was taken aback and replied, 'I came up the stairs.' 'Then go *straight* down them,' said Octavia, and he went, though one thinks he must afterwards have wondered why he did so.

Octavia recovered her gift of happy laughter. Once more the world was full of things to enjoy, the greatest of which arose from the Christian Socialist leaders, the study of their literature was a perpetual inspiration, she slept with a leaflet under her pillow, there were lectures, there were meetings, almost any day one might hear Cooper (the tailor), Kingsley or Ludlow or Furnivall; there were days when these god-like creatures actually came to the Guild. Then there were the opponents of the movement, and all who remember their own youth will not need to be reminded of the very special kind of pleasure to be derived from denouncing the Enemy and shuddering at his wickedness. All this pleasure was Octavia's. 'I am at Finchley with Minnie. I long dreadfully to go to town; I have been very unfortunate in being away from the Guild just at this time. Do you know Mr. Cooper has been there? And Mr. Lewis and the Trustees (Mr. Furnivall) go there so often; and all the bustle, and trying to feel Christian-like to Mr. and Miss——. Oh, would it not have been delightful? I do not at all like Mr.——, or rather I entirely despise his opinions. I will tell you about it when I see you. I will only tell you now that he likes the "subordination of the employed to the employer" and he thinks "there is no tribunal

so proper as the discretion of the employer to decide those
delicate questions of the personal conduct of the employed.
Is it not horrible? Mr. Furnivall I admire more and more,
the more I know and read of him; and as for Mr. Ludlow,
certainly there is not (excepting Mr. Furnivall) such a person in the whole world. He has the largest, clearest, best
balanced mind, joined to the truest, most earnest wish to
help the working classes I ever met with (of course excepting Mr. Furnivall's).' The sense of impotence in the face
of the suffering of humanity was gone, with the resilience
of youth she passed from despair to rapture. 'I am so
happy—so very very happy. I wish you were here with me.
You would so love all my beautiful things.'

The influence of the Christian Socialists was of major
importance in Octavia's life, her work was inspired by
their spirit, and she was deeply conscious of her debt not
only to Maurice, but to all the leaders of the movement.
Many years later (1875) in a letter to Ludlow she wrote:
'It remains true that it was the early connection with that
body of Christian Socialists to which much of my present
work must owe its spirit. It had to find its own form, according to the needs and possibilities of circumstances, but
its spirit must have been influenced deeply by the deeds
and words of all that group of men, among whom it pleased
God to lead me, when life was just first presenting its
puzzles to me.'

Octavia was soon given more responsible work. Mr.
Neale took over from its founder another kind of co-
operative work. This was a business for making toy furniture, which had been started to employ Ragged School
children. Octavia, still herself little more than a child, was
invited to take charge of it. She was naturally delighted at

being offered so important a post though she believed that she was destined to find her life's work in Art, and eagerly cultivated her artistic gifts. She made the designs for the glass painting with loving care; she drew and painted with enthusiasm whenever she could find time. 'I do not let anyone see my drawings, I do not do much. . . . I have such dreams both day and night of what I would do, and when I try what do I see? A little miserable scrap that is not worth looking at.' Yet perhaps because in truth her artistic talent was by no means the greatest of her gifts, she could not be satisfied with this alone. Her maternal instinct clamorously demanded satisfaction, the energy of her spirit required some self-spending task. The toymakers provided all she needed. The business side was no light undertaking. It was Octavia's duty to choose the shape and colour of each piece of toy furniture, to assign the various processes to each child, to price the finished article, to see each suite of furniture neatly packed and sent over to the show room, and finally to pay each child for the amount of work she had accomplished. She had to take stock from time to time and show a balance sheet. This was Octavia's apprenticeship in business methods. She learnt to keep accounts with meticulous accuracy, and to be methodical and punctual in all her work. 'I have often thought of your accounts which would not balance,' she wrote to Mary Harrison, 'and thought what a terrible state I should be in if mine would not, as I have eight or ten different accounts to keep.'

For a child of her age (fourteen), this would seem a sufficiently arduous business even if it had not been complicated by the human problem. It was, however, on the human side that Octavia first revealed to any who had eyes to see, wherein lay her peculiar power. The Ragged School children whom it was her task to control, were of a type not easily to be met in these days of universal education. They were desperately poor and very rough; generally speaking, they came from wretched and degraded homes, some lived in cellars, some were deformed and disfigured by the hardships they had endured. Many of them were older than Octavia, and all were more experienced in wretchedness and vice. They had been accustomed in their work hours to discipline of a repressive kind. On the walls of the room in which they worked hung a list of rules, with the punishment to be inflicted for the breach of each. On her first day in charge Octavia stood before this document, read it through in complete silence, and without a word tore it down from the wall. 'What will you do to us if we are bad?' asked the children, surprised and half frightened at this strange proceeding. Octavia did not reply. She had no fear that they would take advantage of her inexperience. She seems to have had a natural talent for dealing with people which served her better than experience serves many another. The secret of it was that she never (now or at any other time in her life) regarded people in the mass. She had no knowledge of 'the poor', she knew only this man and that woman as friends. So now the little toymakers were not employees, they were Louisa or Clara or Elizabeth, each with her own individuality, each to be studied, each to be treated as an end in herself. 'I know their tempers,' she wrote after she had been working with them for some little time, 'to whom I may say different things, I have to study how to interest each, I connect all they say, do or look into one whole, I get to know the thing they really care for.' She made it her business to know each child's home; and from these early days dates her interest in home making. Every moment she could spare from her other duties was given to planning ways and means of helping those whom she described as her 'dear dear children'. The idiom is Victorian, and though to modern ears it may suggest sentimentality, there was nothing of this in her cheerful and bracing attitude to them.

Of course there were storms in the early days, there were terrible fights between the children, sometimes they combined to defy her. With wisdom beyond her years she made no attempt to coerce them. When they refused to scrub the work tables, she got her sisters to help, and proceeded to scrub them herself under the eyes of the discomfited rebels: thereby, as she remarked in a letter 'doing more to convince them of the dignity of labour than any amount of talk on the subject'. She did not directly attack their swearing, but entertained them by her amusing conversation. She sang songs with them, she made herself a leader rather than an overseer, they began to enjoy their work, and gradually a most satisfactory relationship was established. 'I have no written or fixed laws, simply because in a small business so much has constantly to be altered; but we have a very delightful order, the children all know what they should do, and get into the habit of attending to it.'

Octavia busied herself with everything that concerned the children's well-being. She was horrified at the bad quality of the food they brought for the midday meal which they ate in the work rooms. She suggested that they should all pool the money they spent on such food and prepare and cook a wholesome common meal in the workroom. She discovered that they had not the slightest idea of preparing food for the table, and this seemed an additional reason for carrying out her project. In a very few weeks the whole business was organized, each child in turn was taught to cook the meal; Octavia insisted on a white cloth and civilized table manners. The meal cost 2d. a head a day and at the end of three days there was a profit of 7d. Octavia was triumphant: but there arose a problem which, in one form or another, was to perplex her all her life. 'I am dreadfully grieved, however, that several of the children have absolutely nothing for their dinner towards the end of the week. I was obliged to lend money for six dinners and a breakfast as I could not allow them to go without anything. This must be wrong. . . . I told them I could never lend money again, as I see no end to it; but what to do, I don't know.' It is interesting that already at fifteen, Octavia was facing the ethics of giving and seeing as distinctly as she did at fifty the danger of pursuing the easy path of indiscriminate charity.

On Saturday afternoons there was no toymaking, and Octavia might reasonably have regarded these as precious holidays, but when her heart was engaged she could not but spend herself. The toymakers had no resources within themselves. Nowadays if we have not taught our children how best to use leisure, we have at least provided an abundance of cheap entertainment. This was not so in 1855, and the toymakers had nothing to do but to hang about listlessly either in or outside their miserable homes. Octavia could not tolerate this; she knew the remedy, she would take the children out to Finchley, to Hampstead, to Highgate, where they should enjoy the pleasure she had known in her early days. At first the children hesitated; they were actually afraid of walking in the country, believing there might be wolves and bears lurking in the woods, they had

no interest in flowers and could not distinguish the very
commonest sorts. But Octavia had her way with them and
the expeditions were embarked upon. She was a stimulating leader and enjoyed the outings as much as any of the
party, she led them across country and was not the least
disconcerted when her clothes were caught and torn by
brambles. On one occasion Gertrude, listening in Highgate Lane to the discourse on mosses by a professor, was
taken aback by the sudden appearance through the hedge
of Octavia, who 'joyfully leapt down from the bank with a
staff in her hand, a straw hat on her head, torn by the
thicket, followed by a troop of ragged toymakers, happy
and flushed, each with an armful of bluebells.'

Presently there were more exciting parties. Some of the
Hills' friends, interested in Octavia's work and the origin-
ality of her methods, invited her to bring the children to
their houses in the country for the day. The first of these
invitations was from Mrs. Harrison, Mrs. Howitt's sister.
It was a day of mixed rapture and anxiety. That her beloved toymakers should have the experience of a party
in a house with a lovely garden, should receive the hospi-
tality and kindness of her friends, gave her immense pleasure; that they should behave in a becoming manner, do
themselves justice, and prove acceptable guests, was a
matter of some anxiety. All went well, however. 'I am sure
you will be glad to hear,' she wrote, 'how much we all enjoyed the whole day. The children have never ceased talking about it; the boat, the water, the garden, the flowers are
continual sources of delight.' To Octavia there was another source of delight. It was at this party that she first
met Mary Harris, whose friendship was to become a most
important factor in her life.

It would be difficult to overestimate the importance of Octavia's influence on the children. At first incredulous, they gradually realized that she did indeed care for them, and this in itself brought warmth and colour into their dim lives; instead of a future world of blessedness which they had been promised often enough, she brought them a present life full of interest and possibilities. They responded with whole-hearted devotion.

'Dear Miss Ockey,' wrote one of them when Octavia had gone away for a short holiday, 'we do miss you so dreadfully. I do so long to see you and hear your voice again. The place is so dull without you. . . . I have been agoing to say so often, "Miss Ockey repeat some poetry or talk about birds, or do something".'

Octavia was touched by their devotion, she took her responsibility very seriously, agonized over their faults, and rejoiced over their improvement, yet perhaps, had she but known it, her greatest gift to them was the power of enjoyment, the secret of laughter which all unknowing she imparted to them.

Another important influence on Octavia which dates from this time is that of Ruskin. It is difficult for us nowadays to realize the position Ruskin held a hundred years ago. Of all the Victorians none is less acceptable to-day than he; his matter no longer interests us, his manner exasperates us. It is not only that his style is turgid, with its tiresome repetition, its deliberate straining after effect, but also that his dogmatism, his pontifical pronouncements on art, on morality, on religion fail to impress a generation little accustomed to accept authority on any subject whatever. Yet it is not possible that the immense reputation he enjoyed, the veneration in which he was held was based on nothing more than a constant reiteration of his own rightness. It was not only to Octavia, but indeed to most of her generation that he appeared to be one of the supreme teachers of his day, a prophet with a message for mankind. For he stood for spiritual values in a materialistic and money-making age, for the right of the common man to the good things of the world, chief among which he counted beauty, and education whereby to enjoy it. It may be that in art he worshipped false gods (incontestably they are not the gods of this generation) but the only criticism that can be made of his social doctrines is that they are too obvious to need iteration. In 1850 they were regarded as revolutionary.

Octavia's power of veneration was very highly developed. She had always been an omnivorous reader. In 1852 the first two volumes of *Modern Painters* came into her hands and filled her with reverent enthusiasm for the writer. 'About Ruskin,' she wrote to Gertrude in 1853 just before she was fifteen, 'it matters very little what *The Times* or anything else, says of him. . . . I think there is never a single word he writes which could have been left out without loss, or changed without spoiling an idea.'

A little later she saw him in the flesh. Ruskin was interested in the Co-operative Guild and also in the Consolidated Glass, and came to see the work that was being done. It seemed hardly possible that he should fulfil all Octavia's expectations and be as wonderful in real life as he was in print, but this miracle he achieved. 'Ruskin has been here,' she reported to Gertrude. 'All went as well as I could possibly wish. . . . He gave us some most interesting and useful hints about colour, and ordered five slabs to be painted for him; . . . If you had seen the kind gentle way in which he spoke, the interest he showed, the noble way in which he treated every subject, the pretty way in which he gave his order, and lastly, if you had seen him as he said on going away: "I wish you all success with all my heart," you would have said with me that it was utterly wonderful to think that that was the man who was accused of being "mad, presumptuous, conceited, and prejudiced".'

But even more was to come; in March, 1855, Ruskin invited Octavia to visit him at Camberwell. She could hardly believe her good fortune, 'I do not think any of you can really understand what this is to me . . . first he was only a friend of Mr. Furnivall's, then his books were everything and he nothing; then his name suggested a vision of vague beauty and distant indefinite glory.' The visit took place. Ruskin showed Octavia his statues and his MSS., discoursed about colour, about pleasure and happiness, commended her designs, invited her to come again and sent her home with a heart singing with gladness, glowing with ardent hero-worship and touched with pity for his restless loneliness. 'And now,' she writes to Emily, 'do you or do you not wish to hear what I think of it? that this friendship so happily begun may be a long and growing one; that I have seen a world of beauty, that this might be the opening of a more glorious path; that I would give years if I could bring to Ruskin "the peace which passeth all understanding".'

Ruskin was very obviously interested in his young disciple. He was as ready to teach as she to learn; he sent her work to do for him, and though she longed to abandon all the Guild work for it, this was not possible, and she was obliged to fit it in among other things as best she could. This sometimes irked her, 'I am rather dejected. . . . I often wish now I were quite free and could do what I liked . . . it requires a strong heart to go on working, without anyone caring whether you are longing to do anything else.' On the other hand, there were days when the work went well, ecstatic days when she went to see him. 'It is a very wonderful event for me; and I think always will be . . . he is so inexpressibly kind, so earnest to help everyone, and so generous that one comes home inclined to say "Hush, while I think about it." '

So the busy days sped by. Octavia was working far too hard, she could never do anything with less than her whole energy. Her work with and for her children or her work for Ruskin would either of them alone have given her a full and busy life, together they were more than any one still growing girl should have undertaken: yet Octavia would have refused to contemplate giving up either. She was nearly seventeen, she was the devoted disciple of Maurice and of Ruskin, and her work constantly brought her into contact with both, she was the object of the trust and affection of her own little disciples; life was good. She wrote to her sister in 1855: 'I have my own little room, I have my *nice* books. I have all my writing things; usually some flowers; and I have eleven dear little snails. They are such darlings. I am so happy, so very very happy, I cannot any longer contain my joy.'

Chapter III

DIFFICULT DAYS

'I am felt often to be a pillar to the family in many ways':
OCTAVIA TO MARY HARRISON, 25.4.'56

WHILE Octavia was writing joyfully of her happiness, Fate
was preparing a shrewd blow. Maurice had offered to take
a bible class for the toymakers; Octavia, believing him to
be the greatest teacher in the world and eager that her
children should have the best, accepted the offer with enthusiasm. Maurice was at the moment in the thick of the
Theological Essay controversy, ecclesiastical authority
frowned on him, the timidly orthodox feared him. Among
these was a Mrs. Chamberlayne, described indignantly by
Octavia as 'a strict low-church woman, who enters a room
talking about "the sinful carnal flesh", etc., who wishes all
the children to rise and repeat a text whenever anyone
enters a room.' It was this lady who financed the ragged
school from which the toymakers were recruited and substantially supported the Guild. Horrified at the suggestion
that so 'dangerous' a man as Maurice should teach the
children, she threatened to withdraw all financial support
both from the school and the Guild if it were allowed. The
Managers of the Guild, unable to face the loss of income
involved, asked Maurice to withdraw and Neale, reluctant
as he was to acquiesce, did not feel able to stand against his
Committee.

Caroline Hill was indignant. She opposed the Com-

34

DIFFICULT DAYS

mittee with all her energy 'on very high grounds', writes
Octavia, and finding herself unable to prevail, she resigned
her post in the Guild. It was a difficult decision to take;
leaving the Guild involved the breaking up once more of
their home, the necessity of finding new work, or of becoming dependent on her father. But Caroline had no hesitation. For her it was a clear question of right and wrong,
she had no doubt that Neale was sacrificing principle to
expediency, and therefore she could do no other than dis-
sociate herself from his action.

Octavia, on the other hand, faced the situation with a
divided mind. Her devotion to Maurice made her resent
the affront offered to him with the whole of her vehement
nature, but there were her children: to give them up
seemed utterly impossible. Their love for her, their dependence on her, satisfied both her affection and her
capacity, she felt herself indispensable to them—a grati-
fying feeling to anyone at any age, quite irresistible to
Octavia not yet seventeen. She did not hesitate long, the
children prevailed: but it was difficult and disturbing to
find herself on the side of those who opposed her mother
and Maurice. The very fact that Caroline had never im-
posed her will on her children but had led them to see
things from her point of view, strengthened her influence
over them and made opposition more disquieting. Octavia,
for her own peace of mind, had to convince herself that she
was standing for a principle and not merely clinging to the
work she loved best.

'Mr. Neale has been here to-day to ask me to stay. I had
made up my mind to do so—strong in the Faith that there
is in every body of people . . . a mighty power of self-
sacrifice and devotion . . . the germs of a Fellowship with

35

which we must claim affinity;' perhaps this affinity with the germ left her a little dissatisfied, for she goes on to comfort herself with the reflection that she has chosen the more difficult way, she is ready, even eager, to be persecuted. 'And now for uphill work—I have worked with power, I must learn to work without it—now for struggles, now for faith to keep true to the right, now for strength to give up my bible class, the early service, everything to conform to the regulations of the powers that be, now I must step off my high seat and be as one of the workers, because though I shall nominally be the superintendent of the children, it will be very different when I am under some manager or other.' With her mind not altogether at peace, Octavia took her decision. The difficulties of the situation were perhaps not precisely those she had foreseen, but there was certainly no lack of them; for when Caroline Hill left the Guild, the family finances became again very precarious and Octavia was now of an age to feel herself principally responsible for them.

Dr. Southwood Smith, living in retirement in Weybridge, was ready as ever to receive his daughter and any of his grandchildren into his home, but he was not a wealthy man, having always put the interests of the community before his own, and Octavia bitterly resented the necessity of taking more from him. 'I detest any sort of dependence,' she wrote. 'It is almost hard for me even to imagine a person of whom I could, for myself, ask any assistance.' Yet, for the moment there was no alternative. Florence, whose health had been a cause of great anxiety, had some months earlier gone to Italy with an aunt, Caroline with Emily went to Weybridge, Miranda and Octavia stayed on at the Guild. The work there, however, was not enough to sup-

port the girls; Miranda supplemented her income by teaching, Octavia also found some little girls to teach and helped
Miranda with a French class, but she was very clear that
her allegiance was first of all to the Guild, 'As long as the
Guild stands, I belong to it. No work however tempting,
no position however delightful, could make me think of
leaving it.' But the Guild was not destined to stand for
long; in February, 1856, Octavia reports, 'Its foundations
are rocking', and in the following month it came to an end.

It would seem obvious that now, absolved of her duty
to the Guild, Octavia must abandon her children and find
well-paid work. This, however, was no part of her plan.
'The toys,' she writes, 'are given up entirely into my
hands, my only help being that Mr. Neale will advance a
small capital for me to begin with . . . of course my means
will be very limited. . . . This is, as you may see, a very
daring scheme, perhaps it may seem a rash, impracticable,
unwise one for me to undertake a business without much
connection—or time—or money. But I have first seen this,
I can do it without getting into debt with anyone. I must
make time, I will spend no money but what I receive.' For
the next fifteen months Octavia bore the whole burden of
this business; she did actually keep her children in work
and paid her way. She did more; not content with employing the children on the toys, she ensured that they should
become really self-supporting when they passed beyond
childhood. 'I have been thinking much of the future of my
children, they are many of them great girls too old for this
work, as they can only earn on an average 6s. a week or so.
. . . I am going to see each of the mothers now that I have
made up my mind what to advise them to devote their
children to. . . . One or two will train as teachers in infant

schools, others I destine for printing . . . one should learn some branch of needlework.' This would have been no small labour, had it been her principal occupation, actually she could only devote to it the time she squeezed out in the intervals of earning her living.

The question of how she should earn her living had been exercising her mind for a long time. With what seems like a curious perversity she had set her heart on being an artist, entirely unaware that her creative gifts in that direction were small, while her sensitiveness, her quick imagination and her intuitive sympathy gave her a power with human beings, which she was to use magnificently in the service of her own and succeeding generations. This power she underestimated. 'I hold artistic work and human work should go hand in hand,' she wrote, 'and I am thankful to have found such human work as shall rather aid than retard the main work to which I feel sure more and more of my life will be called.' So completely had she mistaken her vocation!

With this ambition burning within her, she wrote to Ruskin and asked him if he thought she could make a living in art. Ruskin had already commissioned her to design and make him a table in consolidated glass. The description of it reads strangely to our ears to-day, 'a spray of bramble leaves in all their brilliant autumn colours, encircling the centre space which formed a background that was dark at one part and gradually grew lighter and finally changed into soft blue, suggesting storm cloud passing away and leaving a bright sky. Round the edge among the leaves were the words of the Psalm, "He brought them out of darkness and out of the shadow of death, and brake their bonds in sunder." ' Ruskin was delighted with it, and at

38

once offered to give her employment in illumination and to train her to become an artist.

Ruskin's method of training a painter is not one that will commend itself to any school of thought to-day. It consisted simply in copying pictures. 'As to my work,' Octavia writes, 'Ruskin has set me to one which he believes to be the right training for an artist, and he would be glad that at present I did not look beyond it; first, because one must be *contented* to do a work before one *can* do it, and secondly, because he would then be sure I loved art, not only my own ambitious notions; in addition to which he really longs to have things well copied.' With unquestioning docility Octavia set to work to copy, first Dürer then Turner etchings, in pencil, then Veronese and Rubens, in water colours. She worked four or five hours a day, sometimes at home keeping one eye on the toymakers the while, sometimes at South Kensington, where she speedily became the confidante of all the other students, sometimes at Marlborough House where Ruskin was apt to arrive to give her a lesson, often at Dulwich whither she walked most of the way, to save the expense of fares. Ruskin was an exacting critic, he demanded absolute accuracy and Octavia made superhuman efforts to achieve it, and was cast down by his strictures: 'I thought that by some miracle the things I had done were as accurate as human work need be. . . . Now that I know where I am, I don't doubt I can win the battle in time by steady work.'

It was strenuous, but Octavia saw more and more of Ruskin, and this was compensation for any fatigue. He held forth majestically and eloquently on every conceivable subject. She listened spell-bound and wrote long and careful reports of his speeches to her sisters and friends. No wonder her own literary style was affected. The vigorous brisk sentences, describing her real and joyful experiences, were often replaced by fine writing after the manner of the Master expressing sentiments that, no doubt unconsciously, she felt he would think she ought to have. 'The light wreaths of briony not yet transformed into streams of gold, but just changed enough from their summer green to tell you their own individual story, how they grew deep down in the hedge, then climbed up clinging for strength even to thorny branches even to leafless ones; they tell how they thrust themselves and tangle and knot themselves closer and closer, one wreath only impatient for light and sunlight, running up some spray of rose or bramble; and then as if content to be made more and more like that sun, rests on the thorny pillar, and stretches down its golden arms to its friends below, every leaf telling the same story as the whole plant, beginning in darkness ending in light, beginning in life, ending in glorified death; beginning in green, ending in gold; beginning in massive strength, ending in spiritual power.'

It is impossible not to grudge the time and energy Octavia gave to Ruskin's work, to this meticulous copying which wore her out to no useful purpose; but it must be remembered that it gave her great happiness at a time when she sorely needed it; and that, after all, it was Ruskin who later opened the gate for her into her kingdom.

While Ruskin was giving her the work to which she attached so much importance, Maurice was giving her the work which she could do so admirably. One of Maurice's many projects was the Working Men's College. Early in 1856 he had started classes for working women in connection with it, and from the very beginning Octavia had given arithmetic lessons there. When the Guild came to an end, Maurice invited her to become secretary to these classes at a salary of £25 a year. It was about two hours' work a day, and both interesting and responsible. 'We have about 40 pupils,' she writes, 'I sometimes take a class, but my proper work is to keep the books, communicate between teachers and pupils . . . in short, I have the responsibility of all the arrangements. The work gives me the time and power to see much of the pupils of whom I am becoming very fond.' The work also brought her into contact with the teachers of whom she was at first far less fond. She had never before been paid for social work, and she disliked the necessity, she felt herself at a disadvantage with the voluntary workers. 'As I am thrown among "*ladies*" I hope I may discover good in them.' She suspected them of a desire to patronize her on account of her youth and inexperience, yet she felt herself as experienced in the problems of the working classes as any one of them; she resented the fact that when any of them failed to turn up for a lecture she was expected to give it, she felt that they were inclined to exaggerate the importance of the services they rendered. She writes impatiently of the knowledge that 'they will be offended if they think themselves the least in the world slighted, and they think I have no right to be indifferent to what they think. . . . I don't know what there is in the word lady which will connect itself with all the things I despise and hate; first and most universally it suggests a want of perseverance and bending before small obstacles, a continual "I would if——".'

Nevertheless, this contact with social workers was of great value to her, it was important that she should learn to work with them, since in the real work of her life she was to be increasingly thrown with them. It was not in Octavia to regard even 'ladies' for any length of time in the mass, she soon began to distinguish them as individuals, to make friends with some, and to work comfortably with all of them. One important friendship dates from this time; this was with Miss Sterling, the daughter of John Sterling whose life Carlyle wrote. She was the director of the classes, a woman much older than Octavia, and conceived a warm affection and admiration for the eager vivid girl who threw herself with such enthusiasm into the work.

But the secretaryship of the classes and the money Ruskin paid her did not suffice for Octavia's needs. When the Guild came to an end, the Hill family had reassembled itself in furnished rooms in Francis Street. Miranda had pupils mornings and afternoons, Mrs. Hill was writing articles, for some of which she found a publisher, Emily was available to superintend the toymakers when her sister was otherwise engaged, but the responsibility for the family came increasingly on Octavia's shoulders. She managed in addition to everything else to find a certain number of pupils, a drawing class in the school at which Miranda was teaching, as well as private pupils for drawing recommended by Ruskin. She taught other things too, indeed, she never felt able to refuse any pupil offered to her. For by this time Octavia had come to realize the true condition of her father's affairs. There were debts, she discovered, still unpaid, and although she had of course no legal responsibility for these (since her father was a discharged bankrupt) the idea that anyone should suffer loss through her family was utterly intolerable to her. With a full recognition of the burden she was assuming she accepted the debts as hers, and thereafter they figured as a liability in any calculation she made of her financial position; bit by bit, as she was able, she reduced and finally paid off the whole sum, but it was a slow business, and in 1856 she saw herself submerged under a mountain of indebtedness. A further source of unhappiness was the sad state of depression into which her father had fallen. She felt it her duty to go and see him from time to time, and every visit added to the weight of her burden. 'I have been with my father, and what that implies of desolation and despair, God the good Father alone knows.'

She was working eleven hours a day at her paid work; in her spare time she was interviewing possible purchasers of her toys, finding suitable openings for her children, answering every call that came from one or another of them in sickness or any kind of trouble. When she came home she was worn out; little wonder if she was difficult, impatient when her family begged her to do less, irritated if they expected her to join in their relaxations yet a little hurt if they left her out. 'Everyone says I do not need sympathy, I only wish it were a little more true. . . . I am very lonely. . . . They say "Ockey will not be with us" as if I were not longing to join them as they talk or read; but I have other work on hand. . . . I am felt often to be a pillar to the family in many ways.'

Octavia accepted the position of 'pillar to the family' as her right, she would not have been content to relinquish it to another; yet, it must be remembered, she thought of herself primarily as an artist, and as she saw herself obliged more and more to take control of the family finances, more and more regarded as the business man among them, she felt a little resentfully that the sacrifice of her real gifts was being ignored. 'I assure you,' she wrote to Ruskin, 'I am considered the person of the family who is without imagination, poetry, feeling or affection; good only to do a sum, carry a weight, go a long walk in the rain, or decide any difficult question about tangible things. You happen to know the other side of me: all *that's* kept in, that I may do my work, you don't know what a life of calculation and routine and steadiness mine is. I'm told that the best developed organ that I have is that of caution.'

The division within herself, the sense of wasting her artistic gifts, the feeling of being out of sympathy with her family to whom she was completely devoted, added to her financial anxieties and her persistent overwork, produced a strain that became well-nigh intolerable. The more tired she became the more impossible it seemed to call a halt; she was too weary to stop, she even evolved the idea that she had no right to rest, 'that to leave off working was a privilege, to continue a duty, that I dare not claim any time as my own; that I had sometimes felt as if I had earned a time to rest or enjoy leisure: and then had been convinced that all time was God's and to be used for Him.'

When this point was reached, it was clear that something must be done about it. It was Maurice—'through whom I have strength to do all I do . . . whose influence connects all my life together'—who now reasoned with her and finally persuaded her 'that rest was as much a part of God's order as work was, that we have no right to put ourselves out of the order as if we were above it . . . rest is as much a duty as work, it is very self-willed to do without it.' This was in the spring of 1857. Octavia accepted Maurice's judgment, but it was too late to save her from a breakdown; in April she fell a victim to some fever, and in her over-tired state, the illness was severe and recovery slow. Her mother nursed her with devotion, and with wisdom born of deep affection forbore to point the obvious moral. Octavia appreciated both the care and the reticence. She had to have a long holiday and perhaps this break in her work may be regarded as the end of her adolescence. She had time for reflection, she saw her problems more calmly and in truer proportion.

When she came back to London she had achieved adjustment to her family, her work and her responsibilities; she still hoped she might find her career in artistic creation, but she was able to make a more sober calculation of her power of physical endurance. She no longer disdained holidays, she would take long solitary walks into the country when she found a free day, and she was ready to take warning when 'Brother Ass' uttered it. 'I have been ill and people talk gloomy things to me about what will happen if I don't completely refresh myself, and what is more I believe them. Now I do not mean to add one more to the mournful list of women and girls who have rendered themselves incapable of doing anything by their determination to do more than they should.'

In the autumn she faced, sadly enough, the necessity of giving up the toymaking. 'I could not make them pay,' she wrote briefly, 'and ought not to go on unless they did.' It cost her much to make the decision, but once made she stood by it. 'On the morning of the day it was all settled,' writes Caroline, 'Ockey received the sweetest letter from Miss Harris asking what sum it would require to carry on the toys another year; but dear Ockey, very properly I believe, was firm to carry out the change.'

Giving up the toys relieved Octavia of one heavy responsibility, but she still worked extremely hard; she still

45

concerned herself with the girls who had been her toy-makers, since she had established so close and intimate a relationship with them, that none of their affairs could be a matter of indifference to her. She very generally got up at 5.30 to do illuminating or any other work she could do at home, before she went out to her ordinary day's work. She found a way of helping her father too, and though it was a small affair 'I have got him to permit us to lend him books to read, and now they have become a source of great delight to him,' the fact that she could do something, how-ever small, lightened her burden.

Miranda's health now began to fail, and after consul-tation with Dr. Southwood Smith, it was decided that she should go to Italy to join Florence and her aunt, and find pupils there; Caroline took over Miranda's pupils and this, giving her work she really enjoyed, made family life very much easier. Emily too was fully and happily occupied, for she had been nominated by Maurice to hold at Queen's College a scholarship founded in his honour.

Now that Octavia had time to think more about her own surroundings, it seemed to her that they would all be very much happier and more comfortable in a home of their own than in furnished rooms. She persuaded her grand-father to lend them the necessary money, and having found unfurnished rooms in Milton Street, with Emily's help she set to work to make a real home. It was a task which gave her the most intense pleasure, she used all her in-genuity to make a little money go a long way. After her work she would go round the shops with Emily and Ger-trude choosing carefully and economically. She planned and cut the carpet and with Emily sat on the floor sewing it. Once more the house was filled with laughter, and she

recited poetry and chattered merrily as the work proceeded. And at last the home was achieved. It was inevitably Victorian, 'the crimson table cover and chair cover
and green carpet and white walls with roses, make such a
lovely combination. . . . It certainly does give one a most
pleasant sense of simplicity, cleanliness and beautiful
colour.' The sisters waited anxiously to hear their mother's
verdict on their handiwork: she approved completely,
everyone who called upon them admired it. For the first
time in her life, Octavia had acquired household gods and
had arranged them around her in the setting she had chosen
for them, her satisfaction was unbounded. Once more she
faced life with zest and if she had outgrown the rapturous
ecstasy of her early days, she could still write 'I am so
happy, and more so, day by day'.

Chapter IV

NEW FRIENDS

'I get on very much more easily with strangers than I used.'
OCTAVIA TO SOPHIA JEX-BLAKE, August, 1860

'I THINK you will like our dear new home,' Octavia wrote
to Miranda in Italy, 'the prettiness of it is a delight to me,
and I am most thankful for its order and cleanliness. . . . I
am so fond of it.' To Octavia the move from furnished
apartments to a home was a moment of great significance;
it marked the end of their bitter poverty, a period to which
she referred many years later as 'a time when we were so
very, very poor, that I can still hardly bear to speak of it'.
Things were definitely improving; Mrs. Hill was fully occupied with pupils, Emily at Queen's College was rapidly
becoming qualified to earn, Ruskin was paying Octavia
more, and was using some of her work for Modern
Painters; her father was better and happier, and his debts,
though not yet paid off, were being steadily reduced, so
that it seemed possible to foresee a date, not too far distant, when they would be extinguished. She felt so much
better off, that she encouraged Miranda to take music lessons in Italy and assured her that there was no need for her
to think of sending money home.

One shadow, however, marred the two years at Milton
Street. Octavia's health was now a cause of real anxiety.
She blamed herself, 'It is my own fault—I ought to take
things more quietly, not think so very much depends on
my deciding wisely and not nearly break my heart if things

48

go wrong for a time.' There was some justification for the diagnosis, no doubt her spirit drove her body hard, to the end of her life she was to feel joy and sorrow, success and disappointment more acutely than it is given to lesser people to feel them, it is the price paid for the power to 'turn the world upside down', but it was not the whole of the truth. The poverty ('I have only once or twice in my life had to go hungry,' she wrote, contrasting her happy lot, with that of a toymaker), the long hours, the constant response to the needs of others, had put upon her a strain which the most robust constitution could hardly endure. In the spring of 1859 she was heading for another breakdown, and bowing to necessity took a holiday in Normandy with Mary Harrison.

It was her first visit abroad and her spirits rose joyfully the moment she abandoned her work; a 'very rough crossing' which lasted six hours did not daunt her, nor did her rather sketchy knowledge of French prevent her talking freely to all she met, though there was an occasion when she took 'a vehement determination to have nothing to do with a short, stout, repulsive foreigner who sat in the railway carriage opposite to me and who to my consternation was most polite and attentive', but for the most part, her perennial interest in her fellows overcame any such determination and she studied places and people with eager curiosity. She rapidly regained her health, 'I have laughed more since I came to France than I have done for years I think,' and she returned to her work full of vigour. But she could not so easily conquer the results of years of strain. Again and again in her letters, she writes of intense weariness and of bouts of pain that made it impossible for her to stand. She was obliged now to take holidays quite frequently. 'Ockey is rather like a man taking a holiday,' Florence reports. 'She thinks it her duty to be idle and does not quite know what to do with herself.' She found it necessary to restrict the length of her working day, and to forego her long walks to Dulwich, even though this involved spending money on fares. As soon as she had recovered from one of these attacks she flung herself with courageous energy into her work, which every day became more and more interesting.

At the Working Women's Classes she had made herself indispensable, and when, owing to the pressure of her work for Ruskin, she suggested giving up the work there, she was both astonished and gratified to discover with what dismay the proposition was received: 'Miss Sterling said I must know they could not possibly supply my place—it was impossible—the whole flourishing or decay of the classes depended on whom they had in my place; my value could not be calculated in £, s. d. or any number of mechanical performances.'

It was at the Working Men's College in 1859 that Octavia made the acquaintance of George MacDonald who, on Maurice's invitation, was lecturing there on Poetry. MacDonald was not at that time well known in London, he had only recently come there from the North, and did not get easily into contact with this South-country audience, which seemed to him heavy and unresponsive. The lecturer flagged, conscious of a want of sympathy in his listeners, then suddenly his eye fell on Octavia, whose intense concentration and obviously eager interest in all he was saying assured him that one at least of his audience was following and appreciating the argument; much cheered, he addressed himself to her, and regaining confi-

dence made the lecture a complete success. At the end of
it he sought her out, thanked her for her help, and invited
her and her sister to visit him and his family. This was the
beginning of a friendship which was to be of great importance to Octavia, who became devoted to Mrs. Mac-
Donald and to all their children.

They were attractive people, intelligent, vividly alive,
interested in things of the mind, and in their home Octavia
found a congenial atmosphere, freedom from the pressure
of her daily anxieties and inspiration for her intellectual
pursuits. She joined gladly in their activities, sometimes
acting in the plays that George MacDonald wrote, taking
holidays in England and abroad with them, both gaining
from and contributing to the happy family life. Years later,
on Mrs. MacDonald's death, Octavia wrote to one of her
daughters: 'My thoughts kept flying back to the old days,
days when you were all children, days when you were so
good to me, days when your father's teaching was opening
new worlds to me, days when all your mother's sweetness
and unceasing goodness and brightness were such a cheer
and a lesson, days when in sorrow or in joy your home was
always open to me.'

There were other friendships too which date from this
time. In August, 1859, she speaks of a new friend, Emma
Baumgartner, who lived at Godmanchester, where Crom-
well was born. This was one of the quickly conceived
friendships, characteristic of Octavia; 'I went down there,
a perfect stranger, having only seen her twice and her
mother once.' The visit was an unqualified success; the
girls had much in common, Octavia was delighted to discover in Emma 'right views about work and all religious
questions', she shared in Emma's activities—her men's

reading room, her night school for boys and men and her Sunday school—in less earnest moments, Emma taught her to row; 'We drew, we talked of Ruskin and of Mr. Maurice; as well as of her brothers, and my sisters, architecture, and all kinds of things.' It was the beginning of a happy intimacy, broken only by death.

It was in February, 1860, that Octavia first came to know Sophia Jex-Blake. 'I have been giving some book-keeping lessons to Miss Jex-Blake. She is a bright, spirited, brave, generous young lady living alone in true bachelor style.' A sudden flowering of affection was no rare experience to Octavia, and it was no wonder that she was captivated by Sophia Jex-Blake, who was a brilliant young woman, full of energy and spirit, possessed of all the qualities which could not fail to appeal to Octavia. In many respects the two girls were very much alike. Already at the age of twenty, both bore unmistakable marks of greatness; they were built in heroic mould, of indomitable courage and capable of any sacrifice where their chivalry was aroused. Both had the flaming and passionate temperament which is the mark of the pioneer, though Octavia had been chastened by circumstance to subdue her vehement desires to the duty of the day, both had decided views and a difficulty in believing themselves mistaken, both were deeply affectionate. Any relationship between them must have been a tempestuous affair but while Sophia's explosions of wrath relieved her feelings and passed over quickly leaving her restored to good humour, Octavia, who felt her own hardly-won serenity threatened, suffered more from these outbursts than her friend realized. Perhaps no easy intimacy was possible between two such powerful personalities, but the real difficulty lay, not so much in the strength of these, as in the absence of any common background.

While Octavia had been struggling with the bitter problems of poverty, Sophia had been resisting the efforts of her devoted parents to turn her into a well behaved young lady, happy to accept the restrictions considered appropriate to a girl of her class in early Victorian days. She could not be fitted into the mould; she was too full of vitality to accept the role of the daughter at home, fulfilling social duties and visiting 'the poor'. Her parents, loving her deeply, allowed her to have her own way and she was now mathematical tutor at Queen's College. She had no conception of what poverty meant and a life such as Octavia had lived was not only outside her experience but also beyond her imagination. She had been used to people with very clearly defined convictions about the social class to which they belonged. When she was offered a salary for her work at Queen's College, her father protested in horror against her 'accepting wages that belong to a class beneath you in social rank'. She was indeed perilously near to being one of those creatures whom Octavia so greatly disliked, 'a lady', and with the best will in the world she could not see things from quite the same angle as Octavia did. She indignantly repudiated her father's opinions, but none the less her unconscious assumptions were coloured by them.

The friendship began happily enough. In the Easter holiday Octavia stayed with the Jex-Blake family. After the visit Sophia received what she calls a 'loving solemn letter' about one of her family 'rows' and records her reaction, 'Told her by return "Hang you", and bade her remember she was neither nurse nor parson. Dear—dear child though.' In the following July, Octavia, Sophia and her

sister Caroline went to Wales together. It was an enchanted time. Octavia had never seen mountains before
and was enraptured by them. They went to Bettws-y-Coed,
where the Jex-Blakes had a country house; there they entertained all the children of the village, they talked and
laughed and came home in the highest spirits, Octavia
looking 'five years younger and bright as a sunbeam'.
After their return to town they saw more and more of one
another; Sophia's vitality and charm were a constant refreshment to Octavia, who gained much from the intercourse: 'Your magnificent energy does me much good,'
and again: 'Do you know I get on very much more easily
with strangers than I used, all of which I owe to you?' Day
by day they became more dependent on each other, and
when Sophia went abroad for a short time, Octavia missed
her acutely. 'London feels strangely desolate, the lamps
looked as they used to look, pitiless and unending as I
walked home last night, and knew I could not go to you.'

In September Octavia and Sophia began to talk of living
together. Ever since the move into Milton Street had given
them a home, Octavia had been longing for the return of
Miranda and Florence from Italy. She had a deep affection
for her sisters, and in addition she had a firmly rooted
conviction of the importance of family life; even when she
was most acutely conscious of its difficulties and of the
friction inherent in it, she felt that the right way for
people to live was in families. Obviously the three rooms
in Milton Street would be inadequate for the whole family,
obviously their financial resources would not run to a
larger house. To Sophia nothing seemed more delightfully
obvious than that she should share a larger house with her
beloved friend. There were no limits to her generosity;

she would give without any consciousness of conferring a favour, and could not see why there should be any reluctance in receiving. 'She speaks most sadly of the modern fallacy that money must be earned, she thinks it might be given when people are dear friends; she says they've given the most precious things, what difference can a little money make.' Octavia loved her friend dearly enough to accept her view; together they searched for a suitable house; 'Mamma earnestly desired' that they should keep near the Park (Regent's Park), inclined to Harley Street, which proved too expensive, and finally agreed to 14, Nottingham Place.

It was at this point that the first hitch occurred. Sophia's parents expressed complete disapproval of the whole scheme. Mrs. Jex-Blake, whose sensitive understanding of her daughter was an outstanding feature of her character, no doubt realized the difficulties ahead, for Sophia had never found it easy to live in submission to her elders, and Mrs. Hill's was a personality by no means to be ignored. Mr. Jex-Blake's objection was on social rather than on personal grounds. When he had first heard of his daughter's intention to live with the Hills, he had raised no objection, he liked Octavia, and since Sophia could not live reasonably and conventionally at home there seemed no reason to oppose her projected choice of residence. But when he realized that she was to be joint lessee of a house with Octavia, and that a tenant was to be found for the drawing-room floor, he expressed his horror in no uncertain terms. 'You cannot really mean to take a house and let lodgings in direct opposition to your dear mother and me. It would be quite disgraceful, and we can never consent to it. I will not believe, my dear child, with all our love for you, that you will so directly disobey us, or that Miss Hill, knowing our feelings on the subject, can be a party to it. I firmly believed, till the last few days, that you were to live in rooms. I had no more idea of your becoming a lodging-housekeeper than of your keeping a shop.' Sophia's reply is not recorded, but her determination to live with the Hills was strengthened, rather than weakened; it was not too difficult to re-arrange the scheme so that she became a tenant of some of the rooms instead of joint landlord. The friendship between the two girls was too deep and inti-mate to be clouded by the opinions of any third person, nevertheless Mr. Jex-Blake's assumption of superiority added a difficulty to Sophia's relationship with the other members of the Hill family.

Octavia proceeded with the negotiations. Maurice and Ruskin helped her, seeing the landlord and testifying to her 'energy and every estimable quality', Miss Wodehouse, a friend of Sophia's at Queen's College, gave a formal guarantee; by the middle of December the whole business was completed and the family moved in. 'Ockey is im-mensely busy,' wrote Emily to Miranda, 'and quite in her element, buying things, reading over schedules of fixtures and examining plans and carpentering. We have not yet fixed what rooms we are to keep; it must depend on the lodgers . . . we are close to the Park, so the air is very good, and we are about ten minutes' walk from Queen's College. The back of the house is delightfully quiet, because it looks out on Marylebone Church Schools.' The house proved all they had hoped; Octavia rejoiced in its 'wide stone stairs and large light quiet rooms', her one desire now was that her sisters should come back and share it. 'Dearest Andy,' she wrote, 'You know I would not urge

THE FIVE SISTERS.

OCTAVIA HILL.   FLORENCE HILL.

MIRANDA HILL.

GERTRUDE HILL   EMILY SOUTHWOOD HILL

(MRS. CHARLES LEWES).   (MRS. EDMUND MAURICE).

you lightly to leave a work you had undertaken, but I do feel that we ought to be all together again. Life is too short and precious for us to spend much of it separate, we do want all our strength for work here.' This was an appeal not to be resisted, and in the beginning of 1862 the family was reunited.

In May of that year, however, Octavia was again threatened with a breakdown; once more she suffered from bouts of intense weariness and pain, indeed, so wretchedly ill did she feel that she seriously contemplated the possibility of an early death: 'I am like a broken thing, thin and pale, with aching back and hands . . . well enough till I feel or do anything, then feeling like a shadow, a queer feeling as if a slight touch would push me over the brink, however, it is no use talking about it, no one knows but there may be some years of life for me, at any rate, my way is clear, to rest if I can, not to frighten myself anyway.' The means to a rest presented itself most opportunely. Mary Harris was one of Octavia's most intimate and beloved friends. She was a much older woman than Octavia, a member of the Society of Friends. When Octavia first met her, she had been engaged in visiting prisoners at Newgate. Octavia, then only a child, had conceived a passionate devotion for her, and had poured forth all her secret aspirations, her joys and her sorrows. As she outgrew adolescence, the violence of her passion sobered down into a deep and lasting affection, an intimacy most precious to her, which lasted until Mary Harris died in 1893. Like so many members of the Society of Friends, Mary Harris had attained a deep inward peace, which gave her home an atmosphere of untroubled calm. No one could help Octavia as Mary could, again and again Octavia found refreshment in Mary's serene wisdom. By 1861 she was keeping house for her brother, a widower with five little girls, and at this moment, having been ill herself, she begged Octavia to come to her assistance. Octavia responded instantly. She felt a little uneasy at leaving her home with its new responsibilities, but an appeal from Mary, and one moreover which so exactly matched her own needs, was not to be resisted. The Harrises lived in Cumberland, near Derwentwater. The beauty of the countryside, the long untroubled days, the absence of responsibility, the cheerful companionship of the children, above all the satisfying intercourse with Mary brought her the refreshment she so sorely needed. At first she tried to live a normally active life but when she found this was impossible, she cheerfully accepted a passive state. 'I've left off walking again; after the first fortnight I got more and more tired with it, but I persevered till the fever came, and have never resumed it; but the terrace here is my continual haunt.' As the happy weeks went by she began slowly to regain her strength. In July she went with Mary and the children to the seaside where she and Mary sat 'in the sunshine in great peace'.

Meanwhile, things were not going too easily at Nottingham Place. In Octavia's absence, Sophia Jex-Blake felt responsible for the household, but Mrs. Hill felt herself to be the natural head of Octavia's house. Both had very decided views and being separated by a generation and coming as they did from worlds apart, it was inevitable that their views should clash. Sophia had always known very distinctly what was best for everyone, she was never very sensitive to the feelings of other people; she went energetically on her way, only half conscious of the irritation and opposition she aroused. Miranda, who had formed a warm friendship for Sophia, saw the situation from both sides, but was unable to reconcile them. She wrote to Octavia, Emily wrote, Mrs. Hill wrote, Sophia wrote. Octavia, receiving all these letters, felt her spirit quail, she was still far from well, her whole being cried out for peace; the contrast between the simple secure life she was leading with Mary and the complicated contentious existence to which she seemed called was intolerable.

'I hold myself prepared to come when it seems right,' she wrote to Sophia in July, 'sure to be given strength to do my duty, but certainly not longing for anything that will bring me again into a world of contention. All my life long this dread and misery about even the slightest contention or estrangement has taken the form of misery continually saying to itself, "I *cannot* bear it." '

Throughout August and September the letters continued, appealing to her to judge, to come, to 'put things right'. Finally, in October, she was summoned home, and a decision was forced on her. The decision was a hard one, hard on her, and doubly so on Sophia Jex-Blake. Octavia had discovered quite certainly that she could not do her work, could not even live, except in an atmosphere of peace; it was abundantly clear that there could be no peace in the household as it was, and that her family or Sophia must be sacrificed. The sanctity of family life was one of her deepest convictions, she had lived for her family from her childhood, she knew well how much her mother and sisters depended on her, she could not now desert them. She decided that Sophia must go; she would not discuss the question with her, would not try to see her point of view—probably she dared not trust herself to do so, fearing lest her resolution should fail. 'Oh, Sophia, how splendidly you and your mother did act those last few days that now seem so far away,' she wrote a month after the break, 'How deep your forethought was, so loving as to have remembered the very slightest things that might be the least trouble to us, when you were no longer near to take care of us.'

It was a sad ending to an intimacy which promised so much happiness to both. Octavia saw Sophia again, and for the next few years at intervals she wrote her tender letters, showing her affection to be unaltered but she would not attempt any reopening of the relationship, though for years Sophia could not believe this decision to be unalterable. Perhaps it was inevitable, perhaps it was necessary for the sake of the work each was to do, that each should pursue her path alone; but the loss was none the less severe, particularly perhaps for Octavia. In Sophia Jex-Blake she had found a friend who was intellectually and spiritually her equal, one who criticized freely and frankly, who could laugh at and with her. Octavia treading untried ways, creating a new profession, found many disciples but few equals, many to admire, few to criticize her. Her life was the poorer for the loss of Sophia's gay companionship and loving derision.

Chapter V

THE NOTTINGHAM PLACE SCHOOL

'Learning for the sake of learning and knowing is the
only legitimate course':
OCTAVIA TO MISS EMILY DAVIES, February, 1864

THE year 1861 closed sadly enough for Octavia. The
abrupt end to her holiday with Mary Harris and the emotional strain of the break with Sophia Jex-Blake told on
her health and spirits. Then in December, her grandfather, Dr. Southwood Smith, died very suddenly. Caroline Hill was shattered by her loss; the tie between her and
her father had been very close, she had lived with him for
long periods after her husband's collapse, and had been
wont to turn to him confidently for advice, she had indeed
always felt him to be the head of the family. Octavia
grieved for her mother; though she had been little willing
to depend on anyone but herself, and had now for years
been financially independent, his death increased her sense
of responsibility for her mother. She was now more than
ever the only 'man' in the family.

There was, however, no time to waste in mourning, for,
as always, there was much work to do. The whole family
was now engaged in teaching; Mrs. Hill's book on education was fairly widely known among intelligent people,
Emily had emerged from Queen's College fully qualified
to teach, Florence spoke Italian perfectly and had studied
music in Italy, Miranda had been teaching since she was

thirteen: it was not difficult for the Hills to find pupils. At the beginning of 1862 Miranda was head of a school for the daughters of tradesmen and artisans, Emily (or Minnie as her sisters called her) was teaching in a school in the mornings and had two private pupils in the afternoon, while Mrs. Hill was teaching a 'dear little girl'. Octavia's teaching was only one of her activities; she was still diligently drawing for Ruskin, still acting as secretary of the Working Women's College, and teaching drawing there; in addition she had a drawing class of thirty at the Portman Hall, another of ten at Nottingham Place besides 'two tiny boys' whom she taught two hours a day. 'Of course I am growing rich,' she wrote to Mary Harrison, enumerating her pupils; more important still, she was beginning to recover her health and spirits.

It seems to have been almost by accident that the Nottingham Place School, destined to play so large a part in Octavia's life in the next twenty-five years, and to make so definite a contribution to the education of girls, was started. English people were beginning to believe that their daughters needed some sort of education; the movement which culminated in the foundation of the Girls' Public Day School Trust and of other great girls' schools was already stirring the waters; the Nottingham Place School was one of its earliest manifestations. Emily was immensely in demand as a governess, so many of the Hills' friends wanted her that she determined to give up her school work and to concentrate on private pupils, but even so she could not satisfy all the demands made on her. Octavia was asked to receive two children into her house to prepare them for Queen's College. It became obvious that the simplest thing would be to combine all the children who wished to be taught by the family into one school.

Octavia entered energetically into the scheme: she still felt the blank left by Sophia Jex-Blake's departure and welcomed the idea of filling the house with children. 'The work is interesting to me. It supplies an object now that the home is rather broken up.' By the autumn of 1862 the school was fairly started with six boarders and eight day girls. To begin with, Miranda kept her own school and helped at Nottingham Place only in the afternoons, so most of the work fell to Octavia and Emily. Octavia had very definite ideas about the upbringing of girls; characteristically she thought of each one always in relation to a family. Her pupils were to be trained in 'habits of neatness, punctuality, self-reliance and such practical power and forethought as will make them useful in their homes; I think they may be taught to delight in them'. Beyond this, they were to learn their place and function in society by serving others. From the beginning she encouraged them to take an interest in social conditions, to learn at first hand something about their poorer neighbours and to help them when this was possible. 'I so much hope some of the elder ones will manage to spare time for teaching quite little children either on Sunday or some other day.'

It was a remarkable school, though from a modern point of view much might be said against it. The building was barely adequate. In early days there was no real school room, and when later one was made out of a stable in the mews behind the house, it smelt definitely of horse and its windows were too high to see out of; sometimes two lessons went on simultaneously in it, for there was in addition only a small anteroom which one or at most two girls could use for private study. The boarders slept three in a room; after the school room was adapted Miranda's and another bedroom were over it; Octavia and her mother slept together in the back drawing-room. It was a rather spartan life. The Hills cared little for creature comforts, there were no easy chairs, beds were hard, hot water scarce. There was no regulation about the time for getting up; slices of bread and butter were put over night in the school room, and those who got up early were to consume some of these before they began to work. In winter they might light the fire for themselves.

Opportunities for physical development were not forgotten. 'We are so near Regents Park that the girls can walk there every day. We have the key of the private part of the Park and the girls play at running games there in the winter and at croquet in the summer quite undisturbed. In summer instead of dancing and gymnastic classes, the girls row on the ornamental water twice a week; they also get to a swimming bath once a week. Thus we give them opportunity for a good deal of healthful exercise.' How far Octavia was ahead of public opinion may be judged by the fact that some ten years later, the governing body of a girls' school in the same district being asked to provide facilities for 'healthful exercise' for the pupils replied: 'The Council would suggest to the promoters of this scheme, that the needful privacy in the care of girls, causes a wide difference between the concession of a playground for boys and one for girls.' The curriculum was wide for that date. 'The subjects we teach are the English subjects, Latin, French, Italian, German, music (part singing not solo singing), drawing, the elements of Euclid and Algebra also of botany, chemistry, and natural philosophy. In these latter sciences it is only just the first principles which are taught, but we find them valuable as well as interesting to the girls.'

Emily was a qualified teacher, but the Inspectors to-day would look askance at Octavia's equipment. 'I only began my physiology yesterday,' she writes, 'but have done a great deal since; I shall go on with it steadily preparing a lesson each week, and so shall learn much myself.' Latin presented difficulties too. 'Now that teaching has fallen to my share, I regret very much my great ignorance. I want to work very hard at Latin. Minnie and I are thinking of trying whether Mrs. S. or some other good Christian will read it with us. At present I work at it a little alone.' But if Octavia had no academic qualifications, she had an enthusiasm for learning which is worth more to a teacher, since it is infectious. Nor was she satisfied to remain unqualified. In a life already full enough to daunt most women, she managed to find time for private study, and in March, 1864, she could write triumphantly, 'I have my certificate from Queen's College signed, amongst others, by Stanley.'

It was characteristic of Octavia that her concern for the sound education of her own pupils led her to take part in the movement for the admission of girls to University examinations; it was always the need of the individual, known to her, which led her to an interest in a general question. It was part of the scrupulous honesty of her nature that she wanted her work judged by some objective standard; she felt that until some such was established the education of girls would not improve. 'There is no recognized system of examining pupils; I am sure the want is a great one, and very generally felt. . . . I feel the difficulty myself keenly, so keenly that I would not myself undertake pupils here,

6

till I had organized a plan by which their parents might see something of their progress. I provided each girl with a book, in which her answers to the examination questions each half year might be written; and thus her parents can see her progress. But of course the plan is clumsy. The questions are given by the teachers, who must necessarily know where the pupils are likely to fail, who examine, in fact, on their own course of instruction.' As soon as the Cambridge Local examinations were opened to girls the Nottingham Place children were all sent in for them. Their successes were a source of great happiness to Octavia, but she kept examinations in their right place. 'I was extremely pleased with the effect on our pupils. I thought they were much invigorated by the examination; it interested them much; the intercourse with other students gave them a feeling of working with a large body of learners all over England, which was very good, and I think the examination tended to raise their standard somewhat, which, I regret to say, I think is not high. These like all examinations require careful and noble use; people must look beyond them, or they cannot look at them rightly. There are better things to be learnt than can ever come out in them. And to work for one is dangerous; learning for the sake of learning and knowing is the only legitimate course; but a standard that will test our knowledge at last is almost invaluable.'

But no doubt what made the Nottingham Place School unique was the home life which the children shared with their teachers. 'We receive a few girls as boarders between the ages of twelve and eighteen, our reason for not increasing the number is that we wish to keep the arrangements those of a home, rather than of a school.' Indeed, the school life was that of a very happy family. The walks in the Park,

66

the games in the enclosure, the rowing on the ornamental water were all enjoyed together, and gave opportunities to the children to talk freely to the sisters. Octavia was perhaps more stimulating than the others, but Miranda was the most dearly loved: both were good talkers and delightful companions. Lessons were all over by 6 o'clock every day, and then all had dinner together in the dining-room, a room with an apsidal end in which hung a reproduction of Leonardo's 'Last Supper' with the legend, painted by Octavia herself, 'These are the living men, we the passing shadows on the wall.' Very often there were guests to dinner, sometimes people of such reputation as Ruskin, George MacDonald and F. D. Maurice, at other times less well-known people, but all interesting, for the Hills had never had either time or inclination to cultivate 'society'; their friends were always those whom they had met in the course of their work, men and women concerned in public work, in social reform, in all the burning questions of the day. The talk would be full of interest, a valuable part of the education of the girls who listened, and perhaps sometimes joined in, even as Miranda and Octavia had done as children, at their grandfather's table.

When there were no guests, the family would reassemble in the dining-room after the dinner was cleared away—the drawing-room was used on Sundays for hymn singing but otherwise remained untenanted—and the evening was spent in 'social intercourse'. Sometimes they sang together, sometimes the girls would do needlework while Octavia read aloud; she was a wonderful reader, her deep musical voice, her sense of rhythm, her obvious enjoyment of the books she chose made a lasting impression on all who heard her. A six o'clock dinner gives a long evening and a good deal of reading was accomplished in this way. Good talk, glee singing, needlework, reading aloud, a typical Victorian family evening, but those old enough to remember such, will perhaps hesitate to assert that the present generation is altogether to be congratulated on the exchange of these for its varied amusements.

On Saturday evenings all the week's mending was inspected, and every child had to submit the account of her week's pocket money to Octavia, and it had to be absolutely accurate; Octavia also inspected all drawers to see if they were tidy and the owner of one which was not so would find a little note in her drawer, directing her attention to the fact. It was altogether a very happy school. 'You will easily imagine what a busy and merry household we are, with all these young things laughing and playing like kittens.'

In July, 1863, this happiness was interrupted by the very serious illness of Miranda; for some days her life was despaired of, and anxiety lay heavy on the household. Octavia, wearied by grief and long hours of nursing, was touched by the sympathy and kindness shown to them on all sides; she writes of Maurice's daily visits, of Ruskin's constant enquiries, of 'the little children who stole about the house and spoke in whispers, and my children who did their work quite self-reliantly and waited with gentlest service on us; the poor old women who sent to enquire daily, and teachers who offered all service to set us free and friends who drove in to bring flowers and grapes, and servants who were like rocks of strength.' Miranda recovered, and the school found itself bound more closely than ever as one family by the period of anxiety it had lived through.

Meanwhile, the reputation of the school was steadily increasing, more friends wanted to send their children there, others still hoped to receive one or another of the sisters as a governess. One of these was Thomas Hughes (of *Tom Brown's School Days*), who told Octavia that for years he had been hoping to get one of them. 'I was much touched,' writes Octavia, 'by Mr. Hughes' grief about the children's hatred of lessons and finding that they wanted someone to take the children to the country for a month, till they could find a governess, thought that I might take the work, and might perhaps get the little things through some difficulties and so might make lessons pleasanter hereafter.'

Octavia accordingly spent something of a busman's holiday in the Christmas, 1863, teaching the Hughes' children, for she could never resist the call of those in need, and a child who hated to learn seemed to her in sore need of help. In the same spirit some years later, she spent a long summer holiday at Bude, teaching one of the MacDonald children who hated Latin, and as he records 'made him in love, if not with Aeneas and Dido, at least with Latin grammar as well as incidentally but quite permanently with herself'.

The advisability of increasing the number of children at Nottingham Place demanded consideration in 1866. By this time Octavia had begun what was to be the important work of her life, and though it was not at that time possible to foresee the dimensions to which it would grow, it was already absorbing much of her time and thought. To have a big school was no part of the Hills' intention, but it was difficult to refuse friends, difficult to refuse to take younger sisters when parents wished to send them. After some discussion it was decided that Miranda should give up her own school and become head of the Nottingham Place school, leaving Octavia more time for her social work, and increasing the number of boarders to fourteen.

Octavia was glad to hand over the responsibility of the school to Miranda. She was immensely interested in the children, but she was increasingly aware of a difficulty in entering fully into their pleasures. 'You know I've a damping, cool sort of way with them, that just stabs all their enjoyment. I don't think I've any child nature left in me.' Naturally quick and competent, she found it difficult not to be impatient with slow and fumbling efforts of the less intelligent; serious faults and difficulties she could meet with gentleness and understanding, but what she called the 'schoolgirl element', the ordinary silliness that pertains to that stage of development, irritated her; there had been no time for light-hearted foolishness in her own strenuous adolescence, and she did not realize that the normal schoolgirl rarely escapes it.

Miranda, on the other hand, had understanding for every type of child. She was less driven than Octavia, and was by temperament more tranquil. Just as, in girlhood, she had taken the plunge into London more easily, so now she took the follies of youth more lightly; she could detach herself and observe with amusement, while she waited for things to improve in a way always impossible to Octavia. 'We came home to that dear Haven named Miranda,' wrote a friend some years later, 'looking so sweet and rested, and full of delightful sayings and doings of other people. Can't you see her upturned face telling them, a twinkle in her eye at something funny?' She was a natural teacher who taught both child and subject, loving the former and enjoying the latter; she had the gift of making a child believe in her own power, a conviction that the

70

child who failed to-day would certainly succeed to-morrow, she was very gentle and those who did amiss met her astonished gaze, 'her eyes growing larger and larger' till they felt overburdened with guilt. She was full of gaiety and entered wholeheartedly, without effort, into the pleasures and projects of her pupils. No wonder that those who survive to-day, being asked about the school, reply with one voice, 'Oh, it was Miss Miranda!'

Chapter VI

BEGINNING OF HOUSING

'I see no end to what may grow out of it':
OCTAVIA TO RUSKIN, May, 1864

IN 1858 Octavia had written contrasting her 'human work' with the 'artistic work' to which 'I feel sure more and more of my life will be called'. In 1864 she was still of this mind; her ambition was to become a great artist, her professional duty at the moment, to be a good teacher; her 'human work' she regarded as an activity for her spare time. It was natural that she should so regard it, philanthropy as a career was quite outside the range of her thought. She did not, particularly, love humanity, she loved a great many human beings, her toymakers, with whom she had never lost touch, her pupils at the Working Women's College, those who served her in one way or another. Her eager sympathy led her into friendship with many such, and it was natural to her to throw herself wholeheartedly into their lives, to share their interests, their trials and their sorrows and to do her utmost to help each one as opportunity arose. With the hardships of the poor she had long been acquainted, but she had no theory of social improvement, she was too intelligent, and even at twenty-six, too experienced, to believe in any panacea for the evils which existed: what she believed was that one individual could help another by understanding and by unselfish service.

It was natural therefore that when the move into Not-

72

tingham Place gave her the space, she should forthwith institute a weekly meeting for her less fortunate friends. It was the mothers who could most obviously be helped. Week by week they came to the Nottingham Place kitchen and there, by Octavia and her sisters, they were initiated into the mysteries of cutting out and making clothes for their children. Sometimes there was reading aloud, sometimes singing in chorus. No doubt the mothers enjoyed the comfortable kitchen, the evenings of leisure, the quiet and peaceful talk undisturbed by their own families; certainly the Hills did, and after the school had begun the elder girls were allowed to join in the teaching and the singing. On one of these evenings a young mother fainted from fatigue. Octavia in great concern took her home and saw the damp unhealthy basement in which she lived with her family. Such a dwelling was no revelation to her. As early as she could remember she had heard her grandfather speak of evil housing conditions; she had herself visited the homes of her toymakers, and Working Women's College pupils, and had seen how many of them were compelled to live; she knew well that it was not easy to find tolerable accommodation for a family, but nevertheless she thought it should not be impossible to find something better for this one. She searched all over Marylebone, but in vain; children, then as now, were not regarded with favour by potential landlords, it seemed nothing could be done. For a long time Octavia had played with the idea of becoming a landlord herself, of having a model lodging house where families with children would be welcome; this incident accentuated her desire to realize the idea but at the moment it seemed impracticable.

It was just at this juncture that her work took her to

Ruskin. Her mind was seething with the problem of housing families, his, as it happened, with the problem of dis-
posing of the rather considerable sum of money he had
just inherited from his father. Could anything have been
more opportune? It is possible that Ruskin had already begun to have slight doubts about Octavia's artistic gifts,
that he was uneasily wondering whether he had done well
in encouraging her to believe that she should give her life
to art; in a letter to Emma Baumgartner in 1863 about a
visit to Ruskin, she records his praise of her work but adds:
'I was earnestly charged to leave any drawing if I saw what
of help I could give anywhere. "Never argue that it is not
my work," he said. "I believe you have power among
people, which I ought not to monopolize." '

Ruskin very often consulted Octavia about social and
ethical questions, and he now asked her advice about his
father's money. She did not, at the moment, tell him how
well she knew the best use that could be made of it; she
went home and turned the matter over in her mind; sure
as she was of Ruskin's sympathy and generosity, she did
not easily ask for money, even for her most cherished projects. After two days she wrote and put the whole matter
before him. The answer came by return of post:

May 19, 1864

My Dear Octavia,

Yes, it will delight me to help you in this; but I
should like you to begin very quietly and temperately and
to go on gradually. My father's executors are old friends,
and I don't want to discomfort them by lashing out suddenly into a number of plans. In about three months from
this I shall know more precisely what I am about: mean-

time, get your ideas clear and believe me you will give me one of the greatest pleasures yet possible to me, by enabling me to be of use in this particular manner and to these ends.

Affectionately yours,
JOHN RUSKIN

Octavia was delighted. She was perfectly willing to begin quietly and go slowly, she did not even expect to go very far; her idea was 'a small lodging house, where I may know everyone and do something towards making their lives healthier and happier', yet even as she wrote about it, she realized more and more the possibilities opening out before her. 'I see no end to what may grow out of it, our present singing and work will of course be open to any of our tenants who like to come. We shall take the children out, and teach the girls, and many bright friendships I hope will grow up amongst us. The servants and children here are trained for the work, and longing to co-operate.'

The first step was to find the right house. Octavia began blithely enough. Almost for the first time in her life she had no difficulty about money, there was no lack of admirably suitable large empty houses with gardens in the neighbourhood; it seemed a simple proposition to walk out and buy one. It proved far otherwise. Landlords and agents who welcomed the prospective purchaser with eager courtesy, turned cold and disapproving when they learned the purpose to which the house was to be put; they were not willing to spoil their property by accepting such undesirable tenants. 'Where *are* the poor to live?' asked Octavia desperately of an agent, who replied coldly, 'I don't know; but they must keep off the St. John's Wood Estate.' Octavia was disappointed, but not discouraged. Since it was clear that owners of good property would not accept her tenants, she must find property no longer good. There were plenty of Courts in Marylebone, among these she must make her lodging house. William Shaen, her friend and lawyer, heart and soul in the scheme, helped in the search, and did all the legal side of the business. The delays seemed to Octavia almost interminable, but at last in the spring of 1865 Ruskin became the owner of three houses in a Court quite near to Nottingham Place. It was not the house Octavia had dreamed of, since there was no garden, but it made a beginning. 'I am so happy,' she wrote, 'that I can hardly walk on the ground.' Until Midsummer, there was a resident landlord in each house, so that Octavia could not get to work, as she longed to do, at once. She took a holiday in the spring in order that she might be able to do without one when her new work began, and she spent every moment she could spare in thinking out her plan.

Ruskin had urged that the scheme should be made to pay; he suggested that he should receive 5 per cent on his capital, not so much because he cared about the interest, as because he felt that if the enterprise could be made profitable, others would follow Octavia's example and the whole standard of working class housing would be raised. Octavia was not impressed with this argument. 'Who will ever hear of what I do?' she asked incredulously. But she was determined on other grounds to make her houses pay. Her position was perfectly clear. 'A working man ought to be able to pay for his house.' She hated to be dependent herself, and this sentiment seemed to her so human and right that she was convinced her tenants would share it; to force them to live on the charity of others seemed to her an

76

insult; it was because she respected her tenants as human individuals that she was determined to make it possible for them to pay an economic rent. She knew it would not be easy, but she believed that with patience and determination she could succeed. 'The plan promises to pay, but of this I say very little, so much depends on management, and the possibilities of avoiding bad debts. Did I tell you of the purchase of a chest of tea for selling to the women? They save much, and get very good tea. My hope, however, is not in this, nor in any other outward arrangement, but in these as a means of knowing and training the people to work and to trust. It is with me entirely a question of education. My hope is in that.'

Her first three houses were in Paradise Place; a year later Ruskin bought for her 'a row of cottages facing a bit of desolate ground, occupied with wretched dilapidated cowsheds, manure heaps, old timber and rubbish of every description'. It was at no great distance from the original purchase, and though a worse property, it had in Octavia's eyes the supreme merit of giving her space for a playground; at the end of 1866 she acquired 'the four very worst houses I have ever had to deal with'.

It is difficult for us to-day to conceive the character of the property for which Octavia had now become responsible. There are still, unfortunately, 'slums'—an ugly word which Octavia would never suffer to be used about the homes of her tenants; she called them 'Courts' always—but one might safely say that the type of tenant and dwelling with which she had to deal has passed away. Part of the evil was due to the type of landlord in possession. He was generally a man (or woman) of slender means who had bought the house as an investment and meant to make all

he could out of it; he had no capital to spend on his property even if he had wished to keep it in good order, but he
saw no reason why he should do so; drains that a surveyor
regarded with horror he considered to be 'in an excellent
condition for the class of inmates'. He therefore neglected
repairs, and in his dealings with tenants, was uncertain,
now harsh, now foolishly lenient; the arrears of rent were
large, six, seven or eight weeks were due from most
tenants, and some owed very much more. One landlord,
indeed, an undertaker, said frankly to Octavia, 'Yes Miss,
of course there are plenty of bad debts. It's not the rents
I look to, but the deaths I get out of the houses!'

Octavia has recorded the condition of her first three
houses when she acquired them. 'The plaster was dropping
from the walls, on one staircase a pail was placed to catch
the rain that fell through the roof. All the staircases were
perfectly dark, the bannisters were gone, having been used
as firewood by the tenants. The grates, with large holes in
them, were falling forward into the rooms. The wash-
house, full of lumber belonging to the landlord, was locked
up; thus the inhabitants had to wash clothes, as well as to
cook and to sleep in their small rooms. The dust-bin,
standing in front of the houses, was accessible to the whole
neighbourhood, and boys often dragged from it quantities
of unseemly objects and spread them over the Court. The
state of the drainage was in keeping with everything else.
The pavement of the back yard was all broken up, and
great puddles stood in it, so that the damp crept up the
outer walls. One large but dirty water-butt received the
water laid on for the houses; it leaked, and for such as did
not fill their jugs when the water came in, or who had no
jugs to fill, there was no water.' This was the property

78

which filled Octavia with such happiness that she could 'hardly walk on the ground'.

As might be expected, the tenants were equally unpromising. They were living in a state of poverty quite unknown to-day; they were for the most part only casually employed, and at a very low wage; they had large families, and since education was not compulsory, the children spent most of their days fighting or sitting about in the gutters with dirty faces and listless vacant expressions. There was a great deal of drunkenness and fighting, a natural enough result of small irregular wages, discomfort at home and an absence of any rational amusement outside it. The Court had the worst possible reputation, but in the circumstances this is less remarkable than the fact that any of its inmates retained any standard of decency at all.

Octavia went over the houses with the outgoing landlord the last day he collected his rents there, that she might be introduced to the tenants as the new owner. They must have made a curious pair, the man (not, says Octavia, a cruel man, except in so far as variableness of dealing is cruelty) accompanied by a friend whom he hoped his tenants would believe to be a broker, perfunctorily securing what rent he could, so used to the characters of his tenants and the conditions in which they lived as barely to notice them, and Octavia, noticing everything—the vermin, the wallpapers black with dirt hanging in depressing strips from the wall, the sullen hostility of tenants, the general degradation of the whole place. An experienced social worker might be excused for having misgivings, might well quail at the prospect of tackling so stiff a piece of work. What was her reaction? 'I think no one who has not experienced it can fully realize the almost awed sense of

joy with which one enters upon such a possession, conscious of having the power to set it even partially in order.'
So in a spirit of exultation she began her great adventure.

Obviously the first thing to do was to put the property into a tolerable state of repair. Decent sanitary arrangements and a sufficient water supply were the first necessities. The buildings were sound, and it was possible to put them in order very quickly. Octavia was warned by all who knew the neighbourhood that it was useless to replace banisters, or reglaze windows (in one property only 8 of 192 were intact), or to attempt any cleansing operations, since the tenants would at once break the windows, burn the banisters and sully whatever she had cleaned. Undeterred by these prophecies she proceeded with her repairs. The prophets were in part right, things were destroyed again and again and as often replaced. Octavia had infinite patience and believed that in time tenants would learn to respect property that was well cared for.

The business of cleansing the houses was urgent, and though no permanent improvement was possible without a change in the habits of the inmates, Octavia began at once to do what she could. As landlord she was responsible for passages, stairs, wash-houses and yards. These at least she could make and keep clean. She had them all whitewashed and scrubbed thoroughly and regularly, hoping that the dark line of demarcation between the clean passage and the still dirty room would presently arouse the attention and begin to trouble the mind of its inmates. New windows on the stairs made the dark line more visible. At least a standard of cleanliness was suggested, and the provision of sufficient water and adequate wash-houses made it attainable for those who desired it.

But the crux of the matter lay not so much with the buildings as with the tenants. Octavia knew only one way of dealing with people, it was to get to know them as individuals, and to try to help them as one friend can help another. The collection of rents gave her the opportunity of seeing her tenants regularly, but to a less courageous person the prospect of making friends through the weekly call for rent would have seemed somewhat dim. Regularly she called and her reception was hostile. Tenants went out to avoid her, and she had to go again and again to the same door. In one court, chiefly inhabited by costermongers who were out all day, she had to go at night. 'The front doors stood open day and night, and as I felt my way down the kitchen stairs, broken and rounded by the hardened mud upon them, the foul smells which the heavy foggy air would not allow to rise met me as I descended, and the plaster rattled down with a hollow sound as I groped along.' Sometimes looking in at the open door she would find the tenant lying drunk on the floor; the more promising tenants would push the rent book and money through a chink of the door, placing a foot firmly against it lest she should find her way in. The yards were full of men often fighting and brawling. Octavia walked in week after week at all hours of the day, alone and completely fearless, picking her way over the filth and through the rough crowd, noticing everything and saying nothing. She continued to order necessary repairs, above all, she continued to insist that she must have her rent *every* week, she would have no accumulation of arrears. At first the tenants could not understand this, they had not been accustomed to a landlord who could be moved neither by threats nor flattery. More than once a tenant, having admitted Octavia to her room, turned the lock on her, refusing to let her out till some point was conceded. Octavia's technique was always the same. She remained quite unmoved and perfectly silent. This would prove very disconcerting to the tenant, whose voice would gradually drop lower and lower until at last, being unable to deal with someone who did not hurl back violence and insult, she would fall silent too. Then very quietly and calmly Octavia would restate her original position, and since further abuse merely produced a repetition of the scene, there was presently nothing to do but to let the landlord out.

When the rent was not forthcoming, after due warning, Octavia proceeded to take steps to evict the defaulter. At first the tenants imagined this to be bluff, but when they discovered that the proceedings would be stopped only if the rent was paid it generally was produced. Some tenants she lost, of course, and each one was a real and personal sorrow to her, but she was very certain that she could do nothing unless she established the principle that the relation between her and her tenants was one of reciprocal duties; she would do her duty as landlord most scrupulously, and she would demand from them an equally punctual discharge of their obligations. It was not easy for Octavia to insist rigidly on the observance of her rule; she cared so little for money, so much for people that to show leniency to those who had somehow failed to have the rent ready would have been a far more natural and pleasanter course to take. 'It is far easier to be helpful,' she wrote, 'than to have patience and self-control sufficient, when the times come for seeing suffering and not relieving it,' but she remained inexorable, believing that a relaxation would entail 'cumulative evil on the defaulter, and set a bad example, too readily followed by others'.

Gradually the hostility of the tenants softened. They got used to the short sturdy figure which appeared punctually on the expected day, whatever the weather, and moved resolutely and buoyantly across the sordid yards; almost reluctantly they were obliged to recognize the pluck which took her alone, after dark, into places where the police were accustomed to visit only in pairs. It is a significant fact that though many of her tenants were of the roughest and most lawless type, she was never molested or robbed as she walked through them with her collected rent in her bag. Presently they began to appreciate the even justice of her rule and the fact that she never went back on her word in the smallest particular, and when they discovered that she would never walk into their rooms uninvited, the obstructive foot was withdrawn from the door.

When this stage was reached it was possible to attempt to secure the co-operation of the tenants in her schemes for their welfare. She took them into her confidence, trusting their essential reasonableness. She told them all how much money she had to spend on repairs in each house, and promised that if the actual cost of necessary repairs fell short of the sum she had put aside, the balance should be spent on any improvement they desired, safes, washing stools, copper lids or cupboards, the choice should be theirs. At once it became the interest of all to keep the repairs bill low; wanton damage ceased at once, accidents became fewer, and many of the men became interested in doing small repairs themselves to save money. Another form of co-operation with the tenants consisted in the organization of bands of cleaners from among the elder girls, who scrubbed each passage twice a week at 6d. a week. There is always something stimulating about one's first earnings, and the possession of a regular income was a great delight to the children. They became interested in the work too, and took pleasure in the whiteness of their own passages. 'One little girl,' writes Octavia, 'was so proud of her first cleaning that she stood two hours watching her passage lest the boys, whom she considered as the natural enemies of order and cleanliness, should spoil it before I came to see it.'

Octavia next tried to tackle the problem of over-crowding. There were six rooms in each of the three houses Ruskin first bought, and a family in each room. Families were large, and since lodgings were hard to get, kindness or cupidity or a mixture of the two had induced many to take lodgers. An old pupil of the Nottingham Place School remembers being shown a room in which eighteen persons had been living. This was obviously an intolerable state of affairs, and Octavia at once made a rule that there should be no sub-letting at all. As a room fell vacant she tried to persuade one tenant or another to take a second. But many had become accustomed to managing in one room, and grudged the extra rent for another. She made the difference so small as to be almost negligible, still they were unwilling, convinced that they could find better ways of spending the money. Octavia would not insist. She could and did refuse to allow new tenants to take accommodation which she considered inadequate, but she did not feel justified in coercing those who were already established. 'A man has a right to choose the kind of life he will live,' she wrote, and on that right she was determined not to encroach. But as the tenants grew to know her better and increasingly to respect her judgment, it became more difficult for them to hold out against her obvious disapproval.

She tells how a woman with husband and seven children occupying a single room explained at great length all the good uses to which she would put the money which Octavia wished her to spend on a second room. 'I was perfectly silent. A half pleading, half assenting voice said, "Don't you *see* I'm right, Miss?" No, I said, indeed I do not, . . . but of course you must do as you think best.' For the moment the family remained in the one room, but when a little later another room fell vacant, the woman herself asked for it.

The combination of firmness and patience proved irresistible. In a surprisingly short time the houses were in order and Octavia had established a relationship with her tenants based on the recognition of the principle that the duties of landlord and tenants are reciprocal. If, in practice, it was not always perfectly applied by the tenants, Octavia at least joyfully accepted the mass of detailed and often tiresome work it involved. 'I've just come in from a round of visits to the nine houses,' she wrote, 'and somehow its been a day of small worries about all sorts of repairs and things of that kind. I was thinking when I came in, that really it would be a small cost in value to pay any sum however tremendous to get rid of this annoying small perpetual care, if the work could be done as well; but then it couldn't; it is only when the detail is managed on as great principles as the whole plan, that a work becomes really good. And so, I suppose, being really the school of training the tenants most effectually, I must still keep it, and hope that it will not finally make one either small or mean, or bitter.'

Chapter VII

THE TENANTS

'You cannot deal with people and their houses separately':
OCTAVIA HILL in 'Homes of the London Poor',
Macmillan's Magazine, October, 1871

IN the *Fortnightly Review* in November, 1866, Octavia wrote: 'Two kinds of work depend entirely on one another if they are to bear their full fruit. There is first the simple fulfilment of a landlady's bounden duties, and uniform demand of the fulfilment of those of the tenants. . . . Then secondly, there is the individual friendship which grows up from intimate knowledge.' This second aspect of the work had occupied Octavia from the beginning of her experiment. Less technical, though no less exacting, than the management of property, it offered abundant scope to those who could bring little but energy and good will to the service of their fellows. Octavia believed profoundly in the importance of friendly intercourse between all sorts of people and was convinced that those who came to her help had as much to gain as to give from such relationships. She was eager to enlist the help of her pupils, and even before the houses were bought she was thinking out schemes to this end. Every Sunday morning the school produced a journal, to which one or another of the household contributed. It was in this journal on a Sunday in the autumn of 1864 that Octavia wrote: 'I wish to say a little to you about the new work which I hope you feel is as much yours as mine. You know, of course, that I am thinking of the house which I hope will be ours very soon . . . it is about the small practical matters that I wish to write . . . each of you may have her own special work in the house if you will, each may make it a greater blessing to those who live in it—in the friendship and thought and care you may bestow. . . . There are definite actual works to be done for which you will want . . . such regularity and reliability that what is entrusted to you, you will do—without further admonition or supervision. To give an instance . . . we may have a co-operative store opened at our house for our tenants as soon as any one of you has qualified herself to take the management, which means mainly keep the accounts of it. I would manage the rest, but this I could not do. Whenever any one of you feels that I may really trust her, let her come forward and say so. . . . Many, many helpful things of the kind will open out for you."

The girls fulfilled Octavia's expectations and soon found a variety of ways of establishing natural relations with the tenants. The children were an obvious means of approach, and the mothers gladly accepted the help of the pupils who took the children off their hands at busy moments, played with them, sometimes taught them and often mended or made for them. Here was a perfectly natural intercourse, involving no condescension on the one side or subservience on the other. The girls became aware of the conditions in which their poorer neighbours lived, and of some of the social problems which were crying out for solution.

Octavia had defined her business relation to her tenants as one of 'perfect strictness'. It is interesting that, in an age of more clearly defined social classes than to-day, when the Lady Bountiful and the Grateful Poor were still regarded as admirable characters, the word Octavia used to express her ideal for the personal relationship between herself and her tenants was 'perfect respectfulness'. 'I should treat them,' she wrote, 'with the same courtesy as I should show towards my other personal friends; there would be no interference, no entering their rooms uninvited, no offer of money or the necessaries of life. But when occasion presented itself, I should give them any help I could, such as I might offer without insult to other friends, sympathy in their distresses, advice, help and counsel in their difficulties, introductions that might be of use to them, a lent book when unable to work; a bunch of flowers brought on purpose.'

Such a relationship could not be forced; it must come gradually, and all Octavia could do to begin with was to provide some opportunity for making contacts easily. Her first step, taken as soon as she had acquired her first houses, was to turn the stable at the back of her own home into a large room for the use of tenants. She and Emma Cons did the whitewashing themselves and prepared two rooms above it as a dwelling for a blind man and his wife in whom they were interested. Later, when she acquired her second property, she was able to turn one of the shops in that court into a regular clubroom, and the stable room became the school room for the Nottingham Place School. The sewing class from the Nottingham Place kitchen moved at once into the new room, and it was thrown open to tenants. There was some hesitation at first, but no one was pressed to join, and presently one or another dropped in to see what it was like, found it pleasant and stayed, and gradually the numbers increased. Octavia went very warily, eager to meet any need which was felt, chary of forcing anything which was not really wanted. Presently it appeared that singing would be acceptable, then some of the younger ones thought they would try drawing. More and more classes were instituted, and whether she was teaching or not, Octavia was always there. It soon became possible to arrange classes for the boys and girls at times when their parents were not using the room. It is impossible to over-estimate the importance of the room in Octavia's scheme, but it lay not so much in the classes held there, as in the fact that it became a centre for tenants, a place where they met socially, chatted and compared babies. Octavia, sit-ting silent among them, observing them unobtrusively as they talked among themselves, or discussing problems quietly with one or another, came to have an intimate un-derstanding of their point of view which she could have gained in no other way. More important still, the tenants who met there acquired interests in common, they dis-covered themselves to be really members of a community in which each could play a part, instead of units of no im-portance in a great city. Octavia was happy when she heard them use the expression 'one of us', for it showed the growth of real corporate feeling, an ingredient necessary to a truly civilized life. In her realization of the importance of fostering this corporate life, Octavia showed herself not merely ahead of her generation, but so far ahead that we are only now beginning to overtake her, for it is only the more enlightened housing authorities to-day who make a community centre when they build a block of flats or de-velop an estate; there are still far too many working class dwellings built without provision for any sort of social life, to the great loss of the inhabitants and of society at large.

As Octavia came to know her tenants more intimately she found herself more and more able to be of service to them. She realized that the irregularity of employment was the main cause of their perpetual insolvency, and she tried to help them in two ways. In the first place she did what she could to employ them in slack seasons. There was always a certain amount of work on the property, necessary but not urgent, which any tenant was competent to do; this she saved up and shared out among those who were out of work. Secondly, she helped them to save in good seasons. Her method showed her understanding of the essence of the problem. Those who can put aside only very small sums, will not do so unless it is made very easy; to make it so she brought the Savings Bank to their door. Every Saturday evening from 6 o'clock onwards, she sat in the Club Room 'with pen and ink and bags for money at a deal table, under a flaring gas jet' and received such small sums as the tenants wished to entrust to her. Saturday evenings became a time at which Octavia could certainly be found, whenever there was any thorny problem to discuss, advice or help to be sought. The tenants came in increasing numbers, they were delighted to discover how their accounts mounted up, and they learned gratefully to depend on her steady friendship.

The work Octavia was doing was sufficiently remarkable to attract attention. Ruskin was naturally interested in it and talked about it, others concerned with social problems heard of it and wished to see for themselves what she was doing; people began to ask if they might visit her houses. Octavia was bothered by this. 'There is nothing to see,' she said to one applicant, 'only a great deal to do.' She could not altogether refuse to take people round the Courts, but she really disliked having to do it. She was sensitive for her tenants, and could not endure that they should be made exhibits, subjected to the curiosity of visitors they had not invited to their homes. It was not possible to foresee whether a prospective enquirer would treat the tenants as so many cases to be investigated or recognize them as hostesses graciously willing to show their homes to friends of a friend. Princess Alice of Hesse belonged to the latter category. One of Octavia's nieces records her visit: 'She made Aunt Octavia walk in front of her everywhere, as she was anxious to be entirely incog. Aunt Octavia said that she was "perfectly delightful with the people", and she had "never taken anyone who seemed to know so exactly the right thing to say". In one house she discovered that the eldest child's name was Victoria, and told the mother, "I have a little Victoria too", and found they were almost exactly the same age. On hearing that Vicky, before starting to school, had blacked the grate, the Princess remarked ruefully, "My Vicky could not have done that, I fear!" ' (This was, of course, the future Czarina!)

The purchase of the second property in the spring of 1866 made it possible for Octavia to realize a cherished dream. A garden for her tenants had always been part of her scheme and it was only the impossibility of finding a house with a garden that had reconciled her to begin without one. She hated to see washing hanging in the one living room the family possessed, unsightly and inconvenient, she felt the necessity of providing an open space where the children could play in safety and their parents could sit and rest when they had a spare moment. Her new property did not actually possess a garden, but it included a space, covered with mounds of rubbish and derelict buildings, which could be made to serve her purpose. Ruskin had promised her some trees and some creepers to grow against the walls. She planned to have some little gardens, and to gravel the rest of the space, enclosing the whole with a wall.

She quickly set to work on the business of clearing the space, and discovered at once both how difficult and how important the provision of her playground was to be. 'Every moment of my waking time, my whole thought has been of the playground in Freshwater Place, and every second of spare time has been spent there. It is indeed an almost desperate undertaking, whether we shall really succeed with it is still most doubtful, only if it can be made to answer by any power I have, it *shall*, for the difficulties that impede it only prove the need of it.' These difficulties arose from the hostility of the neighbours who resented the clearing up of a waste space, which they had been accustomed to use as a place for fighting or loafing or throwing out their rubbish. 'And the children!' writes Octavia, 'their eyes all inflamed with continued dirt, their bare feet, their wild cries, their disordered hair, and clothes looking as if dogs had torn them all round. There is a poor dejected girl, whom they call Margates, half-witted they say and an orphan—one of five—she wanders over dirt heaps all day, without shoes or stockings, looking so vacant, scolded and rated by everyone, long locks of hair falling over her wild eyes.'

These unhappy people combined to hamper the work of clearing the ground and building the wall round it. They stole the bricks, they threw the rubbish back when it had been cleared out, they interfered with the workers. Octavia appealed to the police with very little effect. From time to time a policeman came and the enemy was scattered for the moment, but the respite was only temporary, and the assailants returned. Less than a week before the opening ceremony, Octavia found that the wall, which in spite of difficulties had been slowly rising, had been pulled down in the night and lay 'one tumbled mass of ruin. A bitter hopelessness filled my heart,' she records, 'I cannot tell you how I had worked and hoped, but with the need came the determination, if not the hope, and vigorously I set to work to repair the evil.' Octavia's invincible courage carried the matter through. She was there late and early. Her builders, fired by her tireless energy, worked furiously at the wall, and a watchman was employed to guard it at night. The opening ceremony took place on the day that had been determined, 70 tickets were issued to tenants and their children and their friends; there was a Maypole, flags, singing and a band from a Boys' Home, and a most happy tea party, in spite of an occasional stone or brickbat heaved over the wall by hostile neighbours.

The playground was there. But now the children must be educated to use it. Octavia was not likely to underestimate either the difficulty or the importance of the task. Long before Education Authorities had discovered the value of games in education, before play-centres were thought of, or the importance of training children to use leisure had been realized, Octavia had been distressed by the sight of children hanging about listlessly doing nothing, or squabbling, gambling, or playing utterly pointless games. That the children must be taught something better, some game that demanded a slight measure of skill, which called for co-ordination of head and eye, and some power of co-operation among themselves, she had no doubt. The Nottingham Place girls were ready enough to help, and could do much with small groups of children who had already been tenants for some little time and had come to know and trust 'Miss October and her young ladies'. But the playground with its horde of untamed boys and girls, children of tenants of the new houses, quite unused to any sort of discipline, was too difficult a proposition for young people to tackle. Octavia therefore must do most of the work herself. Her sisters helped her when they could and she found other volunteers, but hers was the animating spirit, and hers the responsibility. It was difficult and wearying work. 'I have had four hours at the playground,' she wrote. 'It always feels like so many years. No one can imagine the awfulness of the dirt and the disgustingness of the children.' But she persevered. Perhaps it was the flame of her vitality that caught the children and made them wish to do the things she suggested and find pleasure in doing them. She was always devising new occupations for them. One day she hired an organ grinder to come in and play. 'The children's joy was overflowing. The whole ground was covered with tiny dancing figures, each child danced alone, a step rather like a jig. If you could have seen the beaming smiles on the pale dirty faces, and the little bare legs moving so merrily, it would have done your heart good.' Another day she gave them gay rags of stuff and bade them make little flags, then she cut out the initials of each child in another coloured rag and allowed each child to sew her own initials on her own flag. 'Their joy was intense, hour after hour passed, and they seemed never to tire.' For the babies she arranged kindergarten games, for the older children games demanding a modicum of skill. They began to try to play with some regard to the rules and to regard cheating with disfavour. Presently Octavia found that if she had once got them interested in a game they would go on playing it without her direct supervision. Still it was uphill work. Octavia could not herself always be there, and she knew that in her absence there was a good deal of horse play and of bullying. She engaged a superintendent, a Mrs. Simeon, to be in the playground all the time that it was open. This met part of the difficulty, for the children grew fond of her, and she exercised control over the more amenable of them, though naturally she lacked Octavia's animating power.

Gradually the playground got into order. More friends came to help. One, the daughter of a school inspector, had had some experience in managing children, and proved a tower of strength. 'Oh, we had such a successful afternoon there,' Octavia records some three months after the opening, 'quantities of spirited boys and such fine games.' The 'spirited boys' had been something of a problem, being rather contemptuous of girls' games and of activities arranged for the smaller children. Now Octavia found a friend who undertook to teach them to play on pipes and drums, and being happily absorbed in a really manly occupation, they ceased to disturb the other children. When this stage was reached it was possible to extend the use of the playground to other children of the neighbourhood. The local hostility had to some extent died down, it was at least no longer active. When the children's balls bounced over the wall into the yards of the adjoining houses, some at least of the neighbours restored them in a friendly spirit, though others were so fierce that no child dared approach them. Now they were invited to allow their children also to use the playground, and there was an immediate influx of new children, dirty, quarrelsome, violent, and wholly ignorant of games. This, however, was not so difficult to tackle. The tenants' children found themselves to be in some sort hosts and hostesses to the newcomers, and took great pride in teaching them what they had themselves so recently learned. So the playground flourished, and Octavia, looking in when she could spare the time, no longer felt that every hour she spent there seemed like a year. To the parents it was an unmixed blessing, since it afforded them relief from the perpetual presence of their children in their very small houses. Moreover, the children flourished. Having spent hours of happy activity they slept better, they learned to play with other children, to give and take, in a word, under the cheerful and easy discipline of the playground they became much easier to manage, and the parents could not fail to notice this and to appreciate Octavia's work for them.

The playground was a splendid place for parties. May Day celebrations, so dear to Ruskin's heart, took place there, and after the crowning of the little Queen—chosen by lot—the children had cakes, biscuits and oranges; but except for one or two boys, the flowers interested them more than the cake. There were other parties too. Octavia was wont to quote Mr. Sleary's speech from *Hard Times*, 'People mutht be amoothed, Thquire', and she loved to provide these amusements, in the summer at her playground, in the winter in her Room. Sometimes the tenants' children themselves were helped to act simple little plays. Miranda wrote more than one fairy play for them, and then the school worked hard, teaching, rehearsing and making clothes, and the result, however a professional critic might assess it, seemed to the parents at least as perfect as can be expected of human effort: at other times the school provided the entertainment and sometimes Octavia's friends came. Foremost among these was Emma

Cons, always ready to help, and it was perhaps here that she first began to realize the want of good entertainment for those who could afford to pay little for it, a want she and her niece Lilian Baylis were so magnificently to supply later in the Old Vic.

Eighteen months after the original purchase of the houses, Octavia could look back with thankfulness on what she had been able to do. Her scheme had proved financially sound, she had paid 5 per cent on the capital (£838), of which she had repaid £48. Though she had never herself taken any commission on the sums she collected, she had put aside the usual percentage for it, partly because she felt she might at some time need help, but chiefly because she wished to prove that her houses were really self-supporting. Her tenants were flourishing under her rule, there were practically no arrears of rent, and in the winter of 1867–68, when the distress among the working classes was so severe that relief was being widely distributed, none of her tenants needed any help at all.

It may well be asked how so remarkable a result was achieved in an age of large families and low wages, and in the absence of sickness or unemployment insurance. It is impossible fully to explain the success except in terms of Octavia's personality, but it is possible to discern certain factors which contributed to it. In the first place there was her perfect regularity and her meticulous attention to every detail. This gave the tenants a sense of security very precious to those little used to it. They knew they could depend upon her absolutely. No grievance was too small, no problem too trivial for her consideration, and she gave her whole attention to each while she was dealing with it; she never forgot to do what she had said she would do; there was never delay in carrying out her promises; she understood the difficulties inherent in living at close quarters with other people, using washhouses and staircases in common, and was always ready to ease them if it could anyway be done. They knew well that with no other landlord would they find the same unfailing consideration and evenness of rule, indeed, they knew that accommodation even of an inferior kind was hard to find. This made them extremely anxious to keep their homes, and since there was no appeal against Octavia's rule of paying each week, they made immense efforts to have the rent ready when she called for it, and produced it, for it is a fact of common experience that it is generally possible to find the money for what is really believed to be of paramount importance. In enforcing her rule Octavia had certain advantages denied to most social workers to-day. She had the whole business entirely under her own control, there was at this stage of her work no authority over her to whom appeal could be made, no one whom she needed to convince. She could do exactly what she thought right, and she had the immense advantage of being herself completely convinced that her method was right. She had no misgivings. Nowadays the whole question of poverty is less simple. Conscious of privileges which we have in no sense merited, we feel apologetic to those who have never had them, and in an almost shamefaced eagerness to make things more equal, we are inclined to give freely, dismissing as an impertinence the question of the effect of our action on the character of the recipient, unwilling to demand any self-denial from those to whom circumstance already denies so much. Whether this modern attitude is sounder than Octavia's is a matter of opinion, but there can be no doubt that it makes it more difficult to collect rent. Octavia did not feel apologetic, she was deeply conscious of her privileges, but wealth seemed to her the least of these, and to give material things freely would have seemed to her to widen rather than to close the gap between herself and her tenants. She quite simply regarded them as individuals fundamentally like herself, though circumstances had made it difficult for them to keep that independence of spirit which she felt sure they desired. Her function was to help them to regain it or to strengthen it, and therefore she scrupulously regarded their rights. 'I would not set my conviction, however strong it might be, against your judgment of right,' but equally she expected them to respect her rights. The tenants appreciated this recognition of their equality. No doubt they grumbled from time to time, as all English people do; no doubt some, preferring 'bondage with ease to strenuous liberty', left her property and sank into squalor —she found many of these again in the Courts which Lady Ducie bought at the end of 1869—but the great majority responded to her standard, and prospered. In good times she came with her savings bank, helping them to save; in bad times she could often give them work; at all times she was ready to help the children to better education, to training, to apprenticeship, and she could always find a suitable opening for them when they were ready for it.

It must be remembered that the number of tenants for whom she was responsible at this time was relatively small, and it was possible for Octavia to know each one as an individual and to judge how each could be usefully and acceptably helped. Circumstances had made her their landlord, and her personality had made her their friend. This is the explanation of her success. It lay in no theory or method, but in her genuine friendship for each individual, in her confident appeal to the best in each one, in her faith in the unconquerable power of righteousness.

Chapter VIII

INTERLUDE

'I do not mean to add one more to the mournful list of women and girls who have rendered themselves incapable of doing anything by their determination to do more than they should':

OCTAVIA TO MARY HARRISON

It is not surprising that by the summer of 1867 Octavia was feeling jubilant about her houses. All was going so well and the work was abundantly satisfying. It called forth all her powers of mind and heart, there was scope for her practical ability in the care of the houses and the financial side of the business, and for her maternal instinct and pastoral gifts in the care of the tenants. She saw no limit to the possibilities opening for her, but it was becoming apparent to all her friends, and presently even to herself, that there was a limit to her physical power. In addition to the work in her houses, she was still earning a livelihood by teaching in the school and by drawing for Ruskin. It was impossible to go on working at such pressure. She was attacked again by the familiar pain and dizziness, and she was soon forced to recognize that the price of being able to carry on her work at all was a long period of rest and change.

She had learned to accept necessity and proceeded to reorganize her business. She had, of course, far too much on her hands to entrust to any single individual, but fortunately there was no need to attempt to do this. The work lent itself to delegation and there was no lack of willing helpers; Miranda had nicknamed her sister St. Ursula on account of her capacity for attracting disciples and followers. The principal responsibility naturally fell upon her sisters, who had worked with her from the beginning, and were intimately involved in all she did. As her house property had increased, Octavia had already begun to give less time to the school, and now Miranda took over all her work there. This included all that the girls in the school had done with and for the tenants: entertainments in the Hall, activities in the Playground, caring for the children, teaching them on Sundays, taking them for walks and outings on half holidays; this side of the work passed into Miranda's hands. She was helped by Harriet Harrison, a very old friend, who proved most competent in taming the more unruly spirits in the playground. The property management devolved upon Emily, who directed a band of rent collectors including Emma Cons, and some of the old pupils of the Nottingham Place School. Mrs. Nassau Senior, a sister of Thomas Hughes, undertook the accounts, an arduous task made more complicated by a certain haziness in arithmetic in some of her colleagues as well as of the tenants; it is recorded that on one occasion she was called upon to arbitrate in a bitter controversy between a tenant and a rent collector which turned on the question as to whether the rent due was 6s. 11d. or 7s. all but a penny.

Having thus disposed of her business, Octavia set forth to stay with Mary Harris in Cumberland. She found it very hard really to break away from her work. For the first time even the beloved companionship of Mary Harris failed to distract her mind from its problems. She hungered for news of all the tenants, eagerly demanding details about each one from her sisters. On Florence's birthday, when there was a tenants' party, she sent a letter to be read to them: 'You will all know . . . how I have loved my work, and how I have only left it in the full hope of going back to it far better able to do it than I was. So you will understand that I hope we have a great deal to do together in the glad time to come, when I shall be among you again.'

All the summer Octavia was in Cumberland, in the autumn she came South again, but was not able to go back to her work; in October she was sent to Italy to escape the cold and damp of the English winter. Her aunt, Emily Southwood Smith, who, in earlier years, had given a home to Florence, and later to Miranda, was still living in Florence, and eager to entertain her niece. It was Octavia's first visit to Italy, and in spite of her unwillingness to leave her beloved family and tenants, her spirits rose as she crossed the Alps by the Mont Cenis in a diligence. Characteristically—since she had never been able to resist the helpless—she picked up a 'forlorn and stupid young Irishman' who had lost his party, his luggage and his passport, and had never had a word of any language but his own. 'He was very tall and very miserable and I had to take pity on him and do everything for him; but he certainly was very cowardly.' Having rid herself of this incubus at Turin, she fell in with a polite and attentive Italian officer. This encounter proved more satisfactory. 'You know,' she remarks to Emily, recounting the incident, 'it is rather troublesome to have an expressive kind of face: and yet it is, I suppose, rather helpful too.' Helpful undoubtedly it proved; the young man rightly interpreting her expressive kind of face obligingly sat with the windows open though he was very cold, was quick to draw her attention to all the best views, led her to talk of London and her love of it, and by the end of the journey was discussing the eternal verities with her.

The Italian visit was a great success, it gave Octavia that complete change from her familiar surroundings which had become so necessary. She had devastating attacks of home-sickness. 'I hardly dare, even now, to write of home; I think of it as little as I can; the abiding sense of all its pre-ciousness and the heart-hunger for it never leaves me for a minute,' but none the less she was stimulated and re-freshed by it. It was the year of Garibaldi's first approach to Rome. Friends had given Octavia letters of introduction to some of his supporters, and meeting them was to her a thrilling experience. She was, of course, heart and soul with Garibaldi. His idealism, his courage, his spiritual greatness were the qualities to which she inevitably re-sponded, and she felt it a privilege to have known any of his friends. 'I could not help feeling as if *we* who had done nothing for Italy, had no right to be entering into the heri-tage of this accumulated intensity of feeling.' There were all the other joys too, which could not fail to appeal to her. She rejoiced in the picture galleries, and did some copying in them; she walked in the surrounding country up to Cer-tosa, to Fiesole, to other little hill towns, revelling in the views—sunset over the mountains, Florence with her cam-panile, cypresses dark against the sky, olive trees grey and twisted—all in short that delights the eye in that enchanted landscape. She joined the Cerubini choral society and sang Bach and Mozart, she indulged in frivolities—the play, the Corso, a masquerade in which she appeared in a magnifi-cent Eastern dress, borrowed from a friend and univer-sally pronounced most becoming. 'As to me,' she wrote in March, 'I am thriving in the most unaccountable way.

. . . This week I really have had dissipation and it has done me all the good in the world'—clearly it was time to go home.

By the beginning of April, Octavia was back in London finding in her home and in her work no less happiness than she had anticipated. 'I have drifted into the state of intense interest and joy in all the little world I love to work in.' But she had not even yet recovered her full physical energy and she soon discovered that she had less strength than she had hoped. She philosophically accepted the situation. 'Nothing is so provoking as to leave things half done,' she remarked, and submitting once more to medical advice she went, first to Mary Harris, where she spent happy hours in the garden 'mostly weeding—I think that is so interesting, it keeps me out of doors not standing or walking and yet gives me something to do. It is quiet and nice, and I like the smell of the earth and the soothing monotony of the movement and thought.' Thence she went on to the Hydro in Ben Rhydding where the cure was completed, and so back to London in October 'in overflowing health and so merry'.

'We are all assembled again,' she writes from Nottingham Place, 'and very happy. We have a very large number of pupils, as many as we could take in, but these are mainly under my sisters' care. I only teach the girls a few things, I give a few drawing lessons and am managing my dear houses which are getting into such excellent order as to be a great joy and but little painful care.'

Octavia had been away eighteen months, and she discovered to her surprise that there was a change in her attitude to her work. 'I meet the details with less intensity of thought than of old.' It was well that this should be so, and there is no doubt that the interruption to her activities had come at an opportune moment. The success of her method had been proved and the time had now come for her work to be extended so that the general standard of working-class housing should improve. She could not extend her work as long as she was completely absorbed, however beneficently, in a small group of tenants. Her long absence gave her the opportunity not only of seeing her work from outside and in true proportion, but also of realizing how much other people could do for her. She was far too generous a person not to acknowledge and accept this, and too intelligent to insist on keeping all in her own hands. From this time forward she was constantly planning the devolution of her work, learning to give more and more responsibility to others, and keeping herself fresh and alert to see where a new opportunity was opening or a step forward could be taken.

Chapter IX

THE CHARITY ORGANISATION SOCIETY

'I do not think that the influence that the rich and poor might have upon one another has been at all understood by either. I think we have all taken it too much for granted that the giving is all on one side, the receiving on the other':

LETTER FROM OCTAVIA, 1855 (aet. 16)

THE years following Octavia's return from Italy were perhaps the happiest and most productive of her life. Her work was succeeding beyond all hope or expectation. 'Who will ever hear what I do?' she had asked Ruskin incredulously; the answer was being given in no uncertain terms. In her renewed vigour, being to some extent released from the tyranny of the detailed work which had pressed so heavily on her, she had leisure to consider social problems allied to her work, and indirectly affecting her own people.

One such problem was already pressing. A series of bad winters culminated in exceptional distress in the winter of '67–68. Large Mansion House Funds had been collected, relief was freely distributed, but to all who had any practical experience of the working classes it appeared that poverty was increased rather than diminished by this lavish expenditure. All social workers in London were deeply concerned at the rapidly increasing pauperization of their people, and in 1868 a Society known as 'The London Association for the Prevention of Pauperization and Crime' (which has since become the Charity Organisation Society) came into existence. Octavia was inevitably involved in it. Ruskin was a founder and contributed two-thirds of its expenses; William Shaen was a member and its honorary solicitor. Octavia could not be indifferent to the sufferings of her neighbours nor to evils which she saw to be rampant and believed to be preventable.

In 1869 at a meeting of the new Society she read a paper entitled 'The Importance of Aiding the Poor without Almsgiving'. The principles here laid down were implicit in all Octavia's work. She believed in the eternal significance of every man and really held a man's spirit to be of more importance than his material prosperity; the idea, popular to-day, that a man must have his bodily needs supplied before he can be expected to attend to the needs of his spirit would have seemed to her blasphemously untrue. Since then his spirit was of supreme importance, it followed that no man must receive a gift which would not help to make him a better, stronger and more independent person. There were not wanting those who stigmatized this attitude as hard and self-righteous, actually it was neither. Octavia did not suggest that the rich should sit in judgment on the poor, withholding help from all who were not 'deserving': on the contrary, she demanded of them a much harder thing, that they should 'promote the happy natural intercourse of neighbours, mutual knowledge, mutual help'; that they should regard the poor 'primarily as husbands, wives, sons, and daughters, members of households as we are ourselves, instead of contemplating them as a separate class'; that armed with this real understanding, they should use their money in such a way as to make the poor, as soon as possible, independent of them; she believed that no wholesome relationship between people was possible when one always gave and the other always took; what she urged was a far more exacting task than handing out money. Octavia had proved that this could be done, and the comparative prosperity of her tenants in this time of general distress, lent point to her argument.

The Rector of St. Mary's Church in Marylebone was the Rev. W. Fremantle (later Dean of Ripon). He had been deeply concerned by the rapid demoralization of his people, and in May, 1869, he had established the first District Committee of the Charity Organisation Society. He now invited Octavia to take charge of a very poor portion of his parish, the Walmer Street District, and to apply to it the principles she had enunciated. Octavia gladly undertook the work, feeling its importance and foreseeing no difficulty greater than she had overcome in dealing with her own tenants. The parish, however, had been completely demoralized by doles. In the neighbouring districts, where Octavia was not responsible for the visiting and relief, the old system or want of system persisted, and it was still possible for the less scrupulous to thrive on a variety of ill-administered funds. Octavia's abolition in her district of coal tickets, free meals, and every form of monetary assistance, her insistence that any case of distress must be carefully investigated and the entire resources of the family examined before any dole could be given, her practice of offering work instead of relief and withholding relief if the work was not done, aroused bitter resentment, and for the first time in her life she found herself faced with the persistent hostility instead of the friendship of those she wished to help. It was a severe test of her courage and determination but she never wavered. She knew she was right and that to give in would be a betrayal of trust. At the end of the first year, she felt she had made little headway, and in a report of the work made 'while the full sorrow of disappointment was still weighing' upon her, she spoke sadly of the evil feeling and misunderstanding that she encountered. Nevertheless she persevered, upheld by friends who helped and supported her. 'What I am trying to do is simply in my eyes a bit of adult education, or reformatory work among a few people corrupted by gifts.' At the end of the second year things had greatly improved. 'I had to speak last year,' she reported, 'of general misconception, a bitter sense of resentment among the people—I do not wish to underestimate whatever may remain of this spirit . . . but certainly there is this year a strong force telling on the other side, and when I look back on the state of feeling that existed towards me, at the time I closed my last report, I cannot but see the change in a very striking light. . . . There has been some very happy intercourse during the last year, we have come to know each other better, and sometimes the bitterness of feeling has seemed to me wholly gone.'

The success of the experiment encouraged Mr. Fremantle to apply the same principles to the whole parish; Octavia remained in charge of her own District and proceeded to recruit other visitors for the rest of the parish. The choice of these was a matter of great importance. It was their function to get to know the families in their charge, to know them intimately, to understand their difficulties and anxieties, to rejoice in their successes, to establish themselves in short as real friends whose advice could be sought and whose sympathy could be counted on. It was voluntary part-time workers Octavia wanted. She believed that a girl or woman living a normal family life, and having her own domestic problems and responsibilities, her own society engagements and pleasures, would enter more readily into those of other people; she believed so whole-heartedly in the importance of the family, realizing how much she had gained in her work from her own, that she thought no training for social work so valuable as experience of the daily happiness and irritation of family life.

Octavia worked hard for the Marylebone Committee. Nominally she was only one district visitor of many, actually her wisdom and experience gave her a unique position in Marylebone; it was natural to turn to her in any difficult case, to accept her judgment, though it sometimes seemed stern. She became a referee for the C.O.S. and in that capacity her knowledge of the people, of the charitable agencies, of laws affecting the poor, as well as her power of getting on happy terms with fellow workers made her invaluable. Later the Guardians used her as a liaison officer to co-ordinate all the relief, private or public, given in the parish.

Octavia rejoiced in the success of the scheme in Marylebone primarily, no doubt, for the improvement it brought in conditions there, but also because she saw her principles vindicated and believed that other districts would inevitably follow till a sound system of relief everywhere superseded the haphazard and demoralizing almsgiving that had been so general. Progress, however, was very slow. The Society met with bitter opposition. This was partly due to the dead weight of conservatism and partly to a distrust of organization in connection with charity, still not altogether unknown among those whose benevolence is a satisfying emotion rather than a reasonable principle. It had many enemies; all those who felt a pleasant sense of superiority in being a benefactor, and receiving the gratitude of the lower classes, those who, being made uneasy at the thought of suffering, could buy peace of mind with a cheque, those who suspected that they had a duty to their neighbour and wished to dispose of it on a cash basis: all these intensely resented the disturbing activity of a society which demanded, from those who gave, not only money but a little clear thinking.

Such opposition was to be expected, but Octavia had counted confidently on the support of the clergy and their parish workers. The Bishops indeed welcomed the Society, and she was invited to speak for it at Lambeth Palace, at Fulham Palace, at a meeting organized by the Bishop of Gloucester, in parishes all over London, in Bristol and in other provincial towns. She was a convincing speaker who easily got through to her audience, and there was little opposition expressed; committees of the C.O.S. were established in all the Poor Law parishes in London and in some provincial towns but actually the results were disappointing. The clergy were slow to co-operate, they were perhaps set in their own ways, and unwilling to have their own people investigated by an outside body. Octavia regretted this bitterly for the sake of the Church even more than for the sake of the poor, for she dreaded the confusion of temporal gifts with spiritual teaching. 'Religious teaching . . . has suffered of late years incomparably more than it has gained by the confusion. Let the gift stand or fall by its own intrinsic value; if it be helpful in itself, cultivating such right qualities as will make the recipient richer in such outside things as itself, let it be made. If not, withhold it. And for God's sake let His truth stand on its own merits. . . . Preach it by word, by deed, by patient abiding but do not

use bribes or even what look like bribes to make men take
it in.'

In dismay Octavia saw the C.O.S. and the parishes drawing farther away from each other, the clergy content to
complain that the society was all organization and no
charity, the society retaliating with accusations of sentimentality and obstructiveness, each side obstinately refusing to see what the other had to offer and thus destroying
the whole scheme, which depended on co-operation.

'It is of the deepest importance that the C.O.S. should
not become a fresh relieving society, for added societies are
an evil, and besides it can never investigate cases and organize charities as it ought, if it becomes a relief society.
But the C.O.S. must secure abundant and wise relief
where needed, and it must stop that which is injurious. To
accomplish these two ends it must win the confidence of
private donors and relief agencies. Besides this, if its investigations are to be trustworthy and effectual and gently
conducted, they must be watched over by people of education, with deep sympathy for the poor. You cannot learn
how to help a man, nor even get him to tell you what ails
him, till you care for him. For these reasons volunteers
must rally round the C.O.S. and prevent it from becoming
a dry and, because dry, ineffectual machinery for enquiring
about people; volunteers must win the support of local
clergy and support them in the reform of their charities.'

The opposition she met only confirmed Octavia in her
support of the Society. She had in her own work demonstrated the soundness of its principles and, remaining a
staunch member to the end of her life, she fought more
than one battle on its behalf. In 1875 she became a member of the Central Council of the C.O.S. Generally speak-

ing she distrusted centralization and preferred small local organizations, less apt to be bound by red tape, and more able to depend upon the interest and support of the neighbourhood. She was, however, far too intelligent a woman to set any particular value on consistency for its own sake. She supported the centralization of the C.O.S. Fund because she recognized that it was neither just that the rich districts should be asked to help only the few poor people in their own neighbourhood, nor possible that the poor should produce enough for their own needs. She reminded the rich that since they had decreed that the poor should not live unduly close to them they remained responsible for the districts to which they had banished them.

Octavia enjoyed the Central Council; it met to discuss pressing difficulties and to exchange ideas on every sort of social problem, and she found the meetings most stimulating. Moreover, she made new friends and began to take her place among the foremost philanthropic and social workers of her day. They recognized her power and her wisdom and welcomed her co-operation. There was the veteran Lord Shaftesbury who had known her grandfather, Joshua Fitch of the School Board, with whom she had much in common, whose wife and niece were drawn into her work, Lord Stansfield, President of the Poor Law Board who consulted her about the appointment of the first woman-inspector of workhouses and chose Mrs. Nassau Senior on her advice, Langley of the Local Government Board with whom she recorded a 'triumphant meeting' in which she received from the Guardians 'all and more than all I had hoped'. The Artisans' Dwellings Bill of 1875 was in great part her work, for it was based on the report of an enquiry by the C.O.S., in which she had participated, into the whole question of working-class dwellings in London and at every stage her advice was sought and her amendments accepted. It was at the Second Reading of the Bill that Octavia first realized that she had become a public character. She was in the Speaker's Gallery 'leaning back, thinking, when suddenly my own name caught my ear. Mr. Shuttleworth was speaking of the Macmillan article . . . and he read aloud from it the description of the wonderful delight it gave me to see the courts laid open to the light and air. . . . The words recalled vividly the intensity of the longing, and the wonderfully swift realization; a great gush of joy rushed over me. . . . I can't tell you how tiny it made me feel.'

Mrs. Hill, watching her daughter's success, seeing her happily concerned with just such work as had absorbed her own father's days, noticed with satisfaction the esteem in which she was held. It seemed to her eminently right and fitting. 'Octa is so interested in the Sanitary Committee of the C.O.S. All the men who have worked from the beginning are there, and many others besides. Is it not wonderful that Octa should be among them, and able continually to say a word in season! Dear child, the mantle has fallen on her.'

Chapter X

TRAINING OF WORKERS

'In free countries we are not directed from above, as a tool':
OCTAVIA in 'Letter to Fellow Workers', 1874

OCTAVIA, for her part, was more alarmed than pleased at her growing reputation. 'I do feel such a take-in of a person,' she wrote to her sister Emily *à propos* of a dinner party at which she was the guest of honour. 'I wish someone would explode me. It is so difficult to unhumbug oneself, it is all taken for extreme modesty (Fancy, *mine!*) and laid to one's account as so much excellence.' None the less she was very happy. 'I cannot tell you half our success or the vistas of hope that open out before us. May I only have a long life and many fellow workers.'

She was at the height of her power, working easily and confidently, handling each problem that presented itself with a certainty of touch that smoothed out the difficulties; she enjoyed the activity of every day, 'she is as busy as a bee,' writes her mother. 'In and out, in and out and very *like* a bee, and like it too in her happy murmuring when at work and her evident pleasure in the work.' The extent of her property increased steadily, and was indeed limited not by the amount of capital available, but by the number of workers able to manage it. Many of those who saw her work were eager to help; Lady Ducie, to whom she had been recommended as a teacher of drawing, became so much interested in housing that she bought, and learnt from Octavia to manage, a very bad Court in Wigmore Street known as Barrett's Court; Miss Sterling who had helped in the Walmer Street experiment, deeply impressed by what she saw there, managed to buy all but five of the houses in the district, and handed them over to Octavia; nor was there ever lack of money to invest. 'I have never from the first moment paused for capital,' she said in her evidence before the Royal Commission on Housing in 1884. 'I have always a book with a long list of people who offer money for investment. I just put down what amount they offer, and when I have workers and hear of Courts, I only run my eye down the list and choose whoever I think will be the best to work with, and never since 1864 have I had to wait a day for money for houses.'

Besides this money for investment, from 1870 onwards Octavia had considerable sums at her disposal to spend as she thought fit. This was partly the result of her C.O.S. work. Many who accepted its principles and had money they wished to give away, but neither time nor experience to enable them to administer it wisely, acquired the habit of making her their almoner. From 1871 she wrote an annual report, giving an account of her stewardship, recording the progress of her various properties and works, very often setting forth her anxieties, hopes and fears for the future. These 'Letters to my Fellow-Workers', printed and published privately, are full of interest and show the rapid growth of her power and influence. The principles on which she disposed of her Fund are clearly laid down. 'The funds entrusted to me come from two very clearly marked classes of donors,' she remarks in a note appended to many of these 'Letters'. 'The one anxious that their money should be devoted to the direct help of the sick and poor; the other class wishing to strengthen my hands that I may help forward in its difficult stages any great movement.' The money given in the first category was spent either on the corporate activities of the tenants—May festivals, country excursions and other entertainments, plants and flowers, fires and books for Club rooms and classes—or on gifts to individuals or families. These gifts were either in the nature of pensions to those who had ceased to be able to support themselves, or strictly limited to the purpose of making the recipient self-supporting within a reasonable time. The money might be spent on training, apprenticeship or the supply of tools, on convalescence or a holiday, but never on maintaining anyone for an indefinite period. The money from the second class of donor was even more precious to Octavia; it enabled her by a substantial donation at a critical moment to save a promising piece of work from shipwreck, or to embark on pioneer work, when she saw something that needed to be done. 'When an undertaking is first started, expenses often arise which naturally no one is willing to meet until the plan is proved useful.'

In 1873 Octavia's property began to extend beyond Marylebone. In some respects she regretted this. It had meant much to her to have the work centred in her own home, to have her tenants within easy reach, and to keep the intimate family feeling with them, which was possible only when they were near neighbours. But she had little choice in the matter. A block of model dwellings in Lambeth which had been a failure commercially was offered to her. To turn a failure into success was a challenge not to be resisted. The next call came from Whitechapel. One of Mr. Fremantle's curates was Samuel Barnett, later known and

deeply and widely loved as Canon Barnett, the founder of
Toynbee Hall. He had worked much with Octavia in the
parish and had become engaged to Henrietta Rowland,
who was one of her most competent and zealous helpers.
When in 1873 he became Vicar of St. Jude's, Whitechapel,
and the young couple began their magnificent work in a
parish reputed to be at that time 'about the worst, if not
the very worst, in the East End to work', it was natural
that Octavia's heart should go with them. From the very
beginning she shared with St. Jude's any money that came
into her hands, and having now seen in that parish 'a block
of houses that makes me long to take possession of it, with
power to redeem it', she produced the money for it and
became responsible for tenants in the East End. Henrietta
Barnett of course had the experience to manage it, but she
needed help which Octavia gave at once. 'I am sending to
the East my new assistant. She has been more help to me
than any assistant has been for many a long day. I shall
miss her sorely. . . . I am glad to give her to the East, the
need there is far greater, and it is all right she should go.
We must train the new workers.'

This now became a pressing question. Octavia was often
obliged to refuse property because she had not enough
workers qualified to undertake the management, and it was
the essence of her faith that the whole success of housing
the poor lay not in bricks and mortar, but in skilled and
trained management. More and more therefore she gave
herself to the training of her assistants. It involved seeing
less of her tenants. 'I think thou wilt feel as if the poor had
faded much from my sight,' she wrote to Mary Harris,
'but it is not so. I cannot write of them as individuals for
I see little of them. I hardly dare sometimes to think of the

question, it gives me such exquisite pain not to be myself face to face with them in Edward's Place or somewhere. But I know my little life has narrow limits both of duration and of range, and for the sake of the many poor, I have deliberately chosen, for a time at least, to set others to work rather than to work myself face to face with the people in the poorest Courts. I believe the resolution was and is right; I look, however, to the time when the necessity for it shall be over, and to coming back to my own small and well known body of poor.'

The training of fellow-workers was no new task to Octavia. She had always fired others with a desire to undertake social work and had welcomed their help when it was offered; inevitably she had put them in the way of the job she gave them, and working beside her, they had learned how to do it. In early days she had taken it for granted that the elder girls of her school would wish to help—as indeed they did—and had accepted any others who offered themselves; it was not until the beginning of the Walmer Street experiment that she had found it necessary to try to recruit assistants. These, of course, were all part-time volunteers; some could give very little time, but Octavia believed that everyone had a responsibility towards the poor and as much to gain as to give in fulfilling it. She never pressed for more than could be willingly given. 'I feel about gifts of time even more than about gifts of money, that they are such good things they ought to be a joy to the giver and that they cannot be this if they are pressed at unsuitable moments and ways.'

Now in addition to these part-time workers it became necessary to train some who were prepared to give their whole days to the work, who should be able to become completely responsible for Courts. Fundamentally the training for all these workers was the same; they must all learn to deal with people, to understand the conditions under which they lived and the ways in which these could be improved; they must be familiar with the various agencies for helping the people and able to act as agents for Relief Committees, School Board and Guardians; for those who undertook tenants there was the task of collecting rents, superintending cleaning, keeping accounts and advising about repairs, while those who hoped to take complete charge of houses needed also a technical knowledge of sanitary science and the law relating to landlords and tenants. Though the part-time workers had obviously less to learn than the others, it never occurred to Octavia that there should be any difference in their attitude to the work. She expected from those who gave the least time as punctual a regularity and as rigid an accuracy as from those who were training professionally.

To this business of training, Octavia now addressed herself. Her object was to make her assistants independent of her, and this could only be achieved by giving them real responsibility. She subdivided her property, assigning to each worker as much as she could reasonably be expected to manage; there she must make her own decisions and stand by them and face her own mistakes. Octavia would have no hard and fast rules, nothing that could become a system, which might cramp the spirit, lest tenants should be dealt with 'collectively not individually, by routine instead of by living government'. In her own Court or district, each worker was to be supreme. 'Take the initiative yourselves,' she urged, 'manage the details yourselves, think over your problems yourselves, for you alone can;

when you have made yourselves tolerably independent of us then you or we may extend the work but not till then.'

At first the subdivision worked indifferently. It must be remembered that the education of the girls of the upper classes at that date had proceeded but a little way and had not been calculated to develop resourcefulness and readiness to take responsibility. Octavia, waiting in the background ready to give advice, yet constrained herself not to interfere, knowing her pupils must learn by their own mistakes. But the material of their work was human life, and it was not easy to sit back and let them learn. 'I told her to do exactly what she thought right as to helping them with money. But I told her strongly what I believed and urged her to watch the result closely.' Progress was slow. In the Letter of 1874 she laments, 'I do not yet see in most of our courts . . . a powerful rule and will at work among them;' but she persevered. The importance of taking an independent line is urged in one letter after another. 'It is a principle of modern life in free countries that we are not directed from above, as a tool, but have to think out what is best to do, each in his own office.'

She watched anxiously and critically, constantly expounding general principles, never laying down the law in detail, and with the humility which belongs only to the great, she constantly criticized herself no less than her pupils. 'Mary! I do so often tremble lest I should spoil all by growing despotic or narrow-minded, or over-bearing or selfish; such power as I have is a quite terrible responsibility; and so few people tell me where I am wrong.' From all danger of despotism she was saved by her very deep reverence for the personality of every individual, she believed that each one had a unique contribution to make to the work. ' I never find any worker to *replace* another,' she remarked, and she realized fully that 'you cannot get the full benefit of heart and head and active will unless you give those who serve you responsibility, freedom of action and the opportunity of forming and striving to realize their own ideal.'

But though Octavia did her utmost to encourage initiative and freedom of action, in all personal relations, it must not be supposed that she allowed any latitude on the business side. Accounts must be kept exactly right in ink, and checked every week with her at Nottingham Place. This was before the days of fountain pens, and the necessity of carrying a small ink-pot attached to the person as well as a receipt book when the length of a fashionable skirt already occupied one hand, added much to the troubles of those to whom arithmetical accuracy did not come naturally; there were many who dreaded the accounts morning when there was no hope that the smallest inaccuracy would go unchallenged or indeed be suffered to go at all. There was a technical knowledge of drains, of plumbing work, of the law affecting landlord and tenant to be acquired, about which no haziness was permissible, and there was the seeing eye, quick to notice dirt or disorder, to be trained. It was a strenuous business. Though none who knew her could doubt that in Octavia's scale of values the right spirit came first, she was far from allowing it to be a substitute for more mundane virtues. 'It is of no use to have the right spirit, if the technical matters, all the sanitary and financial arrangements, are in a mess. Beware of well meant failures. Have your drainage and your clean stairs and your distempering and your accounts all as perfect as possible.' With a characteristic twinkle she would relate how a tenant had greeted her with the remark, 'Them drains are a feather in your cap.'

Gradually Octavia saw the fruits of her work. Emma Cons was the first to take that complete responsibility which Octavia desired. The friendship between the two women had always been a somewhat tempestuous affair; it had its roots deep in their common past; they saw each other with that devastating clearness only possible to those who have shared experiences at an early age, neither could ever doubt the affection of the other yet it was not easy for them to work closely together. Emma was something of a rough diamond, downright, often tactless. She did not share Octavia's enthusiasm for Ruskin, she thought but little of her artistic efforts, or of her attempts to beautify the Courts and their surroundings. Octavia was always conscious of Emma's indifference to an aspect of the work which seemed to her important: 'It is such a pleasure to me to see things nice; and I am sure it has a good influence on everyone concerned. . . . Miss Cons is sure to consider it quite thrown away labour. Why is this in her I often wonder. She would do a thing of the kind any day to spoil me, but she would think me quite mad to care all the time.' The criticism was just. Emma lacked that sensitiveness to the feelings of other people, which was one of Octavia's greatest gifts, but she was full of energy and gusto and she had her own very distinctive contribution to make to the work. Octavia recognized this. She handed over to her management some Courts near Drury Lane. She 'enrols her own volunteer workers, founds her own classes, clubs, Savings Bank, keeps her own accounts, supervises all the business and all the personal work and reports to the owners direct.' Emma made a very great success of the work, she was an ardent teetotaller and developed temperance organization in her Court. Octavia was genuine in her appreciation of her success. 'I knew she would manage Courts differently from me,' she wrote. 'I thought this rather gain than otherwise. . . . Miss Cons had an ideal. Left to herself she would gladly have sacrificed it to mine in a moment and dwarfed her own nature, power and work. That could not be. . . . I knew we should each learn from the other.'

Gradually other workers became really competent. It was possible to extend the work still further. The first extension outside London was to Leeds. Octavia was invited in December, 1874, to come and describe her method to a company, chiefly of business men. 'I well remember,' writes one who was present, 'the surprise of some of them at the clearness, not only of her opening exposition, but of her spontaneous replies to questions concerning all sorts of matters affecting the treatment of house property, sanitation, repairs and bad debts.' A sum of £3000 was collected at once, and a Miss Martin went to London to live at Nottingham Place while she trained to manage the property. Leeds was the first provincial town to adopt Octavia's scheme, Liverpool followed in 1879, then Manchester. The movement spread as rapidly as Octavia could find workers; within the following decade it had reached Berlin and Munich, Sweden, Holland, Russia and America.

The spread of Octavia's work and the resultant increase in her rent roll did not make her pecuniarily better off, for though she had always put aside from the rents the percentage due to the collector, she had never taken it for herself. Her personal income came still from the school, from occasional private pupils, and from articles she wrote for the press. That it was small was immaterial to her; she had a perfect horror of debt, and would never spend either on herself or even on the projects most dear to her heart a penny more than she actually had in hand, but she could be content with very little and even exulted in her power to make a little money go a long way.

'Somehow personal poverty is a help to me. It keeps me more simple and energetic and somehow low and humble and hardy in the midst of a somewhat intoxicating power. It pleases me, too, to have considerable difficulty and effort in my own life, when what I do seems hard to the people, even though they never know it. . . . All the same, I know very well that if in any way that I call natural and right I found myself above the necessity for effort and denial of myself, I should bless God and feel it a relief and help.'

In 1874 the 'relief and help' came to her in a way that seemed so 'natural and right' that she could not refuse it. She had by this time many friends of ample means who were eager to help her financially, but she had always refused to take gifts of money from them for herself. These now, aided and abetted by her old friend, William Shaen, combined to invest a sum of money sufficiently large to give her an adequate income. Octavia knew nothing about it until the whole business was settled, she was deeply touched by the generosity of her friends and could not refuse a gift so thoughtfully and lovingly made. But she was quite clear that it must not be a precedent for future gifts. She wrote to Mr. Shaen: 'In spite of the extreme kindness and beautiful feeling shown by whoever has given all this help, I must request you not to receive for me one farthing more. The thing is done beautifully, efficiently and abundantly; there really it must rest. I have more than enough for holidays and everything I can possibly want. I do assure you I mean what I say. I can never want or have to earn again, I feel richer than I ever did, and able to do things I never dreamed of doing. But once more and most emphatically I decline more. I have enough.'

For the first time in her life she was relieved from the necessity of carrying a financial burden. She had borne it gallantly as a young girl, doggedly as she grew up, with a steady untroubled resolution as she passed into middle age, but latterly she had become conscious of its weight; now at one stroke it was gone, it was with heartfelt relief and gratitude that she wrote 'I have enough.'

Chapter XI

GROWING RESPONSIBILITIES

'Barrett's Court is still in a dreadful state, but the people are so charming . . . we can do so much with and for them':
OCTAVIA TO MATTHEW DAVENPORT HILL, 1876

THERE is a description of Octavia at this period from the pen of Sydney Cockerell, who met her for the first time in 1871 at the Hydro at Ben Rhydding, 'an unobtrusive plainly dressed little lady' he writes, 'whose face attracts you at first and charms you as you become acquainted with the power of mind and sweetness of character to which it gives expression, a lady of great force and energy, with a wide-open, well-stored brain, but withal as gentle and womanly as a woman can well be, and possessed of a wonderful tact, which makes her the most attractive and pleasantest companion in the whole establishment.' It is interesting to see the effect she produced and to notice the stages of his appreciation; the first superficial glance at a rather unimpressive figure redeemed by an attractive face, the quick realization of power and energy emanating from it, then the warm pleasure in the companionship of a friend.

'An unobtrusive, plainly-dressed little lady!' The words suggest someone very different from Octavia; for indeed her small stature seemed always an accident. She was not small-boned, but on the contrary built on generous lines, her shoulders rather broad for her height, her head massive, her wide brow giving an impression of strength ac-

centuated by the dignity of her poise. All the portraits that
survive suggest a large, rather than a small, woman. Her
features were finely moulded and her large dark eyes
blazed with sympathy or indignation while her feelings
were plainly to be read on her sensitive expressive face.
She was quickly and deeply moved by joy or sorrow, she
felt indeed passionately about all the things that affected
her friends, and it was this depth of feeling that at times
wrought too fiercely on her body. If she was unobtrusive
it was because she deliberately withdrew herself from the
centre of the stage. She hated any sort of advertisement or
publicity, it was part of that womanliness which Cockerell
extolled. She was, in fact, far abler than most of the men
she met, she had proved her own competence and did not
mistrust it, yet in her simple Victorian way, she never
doubted that the centre of the picture was for the man,
that he must rule, take responsibility, lay down the law in
every household, while the woman's function was to work
in the background and accept his authority. It was natural
to her, therefore, in a mixed society to efface herself, to
observe, to listen to others, rather than to instruct. And
she enjoyed this; she had an insatiable interest in other
people, whether those of whom she knew nothing—'The
people in the train yesterday amused me so. How much
more one hears, travelling alone, one sits in the corner and
the people talk on, as if one were not'—or people whom
she knew slightly, whose interests were widely apart from
hers: 'I come in like some queer new being from another
region, but I think it enlarges me even to see and listen to
those whose interests are so different.'

As long as she was allowed to do so she would listen, but
the more intelligent of those who met her soon discovered

that she had much to say that was well worth hearing. When she was drawn into conversation, she spoke freely and without self-consciousness as long as she was discussing any of the subjects that interested her—a wide range— but she was less happy if she found herself involved in small talk. Conventional society frightened her; 'He is just a touch conventional and alarms me in proportion.' She had never had time or inclination to become expert in light society chatter; though far from the affectation of despising convention (indeed she always wanted to do the right and appropriate thing) she was fundamentally unconventional, for she saw things in a fresh and original way and was too deeply interested in them to stop and think about her own reaction to them.

Her clothes were often wrong and there were many of her friends who regretted that she did not take more pleasure in making the best of her good looks. This was partly due to her upbringing, for it had been part of her mother's plan to discourage an interest in personal adornment. 'As a result all skill in dress was acquired in after years; by Octavia never,' Miranda records. 'Not that she could not have dressed admirably if she had ever had the moment of time to think about it; she had no lack of judgment or taste, or even of wish to dress nicely and suitably, but life was too hurried, and more weighty matters pressed, and anything she ever achieved in this line was through friendly hands, in spite of her impatience to be about other things. Her mother often regretted the mistake she had made; the truth being that girls should early be trained to dress neatly and well. They will thus acquire facility and dress well almost mechanically, without devoting valuable time to it.' Generally speaking, Octavia did not mind, probably did not even realize, that her clothes were not appropriate. Sometimes she had a sudden misgiving. Once she was due to lunch with Lady Ducie. She had been going all morning from Court to Court in pouring rain, her mackintosh was streaming, her goloshes deplorable. With a shock of horror she suddenly realized that a luncheon party awaited her, that she had no time to go home and change, and worst of all, that Lady Ducie's door would be opened by a formidable butler. For a moment her spirit quailed, she was sure that the butler would scornfully direct her to the back door, or even turn her away and that there would of necessity be explanations, humiliating to both sides. Then her courage and resourcefulness rose to the occasion. She rang the bell, the door was flung wide, and before the butler had time to realize her appearance she had stepped in, and, lifting one foot, said with hauteur, 'Kindly remove my golosh.' The situation was saved, her status fully established.

In Sydney Cockerell Octavia found a new friend and fellow worker. The acquaintance begun at Ben Rhydding in 1871 ripened rapidly into a warm friendship which extended to all his family. He worked with her devotedly till his premature death in 1877, and when his son Sydney was old enough he took up the work. She became the godmother of his daughter Olive, and a trusted friend and adviser to the whole family. Octavia found in him much to attract her, a quick sensitive intelligence, ready and generous sympathy, and sureness of judgment on which she came to depend. There was so much a man could do for her. Circumstance had forced her to become 'the man of the family', but it was a role by no means congenial to her. It was pleasant to have him look over her books, to discuss the difficulties of her assistants, to show her the easiest and clearest way of arranging the accounts and preparing her balance sheet. He acquired the habit of dropping in on his way home from his work in the City, to go over these matters, and to advise her about her own investments as well as any other financial problem.

There were other things to discuss too. Barrett's Court was a property which gave her a good deal of trouble from the beginning. It stood where now stands a furniture shop in about the middle of Wigmore Street; it was in a very bad condition when it came into her hands, dirty and dilapidated, and it housed a very poor and rough type of tenant. Later it was rebuilt and became St. Christopher's Buildings, but at the moment rebuilding was impracticable and the tenants difficult. There was nothing particularly new to Octavia about this; she at once set to work, and started a Women and Girls' Institute, and introduced her usual improvements. But now her friendship with Cockerell opened new possibilities. She had never before had a worker who could tackle clubs for the men. This was now practicable, and at once together they planned one. Cockerell persuaded a friend, Edward Bond a barrister, to come and help; Octavia dedicated a room in the Court to it, and it began. It was a success from the beginning, the men were invited to manage it themselves, they drew up their own regulations, decided their own entrance fee, organized their own activities. Sometimes Octavia's heart misgave her a little: 'I am fairly alarmed about the order after you gentlemen leave the club, only I tell myself you must see your way to preventing abuses. They tell me that women were admitted last Monday, and that they all danced till $12\frac{1}{2}$. I don't vouch for the truth of it, nor know that there was any harm, but it is a thing you would all feel must not be without notice and supervision. Will you take the matter in hand?' But such alarm did not weigh heavily on her, she had perfect confidence in Cockerell, and she rejoiced at the happy relationship which she saw developing between him and the men. 'Sometimes I think you hardly know how much there your influence tells,' she wrote to him gratefully.

As the club became more popular, men from the neighbourhood who were not Octavia's tenants were also admitted, and rather to her regret the entrance fee went up. 'I can't help a little regretting the increasing scale of fees, it will gradually alter the character of the club, but perhaps all good things must rise with their original elements, and new organizations meet the wants of the lowest, beginning again till the whole is raised. I am sure about all this you must know better than I, and I fearlessly leave the matter in your hands.' But Octavia, willing as she was to give the men a free hand in all club matters, was very tenacious of her own rights over the clubroom. She asked no rent for the room, but she was the manager, not the owner, of Barrett's Court and she felt bound to pay the owner rent, which she took from her donations fund. The School Board, requiring extra accommodation, contemplated renting the men's clubroom for some hours a day, and Octavia was informed that some such proposal was to be discussed by the club, 'and will then in due course be submitted to you.' This did not at all meet her views: 'I dare say it will immediately occur to you,' she wrote to Cockerell, 'that this is hardly the order of proceeding and that should such a proposal reach the club, you will cause it to be forwarded to me direct. The club must be taught to see from the first that the decision is wholly mine. It occurs to me that they possibly fancy the rental would come to swell club funds.

133

This you see would not be the case.' It was to Octavia not merely, or even principally, that such money would relieve her donation fund but far more that the club must recognize that the room was not theirs, it was not a free room since there could be none such, but a room for which rent was being paid although their funds had been relieved of the responsibility.

Another matter in which Cockerell relieved Octavia of an immense amount of work was in the entertaining of tenants. This became more exacting as the number of tenants increased. 'I give one evening every week from October to March, and yet I barely provide an evening's amusement for each of our people. That enables me to meet them at least once face to face, but it does not supply enough happy healthy amusement for the young people.' Yet even this minimum was hard work, for she was by no means content to work off all and sundry in what, in more modern days, is aptly known as a Tea Fight. Her parties must be kept small enough to be a really personal affair, an occasion for meeting her friends. The best thing she contributed to them was her own enjoyment, and this was greatly enhanced when there was someone to do the spadework for her. It was her custom to provide some entertainment. She had many talented friends who gladly came to play or sing, but perhaps her chief allies in this business were the MacDonalds, a family richly gifted, and well known for its amateur theatricals. They were happy parties. Octavia, watching her tenants enjoying themselves, was exercised in her mind about the lack of amusement provided for the working classes: 'How to make amusements self-supporting yet pure and good is the problem.' The solution of the problem was not her work, yet she con-

tributed a small experiment: 'We have begun a series of
paid entertainments in Barrett's Court on successive Saturdays. Last night the season opened with a capital play by
the MacDonalds, the room was crowded to overflowing.
The next performance is to be an operetta by Mrs. Baylis
and her friends.' Modern enterprise, ignoring the second
part of Octavia's aspiration, has made entertainment triumphantly self-supporting, but it was Mrs. Baylis' daughter who at the Old Vic came near to providing the fulfilment
of both parts.

It is a remarkable fact that with all this work on her mind
and on her hands, Octavia still found considerable time for
writing. She had from childhood been a prolific correspon-
dent, pouring out to her many friends eager accounts of all
she was doing and thinking day by day. This habit she
never lost, even when she was busiest; she wrote easily and
with obvious pleasure that communicated itself to the
reader. The same easy readable style characterized the first
of her published articles, an account of the lives of her toymakers, which came out in *Household Words* in 1856. Ten
years later her first article on housing appeared in the
Fortnightly and roused much interest; the public conscience was already uneasily aware of social evils in London; a writer with first hand knowledge of the facts, a vivid
and sympathetic pen and constructive suggestions for
remedies met with instant appreciation, and the more
serious periodicals readily accepted her articles. Octavia
was glad to write. Like the prophets of old, she had a message to deliver and the magazine articles reached a public
otherwise inaccessible to her; moreover, the work was not
exacting, she had her facts and her illustrations at her
finger-tips, and knowing exactly what she wanted to say,

whether about Housing or Relief, she wrote quickly and convincingly. In 1875 five of her magazine articles were published in book form in America under the title *Homes of the London Poor*. Later it was translated into German by H.R.H. Princess Alice of Hesse, who had long been interested in Octavia's work and as early as 1866 had visited one of her Courts. Thus the elements of the housing problem became known, and more thoughtful citizens began to demand of local authority a rather higher standard of public service.

In 1874 Octavia herself was, ironically enough, the victim of one of her own articles. She had described Barrett's Court as it was when she took possession of it. A citizen of Marylebone, outraged that such conditions should exist in his own neighbourhood, drew the attention of the Medical Officer of Health to the article, roundly accusing him of neglect of his duty in having suffered such evils to exist. The Medical Officer's reaction was perhaps natural enough, but certainly not reasonable. He at once ordered the demolition of all the houses in the Court, without stopping to consider that in the interval that had elapsed since Octavia became responsible for the property, she had been busily engaged in making it habitable so that most of the abuses complained of no longer existed. So drastic an order, so manifestly unjust, could not be carried out; it was withdrawn, but the Vestry took up the cudgels on behalf of its officer, who launched a bitter attack on Octavia's management, and presented a report demanding the demolition of some of the houses and very drastic improvements in others. Octavia was much troubled by the attack. She knew the houses in question were not in perfect order; she knew the tenants were not yet ready for some of the improvements required of her, but she also knew that the property was progressing satisfactorily and that she was just beginning to get the right spirit among the tenants; she dreaded this disturbance of the peace.

The local bitterness aroused was very intense. Octavia, who asked nothing but to be allowed to do her work quietly in co-operation with any who would help, without publicity or commendation, found herself the centre of fierce controversy which threatened to embitter her relations with those she sought to help. She was hurt and bewildered at the hostility of those whose office it was to promote social reform.

'Octavia has called a meeting of the Barrett's Court tenants to consult as to how they can keep things in better order, keep front doors shut, etc. She is very sorry it should happen now; but she had fixed the meeting before this vestry row occurred. She fears the tenants will be in a very bad state because of this affair and I fear she will come back very dispirited.' The meeting gave her the greatest anxiety; she naturally turned to Cockerell for support: 'I earnestly hope you will reconsider the question of helping me on that day. I know very well what I want and that you can do it better than Mr. Bond and that it would be much fitter and pleasanter to have you than him. We won't call you Chairman if you don't like . . . if you will come and do what turns up to be done. I needn't explain to you why I am sure you can do what we want if anyone can, but I am quite sure of the fact. Will you try?' Cockerell of course did what she wished, explained the situation to the meeting and brought the opinion of the tenants to Octavia's side. The Vestry Meeting at which the Medical Officer's attack and Octavia's answer were read occurred in the same week, and resulted in a compromise; the report was accepted, but the doctor was directed to consult Octavia as to the measures to be taken. This decision was the result of strenuous efforts of Octavia's friends behind the scenes. 'Mr. Hart had seen Dr. W. the evening before the Vestry meeting and had shown him how utterly untenable his position was . . . and had said that if Dr. W. persisted he would only get into difficulties. So Dr. W. was most anxious to retreat and agreed to have a meeting with Octavia and Mr. Hart to settle measures of reform after the Vestry Meeting.'

For the moment peace was declared, but the Medical Officer did not readily forgive the exposure of his incompetence; his position made it possible for him to hamper Octavia's work, his *amour-propre* made it delightful to him to do so. She had to submit to perpetual pinpricks; he would issue a sheaf of orders about trifles, would announce in the local paper that he was about to submit another Report on Barrett's Court, would threaten to shut this or that house. These petty annoyances were disquieting, Octavia resented them, and resented even more their power to disturb her: 'It gives me a good deal of trouble, more, I believe, a great deal than it ought. I believe if I could make up my mind that I see the right thing pretty distinctly and can do it, and leave the result, it would be far better; but I am apt to go over and over the subject, brooding over it.' The Vestry was kept in a state of perpetual suspicion of Octavia's actions and ready to oppose any new thing she undertook.

There was a Public House, the Duke of Walmer, very close to Barrett's Court, which in her opinion exercised a very bad influence over it. When the time came for the re-

newal of the licence Octavia interested some of her friends
in an endeavour to buy the premises and secure some sort
of disinterested management: finding this impossible she
decided that the only course to pursue was to oppose the
renewal of the licence. Her efforts aroused great hostility.
They were represented as an attempt to interfere with the
liberty of the individual, and to deprive the working man
of his glass of beer with a grandmotherly wish to improve
him. Octavia tried to reason with her opponents. The majority of her tenants by this time trusted her sufficiently to
accept her judgment, and were the less concerned as there
remained other licensed houses within easy reach. Her objection to the Duke of Walmer was not that it was licensed,
but that it was run in a thoroughly disreputable manner
and was doing manifest harm. She approached the question not as a temperance reformer but as an ordinary citizen wishing to remove an abuse almost from her own door-
step. If she could have secured a more enlightened management she might have been led on to consider the whole
question of Public House reform. This being impossible,
she concentrated on getting rid of the licence, in which,
after a bitter struggle, she succeeded. 'The Public House
trial is over, and we won triumphantly and conclusively,
and are very thankful for it. But the spirit of the people was
very dreadful and it doesn't augur well for the future work.
50 vestrymen and 150 ratepayers signed in favour of the
licence. Several vestrymen attended and gave evidence. Sir
J. H. was in a towering rage and tried to annoy me with
things that didn't touch me. But it all points to future difficulties. However, I cannot say I am discouraged. As long
as there was hope of peace from explanation and care I was
full of anxiety; but now we must go straight on.'

It was just while Octavia was fighting against the obstruction and stupidity of an elected body that she was concerned with the Artisans' Dwellings Bill, which gave increased power and authority over working-class dwellings to medical officers and local Councils. Much as she disliked officialism, she was sure that the immense power which is inevitably in the hands of a landlord of working-class property ought to be checked by public authority; the fact that she herself had suffered, was suffering, from a stupid and ignorant Vestry did not deflect her judgment. The conclusion to be drawn from her unfortunate experience was not that officials should be deprived of power, but that they should learn to use it intelligently, that, in fact, the quality of the Vestryman, the Guardian and other local officials was a matter of extreme importance. Here was a service which the educated man could offer to his district. Too often he despised it, leaving the local work to men whose education and outlook made it difficult for them to carry out their duties. Yet the work seemed to her even more practically and immediately important than the work of a Member of Parliament. 'What might not the locality gain,' she asked in an address on Good Citizenship, 'if the administration of its affairs were carried on under the influence of men of education? . . . As Vestrymen how you might be on the side of far-sighted expenditure or the suppression of corruption.' Who can say even now that local elections arouse the interest commensurate with their importance, or that enough able and educated citizens can be found to administer local affairs?

Chapter XII

OPEN SPACES

'The question is—whether there is still any land in England which can be preserved for the common good':
OCTAVIA HILL in 'The Future of our Commons', 1877

THERE was yet another subject to which Octavia gave time and thought during these busy years—indeed it seemed to her as important as any of the work she was doing—this was the provision of open spaces for town people. All her life she had spent much time out of doors, as a child 'always up in the hedges'; as a girl dragging her little toymakers for their good across field and common, teaching them, against all their natural inclination, to enjoy rural sights and adventures; as a young woman seeking and finding refreshment after a strenuous week's work in a thirty-mile tramp across country, and this in an age when convention demanded a costume which must have made even moderate exercise fatiguing, and expected the gentler sex to be unequal to any great exertion. But the harder Octavia worked the more urgently she felt the need of the sight and sound of country things; all beauty moved her, but none so deeply as the beauty of earth and sky, of trees and flowers, of nature whether wild or cultivated.

It seemed to her obvious that what was so great a refreshment and joy to herself must be of value to other people. She recognized that people who live in overcrowded tenements and who rarely experience the peace and spaciousness of the open country, may learn to do without and cease really to desire it, but she was not willing to acquiesce in this. To be content to live a narrow squalid life, without natural beauty, seemed to her far worse than to suffer in doing so. From the beginning of her housing work she had tried to give her tenants access to the sights of the country. She had made little gardens in her courts, she had planted creepers and trees round her playground, she had asked her country friends to send her flowers to distribute. Furthermore, she had arranged walks in Regent's Park, the Nottingham Place schoolgirls were encouraged to take the tenants' children out and to row them on the ornamental water there; and sometimes she made longer expeditions. Often she took parties walking across those fields and commons in which as children she and her sisters had played together. There were also whole days in the country. Just as from October to March Octavia gave an evening a week to a party for her tenants, so from April to September she gave a whole day a week to an outing with them. She liked best to take them to the country house of some friends who lived near London. Her half-brother, Arthur Hill, later Mayor of Reading, sometimes entertained them. A garden party, with a hostess who made them all welcome, provided just the feeling of friendliness, of easy human intercourse, which Octavia always desired for her people. It was a real party not just an excursion, the guests could walk round the garden enjoying the trees and the flowers, could sit about in small groups chatting sociably, or could wander off alone and enjoy the rest that only solitude can give. They were lovely days. But one day in a summer is not really very much, even if you have bunches of flowers in your room and can see the creeper on the playground wall, and Octavia was glad that many of her tenants had learnt from her the pleasure of walking in the parks and in the fields close to London.

In 1875 she learnt with dismay that the Swiss Cottage Fields were to be developed and that building plans were in preparation. She sprang to their defence. There was no open space near London whose destruction would move her more. These were her fields, the haunt of her childhood, the place from which all her earliest familiarity with trees and flowers had sprung. Furthermore, they were the open space nearest to Marylebone, and therefore most easily accessible to her tenants, and she knew well that by them and by hundreds of others they were freely used and great appreciated.

Octavia lost no time in collecting influential people to help to save the Fields and to secure them as a recreation ground for the public. She turned to the Commons Preservation Society which had already done yeoman service for the cause of open spaces. Founded in 1865 with Mr. Shaw Lefevre (later Lord Eversley) as chairman, it had secured the passing of the Metropolitan Commons Act of 1866 and by a series of great law suits, conducted by Robert Hunter its solicitor, it had saved Wimbledon and Wandsworth Commons, Hampstead Heath, Plumstead Common and Epping Forest for the people. Robert Hunter readily placed all his experience at Octavia's service, and they became friends and allies. She became a member of the Executive and remained an enthusiastic supporter of the Society to the end of her life. She found allies also in the Church. Dean Stanley at once supported her; and Mr. Haweis, Vicar of St. James, Marylebone, a man of considerable influence in his day, flung himself into the movement with enthusiasm. The contractor agreed to stay his hand, and a Committee was made to raise the necessary money to buy the Fields.

The sum required was 10,000 guineas, and to raise it in a short time seemed to Octavia a most formidable undertaking. She had never begged, and she did not like begging. The money she had needed for her schemes had come unsolicited; she had to overcome a very real repugnance before she started asking, but there was no other way and the Fields must be saved. 'I feel as if for the sake of securing air and light and beauty for the hundreds I see up in the Fields when I take my own people there, I had resolution enough to nerve everyone else in London for the effort.' She worked for the Fields with all the concentrated energy of her nature. 'I have one idea at the moment, the Fields. Laugh at me as much as you like.'

With the help of Edward Bond, who was her chief support in the effort, and Colonel Gardiner, an equerry to Queen Victoria and one of the Marylebone Guardians, who had worked with her on the C.O.S., Octavia secured influential support. Colonel Gardiner approached 'the Duke of Westminster, Baroness Burdett Coutts, Lord Lichfield, the members for Borough and County and *hosts* of the aristocracy'; while Sydney Cockerell applied himself to names influential in the City. Octavia wrote to *The Times*, and Macmillans published an article from her in August. In the first three weeks £9500 came in, but as in all money raising efforts it was the last £1000 that gave the trouble. August is a dead month for collectors of funds. Octavia became 'a little bitter, waiting for the slow rich people to make up their leisurely minds'. She was puzzled as well as impatient. 'I suppose I *don't* value money very high,' she remarked.

'How strange it seems to me (does it not to you?) that the momentary difficulty is to persuade the owners that there is a chance of anyone (any body of people in London or England) being in the least likely to be inclined to give money for a place which must be a blessing to hundreds now, and hundreds yet to come—a great free gift to this city, the chief city of their country.'

In August her friends insisted that she must have a holiday, and reluctantly enough she agreed and went off to Lady Ducie's house in Gloucestershire, but she could not rest. 'I came down here last night, but I feel leaving my Fields so that I could almost cry. We have got on very well . . . but the vacation has come upon us with its inevitable pause; it becomes a question whether the owners will give us time to try after it.' A week later she wrote: 'The collection goes on slowly, but quite steadily day by day; very well I think for the time of year; but we are in great fear that the owners will not wait. I wonder owners are not a little awed by the possession of so important a treasure, and do not pause a little, before they use it wholly without reference to the people.'

The owners, however, were not the least 'awed'. Their only emotion was incredulous dismay as they saw in the press the steadily mounting subscription list. It began to appear that the 'determined Miss Hill' would actually secure the required sum, and that they would be foiled of the handsome profits of development. This could not be contemplated. In the middle of August they suddenly withdrew their offer. In vain Octavia's Committee offered to guarantee the payment of the whole sum within a week, the offer was absolutely withdrawn, and in due time Fitz-John's Avenue rose on the fields for which she had battled so valiantly. It was a most bitter disappointment, success had seemed so near. Octavia had been so hopeful and had worked so hard that the reaction was very painful. She knew suddenly how tired she was, and went off to finish her holiday in Ireland feeling flat and disillusioned. 'For the moment I am a little broken by the loss, and it would be difficult to begin just at once, to work again.'

But this mood was transient. Even in the moment of defeat she had felt that the generous spirit which her supporters had shown need not and must not be wasted. Most of the subscribers to the fund chose to leave their donations in the hands of the committee, and when Octavia came back from her holiday it became necessary to consider how best to use it. By common consent the decision was in her hands, and there were many suggestions made to her for this space or that. Octavia refused to be hustled. The battle for the Fields had been thrust upon her, she had fought it on grounds personal to herself and to her tenants. That was over. It led her to consider the whole question of open spaces on general principles. 'I do not purpose pledging myself to any one spot, until I have carefully prepared a general map, to see where space is most needed. My impression is that I shall care most (now that the Swiss Cottage Fields are gone) for small central spaces; but this may not prove to be the case. . . . I can work for them gradually, quietly and less personally.'

The small central spaces, 'open air sitting rooms for the poor', became her immediate objective. She had always been appalled at the lack of space available for the poor; as she looked into the Courts 'the children are crawling or sitting on the hard hot stones till every corner of the place looks alive, and it seems as if I must step on them if I am to walk up the Court. Everyone looks in everyone else's way.' She reflected that it was strange that it should be necessary to fight to recover for Londoners 'the healing gift of space'. 'To most men it is an inheritance to which they are born, and which they accept straight from God as they do the earth they tread on, and light and air its companion gifts.' For those who had been deprived of this birthright she now demanded four things: 'Places to sit in, places to play in, places to stroll in, and space and place to spend a day in.' The fields she had lost had been a place to stroll in, it was not till some years later that she set to work to procure the places to spend a day in; it was with the first two that she was now concerned.

The important thing about the 'open air sitting rooms' was that they should be quite close to the crowded homes; it was not necessary that they should be very large, but they must be gay, well distributed, and abundant. London, overbuilt as it already was, was not really without such spaces; there were disused burial grounds, small church yards, derelict patches here and there, railed off so that the public could have no access to them. It was the burial grounds Octavia attacked first, in spite of a certain amount of opposition from those who felt there was something irreverent in the suggestion that the living should in some small degree share in the quiet of the dead. She tried to get those who had control of them to lay them out as gardens, to put seats in them, and to throw them open to those who so sorely needed them. She looked longingly at the various Square Gardens, reserved for those who had ample space. She begged that they might at least be opened in August and September, when the houses around them were empty and the privileged owners enjoying themselves in the country. It is an interesting fact that the appeal she made in 1875 is still repeated as summer comes round, and still (1940) meets with little response.

Octavia approached Corporations, City Companies, the Metropolitan Board of Works, with requests that they should buy open spaces, and keep them open, that in making new building schemes they should keep some parts of their sites open. For places to play in, she tried to prevail upon the School Board to keep the school playgrounds open in the evenings and on Saturdays. This seemed to her more difficult to arrange since she knew by her own experience that a playground to be useful must be staffed, that someone must supervise the children, must teach them to play, and must take real responsibility for them.

For a time her efforts met with very little success. In her report of 1876 she wrote: 'We have tried earnestly this year to secure small open air sitting rooms for the people in various parts of London, hitherto without one atom of success. I think I never spent so much heart, time and thought on anything so utterly without apparent result. We tried for an East End boulevard with an avenue, and with spaces of green and flowers, an East End embankment as it were, where the people might have strolled on summer evenings and sat out of doors, and we failed. We tried to get a Churchyard planted and opened in Drury Lane, and the matter has not progressed very far as yet, we tried to get trustees to act themselves in regard to other spaces and we hear little from them. We tried to get leave from one nobleman to plant trees along an East End road, where he is lord of the manor, and he postpones the question. We tried to get the Board-School playgrounds open, so far without success. We tried, oh how we tried, to get the Quakers to devote to the service of the poor their disused burial grounds, and they, even they, have decided to build over by far the most precious of the two; a spot which might have been perpetual joy and rest to the people, now is gone, I suppose for ever.' It was a melancholy review; Octavia felt particularly the action of the Quakers, for her friendship for Mary Harris had given her the greatest confidence in their wisdom and generosity. She wrote to *The Friend*:

... 'I am imagining for a moment that, in accordance with what I know to be the high minded and generous character of your Society, you are looking at the question from the people's point of view, and feel that your possession of land there, which has never yet brought you in rent, and was purchased by your ancestors with money devoted to their beloved dead, is in some sense a trust which it would be well to use for great ends of blessing the living. And I say unhesitatingly, from my experience of the locality and the poor, that a garden for them all would there help them more than dwellings for a few. . . . Then lastly, with regard to the portion of the ground accorded to those of your dead whom you seem to think worthy of honour enough to leave them in their graves, are you going to shut them up in possession of their space? Because, if so, you will soon find oyster shells, and old pots, and butchers' refuse accumulating over them too; and very likely, having inured yourselves by moving half your dead, you may feel less hesitation in moving or building over George Fox too. And so you may fill up the little gap between the houses which now you are going to halve in size, and the buildings, closed in, shall leave no trace of what was once your burial ground. The unused is always abused. Plant your trees there, sow your flowers, place seats in what you preserve of your land, invite the neighbouring poor in to rest and breathe fresh air, and, if it may be, to work a little in your garden, and it will be cared for, and look cared for too, as if it were a sacred place.'

When even this appeal was fruitless, she had to remind herself: 'It is a bad thing trying to see other people's duties, they alone can judge what they are.' The struggle was exhausting to her, partly because she so ardently desired success, partly because the method she had to use was alien to her. She had been wont to get her way by persuading individuals with whom she had personal contact, of the reasonableness of her demands, now she was fighting the inertia of a mass of people who meant nothing to her: 'My work becomes less home-like, more struggling; there is in it necessarily more of opposition, it brings me into contact with people further off whom I do not know well, nor care for at all.' She felt this opposition sorely. She had always worked with, not against, others, and she feared lest she should grow too militant, and should lose her sympathy with those who had a different point of view. 'The more opposition I have myself to do, the more it has been necessary to me to dwell on the duty not only of patience, but of gentleness. When I cast my bread on the waters, I have had to make sure that it *was* bread, not a hard stone cast at a brother, but bread to feed him, though he does not see it now.'

However much opposition she met outside, Octavia was always sure of help and sympathy in her home. Her sister and the school were always behind her in all her projects, and Miranda made it her concern to keep her pupils interested in all Octavia was doing. In December, 1875, therefore, when the apparently fruitless struggle for small open spaces was at its height, Miranda read a paper to the girls addressed to 'those who love beauty'. She quoted Mr. Barnett who had said, 'It is not the poverty that is such a weight upon everybody in the East End, it is the ugliness,' and proposed to start a society which should be called 'The Society for the Diffusion of Beauty'. It was to be a modest domestic little affair. 'I propose to learn as far as I can what has been done and what wants doing in the way of beautifying in poor districts, to write a short account of the work done and required every month, and to send it to the members of this society.' She asked for no subscriptions, merely for an expression of interest in the subject from those who chose to join it.

Octavia was delighted with the paper and with the project and she had the paper printed and circulated privately. It met with so warm a response that she persuaded her sister to read it to the National Health Society. 'The room was quite full; and the hearers were just those in whom the thoughts would be likely to bear abundant fruit.' From this meeting sprang the Kyrle Society, so called after Pope's *Man of Ross* who with an inconsiderable income yet beautified the streets and increased the amenities of his native town. Donations poured in. Octavia became the treasurer, while Miranda remained the chief organizer of the Society. Its purpose, as Miranda had originally planned, was the 'diffusion of beauty', an activity always dear to Octavia's heart. The Society took over the business of collecting flowers for poor homes, of planting small gardens, of providing entertainments for poor parishes. It ran a choir which sang at services in poor parishes, and found volunteers to take singing classes. Another of its labours was the decoration of all sorts of blank walls in school rooms, club rooms or Churches. Its members painted panels, illuminated texts, and 'carved brackets'. It is probable that we should to-day regard much of this decoration with disfavour, but Octavia cared very much about it, and took it very seriously. She believed in making people familiar with beautiful words and felt there was real value in having a motto in places where people could not fail to see it. There was one piece of decoration which gave her the greatest happiness. She put it in Freshwater Place, along the faces of the houses in the Court. The words she chose were 'Every house is builded by some man, but He that built all things is God', and she wanted 'to make the sentence very lovely in colour, that the mere brightness of it may be a joy to everyone that sees it. It will be done in tiles, so that every shower of rain may keep them clean and bright.' Alas that London rain, laden with smuts, fails to fulfil this function. She chose De Morgan tiles, and invited all her closest friends to give a letter of the inscription. She planned the work with joyful care, and discussed with an ingenuous earnestness the particular word or letter which each donor might give. She was delighted with the result; and felt sure it would please Ruskin who 'taught me to care for permanent decoration, which should endear houses to men, for external decoration which should be a common joy.' In her relation to Ruskin there was always something of the earnest child, she remained his disciple to the end of her days.

There were other inscriptions that Octavia wished to see blazoned along blank pieces of wall; she suggested that Kingsley's words 'Do noble deeds' should be put up on a wall near Waterloo Station. Doubtless this is not a form of decoration that commends itself to a modern mind, but it must be remembered that the streets of London in Octavia's day were dark and dreary to an extent hardly to be conceived to-day. There is much to be said against advertisements but no one can deny that the posters and the neon lights supply gaiety and colour to our streets. It is possible that, deprived of these, we should welcome even rather sententious quotations if they were executed in sufficiently bright colours.

The Kyrle Society had a sub-committee to deal especially with open spaces, and within a year had achieved substantial success. 'Drury Lane Churchyard has been planted and opened, so has St. John's Waterloo Road, . . . St. Giles Churchyard, a capital bit of ground running down to Seven Dials, its wilderness of tall rank grass and shivering leafy trees would, even if untouched, be something green for the people to look at, if the great wall which hides them were but down, and should the untidy neglected looking graves, and green damp paving stones, be put in order, and bright beds of flowers made in the grass; should the great gates be opened . . . what a possession the place would be to the residents near! This I trust may be done, for on every side the subject seems awakening attention, churchyard after churchyard is spoken of as likely to be planted and opened. The School Board has considered a scheme for opening its playgrounds to the children on Saturdays and after School on week days.'

While Octavia struggled for this space or that, she never lost sight of the more general question of the disposal of all commons and open spaces. 'The question before the country, and it is well we should realize its magnitude before important decisions are made, is whether consistently with all private rights there is still any land in England which can be preserved for the common good. . . . Are we, as a nation, to have any flower garden at all? Can we afford it, or will we have beetroot and cabbages only? In other words, is all the land as far as the people are concerned, from sea to sea to be used for corn growing or building over only?' She urged that this question should be faced and answered intelligently, that it should not be possible for commons and foot paths to be filched from the poor man by chance, or by the inertia of those who should act as his trustees, but that Parliament should show not less concern about its estates than a landowner does in planning what proportion shall be devoted to crops, and how much to the pleasure garden. She was, characteristically, anxious to preserve the rights both of the landowner and of the plain man, and to insist that it was not only rights which could be financially assessed which must be protected. . . . 'It must be observed that the nation, as a nation, is not held to possess the open uncultivated unappropriated land of England. True, generation after generation has passed over much of it freely, but it seems that the people are not thereby held to have acquired a right to do so. Perhaps this is because such right has no money value for rights of way, rights of light, rights of possession of soil, even rights on these very open spaces of pasturing cattle, cutting furze and of playing games are recognized by law where they have long been enjoyed. Had the right to wander freely, and to enjoy the beauty of earth and sky been felt to be a more distinct possession, it may be that these rights also would have been legally recognized.'

She never ceased to insist on the danger of underestimating those values which were not material, but she did not commit the folly of declaring that they were the only

154

valid consideration. She fought against the scheme for
making Thirlmere the reservoir for Manchester because she
felt the value of the beauty of the Lake and Valley was being ignored, and she insisted that the scheme ought to be
laid before some tribunal which would at least allow weight
to that value as well as to others in assessing the need of
Manchester. She failed to get her way, Thirlmere was
handed over to the engineers, and Manchester secured its
water. Perhaps she was wrong to wish it otherwise, but few
nowadays, regarding the haphazard development of estates,
the hideous eruptions of bungalows in places which were
once really beautiful, the enormous undirected growth of
London and its suburbs, can doubt that she was right in
working for some planning of our English countryside.

In this, as in so many things, Octavia was not only ahead
of her own generation, but ahead even of ours.

Chapter XIII

A LONG REST

'I could have done nothing but for Miss Yorke':
OCTAVIA TO EMILY, 1878

In these busy years there was one helper on whom Octavia had come to place more and more reliance. This was Edward Bond, the friend whom Sydney Cockerell had brought to help in the Club at Barrett's Court. He was a most valuable helper there, strikingly tall and good looking, he was of the type to appeal to young men, and he exercised a salutary influence over the roughest of them. He was interested in all Octavia's work, and at her instigation introduced C.O.S. methods into a parish in Hampstead where he lived. In the matter of open spaces he was particularly helpful, he fought at her side in the battle for the Swiss Cottage Fields, and was always ready to look into the legal side of any of the problems that arose, to interview those responsible for churchyards or the trustee of any open space. Inevitably Octavia saw a great deal of him and very much enjoyed his society. It was much the fashion in those days for parties to go for walking tours, and Octavia and Edward Bond often took part in these expeditions. He was so tall and she so very small that their friends were always amused to see them together. Since all of them disdained umbrellas and braved any kind of weather they often arrived at their destination looking so deplorable that on one occasion they were even refused admission at an inn. She found him stimulating. 'We had a long talk,' she writes in 1873, 'one easily gets on subjects with him, and seems to have much to say; there is a pleasant sense of friction and stimulus, though none of peace.' One of the subjects they were apt to 'get on' was religion. Edward, like most young men of the '70's, had religious doubts, which he liked to discuss with her. She was interested, eager to help, sometimes a little uneasily uncertain whether he was not more anxious to contemplate his doubts than to resolve them. In the early days of their friendship she sometimes asked herself why she liked him more than other of her friends whom she admired more. 'He is *very* helpful, *very* interesting, kind but not self-sacrificingly so, I cannot quite feel I trust him, yet one may trust him for response or help or kindness to any extent.' The struggle for the Swiss Cottage Fields brought them closer together, gradually her doubts about him faded away, she found increasing pleasure in his society, their intimacy grew. In July, 1877, somewhat to the surprise of their friends, they became engaged. It was a brief engagement.

Edward Bond's mother was a woman of 'proud cold conventional reserve'. She was a widow and he an only son, and having till now lived in complete docility in his mother's house, it was natural enough that she had come to take it for granted that he would do so to the end of her life. It had probably never occurred to her that he might wish for a home and life of his own. When therefore he told her that he intended to marry Octavia, she left him in no uncertainty as to her attitude to the proposition. Edward had always done what his mother thought good, he was not very courageous, he was not ready to defy her; like most men he dreaded a scene and felt that with patience and tact she could be brought round and he could have his heart's

desire without alienating his mother. But he had not understood Octavia. It had not been easy for her to accept him
as a suitor, she was no longer a girl, to marry meant a real
sacrifice of her independence (which was very dear to her)
for her Victorian view of matrimony would have involved
a real submission to her husband. She was ready to make
this sacrifice, but only because the man she loved was one
whom she could wholeheartedly respect. The Edward
Bond who came to her apologetic, hesitant, counselling delay, obviously afraid of his mother, was not the man she
had come to believe him to be. She realized then that their
outlook on life and its fundamental values were different
and, facing all that this meant, she ended the engagement.
She dismissed him once and for all, but what it cost her no
one ever knew; she held his memory sacred in her heart to
the end of her life. How much Edward Bond suffered none
can say. They never met again, and he died unmarried.

For Octavia it was an experience of intense bitterness.
The conventional side of the affair meant little to her.
Actually very few people knew of the engagement. The
Nottingham Place School girls who had been told of it,
were told the next day that it was a mistake and they were
not to talk about it. Young as they were, they were completely and loyally silent, not even discussing it among
themselves; there was no talk among any of Octavia's
circle. Her hurt was deeper than that, she had always felt
joy and sorrow very intensely; where she loved she loved
whole-heartedly, where she trusted she had no doubts. She
had staked her all on Edward's worthiness, he had proved
himself less than a man. It was a thought that kept her
awake at nights, and made her, for a time, wish to cut herself off from all her intimates. She acted, however, with

perfect dignity, she would not allow the wound she had received to deflect her from her course. She went to Lady Ducie's in August and there tried to rest her shattered nerves and weary body. The pains in her head and her back, to which she was always subject, attacked her again; she felt only partly alive, and though she longed for rest and solitude, she found she could not get the one nor easily endure the other. 'I suppose what there is of me will return to the old places and work. . . . I count the hours and days till I may slip back there—life is easier with the old duties and with the people to whom one is nothing but a person to be used. . . . Rest can't be procured by will . . . we can't make any but physical rest for ourselves.' In the autumn she was back at work as usual, holding her head high and dealing with each problem as it came with her usual thoroughness and sympathy, but she was very obviously ill. Her friends begged her to go away for a long rest; she replied: 'For the moment my place is here, and here, cost what it may, I must be.'

At the end of the year a new grief fell upon her. Sydney Cockerell had been taken ill at the end of July, and throughout the autumn anxiety about his health persisted; just before Christmas he died. To Octavia this was an irreparable loss. In her weakened and lonely state it seemed that the very foundations of her work were rocking, she did not see how the Club at Barrett's Court could survive, she doubted if she herself could go on without his ready help; she had come to depend much on his wisdom and experience, and more on his 'exquisite sympathy and goodness' which never failed her. It was a crushing blow, and it was only her strong religious faith that strengthened her beneath it.

Yet a third blow fell upon Octavia in this most unhappy autumn, this was the breach of her friendship with Ruskin. Octavia's relationship with Ruskin had been an important part of her life. She had been captivated by his idealism and eloquence when she was little more than a child, and the spell he cast over her had never been broken. Though she was perhaps more deeply and permanently influenced by Maurice, whose judgment she trusted more completely, it was Ruskin who brought romance into and cast a glamour over her most difficult days. Moreover, he had helped her at a crisis in her life. He had accepted her as a pupil and had put her to work for him. For ten and a half years he had employed her to copy pictures for him and provide illustrations for his books. In these years she had seen him constantly. He had ruthlessly criticized her work, and she had accepted his strictures with docility, stretching her powers to the utmost to satisfy him. It had been for both a satisfactory relationship. Ruskin in his restless unhappiness found comfort in the companionship of the intelligent girl, whose admiration was unbounded and who believed him always right. He spoke very freely to her, and could unburden himself of his sorrows, and propound his social and artistic theories, sure of her enthralled attention. It pleased him, naturally enough, to realize how easily he could give her pleasure, and how much she was conscious of her debt to him. Her steady confidence in the supremacy of righteousness, her conviction that all evil and suffering could be turned to good, seemed to him rather touching—a childlike faith suitable to an inexperienced girl. He felt incredibly old, weary and disillusioned (actually he was not 45), her unruffled serenity soothed his tortured mind.

When Octavia gave up her painting and turned to the management of house property, at first it made no change in their relations. Her work was still work for him, and he took a very great pleasure in his houses and followed all she did with interest and approval. It was a gratification to him to see the success of the work he had initiated. But gradually things altered. Inevitably Ruskin saw less of her, and as her work progressed and she became more experienced she turned less eagerly to him for approval. She was not working simply for him, but for a variety of other people. She grew older. Unconsciously Ruskin was fretted by all these things. Like so many fundamentally unhappy people who feel themselves misunderstood, he wanted disciples, young people who would hang upon his words and admire all he did. Octavia had outgrown this stage, but she still wrote to him simply enough about the houses and the tenants. Unfortunately he no longer took her as simply. The optimism which had seemed charming in an inexperienced child became irritating when it survived contact with the sordid misery of the very poor. 'I cannot understand,' he wrote irritably, 'how you maintain your faith in good coming out of evil to the person themselves . . . please send me word what you *mean* at all events, whether you tell me anything of what you speak of as evidence or not.' In answer to her attempt to tell him what she meant, he replied: 'It is very like Maurice, and to me—a poor moth lying singed under a candle which, as far as I know, doesn't light anyone—it is all very wonderful. But a nice frame of mind to work in. It will enable you to do much good in the future as in the past.' Octavia was saddened by Ruskin's bitterness, but she answered his letters with simple sincerity and sometimes he wrote with all his old tenderness and affection. Whether he wrote bitterly or kindly she still felt for him nothing but gratitude and love. Her reverence for him never wavered. She still believed him to be a supremely great man, whose vision was true and glorious, though sometimes it was sadly obscured.

The close intimacy, however, had gone. Octavia's work expanded in various directions in which Ruskin had no particular interest. He became more and more despairing of mankind, and began to think that no improvement was possible. When in 1875 Octavia wrote to ask him for a donation to help her save the Swiss Cottage Fields he declared: 'London is utterly doomed—as utterly as Gomorrah. That is no reason why *you* should not open a window or buy a field to give a moment longer breath to her plague-stricken children.' As the months went on Ruskin's gloom deepened, and by 1877 he was in a state of settled despondency, seething with indignation against mankind. In his restless unhappy state, a quite trivial incident was enough to set him ablaze. It was such an incident that provoked his quarrel with Octavia. Some busybody told him she had spoken of him as a visionary whose teaching could not always be taken literally. Ruskin was outraged. He did not stop to enquire into the context of the remark, or the spirit in which it had been made. It aroused him to a passionate belief in his own practical gifts, so that all his teaching seemed suddenly a small and negligible matter beside the solid reforms he had accomplished. More than this, it was he, the practical man, who had enabled her, the visionary, to translate her ideals into action. That she should turn against him, undervaluing all his life work, was intolerable. It was disloyal and ungrateful. In a torrent of rage he wrote to her demanding that she should forthwith substantiate her accusation. Octavia, unconscious of having made any accusation, replied as best she could, but quite firmly declined controversy. This added fuel to his indignation, and in a second letter, he threatened to publish the correspondence unless she would satisfy him. Octavia could not do this. There was really nothing she could say that he, in his excited condition, could hear. Ruskin therefore published the letters in *Fors Clavigera* in which at that time he was thundering forth his disapproval of all mankind.

Octavia maintained complete silence, but she was deeply wounded. She did not know that Ruskin was on the verge of his first attack of insanity, and she could not fail to suffer acutely at this public attack by one whom she still deeply loved and venerated. At any time her sensitive abhorrence of publicity would have made the incident very distressing. But it came at the moment when she could least bear it. She had forced herself to resume her work after the sorrows of the summer, but it was only by a great effort of will that she was able to face her friends and colleagues. In her busy days she found an escape from her unhappiness, but at the end of the day her tormenting thoughts attacked her again and robbed her of rest. 'I feel as if eyes and eyes and eyes had been on me for months, and my own never closed.' No wonder her family and friends became increasingly anxious about her.

Apart altogether from the emotional strain she had undergone there was every reason for her to be on the brink of a physical collapse. For ten years she had been accumulating more and more work. She had done it all with the whole of her generous nature, she had been obliged from time to time to give up one bit or another, but she did this only reluctantly to make room for something new. 'It is strange, but the strain of responsible schemes under my continuous charge,' she had written in February, 1877, 'the thought necessary for dealing with all the new large plans before me, and starting them wisely and well, the ever flowing stream of persons with whom I have to make appointments on business, and the incessant buzz round me of my assistants and immediate fellow workers, leave me in a state of exhaustion on a Saturday night which makes perfect stillness the only possibility for Sunday. . . . I know you will begin to tell me I ought to give something up. And I could only answer my whole life is giving up of work. I part with bit after bit, often of that I care for most . . . but it is the nearest of all duties, added to the large new questions, in which a little of my time goes a very long way, which thus engross me.

In the following months the work had only increased, and it was obviously not possible in the midst of such incessant activity for Octavia to regain her strength and to recover from the emotional stress she had undergone. Early in January, 1878, the doctors decided that a complete break was imperative, that only a change of scene and change of companionship and a long rest would make her recovery possible. Octavia accepted the decision with docility; her vitality was so low that she hardly cared what was done to her. The devolution of her work, which she had carried out so consistently for the last ten years, made giving it up now an easier matter. She had tried to make the managers independent of her; now they readily accepted real responsibility. Some of her business friends volunteered to audit and supervise the accounts, and all were asked to report direct to the owners of the Courts, and obtain their decision on all important matters. Her

OCTAVIA HILL IN 1882.

sister Gertrude acted as a liaison officer between all the workers, and Minnie took over the administration of the donation fund.

But obviously Octavia could not travel alone, and now a new friend appeared who had the means, the leisure and the will to be her companion and to help her through the long dreary months to recovery. This was Harriot Yorke, a woman of about her own age with whom Octavia had had no previous intimacy; perhaps at that moment it was easier for her to be with someone who did not belong closely to the everyday life she had been leading, with whom she could live on the surface. They started little more than acquaintances. Harriot Yorke was a splendid travelling companion, she talked very little, and was quietly competent and effective in all she did; there were no contretemps, no last minute scrambles, when she was directing affairs. 'She knows at a glance,' wrote Octavia, 'which carriages are large enough, what hotels are suitable, which drays are strong enough, at which places we may leave luggage unwatched, what men will fulfil engagements without supervision.' Moreover, she possessed that most valuable gift—the power of taking a genuine and lively interest in all her fellows. She was one of those people who inevitably hear the histories of all who serve them, and who remember them, so that when they come back to places they have visited before they are greeted with enthusiasm by every driver, porter and chambermaid. Such travellers are always well served. Octavia had never been looked after before. She found it wonderfully pleasant; more and more she learnt to depend on Harriot, and she became conscious of a deep and subtly expressed sympathy which was blessedly healing. Thence arose a satisfying friendship which became

the most precious possession of them both. It was such a
relationship as is supposed to be peculiarly characteristic
of English spinsters. For the rest of their lives they shared a
home, and for 'Ottie' making the way smooth for Octavia
became her principal business. She made herself the guardian of Octavia's health, noticing when her energy was beginning to flag, and saving her from over-fatigue. Octavia
laughingly nicknamed her Keeper, and she retaliated by
the name of Lion. She was well content that Octavia should
be the Lion, while her unobtrusive ministry ensured that
all her friend's energy should be released for its work. Her
relations with the Hill family were most harmonious, and
for Miranda particularly she conceived a warm affection,
but it is characteristic of her deep reserve that she remained 'Miss Yorke' to all of them to the end of their days.

Octavia's recovery was a slow and tedious business. The
history of the next three years can be briefly told. When
she started off with Miss Yorke in January, 1878, she was
in an almost completely passive state. The eager interest
with which she had been wont to greet new places and new
people, the readiness with which she had entered into discussion with chance fellow travellers, the hunger with
which she had demanded detailed news of her family and
tenants, were all gone. She could not walk at all, she had
no energy to sketch, nor any spirit to meet adventures. She
was quietly grateful to the George MacDonalds, with whom
they stayed at Nervi, for their kindness, but nothing had
the power to stir her very much. She was taken from Nervi
to Genoa where she met some disciples of Mazzini's and
was touched by their zeal for his memory; she wished to
show her sympathy, but was painfully conscious of her
lack of energy. 'I could have done nothing but for Miss

Yorke, who was so kind, she knew less than I did, much! but she took such pains and asked everything I asked her.'

Gradually as they went through Italy to Switzerland and the Tyrol her strength increased. She was able to drive and sketch a little, and take an interest in local customs and ways of life. A short visit home, and a consultation with her doctor sent her away again to France and Italy, but though during this second trip her letters show that she was sufficiently recovered to concern herself with some of her old interests, specially the work of the Open Spaces Committee of the Kyrle Society, and her sketches show a revival of her artistic energy, it was not until her third journey abroad that an eventual recovery began to appear probable. In this third trip they went to Greece, a sufficiently adventurous undertaking for two unescorted women in the year 1880. Upon this expedition Octavia entered with something of her old zest. 'Though she does still feel writing letters and all thinking very tiring, yet she is unmistakably better . . . one almost feels as if she would care to stay and work. And she said "I begin to look forward to this Greek journey". She is really able now to enjoy many things.' A symptom of her recovery was her determination to learn modern Greek as soon as she reached Athens, to read Geology on the way there, and to take paraphernalia for pressing flowers. The trip was undeniably a success. The Greeks were at that time still recovering from the long Turkish domination from which they had but recently (as the life of nations goes) escaped. Octavia became at once intensely interested in the work of reconstruction, her letters are full of accounts of the Greek interest in education, of the various measures of reform being instituted. She pushed on with her study of Greek, feeling it intolerable that she should not be able to talk to the natives. She listened to a debate in the House of Deputies and regretted bitterly her inability to follow all that was said. Though for most of the time they stayed at Athens, she and Miss Yorke made thrilling expeditions into all parts of the country, riding on mules or in very rough carts, enchanted to see scenes famous in Greek history, and particularly impressed by the German excavations at Olympus. 'She is evidently thoroughly enjoying it,' writes Miranda to Mary Harris, 'she is very far on towards recovery now.'

They journeyed by Constantinople and up the Danube and through Germany. A stay at Nüremberg opened her eyes to an English abuse, which she felt must be combated on her return. 'Trees grow among the houses, and children play round them, and clean industrious women knit at their doors . . . and still these gardens for the people look reproach at me, when I think of England; every tree and creeper and space of green grass in the town reminds me of our unconsumed smoke, and how it poisons our plants, and dims the colour of all things for us.'

A second less happy idea struck her also in this town. 'We hope to make a few useful outlines here for windows, etc., in possible future houses in London.' It was part of Ruskin's doctrine of the picturesque that made it seem possible and desirable to 'make a gift of a window here, or a cornice there, or a balcony in the other place' . . . in the hope of teaching English people to like 'what is home-like, quaint, pretty'.

By the summer she was home again, and spent September in Harrogate. 'If you were to spend all the time from now to Christmas in guessing what Octavia was doing' (writes Mrs. Hill to her daughter Emily) 'you would never guess aright, so I will tell you. She was acting to a Harrogate audience the part of Piety in the MacDonalds' "Pilgrim's Progress".' Octavia had undertaken to do this at a moment's notice, owing to the sudden illness of Grace MacDonald; she 'learned her part (eight pages) that night. I cannot tell you how beautiful she looked, and how lovely her voice sounded.'

It seemed to her delighted family that she had recovered. Indeed, virtually she had done so. She had to go very slowly at first, since any anxiety was apt to bring a return of the pains in her head and of sleeplessness. Sometimes noise tried her beyond endurance, at other times she felt unequal to the fatigue of meeting many people. She who had always faced her work so calmly now found herself worrying about a meeting for which she was responsible, nervous if she was going to speak. But these disabilities were transitory, gradually they ceased to worry her, and she was able to bring to her new problems her old energy and confidence.

For the moment she left her housing work to those who had managed so well in her absence, and since she was no longer working in daily contact with the poor she left also the administration of her donations fund to her sister Emily.

It was the easier for her to make up her mind to do this, since there was a great deal for her to do in her home. Florence had been for some time subject to a form of nervous debility, which gave her sisters much anxiety, and Mrs. Hill, now over seventy, though still wonderfully the centre of the household, began to find its ordering something of a burden. Octavia therefore busied herself with her domestic duties, and with work which she could do from home. It was a real deprivation to her to be obliged to cut herself off from the tenants, and from that daily contact with them which gave her so much joy, but she accepted the necessity quietly. 'I am obliged to keep very much out of all even thought of work. The home claims are very strong just now, and my own strength not very great. It is very strange to have to put the old things so wholly second.'

Her principal work at this time therefore was with the Kyrle Society, since this centred on Nottingham Place and could be done from there, and her first enterprise was the struggle against Smoke, to which she had vowed herself in Nüremberg. The Kyrle Society was obviously the right body to take the matter up. 'It appeared a natural sequel to what we had tried to do to secure open spaces, when once the world seemed awakening to the necessity of obtaining them, to endeavour to make them such as trees and flowers and grass would grow in and show their natural colour and brightness.' Accordingly as soon as she got home a subcommittee of the Kyrle Society was formed to deal with the subject of Smoke Abatement. Octavia saw clearly how the problem must be approached, first public opinion must be aroused in the matter, people must desire cleaner air and be convinced that to secure it was practicable; then smokeless fuels and smokeless grates must be made available in a form both cheap and easy to use. She conceived the idea of having an exhibition to show what could and should be done. She worked hard. The Commissioners of the Exhibition of 1851 lent its building at South Kensington, the exhibition was held, and there was a numerous gathering at its opening. Manchester sent a deputation to see it and planned to have a similar exhibition. English manufacturers produced improved grates; improved fuel was on show. Professors and other scientists supported the Committee. Octavia discovered to her surprise that 'the law *does* forbid smoke, so far as it can be prevented, issuing from factories large and small, from steamboats, and from all chimneys other than those of private houses'. It all seemed very promising. 'The saving ought to be enormous, the smoke all consists of unconsumed fuel. Some scientific men say that as much as three million out of five million tons used annually flies away in smoke, and so does harm and not good. Be the proportion what it may, the waste in mere fuel is considerable, to say nothing of the cost of the extra washing, and the artificial light required in day-time. But, independently of any question of saving, many of us would, I believe, be ready to make an effort to diminish smoke, were it only for the beauty and comfort and cleanliness, and for the life of the flowers we might then preserve round us.'

The case for smoke abatement was and is unanswerable, yet London and all our great cities remain extravagantly dirty and the citizens still endure fogs which deprive them and their children of the health-giving sun. Octavia gave the first impulse to the movement, at the moment she lacked the strength to pursue it, and later other and older claims recalled her. It was forty years before another smoke abatement exhibition was made. We still await someone with Octavia's force to carry out the reforms she so wisely foresaw and so greatly desired.

Chapter XIV

HOUSING AGAIN

'Remember that singly people must be dealt with':
OCTAVIA HILL, 'Letters to Fellow Workers', 1883

THOUGH Octavia found quite as much to do as her strength would allow in her household affairs and the Kyrle Society, her heart hankered after her real work, the daily contact with tenants and all the human intercourse it involved. It had always been her custom to have a tenants' party on her birthday, and in 1881, when Miranda suggested that she should invite the Paradise Place people to celebrate it, Octavia replied: 'No, I have nobody under my charge now. I think I shall have to invite sugar-jars to my birthday party, those are my only charges.' 'She could not help laughing as she said it,' Miranda records, 'but she had tears in her eyes.'

Though she was not in charge of them, the Paradise Place people had become her tenants. When she came home from abroad and began to survey the work that had been done in her absence, she felt unhappy about her first two properties, Paradise and Freshwater Place. These Courts still belonged to Ruskin, but since the state of his health made it impossible to appeal to him for any decision and since Octavia herself was not in a position to decide anything, she perceived that all the worst evils of absentee landlordism were springing up. The only remedy seemed to be for Ruskin to sell the property. Octavia had tried, almost as soon as she came home, to suggest this, but Ruskin was not easy of approach, and in the winter of 1880–81 he had fallen ill again and any discussion of business was impossible. It was therefore a great relief when in May, 1881, she heard, from Ruskin's man of business, that he was anxious to sell his houses. She had no doubt at all as to who should buy Paradise Place. It was the first property she had ever managed, it was within a stone's throw of her own home, many of the tenants had been her friends and neighbours for years. She at once bought it herself. 'That is now my very own; and I am thankful that the fact of ownership implies a continuous duty towards the people there, which must always claim due fulfilment, even when home duties are many.' It was a sort of guarantee to herself that she should not for ever be cut off from her tenants, that it would never be her duty to give all her energy to her own home.

Freshwater Place presented more difficulty. Octavia could not herself afford to buy it, but she cared for it as much as she did for Paradise Place, and could not lightly contemplate the loss of the playground which contained the first trees she had ever planted in London; yet unless the right owner could be found, it was indeed in peril. 'To anyone not trained to think first for the people, and temporarily to accept 5 per cent only, and let the balance be spent —or renounced—for their good, there would certainly be an overpowering temptation to build on the playground and cut down my trees.' This danger was averted by the purchase of Freshwater Place by the Shaens. Nothing could have pleased Octavia better. He had been a staunch friend from the beginning, he had been with her through all the difficult days and had expressed confidence in the plan when no one else except Ruskin had believed in it, and had given strong support and valuable help in business, in all the Courts. This new evidence of friendship touched Octavia very deeply, for she knew well that it was for her sake, even more than for the sake of the tenants, that he had made the investment.

For the present Octavia had to content herself with the thought that she had tenants of her very own and to look forward to the day when she would once more be in and out of the Courts. Meanwhile there was much that she could do in ways other than direct management. She kept in touch with the detailed work through her assistants, and particularly through Miss Yorke who was now managing, for Lady Ducie, her property in what had been part of Barrett's Court, but was now rebuilt and known as St. Christopher's Buildings. The name was Octavia's choice and very characteristic. 'I think in Barrett's Court we all want to be reminded that the Devil himself is afraid when he sees the good thing.' To her great pleasure Miss Yorke now undertook not only the management of the new Buildings, but also the rebuilding of the blocks that still remained. This included the building of a new hall, which did for St. Christopher's what Octavia's original club room had done for her first tenants. There were evening parties there every week, known as 'Socials', which supplied every sort of pleasant entertainment. Miss Yorke hardly ever failed to be present, and Octavia often went with her. There was dancing and music and some friends. Mr. Sam Hamer and his sisters trained the tenants to act and sing in Gilbert and Sullivan operas, for which Arthur Rackham painted the scenery.

Furthermore, Octavia found that she was able to be useful to the tenants in all sorts of indirect ways. 'The truth is, that though just now I am not and cannot be responsible for any work among the poor, I am in such close and constant communion with those that are, and the years of work in courts have given me such radical knowledge of them all, that I am really able to help in fifty small ways without feeling fatigue, and now and again I am called in about great matters where my experience is useful.'

By almost imperceptible degrees, she passed from this advisory role into full work again. But the work was somewhat changed in character. Its value was widely recognized and her reputation established. She was increasingly accepted as an authority on housing and other social problems. There was henceforth more contact with Royal Commissions, public bodies and dignitaries, less intimate intercourse with the very poor and the disreputable. There was more committee and less personal work, more organization, less improvisation. And in Octavia herself there was a change. Experience had only confirmed her faith in the principles on which her work was founded, there was no change in her outlook, no wavering in her principles. But the buoyancy which had distinguished her, the gallantry which had made of each day a new adventure, the gaiety which had lighted up the dreariest task—these were gone. What is this but to say that as the pioneer had become the accepted authority, so youth had passed into middle age? Octavia was now in her forties, and the change was natural enough. But before her breakdown it had seemed as if she might retain the quality of youthfulness to the end. It was not to be. She learned to be happy again, and to enjoy her work, her friends and the old pleasures, but she was always a little withdrawn into herself, a little aloof. It was only to her very intimate friends, her sisters and her nieces that she could reveal herself. To others she was a little alarming, almost unapproachable—a person to be greatly admired and revered, but not easily enjoyed. Her greatness was more apparent than the simplicity and tenderness which underlay it. She was wrapped in an impenetrable reserve which made intercourse difficult.

The general situation of housing had altered to a considerable extent during her absence abroad. The evils against which she had struggled, crowded insanitary houses, grasping and negligent landlords, had become more generally recognized and had shocked the public conscience; there had been a great wave of rebuilding. 'The Courts are numerous, the money for their purchase practically unlimited; . . . while I have been away everyone has been buying Courts.' There was now no lack of accommodation for working-class families, and though this was, in itself, a desirable state of affairs, it did not really promise any permanent solution of the housing problem; for, as Octavia was never tired of insisting, to regard the problem as one of bricks and mortar was to miss its whole significance. 'In all the late stir, the cry has been as to the dreadfulness of the houses and landlords. If all that is true under this head were remedied to-morrow, the public would see . . . that a large class would remain, which could not, without education, be drafted into better houses.' In some ways, indeed, the increase in accommodation made Octavia's work more difficult. 'The great supply of tenements, though much to be rejoiced in, on many grounds, has this drawback, that it makes the rampant and disorderly tenant tenfold more headstrong, it becomes almost impossible to exercise any just or wise rule or to secure any order.' In the

old days it had been possible to be pretty certain of paying
5 per cent on capital invested in the Courts, since she could
always let them and she had always found it possible to
train her tenants into orderly ways. Now that there was
alternative accommodation at hand, those who found regular payment of rent and observation of regulations irksome,
could move into new buildings, converting them rapidly
enough into a new slum. Octavia felt she could no longer
'with confidence recommend to those who are unac-
quainted with business and who depend on receiving a fair
return for their capital to undertake now the responsibility
of purchasing houses'.

It seemed to Octavia that it was necessary to discriminate
between two types of tenants. The reasonably prosperous
artisan could and should be housed by the Building Societies—of which there were now many—who could build
dwellings and let them at an economic rent to those who
were regularly employed and had attained a reasonably
high standard of living. It is fashionable now to assume
that all working-class flats must be given the conveniences
and modern devices which are to be found in the best of
them, but Octavia was a realist. She knew that there were
tenants of a less prosperous type, living on the edge of
poverty, the despair of any commercial Housing Society,
who could be dealt with only by landlords who were prepared, either personally or by proxy, to take the trouble to
educate their tenants as only fully trained managers could
do. These did not need new buildings and modern con-
trivances. 'I should make everything as strong as I could
and above all as simple as I could,' she said, to the Royal
Commission on Housing. 'These people are not at all accustomed to the use of appliances of any kind and any-

thing of that sort is a difficulty to them and I am quite certain that we ought not to give them elaborate appliances for a long time yet. For that reason I think old houses far better than the new for training them in.' For this type of tenant there was need to train managers and more managers as quickly as possible. Octavia appealed to all who were interested in social work to choose this branch of it; 'Let them come quickly,' she wrote in her letter to fellow workers of 1881, 'for the need is great.' She herself undertook the training of one volunteer, and there were now so many of her workers fully responsible and able to undertake the training of others, that she felt confident that if there were material there, a very large number could be trained within a reasonable time.

Octavia's appeal met with a generous response. By the end of 1883 she had a larger number of workers in training for management of houses than she had had for many years, and she had enough ready trained to take over two or three more blocks or Courts. She was anxious that these should be old houses full of the poorest and least desirable kind of tenant. The years had not changed her essentially; it was those who had failed, whom she chiefly wanted to help. 'One can meet and help a lower class of people than in any new buildings, however cheaply they may be let. . . . In letting to new tenants, one must ask for good references; the drunkard, the dirty thriftless woman cannot be accepted; the poor may be received, but not those whose character is doubtful; the preference is fairly and rightly given to the sober, industrious and clean. But buy up, take over a court full of the less hopeful tenants, and it becomes your duty to try them, some of them always respond to the better influences, and are permanently saved; . . . with that

178

class, we, if anyone, must deal. I would earnestly ask those who are working with me, not to lose sight of that fact, not to be led away by tempting plans of rebuilding, but remember that singly people must be dealt with, that face to face only can their education be carried on, that it will take years to accomplish, and many workers will be needed for it.'

By 1884 Octavia was fully immersed in housing work again. To make this possible some readjustment of her home life was necessary. She had willingly enough accepted 'the duty of weighing out sugar or correcting washing books', she really enjoyed 'shovelling away snow on the leads, or superintending the carrying of pails of water to the cistern which is obliged to be filled by buckets carried in from the street—our pipes being frozen from the main pipe', she found some pleasure in 'helping the girls with their drawing' and doing a certain amount of teaching, but, as Miranda remarked, it was 'plainly absurd for her to be prevented from advising a Royal Commission' by such homely tasks. Miranda's solution—that *she* should 'take the whole charge of the household and school matters' was obviously not one that her sister could accept. Florence, never very strong, longed for more privacy and freedom than was compatible with life in a school, and Mrs. Hill had reached an age when the perpetual presence of young people becomes inevitably wearisome. It seemed that the obvious solution was to close the school, and this, after much serious thought, the sisters decided to do at the end of the summer term of 1884. 'Octavia thinks we can manage now to live very simply on our little savings, if we let part of the house. Of course we shall be much poorer in money than now, but richer in time.' Even Miranda, who loved

the school, and knew she would miss the girls, felt that the
freedom from anxiety and responsibility would be a great
relief. For Octavia the decision was an unmixed blessing.
Not only did it give her greater freedom, more space for
her work and more quiet leisure, but what was even more
important it released Miranda to work for her. The two
had always worked together with so intimate a sympathy
that Miranda knew Octavia's mind, her hopes, her intentions as if they were her own. There was no need of elaborate explanation, Octavia completely trusted Miranda and
left much in her hands. Miranda had a lighter touch than
her sister, a graciousness and charm that conquered all who
met her. 'Miranda's sweetness with everyone,' writes Octavia, 'is beyond expression and also her merry fun over
all that takes place. She is quite delightful as a coadjutor,
bringing all the people so sweetly together, and never making difficulties over anything and all her spirits and power
come out.' She was happy if she could make the path easier
for her sister, and she made it her first business to relieve
Octavia of all domestic responsibilities and to give her
complete peace in her home. 'It feels like home now that
Miranda has come back,' writes Octavia to her mother. 'It
is wonderful to me the atmosphere of love and peace and
duty she spreads round her.'

There was yet another advantage to Octavia in the closing of the school. Emptied of the girls the house was too
large for the Hills alone, and they invited Miss Yorke and
another of Octavia's colleagues to live with them. It was
convenient to have her fellow workers at hand, but the real
advantage to Octavia was the close companionship of Miss
Yorke which she thus received. The latter, wishing to have
a home in the country, which should also be Octavia's

home, bought a field at Crockham Hill, close to the Warren where her sister Gertrude Lewes and her family already lived. 'They went down yesterday to see the ground that had been staked out. The owner of the field says the ground is so stony he can make nothing grow, and that he does not at all mind giving up the field. Octavia and Miss Yorke think the freehold may enable them to defend the common, if it is threatened by the Lord of the Manor.'

The planning of the house, which was called Larksfield, and the making of the garden, filled many happy hours. Octavia had always loved gardening, and the stony field which might have been discouraging to some natures was to hers a challenge. She positively enjoyed struggling with thistles—'my beloved thistles', she calls them—moving stones, collecting a little earth to make a grass plot, and she gloried in every flower that she persuaded to grow. Larksfield became a haven of rest to her, a place where she could always find peace and strength which enabled her to carry on her work.

In March, 1884, Octavia was invited to take charge of forty-eight houses in Deptford; in May of the same year the Ecclesiastical Commissioners asked her to manage some of their Courts in Southwark; in November they put more of their property in her hands; and in January, 1885, she accepted the management of eighty-five more houses in Deptford. The Deptford property was as bad as even she could wish. It had been neglected, the tenants had been badly mismanaged. On her first visit, she found a woman lying at the foot of her own stairs. She had been beaten by her husband, and had lain there from Saturday night to Monday morning too badly injured to move, since none of the neighbours had dared to send for a doctor for fear of the husband's vengeance. The tenants were quarrelsome and destructive, many of the houses were empty, and it was difficult to get new tenants not only because the houses were in a shocking state of disrepair, but also because the street had so bad a name that respectable people were unwilling to live in it.

Octavia tackled the street with all her old zest. She had Miss Yorke to help her, and an American, Ellen Chase, who had come from Boston to learn how to manage property. She was a worker after Octavia's own heart; she could see good in the most unlikely tenants, but was entirely unsentimental over them; she attacked Queen Street, Deptford, in a spirit of adventure and found much to laugh at even at the worst moments. And there were very bad moments. Octavia put the houses into thoroughly good repair, and thieves broke in and carried away the pipes of the new water fittings before anyone had time to use them, and one left a caricature of Octavia in chalk on the door. The Vestry was unsympathetic, but rather through stupidity than illwill. They served notices that the houses were in so filthy a condition as to be dangerous to the neighbourhood. Octavia, who had put the houses thoroughly in order within the preceding two months, and knew they had not since been inhabited, naturally enough protested. The Vestry was apologetic, they had no wish to be unreasonable, but the Metropolitan Board of Works was urging great attention to sanitary matters and they had felt bound to 'do something', perhaps Miss Hill would see her way to 'a plentiful use of whitewash and the putting down of a little gravel near the yard doors'.

The difficulties remained very serious, Octavia could not get the public opinion of the street on her side. Ellen Chase reports of one tenant: 'He had torn his garden all to pieces and broken off all the fence and windows here and there and did not show himself at all. We were nonplussed. First I hoped to slip a notice under his door, but the weather board was too close (that is a reason against putting them on), then we debated how legal a service would be, pinned to the back door, but Mr. P. thought it would be awkward, if I was summoned for breaking in on the premises; and to post it we thought would not be customary; so we were baulked, and Mrs. Lynch smiled sweetly all the time from her door.'

For years Octavia seemed to make no headway at all—sometimes she feared that the owner would feel she had failed and take the work from her hand. 'That was the only fear in her gallant soul,' writes Miranda. 'She seemed quite undismayed by all the trouble and difficulty, while Miss Yorke, who has faithfully and ungrudgingly spent three whole days of every week at Deptford with Octavia, toiling on in the midst of abuse and discouragement, murmured that she should be *glad* if the work at Queen Street came to a natural end. I felt and said the same, until I saw how Octavia longed to go on and dreaded failure.' She went on courageously. Part of the difficulty lay in the distance between Deptford and Nottingham Place, no trivial journey even to-day, with Tubes and motor buses to help, a weary business when there were none such. It was the first time she had undertaken a work at a distance from her home. She did not grudge the time she spent getting there and back, she gave three or four days a week, but she felt that the tenants needed more constant supervision than she could give at such a distance. She tried many expedients, she got a suitable superintendent to live in the street, she did all the things that had helped with other tenants but the 'black sheep' remained discouragingly black. Year after year she records in her 'Letters to Fellow Workers': 'Deptford is still far behind.' 'Deptford is still a cause of sorrow.' 'My poor Deptford.' She was puzzled as well as distressed, for she felt her workers were admirably equipped and were putting in such solid faithful work, that it must be telling, even though the result did not appear.

'The street is disgraceful,' she writes sadly in 1890, 'what more to do I do not know. I don't want to throw all the blame on the tenants, of whom I am fond, whom we have failed to help to be better. I have had good workers there, better couldn't be, but of course it is a *great* drawback that we work from such a distance. Whatever be the cause (I am quite willing to think it is my own fault, only I do wish I could see how, and set to work to remedy it) I am bound to record this street as a failure up to now, as far as human eye can see.' It is only the truly great who can recognize their own failures, record them with simplicity and without bitterness and believe that they may be their own fault.

Deptford began to improve when Octavia found an old pupil of her own who lived at Blackheath, within walking distance of Queen Street, and who was willing and able to learn to undertake the property. In the 'Letter' of 1892 a glimmer of hope appears: 'Poor Deptford, our black sheep continues black—at least I fear it does—I am, however, full of hope about it. . . . I have secured one who, if I mistake not, will make her mark there before the year is out. But we shall see. It is slow and uphill work.' Thenceforth Deptford went forward steadily, so that when, in 1900, a great accession of new work made it desirable, Octavia could without misgivings herself give up Deptford entirely.

The course of the work in Southwark was entirely different. From the beginning it went well, local people were friendly and helpful, and the fact that Octavia was representing so august a body as the Ecclesiastical Commissioners gave her a certain standing in the district. There were difficulties of course. She had never before worked for a corporation and she was not very sure that she should like it as well as working for an individual, she always felt more competent to manage one person than a Committee. Actually, the Commissioners were as clay in her hands. She had by this time so clear a view of what was the right thing to do with houses and tenants and so convincing a manner of presenting her case, that it was impossible to withstand her. Yet it is doubtful if she ever realized the strength of her position; the humility which characterized her attitude to Deptford made her underestimate the immense reputation she had achieved, which gave her an unassailable position in all housing matters. She was genuinely astonished, as well as pleased, when the Bishop of London (Temple) in the course of a speech at Fulham Palace said of her: 'When she had talked to us for half an hour we were quite refuted. I never had such a beating in all my life! Consequently I felt a great respect for her. So fully did she convince us, that we not only did what she asked us on that estate, but proceeded to carry out similar plans on other estates.'

There was no difficulty in finding volunteers for Southwark, and Octavia soon had a useful body of workers there, ready to train others as the work expanded, which it rapidly did. 'Our last batch of work,' Octavia remarked to Miss

Yorke in January, 1885, 'after this we won't expand any more.' Nevertheless the expansion continued, for business men and companies who owned property now showed increasing readiness to put their houses under her care, and with her views on the importance to the tenants, as well as to the owners, of good management, she could not refuse them, if she could supply competent workers.

The work in Southwark followed the usual lines, but the extent of the area controlled by the Ecclesiastical Commissioners gave scope for more large scale planning than had hitherto been possible to Octavia. On the occasion to which the Bishop of London referred when she had given the Commissioners 'such a beating', the point at issue was the provision of open spaces for the tenants. In the course of a reconstruction scheme, many small buildings had been swept away and replaced by blocks, thereby 'destroying so many small cottages with tiny yards or courts which were not thoroughfares that they (the Commissioners) had deprived the children of play places and the women of spaces for sitting out of doors.' Octavia was able to convince them that this loss must be made up to the tenants; not only did she secure a garden in this particular estate but also established the principle that in any rebuilding scheme space for recreation was no less important than space to live in.

She got her garden. Like her first playground, when she took it over, it was a waste desolate place, but Octavia saw possibilities from the beginning and planned to do more than make a playground. To clear it was the first step and she attacked it with all the zest characteristic of her whenever she brought order out of chaos. None knew more clearly than she, that the unseen spiritual results were the more important, but there was, all the same, a very positive joy in visible tangible results which could be measured and assessed; her account of the transformation of the waste plot into the garden breathes the same spirit in which years earlier she had reformed her toymakers' dinners, more recently had cleaned up her first Courts, even then was pulling thistles out of the field that should be Larksfield. 'There had been a paper factory on one half of it, which had been burnt down. Four or five feet of unburnt paper lay in irregular heaps, blackened by fire, saturated with rain and smelling most unpleasantly. It had been there for five years and much rubbish had been thrown in . . . our first work was to set bonfires alight gradually to burn the mass of paper. This took about six weeks to do though the fires were kept alight day and night. The ashes were good for the soil of the garden, and we saved the whole cost of carting the paper away. Our next task was to pull down the warehouse, and let a little sun in on our garden, and additional light, air and sight of sky to numerous tenants in the blocks in Red Cross Street.'

She describes the whole plan in loving detail; the covered playground for the children, with its flat roof approached by a wide staircase, making a terrace for grown-ups, the paved arcade with a drinking fountain of grey granite, the gravel playground for the children which 'melts off irregularly into the garden proper' with its winding paths, a small pond, crossed by a bridge—rustic no doubt—lawns and flower beds and 'bulbs in plenty'.

Another question arose over rebuilding schemes. The enormous value of London sites made it obviously expedient to replace cottages, of which there were many in Southwark, by blocks of flats. Octavia bitterly regretted this, having no doubt that though the cottages looked less impressive than handsome new buildings, they actually made far better homes for working people. 'The old cottages look shabby, those who do not know the life of the people object to owning them, and they are looked upon without favour; but well managed, and essentials secured, they are an inestimable boon to those who live there, and any one that can be preserved, with security for health, should be jealously guarded. The separate yard for chair for invalid, swing for child, place for creepers and bulbs, space for man to make a little workshop, the separation from other families make them incomparably better for a family than anything however spick and span we can build now. And so you will find the respectable working man knows well. He will prefer them for his family to anything we can provide unless he can afford a *new* cottage.'

They were always in demand, and Octavia worked hard to persuade the Commissioners to save as many of the old ones as possible and when they planned any new development, to devote some small part of the site to cottages. She prevailed. Near her new garden first three cottages were built, then six more, then as still more were demanded, twenty-four more on a neighbouring site. They were all four-roomed cottages with a small yard or garden and none was ever empty for a day. Some of her friends began to build cottages in other districts, and Octavia was delighted when one who was building them in Lambeth and had borrowed her plans from the Commissioners, reported after her interview with them, 'You *have* fired them with interest about building cottages.' The fact that with the ever increasing pressure on space in London, cottages become fewer and huge blocks of flats are larger, is one of the many arguments for replanning the metropolis and de-creasing its size. So the work in Southwark took root in a most satisfactory way; everyone was kind and interested, there was no lack of helpers and therefore no limit to what could be accomplished there.

Chapter XV

SOUTHWARK—A HAPPY FELLOWSHIP

'All classes were so entirely gathered in, each to do what in
them lay to accomplish the good work':
OCTAVIA TO SYDNEY COCKERELL, July, 1890

CLOSE beside Octavia's cherished garden was another site,
occupied by 'an old dilapidated skin factory, by no means
a pleasant adjunct to a garden'. Here she was determined to
build a Hall for the use of her tenants and a few cottages.
Elijah Hoole was her architect. He was an old and tried
friend who had helped her in all her buildings, often giving
his services with the utmost generosity and always taking
endless trouble to meet her wishes. He now laid out the
site, planning the garden and the cottages and a hall which
he estimated would cost £2500. For this Octavia now appealed in *The Times* of March 12, 1887. Even she, accustomed as she was to the generosity of the public, was astonished at the rapid response; she received £2105 on the
following day—of which £2000 was the gift of the Hon.
Henry Cooper—and the whole sum before the end of the
month.

Needing a secretary to the fund, she turned to Sydney
Cockerell (later Director of the FitzWilliam Museum at
Cambridge and now Sir Sydney), the son of her old friend.
He responded readily, having a hereditary right to the
office; had he not gone with his father to Barrett's Court
and 'appeared in a little holland frock, at the age of five, in

a play in which Octavia took part'? He became secretary to the fund on March 14, and thereafter Octavia's right hand in all that had to do with the Hall and the work among men and boys there.

The Hall was called Red Cross Hall, and the development of the whole site gave Octavia the greatest satisfaction. It all went so easily. Within a very few months she could record: 'the walls of my Hall begin to rise, and three of my cottages are getting their roofs on.' The cottages had 'pretty gables', one had a bow window and all looked over the garden. Expenses were kept as low as possible, and in building the covered playground and terrace Mr. Hoole made ingenious use of the warehouse walls which still stood, and used material he could find there for the balustrade and garden bridge. Walter Crane designed panels, each depicting some deed of heroism, for the inside decoration of the Hall; Lady Ducie paid entirely for the laying out of the garden, and the Kyrle Society did the work; the local authority co-operated, and all the neighbours in Southwark were eagerly interested in it all, and felt so much that the garden was theirs, that they treated it with respect and destroyed neither flowers nor grass, but by common consent preserved its beauty.

Friendly as the local authority was, Octavia did not wish her Hall to pass into its control; she collected enough money to endow it and vested it in Trustees, of which she was one, in order that the Hall might always be used in the way she thought well. There was a formal opening of the Hall and garden in June, 1888. The Archbishop of Canterbury performed the ceremony and Octavia enjoyed every moment of it. The sun shone, the place was decorated with lovely flowers and green boughs sent up by friends in the country, the warehouse wall over which the creepers had not yet grown, bore a large inscription in red letters on a white ground, framed with garlands: 'The wilderness shall blossom as the rose;' the Kyrle Society choir sang, Mrs. Hill was able to watch the proceedings from a little room in one of the new cottages. Octavia's cup of happiness was full.

The activities in Red Cross Hall were soon in full swing, and it is interesting to notice that here Octavia did on a larger scale exactly what she had done for her very first tenants in the white-washed room over her stable in Nottingham Place. The years had only strengthened her conviction that any group of tenants must have a centre of corporate life, a heart as it were, to make a civilized community. In the old days when tenants were comparatively few and all in Marylebone, her own home had served the purpose; she had extended her work farther afield with some reluctance, just because she could not see how to keep that home-like neighbourly relation with people at a distance. The Red Cross Hall solved the problem. In it she saw her ideals worked out on a scale which had hitherto been impossible, and the work there seemed to her, perhaps, the greatest reward of all her years of strenuous toil. There was no end to the activities which centred in the Hall and garden, there were classes, lectures, entertainments, gatherings of all sorts, girls' club, boys' club, men's club and gymnastics with movable apparatus and a sergeant capable of instructing. The activities were planned by those who took part in them, and again she collected friends to come in and help. Sydney Cockerell acted as Secretary to the Men's Club, and it must often have seemed strange to Octavia to find herself discussing with him ex-

CAROLINE SOUTHWOOD HILL
(MOTHER OF OCTAVIA HILL).

(*From the Portrait by Miss Baldwin Warn*).

actly the same problems as she had discussed with his father. There was again the question of club-room rent, and again Octavia's insistence that the men must recognize the truth of their financial position.

'I can quite understand that the Club would like to feel that it paid its own rent, and also can fancy that the rent asked might seem high. . . . I hoped that the suggestion of their having the hall on a stipulated number of nights would amply make up to them for paying a rent which, though we could have got it, always seemed to me high for the room for them, but they are much the best judges of their own business, and if they don't think it does, we must see if we can think of a plan they approve.' And later: 'I feel that the Club should either *punctually* pay for the room or give it up. This half and half responsibility is very unsatisfactory.'

A satisfactory feature of work in the Hall was that many of the helpers were Southwark residents, who being close at hand were most valuable in a variety of ways. Nor was the usefulness of the Hall confined to the tenants, it really became a centre for the neighbourhood. From 1893 onwards there was an annual flower show, which became a kind of garden party for the district. There were two bands, dancing, refreshments, and all who lived in the neighbourhood were invited to show the plants they had grown. It was a great success. On Sundays too the Hall was a meeting place. 'On Sunday afternoons we have opened the Hall free to all grown-up people who like to come; by the great kindness of friends we have been able to provide really beautiful music, Sunday after Sunday. . . . Always we have been supplied with flowers and the Hall looks really lovely all lighted up, with its three great cheerful fires, which are a great attraction, specially when one turns in from the mud, fog and general dinginess of Southwark.'

There were dramatic performances too; a real stage made it possible to give serious plays. The MacDonalds as of old came and acted again and again and other friends, old and new, came to give Southwark the advantage of their talents. Octavia enjoyed the plays, as she had always done, but she was not altogether content until she had got the tenants themselves to act. She knew the value of 'the learning, the discipline and the working together'. It was some years before the children of the Southwark tenants gathered enough courage to act some of the charming little plays that Miranda had written, but having once broken the ice it became an annual event. There were concerts as well as plays, and Mrs. Julian Marshall who organized many of them also started a violin class for the tenants' children. Octavia, who in her youth had recognized with mortification that the conductor of the Choral Society at the Working Women's College did not consider her good enough to sing in it, rejoiced that these children should be given the opportunity of making music, knowing that whether the listeners gained much or little from hearing them, the performers were satisfying an imperative need of their being.

There was soon a library too in the Red Cross Hall. This arose from a suggestion of the Men's Club, which Sydney Cockerell put before Octavia. 'You don't say,' she replied, 'whether the men want a small lending library of their own, or a nucleus for a reading room hereafter, nor whether they have space and a librarian. If they are ready to receive books I should propose to make their wants known in two or three quarters.' A combination of library and reading room was decided upon, and Octavia made its wants known to Cassells, who responded with a generous gift and this was supplemented by presents from the Trustees of Dr. Williams' Library and from Octavia's friends. 'The Hall is open for two hours daily as a reading room. In summer with the doors to garden wide open, it forms a very pleasant place for men in the dinner hour or children between morning and afternoon school.' In its first few weeks members paid 8s. for books taken out, at the rate of $\frac{1}{2}d$. a volume, which showed to her satisfaction that a considerable amount of reading was being done.

In 1888 Octavia was concerned with a new venture. Anyone who has attempted work with young people knows that the boy from fourteen to eighteen goes through a difficult and tempestuous stage, particularly perhaps in a town where there is little scope for the energy of the exuberant, and an abundance of temptation for the idle; he is apt to be resentful of discipline, suspicious of any attempt to improve him, desperately afraid of appearing unmanly. Octavia, recognizing this, had always tried to provide gymnastics, and to persuade young men of her acquaintance to play football with her big boys and to encourage them in outdoor recreation. It was W. Ingham Brooke, secretary of the C.O.S. in Southwark and one of Octavia's most faithful supporters, who having seen the working of a Cadet Corps at Toynbee Hall, suggested to Octavia that Southwark should have such a corps. She took up the idea eagerly, found Albert Salmond, a Captain in the Derby Militia who was willing to organize the corps, and thereupon approached the War Office with the result that Lord Wolseley himself presided at an inaugural meeting; the Corps was fairly launched in 1889 with 160 recruits. Octavia took the greatest interest in it, she took the chair at the Council of the officers, and in *Changes and Chances* H. W. Nevinson gives an interesting picture of her on these occasions: 'I used to compare her in my mind to Queen Elizabeth among her pirates and explorers. For the solid little figure with powerful head, masses of loose grey hair, large, benign but watchful brown eyes, and mouth closing tight like an unyielding steel trap when she was displeased, displayed all the great Queen's indomitable resolution, power of command, personal affection or dislike, scrupulous regard for every halfpenny spent or received.'

The Corps flourished from the beginning: in the course of its first year it was necessary to halt the recruiting because there was not enough money in hand to supply more uniforms and equipment. The money was quickly subscribed by Octavia's friends to the great satisfaction of the would-be recruits. The uniform of the Corps to which the company was attached was dark green. Octavia wrote to the War Office asking that her boys might wear scarlet instead, both because she loved strong bright colour herself, and because she felt the streets of Southwark needed cheering, a choice very greatly approved both by the lads and by local opinion. The Corps began without a band for reasons of economy, but Octavia's generous friends soon supplied that need and also funds to enable it to go to a camp for a fortnight. In 1890 it marched in the Lord Mayor's Procession, a great satisfaction to Octavia who believed that taking part in municipal or other public functions would help the lads to realize that they had a stake in the country and locality. The Corps became the 1st C.B. of the London Regiment and the senior Infantry Cadet unit in the army.

The question of financing the corps presented some difficulty. It was necessarily a somewhat expensive business. Though Octavia received generous gifts for it in its early stages, she did not feel that she ought to keep it permanently on her donation fund. Many of the public schools were already supporting missions in poor parishes in London and it seemed to Octavia that the Cadet Corps was exactly calculated to appeal to schoolboys, and that to link the Cadets with the great schools might be of great benefit to both. She consulted Edward Stone, then a Housemaster at Eton. Her friendship with the family dated from the very serious illness of Mary Stone while she was a pupil at Nottingham Place. Her mother had spent the critical days of her illness there, and out of their common anxiety for the child's life, an intimate friendship between her parents and the Hill sisters had arisen. Octavia stayed with them frequently at Eton, and their youngest son Christopher was her godson. Mr. Stone was extremely alive-to social problems and readily enough put the subject of the Cadet Corps before his pupils. The boys responded with real interest, and this was the beginning of a regular connection between their O.T.C. and the Cadet Corps.

Southwark was the first of Octavia's districts to have a Cadet Corps. It proved so useful there, that she encouraged its spread to other properties under her control, more especially to those which she found difficult. In 1911 when she was tackling a very thorny bit of work in Notting Dale, a notoriously bad neighbourhood, she put much energy into a Corps there, to which she was wont to refer affectionately as 'my Benjamin'.

There were not wanting those who disapproved of the Corps on the grounds that it encouraged a militaristic outlook, which might tend to support war. Octavia was no chauvinist, she had too tender a feeling for the Society of Friends to be able to disregard this criticism; she considered the matter carefully and wrote her conclusion: 'I do not feel any doubts about the Volunteer Cadet Corps. . . . I do feel defensive war is right, if by sad necessity it should ever be called for, which I doubt. The Volunteer movement seems to me a helpful form for preparation to take, contrasting with all standing armies. . . . I do so clearly see that exercise, esprit-de-corps, camping out, manly companionship with the gentlemen who will be their officers will be to our Southwark lads the very best possible education. I see how it fills a gap in their education. . . . I do feel that neither Mr. Barnett nor Mr. Brooke, who believe this movement reaches a sort of boy that nothing else does, and reforms him, are men to desire to strengthen a love of war. In fact, I see what they, who know the lads better than I, say most emphatically, that all the temptations to war are entirely absent from the boys; they are cowardly and wanting in power of endurance, wanting in power of standing together, worshippers of money. All which the volunteer movement will teach them, will, I believe, be helpful.'

Octavia indeed regarded the Corps simply as an instrument of education, in her mind its value lay in what it could do for the lads who composed it, not in what they corporately could do in the army, on questions which might bear on its military efficiency she refused to offer any opinion; when the desirability or the reverse of a camp at Shorncliffe arose she wrote: 'It is a question I am wholly incompetent to decide. . . . The only duty I have is to remind you . . . that our object is to train good useful and healthful men, capable of becoming volunteers, but that we are pledged, by our own lives and convictions and by the trust reposed in us by others, not to weigh for a moment military training against good, natural, healthy influences.'

The Red Cross Hall therefore continued to be the centre for the Corps and for all the other activities. It stands in Southwark still, and if to modern eyes the garden seems smaller than Octavia's enthusiasm would lead one to expect, and the Hall less full of vital activity, it is perhaps because there are, thanks to her, more open spaces and more opportunities for young people, of social contacts and healthful recreation all over London to-day. Yet no doubt in part the abounding life of Hall and garden was derived from Octavia's own passionate energy. 'Since she came back,' wrote Miranda after one of Octavia's absences from home, 'everything has been astir again. I always think her return on the scene brings about what Tennyson describes as happening when the Sleeping Beauty awoke:

> "And all the pent up stream of life
> Roars downward like a cataract."

Things seem asleep till she comes, then all is life and movement.'

Chapter XVI

POVERTY AND INDEPENDENCE

'If the poor are to be raised to a permanently better position,
they must be dealt with as individuals and by individuals':
OCTAVIA in 'Homes of the London Poor', 1872

FROM 1884, when Octavia became responsible for property
of the Ecclesiastical Commissioners, her work was mainly
in South London, but not exclusively so. In Marylebone
her old Courts and houses gave her very little anxiety, but
in 1886 she embarked on some property there which involved quite peculiar difficulties.

For some time a Criminal Law Amendment Bill, backed
by the leaders of all religious bodies and rescue societies, designed to prevent traffic in girls, had been before the House.
The age of consent at that time was thirteen and the sale of
children for immoral purposes was an easy and lucrative
undertaking. In 1885 Gladstone's government, shaken by
the tragedy of Gordon, and facing the prospect of an early
dissolution, proposed to jettison the Bill. W. T. Stead, then
editor of the *Pall Mall Gazette*, a man deeply interested in
social questions, determined that public opinion must be
aroused to prevent this. Accordingly he started a crusade
in a series of articles entitled the 'Maiden Tribute of
Modern Babylon', in the course of which he revealed that,
in order to prove how little protection the law afforded to
a child, he had bought one from her parents, who lived in
James Street, Marylebone. Stead gained his end, for the

pressure of public opinion forced the passing of the Bill, but he was prosecuted, and having overlooked the necessity of getting the consent of the parents in writing, he was convicted and sentenced to three months' imprisonment. The trial received an immense amount of publicity, and James Street, which had at no time enjoyed an enviable reputation, now became so notorious that no respectable family would willingly live in it.

It was at this moment that Octavia was invited to manage a block called Christchurch Buildings, in the street. She accepted at once, since the work obviously needed doing, and was one which demanded the qualities she could bring to it. It was manifest that the standard of the whole street must be raised if her block was to be a success. Her first step was to weed out from Christchurch Buildings all evil-living tenants and to keep their rooms empty until she could secure others whom she knew to be respectable. The whole street was structurally in a bad state and ripe for rebuilding. Octavia therefore obtained possession of as many sites as she could, and knowing the attractive power of cottages, she got her friends to build some there. The charm of a cottage and Octavia's reputation for good management gradually overcame the reluctance of respectable tenants to settle in the street; when it had receded from the forefront of the public mind, Octavia persuaded the London County Council to change its name, and its past history sank into oblivion.

While James Street, Deptford and Southwark were occupying so much of her time and energy, Octavia's mind was full of anxiety about the problem of Poor Relief, which had given her concern since the early days of the C.O.S. 'The days are full of difficulty,' she wrote in 1885, 'the

temper of the poor is difficult, the old submissive patience
is passing away, and no sense of duty has taken its place;
the talk is of rights, not right. The ideal the poor form for
themselves is low, and the rich support them in it. The
rich, on the other hand, while they are continually coming
forward more and more to help the poor, are thoroughly
cowardly about telling them any truth that is unpalatable,
and know too little of them to meet them as friends, and
learn to be natural and brave with them. We have great
relief funds, and little manly friendship, idleness above and
below and an admiration for what is pleasant, which de
grades all life. This temper makes work difficult, and sometimes fills me with wondering awe about the future of rich
and poor.'

Wages were still low, and unemployment a steadily increasing evil, the rich had become more conscious of the
poverty which surrounded them, 'slumming' was becoming fashionable. It was true that the rich were 'coming forward more and more to help the poor', but the help did not
take the form of intelligent service, it expressed itself in
streams of money which flowed in answer to any appeal.
Again there was an immense Mansion House Fund; in
January, 1886, it amounted to £20,000 administered by
Parish Councils, few of which attempted any rational
method of distribution. 'I hear that the working men on
the Committee are the greatest help in the only four
parishes where any order is attempted. As a rule the most
utter confusion prevails, the crowd of regular roughs awe
some into giving soup tickets, so low have we got with a
fund the only excuse for which is that the distress has
reached a higher class than would ever apply. Men in work
are getting the relief unknown, vestrymen and publicans

initial papers which are treated like cheques, which must be honoured. People who ought to have £5 have 3s. tickets, and tickets are sold for drink. Five Committees meet in one room to decide cases, the only data being statements written by clerks at the applicants' dictation. The City Missionary at Deptford says that if the money had been thrown into the sea, it would have been better. . . . Everyone is praying for the Fund to be exhausted.'

The scandals arising out of the Mansion House Fund had hardly died down before another wave of emotional almsgiving was aroused by the publication of *In Darkest London* by General Booth of the Salvation Army. The book, with its horrifying descriptions of squalor, poverty and sordid misery, made a painful impression and once more money flowed into the relief fund it initiated.

The C.O.S., warmly supported by Octavia, protested in vain against this indiscriminate distribution of funds. She and C. S. Loch, the secretary, worked indefatigably together, holding meetings, speaking and writing with little result but the increased unpopularity of the Society, an unpopularity in which Octavia, to her immense annoyance, did not share: 'She said how much she wished she could share the opprobrium that fell on the Society,' reports Miranda, 'but having other work as well, she seemed to escape it. She took the opportunity of saying publicly how much she would like to share the unpopularity of the C.O.S. and how she honoured the men working on it.'

There were two grounds on which Octavia founded her criticism of the Salvation Army fund and both were characteristic. The first was that it suggested that all could be put right by money, and permitted the rich to say: 'We give the money, the Salvation Army can give thought and care.'

This idea that the duty of the rich to the poor can be commuted for cash was always anathema to her. The second was that the Fund was administered autocratically by the General, and she saw real danger in the 'placing in his hands of the despotic control of a machine so huge that it cannot be rightly watched and guided by one human being'. The conviction that money can only be given and received without degradation when the giver cares for and understands the need of the recipient was fundamental to all her work.

But it was not only the big charitable funds that filled Octavia with anxiety; what seemed to her even more dangerous was the tendency of the legislature to extend all forms of out-door relief and to make it easy for all to claim it without any very serious consideration of the circumstances of the recipient. This effort 'to get rid of charity and substitute a rate distributed as a right' seemed to her doubly dangerous in that it not only destroyed a man's independence but also concealed from him the fact that it was so doing. Nowadays our conception of independence has changed; it is too often assumed to be threatened if any questions are asked before money is given to the needy by the State. This makes it difficult to understand Octavia's point of view. It has been said of her that her fear of pauperizing the working man amounted to an obsession, and it is suggested that this is somehow an insult to the worker. Actually, she ascribed to him the sentiments that animated her; it was because she respected him that she assumed that for him, as for her, independence meant providing for himself and his family. She valued money and all it can buy very much less than we are accustomed to do. She really believed that poverty was not in itself a very serious evil, and it must be remembered this was not the facile sentiment of one who has always had enough, but the deliberate judgment of one who had felt the full bitterness of real poverty; there had been times in her life when she had had barely enough to eat, and had been obliged to deny herself what we, to-day, should consider necessaries; yet she still believed that independence was far more important to happiness than affluence.

It was obvious, of course, that in too many cases wages were so low that a man could not provide for the bare necessities for his children, and it was for this reason that she constantly urged the raising of wages, and the provision of facilities for education and training which should enable a man to command a higher wage and to start his children in well-paid work. The evil of supplementing wages by poor law relief had been recognized in the abolition of the direct rate-in-aid of wages by the Act of 1834, but it seemed to Octavia that the same effect was produced by the provision of houses at an uneconomic rent, of free meals and of various kinds of out-door relief. All the old abuses seemed to her to be re-appearing. Her view was that if a man was obliged to manage without subsidies his employer would be obliged to pay an adequate wage. 'There is no reason why these people should earn twenty shillings, or a guinea or eighteen shillings a week. If their rent is at a given figure, their wages must and will meet that.' The assumption that it was the business of the State to provide those desirable things which a man could not provide for himself kept wages low and tended to discourage the worker from making any effort to improve his skill or husband his resources. If Octavia's conviction that employers could pay wages which would obviate the necessity of state assistance sounds strangely to us to-day, accustomed to falling export trade and large scale unemployment, it must be remembered that in her day the country was still supreme in trade and enjoyed a degree of wealth and prosperity which it is unlikely to regain. 'If you desire to equalize incomes, I should advise you to do it by giving liberal wages, arranging for reasonable hours of work and taking a large view of your duties to all men, and by making large well-considered gifts, not by giving from a compulsory tax upon your poorer neighbour as well as yourself. If you wish to take from charity its patronizing tone, see that you yourself from your hearts believe that what is helpful to any man is verily due from you, as far as you can render it at any sacrifice.'

Dealing with poverty through each individual, treating each case as a man, is a slow business. To Octavia it was the only way, since she regarded each individual as a child of God, who in poverty as in prosperity might grow in grace, and the slowness mattered little since the growth was all. To those who believe that material conditions are all-important, and that the spiritual is so intangible as to be better ignored, a short cut to prosperity is essential. Jerusalem must be built at once in England's green and pleasant land on a foundation of good sanitation, free social services and subsidized houses, without any superfluous mental strife. 'Some men sit down in their studies and imagine a world all different or speculate as to whether, if they turned it all upside down, selfishness would not vanish because comfort had come. We don't know what this world might be if it were altered, but we do know that God has given it to us, whom He has put near us, where He has called us, what power He has given us.'

206

This reflection is very characteristic of Octavia. She was no speculative thinker, her work had always consisted in serving those who were 'put near' her, and all its ramifications had arisen naturally out of the needs of one or another of them. She knew only one way of building Jerusalem, and the first step was to find out the truth and face it unflinchingly; it was what appeared to her the very general desire to ignore all that was unpleasant, that filled her with forebodings. It was sufficiently dangerous to make a habit of supplementing wages by relief, to conceal the fact was far worse. It was for this reason that she protested against the use of the word 'free' as applied to 'free meals', 'free medical services', 'free library'. In actual fact these things were not and could not be free; meals, doctors and libraries must be paid for, and were being paid for by rates and taxes or private charity; the use of the word 'free' encouraged the recipient to think of the State as a super-organization which, out of some bottomless horn of plenty, supplied all needs without expense to anyone, and this conception led a man unthinkingly to accept benefits, which he could and should earn for himself, ignoring the fact that he was living on his thrifty and hard working neighbours. Whether this might or should have been avoided is a matter of opinion, but it would be difficult to deny the existence of some of the evils she foresaw; a certain extravagance in the rates, owing to a vague idea that there is plenty for everybody, and a tendency among the least substantial rate-payers to vote for those who promise the greatest extension of benefits.

Octavia felt very deeply the importance of combating the ignorance of the voter about local finances; 'I dread these large loans, lightly voted by thousands who little know what they mean in the future, and I think the greatest blessing, as well as the greatest justice, would be for those who vote for the expenditure to feel that it mattered, and that economy benefited them.' Octavia considered deeply how she could teach her tenants this important lesson; she knew well that no amount of talk on so complicated and technical a matter would be the smallest use; that they could only learn by practical demonstration. Her cottages were always full and in demand, since there was not alternative accommodation of the same type; it was therefore possible for her to make an experiment with tenants of cottages which she could not apply to those in tenements. 'In all my new cottages,' she wrote in 1894, 'I am introducing the plan of arranging that the tenants should pay their own rates, the rent being fixed much lower to enable them to do this. Now that the rates are steadily rising in all parts of London, and threatening not only to be a heavy incubus for the current year, but to lay a burden of municipal indebtedness for sixty or eighty years, which may seriously cripple the future; now that the expenditure is decided on by multitudes of voters little trained to look forward, keen for immediate results; in pity for those thousands of poor who depend so much for their prosperity on sound and far-seeing finance, I feel such an arrangement of very deep moment to our city. . . . It has not, even on the present small scale, been without result, as our tenants are now keenly alive to many of the facts about the rates which they, and only they, can alter—the plan of making weekly tenants responsible for rates is very difficult work; not being general, the machinery and arrangements do not help us. But I have felt it to be so important as to be well worth a great effort. . . . I hope that if we lead the van, others may follow, and co-operation may come—in time—from officials.'

Others were slow to follow, for many years Octavia struggled with the difficulties. In 1896 she and C. S. Loch met representatives of the Societies for improved buildings for working people, to try to find a way of applying the system to tenants in tenements. All agreed on the importance of the matter, but they could not devise a plan acceptable to some of the larger bodies represented. In 1901 the Southwark Borough Council decided to reduce the allowance for compounding rates so drastically that the owners determined *en masse* to cease collecting them, and thus at a stroke the tenants became responsible for their own rates. Naturally complete confusion ensued, three thousand summonses were issued on one day, many to those who had actually paid their rates.

Octavia's feelings were mixed. 'We are not the leaders in this sudden and extended movement. Personally, I should have preferred, for the poorer tenants, some intermediate step, with a fixed rent and a movable rate collected weekly, at any rate for a time. But if the far more educational plan can be at once carried through—and it is marvellous how soon our people learn things—it will be incomparably better, and may save London from much waste.' She at once took steps to make the position absolutely clear to her own tenants, and had very little difficulty in the matter.

The plan was, however, very unpopular, and remained so; applied generally and without preparation, it could not succeed. There were tenants who accepted the lower rent till rates fell due, and then absconded, which, observed Octavia, 'is bad for them, their landlords and the local authority'; the fact that the rates were always demanded in advance meant also that the ratepayer had to forestall his income, a real hardship to a small wage-earner.

These things considered, though she preferred the direct payment of rates as more educative, Octavia made a different plan for the majority of her tenants. 'I propose to diminish the rent by the amount of the present rate, then to collect each week, the amount of rent plus a varying rate to be calculated half yearly. The tenant will see how large and how steadily rising is the sum he pays for rates.' This subject of commutation of rates is technical and, to the lay mind, somewhat tiresome, but Octavia's attitude is interesting; the immense amount of time and energy she spent on the matter shows how important she felt the ratepayer's recognition of his responsibilities to be; it was by dealing faithfully and justly with details that Octavia hoped to train her tenants to become useful citizens.

Chapter XVII

SETTLEMENTS

'I much delight in thinking one may link their young life with the houses and hall and garden in Southwark':
OCTAVIA TO HER MOTHER, April, 1889

ONE of the features of social history in the latter part of Queen Victoria's reign was the rise of Settlements in the poorer parts of the great cities. The first of these was founded by Octavia's friend and colleague, Samuel Barnett. Its purpose—to bring rich and poor together in mutual understanding and sympathy—was one which strongly commended itself to Octavia, and from the beginning she was concerned in the movement.

'Young men who are leaving Oxford,' she wrote to Mary Harris, 'are to come and live in Whitechapel instead of living in the West End, and their evenings are to be spent in social intercourse with the working people.'

Early in 1884 on the invitation of the Warden of Keble College (later Bishop Talbot) Octavia went to Oxford to speak to undergraduates about work in the East End. At a tremendously successful meeting, attended by more than nine hundred undergraduates, Octavia was received with enthusiasm, but she was left with some misgivings. She had hoped greatly that the result of the meeting would be to strengthen Mr. Barnett's settlement, she received the impression that the new movement was intended rather to rival it. This was to some extent true. Canon Barnett was largely supported by Balliol men, of whom many were believed to be 'sceptical or at least very free-thinking', certainly he made no conditions and asked no questions as to the faith of those who worked with him. The settlement (afterwards Oxford House) which Octavia somewhat unwillingly inaugurated, embodied a different conception. Those who worked in it were pledged to the faith of the Church, believing that by witnessing to the faith in a life of corporate worship, they could best serve their fellows and gain the strength for the work they were to do. Octavia perhaps failed to do justice to their point of view. She saw the mass of work to be done, she believed whole-heartedly in Canon Barnett's wisdom and goodness, and abhorring all religious exclusiveness, she felt it intolerable that all men of good will should not be united to further the work already begun. 'Octavia spoke *most* strongly about the importance of co-operating, and said the men with faith must do good in going among the others . . . she does seem to have spoken so strongly and bravely and to have vindicated Mr. Barnett and told them he certainly wished a religious spirit in the work. But her impression is that though they appeared to agree somewhat, and listened most respectfully, they mean to go their own way.' And so it was. Oxford House was founded in Bethnal Green, and Toynbee Hall, in Whitechapel, went on its way and no doubt there was room for both.

In Southwark the question of settlements touched Octavia more nearly both because of its proximity to her own work and because it was a settlement for women. She was not predisposed in its favour, for she believed so passionately in family life, that a collection of women, living together without family ties or domestic duties, seemed to her unnatural if not positively undesirable. She believed the part-time voluntary worker, who was fulfilling obligations to her home and family, had something to give which no professional social worker could supply. She was therefore a little doubtful about the Women's University Settlement, Southwark, whose Committee she joined in 1889, 'not because I have very much confidence in the beneficial result of large or many settlements of workers bound together by no family ties, with no natural connection with a district; but because their settlement is the practical outcome of a very large association, and because a small group of these, settled in the heart of the South London poor, may be of the greatest use.'

Miss Sewell became the Head of the Settlement soon after Octavia joined the Committee, and a warm friendship, based on mutual respect, developed between the two women. They cared for the same things and had the same values. Octavia became more and more interested in the young people who came to work there: 'They are all very refined, highly cultivated (all I fancy have been at one of the Universities) and *very* young. They are so sweet and humble and keen to learn about the things out of their ordinary line of experience. I much delight in thinking one may link their young life with the houses and hall and garden in Southwark.'

Gradually she was conquered by the settlement: 'I look upon it,' she wrote in 1892, 'not only as a great added strength to my management of houses in Southwark, but still more as a most promising centre for that training of workers to which must be devoted so much of the energies of those who would see wiser methods of work among the poor prevail.' She and Miss Sewell together planned a Training Course suitable to all social workers whether voluntary or professional, and Octavia appealed for financial help for students wishing to undertake the training. As usual her appeal met with immediate and generous response, and two scholarships were given. Altogether the connection with the Settlement was thoroughly happy and successful: 'I find there the Training for many of my new volunteers, while, as they grow in knowledge they return to form some of my best workers. I think the Settlement finds my work, too, one of its best training fields, and a sphere that would afford scope for some of its well-trained workers.'

In 1894 it became evident that the Settlement needed more and better accommodation. Octavia went into the question very seriously, she was determined that the residents must have a home in which they could have quiet and airy rooms. Nelson Square appeared the only place in the district where such conditions could be secured. There were difficulties about getting a freehold here, and when Octavia had overcome these and had bought the house in which the Settlement was living, and the two adjoining houses, there were still difficulties to face. Adapting old houses is always a costly and tiresome business, but it was the kind of work Octavia enjoyed; she exercised all her ingenuity on it, and was well pleased with the result. In the following year, the freehold next door was for sale, and Octavia was faced with a fresh difficulty. The Committee had no wish to enlarge the Settlement, and did not feel justified in spending more money on its buildings; on the other hand, it was of the utmost importance to them to secure unobjectionable neighbours, especially as the back garden or yard might have been built over, the Settlement thus deprived of sunlight and two large plane trees, visible

from all the Settlement windows, sacrificed. It was therefore a great relief when Miss Yorke volunteered to buy the
house. With the trees and the sunlight secured for the
Settlement, Octavia felt satisfied, and Miss Yorke shared
her contentment.

But before this rebuilding, Octavia had been faced with
the necessity of making a very serious decision about her
own home; this was no less a matter than the decision to
leave Nottingham Place, where she had lived so long and
so happily. It was not easy for her, she had lived in it for
thirty years and loved her home in a way scarcely compre-
hensible to this nomadic generation; leaving it was a
wrench. 'We are to leave the old home in March. It is so
crowded with memories, that it seems quite alive with
them; and there isn't a sound of latch or bell, an echo or
footfall, that has not associations which wake the years that
are past. The little tree that is near three feet high, which
has grown outside my window from the acorn I planted
there long ago, and which for many years gladdened me
with its fresh green in spring, is going to Crockham, so as
to be set free from London gloom.'

The house, much as she loved it, had become really too
large for their needs. Florence's health had so far deteriorated that the noise and bustle of London and the incessant activity of her sisters became too great a strain.
Mrs. Hill also needed a quieter and more peaceful life. The
sisters decided therefore that Florence and their mother
should move to the country, and they went first to Pinner
and later to Tunbridge Wells.

Having made up her mind to leave Nottingham Place,
Octavia looked about for a new home, and it was at the
point while the future was still undecided that Miss Sewell

invited her to establish her household in the Settlement, and to become herself the principal worker there. By this time most of her own work was in Southwark, and she was deeply interested in the training scheme which she had just inaugurated. There was much in the suggestion to attract her. She wrote to Miranda: 'I cannot tell whether dear old Marylebone or Southwark will seem the most natural working centre, nor how far such a body as the Settlement would leave you with enough sense of home.'

Octavia thought over the proposal very carefully; the fact that the suggestion had come just at the moment when she had decided that she must be uprooted, and did not know where she should be replanted, made her wonder whether this was a call for a new kind of life. It was nine months before she had fully made up her mind; her decision was given in a letter as revealing as any she ever wrote. 'I can't help thinking it would be turning my back on the principles of a life-time. My sister and two of my friends here have all their work in this neighbourhood, it has gathered around this home and will continue centred round the new one. My own traditions for more than fifty years are with Marylebone, and though my *main* personal work among the poor has been for some six or seven years in the South of London, it has always been planned in the sort of way one does plan work at a distance, that is much in connection with other workers. So, if we moved, I should uproot and alter the whole character of three people's work, and change my own; improve my own, no doubt, in some respects very vastly, but it would not be all gain even to it. For, I ask myself, is not this work a new one? Is it not right that it should develop much in accordance with the aspirations of a younger generation? Will not they care for it more if they themselves in a large measure mould it? Is not my work really to help them to make it what they would have it to be, taking care to bring before them the great old truths known in the past, but still rather initiating and guiding than being myself the centre? Will not this very limitation of not living there keep my rather overpowering presence just far enough away to foster native growth? And at the same time respect the work of all here which I have helped to originate? I've plenty of vigour and might live to work, work strongly for many a year in Southwark, but don't we all lose by too much uprooting and change in this age?'

The letter reveals the unique quality of Octavia's greatness. The training scheme she had initiated, seemed to her of paramount importance, she had given the best of her thought and energy to it, yet she was able to believe that it might rightly develop on lines other than hers; she was willing, even anxious, to leave the real responsibility in the hands of the younger generation that they might mould the work according to their own aspirations. There are few who, having the opportunity and the power to dictate, are wholeheartedly glad to abdicate, and to remain in the background ready to advise but resolutely determined not to interfere.

The decision made, a house was sought in Marylebone. 'We have found a house that we very much like in the Marylebone Road,' writes Miranda. 'It is smaller than this, with much smaller rooms; but it is quiet, light and cheerful (having its chief rooms with a South aspect) and cheap. It has a garden in front—and a yard behind—to our great delight; a little light and space and quiet being our chief requirements. There will be room for Octavia and me with Miss Yorke and two of the friends now living with us, Miss

Pearson and Miss Sim. It would be a great sorrow to part with them; so we are thankful to get a house large enough for us all.'

The five women moved in in March, 1891, and as usual Octavia took the greatest pleasure in settling in with her household goods. 'My room has been our last household pleasure,' she writes to her mother. 'It has turned out so pretty; and I am so astonished, because it was the room where all the leavings naturally gravitated. But you know it has a pretty bow; like the back drawing-room; and my one extravagance has been a very nice brass curtain rod. On this, with large curtain rings, which draw easily, we have hung the curtains which Minnie gave—crimson—and they look so bright in the Western sun and so snug when drawn at night. Then I have my writing table in the bow, my pretty dark book-case, and the old drawing-room carpet from Nottingham Place, which looks quite handsome as good things do. My photographs group themselves prettily on the walls; and altogether it is very nice.'

'Miranda gave me a beautiful piece of crimson plush,' she had written at the age of four, and now as she drew her crimson curtains, contemplated her dark book-case, a gift years ago from Mary Harris, looked at her handsome carpet which had come from Nottingham Place, she knew that she had done well to choose this home.

Miranda took over the running of the house, 'a little domain . . . to work in my own way,' and gave it that atmosphere of peace and love which she always created. The house became the centre of Octavia's activities, a meeting place for their many friends. It was a happy place as all Octavia's homes had been, a stimulating place, where all occupied in social work, and others, might come to seek

MIRANDA HILL IN 1895.

counsel and refreshment. Mary Harris came to stay there. 'She was delighted to see Octavia,' wrote Miranda to her mother. 'She said she felt her so life-giving.'

Chapter XVIII

COMMONS, FOOTPATHS AND THE
NATIONAL TRUST

'A song of thankfulness seems to be singing on in my heart for having been given power to have some hand in devoting some of the lovely places to the people for ever':
OCTAVIA TO HER MOTHER, October, 1902

'WHEN I first began to work,' Octavia remarked to Miranda, 'people would say: "I'll give you money for necessaries for the poor, but I don't see what they want with recreation;" then, after a few years, they said: "I can understand poor people wanting amusement, but what good will open spaces do them?" and now everybody recognizes the importance of open spaces.' This change in public opinion, largely due to her own work, was of course eminently satisfactory to Octavia but unfortunately it did not go deep enough. There were still too many landlords and directors of commercial undertakings who, readily admitting in general terms the importance of open spaces, were convinced that any space they themselves coveted might well be sacrificed; and those who professed enlightened views on the subject were not always ready to take active steps to save gardens, commons and footpaths for those who most needed them. For these Octavia battled ceaselessly and with a large measure of success.

There were two Committees occupied in this work; the Open Spaces Committee of the Kyrle Society and the executive of the Commons Preservation Society. The former was particularly her own conception; her brother-in-law, Edmund Maurice, was its Honorary Secretary and its function was to keep public opinion alive to the importance of preserving open spaces, to raise money for the purchase of those that were threatened and, having secured them, to put them in order so that the local vestries would take over and maintain them. The Kyrle Committee worked hard and very successfully; year after year in her 'Letter to Fellow Workers', Octavia was able to record one or another church yard, burial ground or garden saved for the use of the public.

The C.P.S. dealt with the legal aspect of the problem; it had been founded to protect the rights of the public and to fight actions when necessary. There was much to do; the foe was insidious. The difficulty was partly at least that those who wished to absorb open spaces were generally public or quasi-public bodies, while those who most needed them were just those who had neither money nor influence to fight their own battles. It was for these that Octavia was passionately concerned. 'An effort on the part of small shopkeepers at New Cross to save a hill near, which belongs to the Haberdashers' Company, does not seem likely to succeed,' she lamented in 1883. 'In fact it is strange to notice that though other towns in numbers have had Parks given to them, the thousands of rich people who owe their wealth to London, or who avail themselves of its advantages, have not, as far as I know, given one single acre of ground that could have been sold for building over, to Londoners for recreation ground or Park, if we except Leicester Square.' This remark would appear to have fallen on fruitful ground, for a year later Miranda, speaking of the work in Deptford, writes: 'For the *first* time a London landowner has offered to give land he could build on for an open space for the people. It is Mr. Evelyn who has done this;' and later, as has been seen, Octavia managed to persuade the Ecclesiastical Commissioners to make a practice of doing so.

It was necessary then to be ceaselessly vigilant. In 1883 the London and North Western Railway threatened to take possession of a small burial ground near Tottenham Court Road. The site was in a populous neighbourhood, immediately overlooked by a row of houses and a hospital. Urged thereto by Edmund Maurice, and supported by the C.P.S., the Vestry of St. Pancras decided to oppose the Bill in the House. It passed the Commons, however, and was only defeated in a Committee of the Lords, before which Octavia gave evidence; 'Octavia was under the impression that her evidence had not been of much good; but she has been complimented by the gentlemen of the C.P.S. and the report goes that "Miss Hill was more than a match for the Counsel of the L.N.W.R. who is looked on as a rather formidable antagonist".'

It was a notable triumph for St. Pancras and its supporters, but the space had been saved only because the Vestry had been willing to fight a long and costly action and because it had powerful supporters. To Octavia the necessity of dealing with each threat as it arose and the uncertainty of the result, seemed most unsatisfactory. She urged a more general policy, and some amendment of the Building Laws to prevent haphazard development. With the C.P.S. she tried to work out some plan of treating London and its suburbs as a whole. A memorial on the subject to the Charity Commissioners, presented by the Kyrle Society, the C.P.S. and the Metropolitan Gardens Association in 1887 was largely her work. 'I was occupied for a good deal of the autumn in getting facts for the Memorial, and the more I looked into the matter the more I was impressed with the fact that unless some very much larger view of the quantity of open space needed should be taken by the authorities, and some really great scheme be adopted for purchasing important land *at once*, the time would go past very rapidly when it would be possible to save what in the future would be felt to be almost essential to the health and well-being of Londoners. To secure the support of the public in pressing forward large schemes, and that at once, I must use all ways open to me.'

There was one scheme very dear to Octavia's heart which the C.P.S. warmly espoused. This was the securing of paths which should make walking pleasant to Londoners. There were the tow-paths along the river, Traitor's Hill which gave access by fields from Kentish Town and North London generally to Hampstead Heath, as well as many footpaths and walks round London, connecting one common with another. Octavia always enjoyed a map, and now she invited volunteers to help her to make a map to show what walks existed and what commons they would connect. She was, in fact, trying to secure that Green Belt for London which in 1940 we are beginning to think may be desirable.

Besides the small spaces and the footpaths, there were two large spaces in London for which Octavia fought to a victorious conclusion. The first was Parliament Hill, and the battle was opened in 1884 when Octavia read a paper on the subject at a meeting at the Duke of Westminster's house. The space was large and very costly; it seemed to Octavia reasonable that the local authorities should contri-

bute some part of the purchase money, a most satisfactory
way of spending rates for the benefit of the ratepayers, but
since many ratepayers were poor, she thought the rich
should be ready to add donations. 'I cannot but think in
the Metropolis where rates press so heavily on the poor
there should be many a rich and generous-hearted man who
would like to contribute something above his share of the
rate to give his fellow townsmen some few acres of sloping
grass with stately trees. . . . I should like myself nothing
better, if I had the money, than to make so great and lasting
a gift to the public.'

The ratepayers had to be convinced of the soundness of
this scheme. The Hampstead Vestry refused by a majority
of 21 (out of 55) to subscribe anything the first time the
scheme was laid before them but on the next occasion they
voted £20,000 by 45 votes to 20. It will be readily believed
that this change had not taken place without much hard
canvassing behind the scenes. The Metropolitan Board of
Works had also to be converted and Octavia was full of
anxiety. 'The Metropolitan Board are to consider the Parliament Hill scheme to-morrow,' writes Miranda, 'and no
time is to be lost in getting the Press to tell them. Octavia
is very hopeless as to the result, but must do all she can, as
usual.'

The Board, however, proved amenable, and Octavia was
left with the task of raising £52,500 by private subscription. She was not dismayed by this, for she was never faint-
hearted about money; she had £2000 promised when the
appeal was launched, in nine weeks the fund had risen to
£45,500. When it was suggested that she should approach
the City companies for the last £7000, she replied that she
felt they 'should be reserved for more difficult schemes

than this now is. I should like to see some of the rich of London proud to share the remaining part of a gift which will be, so far as we can see, a great and lasting and a visible blessing to thousands.' Octavia's confidence was fully justified, for she received not only the necessary £7000, but a surplus large enough to justify a meeting of the whole Committee to decide how it should be spent. There was a proposal that it should be devoted to the purchase of the field way between Kentish Town and Parliament Hill Fields. Octavia, anxious as she was to preserve it, yet urged strongly that the balance should go to the general movement for preserving open spaces. She knew well that it was far easier to raise money for some particular space, for which one could appeal to local sentiment, than for a general fund, and she felt very strongly the importance of having some money in hand which could be produced at a critical moment when any sudden need arose.

Vauxhall Park is the name to-day of the other space of which mention must be made. Octavia knew it as 'the Lawn', the home in Lambeth of Henry Fawcett, Postmaster General in Gladstone's Cabinet. When in 1887 it came into the market, she set her heart on securing it as a park for Lambeth. She wrote to the Press about it, and was very much cheered to find that the working men in the district were themselves pressing for its purchase. She and Miranda went to an open-air meeting in Lambeth. Standing in the crowd among the audience, listening to the working men speaking from the wagons, they were very much encouraged by the unmistakable determination of the people to secure the park for themselves and their children; it meant that the movement for open spaces was really taking hold of the public mind. It was never her way to thrust herself upon those who were already doing effective work, so it was as an ordinary member of the public that she attended a second meeting on the subject in Lambeth; but 'when the chairman found she was present, he insisted on bringing her up on the platform that he might at least show her to the people if she would not speak, and the audience —chiefly working men—greeted her with rounds and rounds of cheering; it seems they look on her as the author of their scheme, because she first wrote to the papers about it, and roused public attention.'

While the Lambeth people were organizing local opinion, Octavia was appealing to a wider public. The Archbishop lent Lambeth Palace for a meeting, at which the Dean of Windsor (Randall Davidson, known to this generation as *the* Archbishop), Mrs. Fawcett, whose daughter Philippa had recently defeated the Senior Wrangler at Cambridge, and an eloquent engine-driver spoke; but what pleased Octavia most was a 'beautiful letter' from Florence Nightingale. 'She,' said Octavia, 'of all the people who have spoken or written on open spaces, has got most to the heart of the matter.' The sympathy of one pioneer of women's work was dear to the heart of the other.

The Lawn was formally opened in July, 1890, by the Prince of Wales; Princess Louise, who had followed Octavia's work with interest and sympathy for many years, was present. It was not the kind of party Octavia really enjoyed: 'I am much distressed that, in spite of almost superhuman efforts, I am unable to escape being taken up by the necessity of "receiving",' but she took immense trouble over the organization—'three weeks' hard work' she said—and all went without a hitch: the Cadet Corps made a Guard of Honour, the stewards fulfilled their duties punc-

tually and exactly, Miranda in the house was a most happy
and useful hostess, and the Prince of Wales, according to
his custom, captured all hearts by his easy graciousness and
expressed his complete satisfaction with the whole ceremony. Octavia retired to Larksfield exhausted but triumphant. 'It was to me a very solemn scene, because all
classes were so entirely gathered in, each to do what in
them lay to accomplish the good work: and now it is done:
and for long years as long as our people need it and wish
for it, flowers will grow and sunlight have leave to pene-
trate there.'

It would be tedious to enumerate the various parks and
gardens which London owes to Octavia and the C.P.S. The
method in dealing with each was fundamentally the same:
when any place was threatened, Octavia at once wrote to
the Press and proceeded to mobilize public opinion; the
C.P.S. looked into the legal side, a scheme was proposed,
and the Local Authorities concerned canvassed to provide
part of the purchase money. When public bodies had expressed readiness to do their share, Octavia undertook the
raising of the rest.

Sometimes Local Authorities were difficult. There were
forty-five acres known as Hilly Fields to the south-east of
London. The L.C.C. and the Greenwich District Board
offered between them to pay about two-thirds of the cost
—Lewisham refused to contribute. 'The action of the
Lewisham Board in refusing to vote anything, though the
land is in their parish, appears to me disastrous both as a
precedent for other Boards and also as forming a very valid
reason why many persons will not give. We have hoped to
the last that the Lewisham Board would reconsider its decision, and have done our utmost in raising subscriptions

in which effort the public has been most generous, but if now, in spite of all this liberal aid, the Board still refuses, the failure of the scheme must rest on their shoulders.' In such a case the only hope was to persuade the ratepayers to bring such pressure on the Board that it could not persist in its refusal, and ultimately, though after a long struggle, this was achieved.

In 1891 Octavia's work for Open Spaces had developed on another side. It was perfectly clear that the part played by the ordinary citizen in these matters was very important, and she was determined that he must be roused to exert his influence in fighting against any sort of encroachment on the land; it was not only commons, parks and fields; there were footpaths, rights of way, roadside strips of grass in danger. It was natural that she should first consider her own county, Kent, and to encourage its residents to help in the good work she founded the Kent and Surrey Committee of the C.P.S. 'It is the first attempt,' she wrote, 'to work in greater detail with regard to all the numberless small encroachments on public rights which are going on in country neighbourhoods.' The essence of the scheme in her eyes was that it should combine all the residents of the county, rich and poor, rural, suburban and urban, as guardians of the common land. All residents were invited to enrol, at a fee of 1s., and to make it their business to report to the executive any threat of encroachment as soon as it was made. Almost at once the Committee had a success; some of its members were summoned for exercising common rights which they were convinced were theirs. The Committee's support was so effective that the summonses were all dismissed and the costs given. This was most encouraging and new members enrolled; 'The agricultural labourers have found us out. Many a hard-earned shilling reaches us in postal orders from a village, many an illiterate but burning letter.' Unfortunately, the enrolment of the wealthy did not keep pace with that of the poor, nor were volunteers forthcoming who could give time and thought to the work. This seemed to Octavia difficult to understand. 'I cannot think why . . . a larger number of young and ardent men, politicians and others do not come forward to try to secure for the agricultural labourer in his daily life, for the Londoner in his holidays, the safe and undisturbed possession of the common, the green wayside strip, the thousand footpaths which lead him to pleasant places. . . . Why must the organizing, or rather the vivifying, come all from me and my few tired fellow members, already over-taxed?'

Since volunteers did not appear, Octavia had to carry on the struggle; it was hard work and often discouraging: 'I have myself withdrawn all my strength from London open space work, which is progressing, to devote it to the country, which is losing day by day. Many are doing the same, though it is most disappointing to meet with so little immediate result. Still, I look to the time when these efforts will tell—they *do* tell already by encouraging many people —may tell indirectly in discouraging some enclosures. We are gaining friends, perfecting our machinery . . . but for tangible results, for visible victory, we must wait.'

It was easier to find money than helpers. Octavia was never in any of her ventures defeated for lack of money. Her donations fund had been increased by more than one legacy left to her to be spent at her discretion. She felt her responsibility to the donors deeply, but she never hesitated to spend freely, even when she expected no visible results.

Law suits must be lost sometimes and paid for. 'We have not succeeded in preserving the footpaths to which I referred last year. This has not arisen from any want, however, of our being heartily supported, and being able to fight for it up to the last. We had enough money given us to carry the case up twice to Quarter Sessions. Once we were successful, owing to the irregularity of proceeding on the part of the enclosers. The second time the matter went to a jury who took into consideration the relative value of the widening of a road. . . . I hope those who trusted us with their money will not feel too disheartened. I think myself that it was by no means thrown away—I believe that the fact of a fight is a help in preventing closure. I also think that a point was secured by the first trial, when the landowner had to pay costs and to begin again in proper legal form. Besides this, I feel that we cannot always foretell the result, and must advance in hope of a victory, when sure that, whether it come or not, we ought to struggle for it. . . . It is on the defeats that victories are built, as a bridge upon piles out of sight. May I be with the defeated in the early struggles of a great cause! Never shall I be more useful.'

There was work other than litigation. Octavia was directing a methodical survey of Kent and Surrey, and maps were being prepared showing all the footpaths, rights of way and commons in the counties. She took endless trouble to discover what paths there were and had been, enquiring into the early recollections of all the oldest inhabitants, and pursuing investigations with tireless zeal. 'Gertrude's coachman,' she writes, 'is very helpful about Chartwell. I saw him last night. He knows another path better, but recognizes this and will look and see how far his own evidence will go. He will speak to several working people there, and to his brother-in-law, now a gardener at Wimbledon, who was born at Toy's Hill.' Friends who stayed at Larksfield were often taken for walks over little used tracks, through hedges, across the park and past the front door of the Lord of the Manor, that a right of way might be asserted and maintained. To the conventional it was perhaps a little disconcerting, but to Octavia a splendid justification for taking the kind of walk she had from her childhood most enjoyed.

While Octavia was most intimately concerned with the fight in Kent and Surrey, she was always ready to help any who were carrying on the same struggle in other parts of the country. 'We are very much interested just now in the defence of footpaths in the Lake District. Some landlords are shutting up old rights of way and preventing people from ascending the mountains. A very brave clergyman, a friend of Octavia's, who has a parish at Keswick, has taken up the defence of these rights, and is threatened with a very expensive lawsuit. Her other "defenders" are appealing to the public of large towns to help with a guarantee fund. A meeting was organized at Hampstead, which turned out very successfully.'

Gradually the work of the Societies began to tell, and slowly public opinion became educated and the general public became alive to their responsibilities. In 1896 the Parish, District and County Councils became the guardians of these public rights and enlightened members of these bodies found in the C.P.S. and its allied Committees valuable allies, who were a mine of information about the law and procedure in these matters. In 1897 Octavia could write of her Societies, 'they appear to me to be distinctly growing in power and influence: their organization seems to me far better and on a sounder footing. . . . Public opinion is growing, it now has a legal organization through which to act, and I am hopeful.'

In all this work Octavia's staunchest ally had been Sir Robert Hunter. In 1881 he had become the solicitor to the Post Office, and though this had obliged him to resign his official position with the C.P.S. it had by no means lessened his interest in its work. His friendship with Octavia had been strengthened by their work together. They were mutually sympathetic for like her he was an idealist, possessed of great width of vision, and of the same kind of solid common sense. As early as 1884 he had been convinced of the desirability of founding some corporation which could hold land and buildings in trust for the people, and had read a paper on the subject in Birmingham. Octavia was in full sympathy with the project, its importance was brought home to her in the following year when Mr. Evelyn, a Deptford landlord, wished to hand over to the people Sayes Court with its large garden and was unable to carry out his scheme in its entirety, because there was no public body able to hold both building and land. Octavia was convinced of the practicability of the scheme and discussed with Robert Hunter a suitable name for the proposed body: 'A short expressive name,' she wrote in February, 1885, 'is difficult to find for the new Company. What do you think of the "Commons and Gardens Trust" and then printing in small letters "for accepting, holding, preserving and purchasing open spaces for the people in town and country." I do not know that I am right in thinking that it should be called Trust, but I think it might be better than "Company". You will do better, I believe, to bring forward its benevolent than its commercial character. People don't like unsuccessful business, but do like charity when a little money goes a long way because of good commercial management.' Across the letter Sir Robert scribbled in pencil '? National Trust'. Another friend was soon called into council. This was Canon Rawnsley, 'the very brave clergyman' from Keswick, who had successfully secured the access to the lakes and mountains in his own district. He made a worthy third to Octavia and Robert Hunter, he entered enthusiastically into the project, and became its Honorary Secretary long before it was a properly constituted body.

Meetings were organized over which influential people presided, and there were distinguished speakers, but it was Octavia who held the audience and made an impression not easily effaced. Power flowed from her, for she spoke with an eloquence derived from her passionate belief in the gospel she was preaching. Her love of nature was no conventional sentiment, no facile pleasure in free days in the country, it was of the very fibre of her being, in some ways akin to Wordsworth's. She looked at the world with the eyes of a child, and saw the rebirth of each spring, the coming of fruit blossom, of flower, of leaf with a delightful shock of surprise. When she spoke of the hills, the headlands, the commons, her hearers saw these through her eyes, and perhaps recaptured some happy memories of earlier and easier days. They were convinced of the importance of saving them for all time. She wrote articles, too, which were readily accepted and gradually the idea of the National Trust took root in many minds.

No part of her work gave Octavia more happiness and less anxiety; from the beginning her colleagues were congenial, and since the function of the Trust was to receive and to hold gifts rather than to force unwilling authorities to cede them, there was no friction about it. 'The work would be delightful to one who cared for it,' she wrote in 1896, when she was looking for a new secretary, 'all the good result of the Commons and Footpaths work, with little or no fighting; on the contrary, calling on the generous good people.' This new secretary, Mr. Nigel Bond, has given a vivid sketch of the three founders of the Trust. 'If the Committee of the National Trust were faced by an awkward fence, it would be Sir Robert Hunter's way to say very little, but to go quietly away and turn his brain to the solution of the problem—how to get round that obstacle—and it was very rarely that he failed to find a way. Canon Rawnsley was different. He did not claim to be a business man, but he was a great enthusiast who did not know the meaning of the word "No", and it would have been his way to have said "There is no obstacle there, go on", and he would have given a leap and nine times out of ten would have landed safely the other side. Miss Hill would see the obstacle, she would not bother to find a way round, but she would say "This is an obstacle we have got to face, we will build a ladder and we will start on a sound foundation, climb up, get over and go down on the other side".' With such a Triumvirate in command, it was no wonder that the Trust made headway. Mrs. Fanny Talbot was its first benefactor giving to it the cliff at Barmouth. 'We have got our first property,' said Octavia to Sydney Cockerell with a smile, 'I wonder whether it will be our last.'

But she never for a moment believed it would be the last. In the following year the Trust was able to buy Barras Head at Tintagel, a headland dear to Octavia on account both of its wild beauty and its literary associations. 'It is not quite the first, nor will it, I hope, be the last of such places which shall thus become in a new and very real sense the Common Land of England. But it is the very first which has been, not given by one far-sighted and generous donor, but purchased by the combined help of many— rich and poor, near and far, American and English—giving each in their measure to buy a bit of England as the common playground, study, resting place, vantage ground for seeing the holy things of nature. Surrounded on three sides by the great sea dashing among its black rocks, hollowed into great caves like that of Merlin just opposite into which the Atlantic waves roll, sailed over by sea birds, set with great clumps of heather, gorse and sea thrift, looking across the narrow space of King Arthur's cove to the Island rock, with ruins of Tintagel Castle so dear to us all from legend and poetry, bound up with noble thoughts of British history, of British legend, it seems a fitting first fruits of the combined gifts of members and friends of the National Trust which has been founded to keep for her people for ever, in their beauty, accessible to all, some of England's fairest, most memorable places.'

In a letter of jubilation while she was still collecting money for Tintagel, Octavia wrote: 'To-day we need only £23, so I almost see it ours. Is it not delightful? I must set to work now about Alfriston, a *much* more difficult problem, and hampered by mistakes and delays before we touched the matter. Still, into a safe state it must be got.' Alfriston was a pre-reformation Priests' House, which had been converted into labourers' cottages and allowed to fall into a state of complete disrepair; it was in very immediate danger of being demolished. The difficulties here

235

were not financial, since £10 bought the building, but the restoration was difficult and expensive. It was, however, accomplished, and was the first Building which the National Trust held. It was shortly followed by a beautiful fourteenth-century Court House at Long Crendon in Buckinghamshire, and by an old house in Tintagel. Octavia's appreciation of the picturesque and of all that was historically interesting made her rejoice in these acquisitions, but they never gave her quite the same rapturous satisfaction as the possession of large stretches of open country.

These, however, followed, each giving her a thrill of pure joy. To the end of her life she felt quickly and acutely, and her happiness would flame up within her at each evidence of generosity; she would clap her hands joyfully like a child when good news was brought to her, sorrow, hard work and anxiety had never been able to crush the child whose ringing joyous laughter had been described as the 'happiest, sweetest ever heard'.

After Tintagel there were two districts in which the Trust's acquisitions particularly rejoiced Octavia's heart. There was first her own county of Kent, and there, on the top of Toy's Hill, a 'small bit of terrace-like hillside' was given, 'the first beautiful site in England dedicated as a memorial.' It was a very little property, but it looked over the weald of Kent, and Octavia, delighted with the idea of making such a gift as a memorial, took a great deal of trouble to make the most of it. 'Seats have been placed where villagers and visitors can sit and watch the lights and shadows over the whole magnificent sweep of county of which the terrace commands a view. A small tiled roof is being put over the village well, dug by permission of the

Trust on its ground; heather, broom and other wild flowers are being brought in and planted, so that the little place will soon look dedicated to all in memory of one who would have rejoiced that a memorial should take a form so helpful, so unobtrusive and so lovely.'

Toy's Hill was a beginning; Ide Hill on the same range of hills, between the North Downs and Ashdown Forest, was the next objective. The option of the purchase was secured at once and within a year, without any pressing, the necessary money had been subscribed. 'It is really bought, conveyed to the National Trust for the people of England for ever, my own faithful friends helped; the press helped cordially, we appealed widely; the Kyrle Society . . . gave great support . . . so it is saved, the breezy hill, wide view, woodland glades, tiny spring, all yours and mine and every citizen's for all time to come.'

But no acquisition by the Trust could give Octavia more pleasure than that in the Lake District. It was of course Canon Rawnsley's own countryside, the unique character of its scenery made it particularly desirable that it should be saved for the people, Octavia herself had the tenderest associations with it, for it was there that she had sought refuge again and again with Mary Harris when the strain of her work became intolerable. She had spent happy weeks there too with her mother and her sisters. When in 1900 Brandlehow near Derwentwater came into the market she had every reason to rally all her friends to its defence. She made the appeal, and the money poured in with incredible rapidity. 'The £7000 we wanted seemed so large a sum; the gifts, welcome as they were, seemed to make so little impression on it; the time for collecting passed so rapidly, the year was said to be so bad a one for collecting money. On the other hand, I had such hope; so many things in my life which had seemed impossible to do had got done in time . . . the English public had always seemed so appreciatively responsive. . . . Day after day Canon Rawnsley and I kept receiving letters, one more delightful than the other; some from the young in their exuberance of life; some from the old, rich in memory; some from the rich with solemn sense of duty, some from the poor, eager to contribute their mite; some from the North, from sense of neighbourhood; some from the South in gratitude for holiday; some from America, from friends and in thought of kinship and common inheritance of literature; some from our colonies abroad in thought of English loveliness and dearness. And at last by the multitude of gifts, the large sum was amassed.'

Octavia's pleasure in the work of the Trust was no doubt partly due to the opportunity it afforded for a multitude of small gifts, it seemed to her so great a privilege to help to secure some lovely acres of England in perpetuity to the people, that she longed for as many as possible to share it, and the fact that many of those who subscribed had little enough to give touched her very deeply. 'All my life I have longed to see the lakes,' wrote a factory worker sending 2s. 6d. 'I never shall see them now, but I should like to help to keep them for others.' Letters of this sort were ample reward for much hard work, that giving should be a real pleasure seemed to her a right and natural thing and she never begged over-insistently, lest she should, by pertinacity, extract a gift half-willingly given. 'The last thing I would wish, is to spoil the joy of the gift by undue asking or pressing.'

Brandlehow was formally dedicated to the public in

October, 1902. It was a day of supreme and triumphant happiness to Octavia. She wrote to her mother: 'I have just come back from the great opening, and want to tell you about it. It was very successful, very simple, real and unconventional. The place was looking very lovely. I never saw the light more beautiful, it was not what people would call fine, but it was *very* beautiful and it did not rain. The wind was high and tore the tent to ribbons when it was being put up, but I think it really did better, because the simple little red dais was out under the free sky, with the great lake lying below, and all the purple mountains opposite, and the golden fern-clad slopes of Catbells above. It was very funny and primitive and the nice north country folk were quite near and saw and heard all. The Princess was most friendly and kind, and really did show deep and intelligent interest in the National Trust work. She asked me whom we were going to make President, and added, "I hoped you would ask me, I should like really to do more for the work, and I should like Lord Carlisle as Vice President." She then went on to tell me of some beautiful old houses she wants us to try to save. She really does care and know I think . . . I feel almost overcome by the extreme beauty of everything here, so bountiful in making and giving is the great Creator, and a song of thankfulness seems to be singing on in my heart for having been given power to have some hand in devoting some of the lovely places to people for ever . . .'

This 'song of thankfulness' is audible in all Octavia's writing and speaking about the work of the National Trust.

Chapter XIX

PLANNING THE FUTURE

'Almost the worst house, if the household be wisely managed, is better than ever so costly a one ill-managed':
OCTAVIA in 'Letter to Fellow Workers', 1907

IN 1884 Miranda writing to Mary Harris about Octavia's work exclaimed, 'It *has* come to a point!—when two peers and a cabinet minister call and consult her in one week. She had Fawcett here yesterday, Lord Wemyss the day before to ask what he should say in the House of Lords and the Duke of Westminster on Wednesday to ask what the Prince of Wales could do in the matter.' (Open Spaces.) Miranda exulted in her sister's growing reputation, Octavia herself remained curiously unaware of it; when she was offered a seat in the Abbey for Queen Victoria's Jubilee she was simply astounded. 'I cannot think why I, who have done so simply, and at no great cost, just what lay before me, should be singled out in this kind of way,' she wrote to her mother, and this was no affectation but a settled attitude of mind. The art of publicity had not in those days the vogue it has since acquired. Octavia knew nothing of it, and with what to modern minds must appear a strange perversity, took as much trouble to avoid being in the public eye as many take to-day to be in it. She felt 'an irresistible longing to be out of sight as much as possible, a deeply rooted sense that it is better, more blessed, quieter. Of course,' she added, 'when a great cause has to

240

be helped or any bit of positive work to be done, one must go straight on and never mind whether it be public or private, but when one may choose I, for one, long to get back to silent obscurity.' It was this irresistible longing which made her refuse to have any block of buildings, even in her own beloved Barrett's Court, called after her, and led her to write to Sydney Cockerell, 'I see by the papers that Mrs. Barrington proposes giving my portrait to Red Cross Hall. Now I can't have this done, and I write to ask you, as a friend, to help, so that the Committee should respect my wish about it and back me up in saying it cannot be.'

Octavia, however, could not always have her own way. There comes a point when to refuse to friends the opportunity of expressing their affection and appreciation in the way they desire becomes ungracious and ungenerous. Octavia could never be either, and when in 1898 some of her most intimate friends led by C. S. Loch and Lady (Frederick) Pollock asked her to sit to Sargent and accept the gift of a portrait of herself, it was impossible to refuse. She accordingly gave the sittings and the portrait, which now hangs in the National Portrait Gallery, was painted, and on 1st December at Grosvenor House in the presence of a multitude of her friends, it was formally presented. The speakers were Dean Fremantle, for whom she had worked thirty years earlier, and C. S. Loch who was working with her then, in her maturity. They both spoke of her strength, her courage, her indomitable will; 'they hoped,' reports Miranda, 'that as the picture was the work of a great artist, it might speak to those who should look upon it, and that it should bring them something of the strength which she had brought her friends.' Admiration for what she had done but even more, affection for what she was, were expressed in no small measure. To Octavia this gathering of her friends to do her honour was a deeply moving occasion. Some of them had been with her in the early days when difficulties seemed great and success precarious, others had known her only when she had achieved a position of security, but all were staunch allies upon whom she could depend for active support in all her undertakings, without whom, indeed, she would be powerless to accomplish anything. 'I look upon it, not as a memorial of my own work, but of that joint work to which they have all, each in their various ways, contributed and that in so large a measure that we can none of us say "This is mine" and "that is yours", but all of us may say "it is ours".' In her speech of thanks for the portrait, Octavia looked back over the work which she had been able to accomplish and forward to what the future might hold, not for herself, but for the causes in which she had laboured. Characteristically she was not the least concerned that her part should be recognized or her methods perpetuated. 'When I am gone, I hope my friends will not try to carry out any special system, or to follow blindly in the track which I have trodden. New circumstances require various efforts, and it is the spirit, not the dead form that should be perpetuated. When the time comes that we slip from our places, and they are called to the front as workers, what should they inherit from us? Not a system, not an association, not dead formulas. We shall leave them a few houses, purified and improved, a few new and better ones built, a certain record of thoughtful and loving management, a few open spaces, some of which will be more beautiful than they would have been, but what we care most to leave them is not any tan-

OCTAVIA HILL IN 1898.

(*From the Portrait by Sargent and by kind permission of The National Portrait Gallery*).

gible thing however great, not any memory, however good, but the quick eye to see, the true soul to measure, the large hope to grasp the mighty issues of the new and better days to come—greater ideals, greater hope and patience to realize both.'

Octavia was now sixty. Like most people of abounding vitality she had been too much absorbed in living to realize the passage of years; she had noticed in 1889 with some amusement that she seemed 'quite a veteran' to the young students at W.U.S.S.; to herself she seemed much the same as she had done at any time since she grew up. Most active vigorous people as they pass from middle age into the ranks of the elderly notice with surprise how considerably their contemporaries have aged; they are slow to believe that they themselves have become part of the passing generation. This was brought home to Octavia by the public recognition, the portrait, the speeches at Grosvenor House. She had achieved in principle all that she had set out to do, henceforth her work would consist not so much in launching new attacks as in consolidating the position she had secured and in planning for a future in which she would not take part.

Ruskin's death in 1900 accentuated for her the sense of belonging to the older generation; it brought to an end a relationship which had been precious to her for over forty years. Though in the last twenty years there had been little contact, only 'some news now and again from out of the death-like silence into which the friendship of nearly a lifetime has fallen', she felt the loss acutely. 'To me, personally, the loss is irreparable. I have loved to think of the master and friend of my youth in his lovely home, to feel that he was among us still.' For nothing had been able to take from her the deep veneration for Ruskin which he had inspired in her girlhood. The breach in 1877, much as it had wounded her, had left no bitterness in her heart, it had not even diminished in her eyes his essential greatness. 'It is a high honour and great blessing which has come to you both,' she wrote to Sydney Cockerell when he and his sister Olive were going to stay with Ruskin. 'I believe you will walk worthily of it in the time to come, with, as it were, your shoes put off your feet, for indeed the spirit which will be near you will make the place holy ground.' It is curious to notice how the very thought of Ruskin always moved her so greatly that for the moment she lost the lucidity of her speech, and in a flurry of Ruskinian rhetoric could exhort her young friend to walk in the time to come with his shoes off his feet.

Sydney Cockerell, much as he admired Ruskin, was not blind to the injustice he had done to Octavia, and being a young man of very great courage, he was determined to attack the great man on the subject and get some kind of acknowledgment of error from him. 'Thou knowest,' writes Miranda to Mary Harris, 'what a great admiration Sydney Cockerell has for Ruskin and how fond Ruskin is of him. Ruskin invited him and Olive down to stay with him and read them the next unpublished number of *Fors*. Sydney is so loyal to Octavia too, and he has expostulated with Ruskin about his attack on her, and got Ruskin to re-read what he had written, and Ruskin appears quite grieved and shocked at himself by Sydney's account. Sydney wants Ruskin to make a public recantation, but Octavia urges Sydney to let the matter drop. The young man's intense enthusiasm for Ruskin and desire to get him to do the right thing is a very beautiful combination.'

There was no public recantation, but in a private letter which Cockerell was able to show to Octavia, some amends were made. 'I return the valuable letter. . . . I think he is right about the forgiveness, and I think it *is* hard you should any of you expect a man, who had the place in the world he had, when he knew me as a girl of not fifteen years, should ask forgiveness. Not for a moment do I myself wish it, unless in any way it took away from him the sadness of the memory of what he did, I tell you most distinctly I do not think there is very much in the whole affair, that is, when the imperfections and limitations of earth and speech are taken away I do not think there will be very much to clear up between Mr. Ruskin and me. Till that time, touched as I am by your chivalrous kindness about it, I do seriously assure you I think a merciful silence is at once the best, and the most dignified course for him and me. . . . Be at peace about it, I am. I hope Mr. Ruskin is. He may be. The thing is past, let us bury it, that which the earth will not cover, which is not of it, lives on in the eternal kingdom and in the thought of it, earthly imperfection or mistake seems a very small thing.'

Ruskin was gone, and the world seemed a poorer place to Octavia for his going, but two years later she sustained a still heavier loss in the death of her mother. That remarkable woman was ninety-two when she died, but had retained to the last all her mental faculties, all her eager interest in the work of her daughters. 'No more on earth,' wrote Octavia at the end of her 1902 Letter, 'can we carry to her our completed work for her approval, nor turn to her for sympathy in its progress.' Caroline Hill had had a hard life, but she had never failed in courage or resolution and she had been richly rewarded in the lives of her daughters; she had left them as free as it is possible to be in their girlhood, and as they came to womanhood, she had been content to let them make their own lives in their own way, while she followed all they did with loving understanding and sympathy. She was the least exacting of parents and reaped the reward of such, the trust and confidence of her children. 'I think there never could have been any mother,' wrote Octavia of her, 'of whom it was so true that she desired no personal nearness, so that she was entirely one with what her children did.' She never asked, advised or criticized, but she watched and her comments on them in her letters are always illuminating: 'Octavia thinks she has laughed more this week than in a year at home; but I don't think she knows what a frequent occurrence that is.' To take her away for a holiday was very real joy to any one of them, to have a quiet time to sit with her was always a refreshment. Old Pupils of Nottingham Place remember her as a very little old lady, smaller than any of her daughters—all of whom were short—who was always ready to speak of them, and had many tales of their childhood to tell.

Perhaps she was closer to Octavia than to any of them, for in her she saw again her own father, Dr. Southwood Smith. It was her father's work her daughter was carrying on, his serene courage and sleepless energy which animated her. Octavia, for her part, found in her mother a wise counsellor and beloved companion whose great qualities she appreciated more deeply year by year. 'I think the thing I most failed to convey to thee of all I had wanted thee to know,' she wrote to Mary Harris in 1875, 'was the intense blessing Mama is to us all. . . . I think the sense of life is a joy to her; while often she puts before me principles bear-

ing on questions under consideration, most beautifully.'
Her death therefore was a very great grief, and since grief
is not logical, was in no great degree lessened by the fact
that at her age it could not be expected that it should be
long delayed. Octavia felt it acutely and experienced too
that desolation which comes to most people on the death
of the last person who has known them as children; it
marks very definitely the beginning of the last chapter.

Octavia's Letter of 1902 shows the spirit in which she
entered the last phase of her work: 'The work which I have
to chronicle is rather a steady development on the old lines,
than any new departure; it is growth rather than change.
And this is best so, provided we are all sure that we have
kept ourselves attentive to the low whispers which should
teach us where and how we were wrong or how the new
times call us to different methods. We who grow old
specially, should strive to keep an open heart, a quick eye,
and a ready ear for the facts which should teach us how
"New occasions teach new duties. . . . I do not regret to
have no new special departures to record only let us be sure
that there is growth and that the absence of change is not
because of dullness of apprehension of the new needs which
life must bring."'

'We who grow old.' From now on, Octavia, as she went
about her work, was consciously preparing for the time
when she must leave it to others. It was always expanding,
the work for the Ecclesiastical Commissioners alone was a
tremendous business, and as leases of working-class houses
on their property fell in, they handed them over to her
management. The question as to who should be responsible
for all these houses and tenants was one which needed careful thought. Hitherto Octavia's colleagues had been largely

volunteers and the work had been very much a family affair: Octavia, her sisters, Miss Yorke or some other intimate friend, had been the responsible person to whom property owners had entrusted their houses, from whom they had received reports; under these, part-time voluntary workers had taken charge of small groups of tenants, as many as they could manage in the time they were prepared to give. Whenever it was possible, Octavia had encouraged those who bought houses to learn to manage them themselves, or to persuade members of their families to do so; she believed this to be the ideal arrangement, since it made possible a natural family relationship between tenant and landlord, and helped the more prosperous to arrive at a real understanding of the problems and circumstances of those who were less so.

There were of course some professional workers among her colleagues, as well as some who, like Emma Cons, had long been established in centres for which she herself had no responsibility. As early as 1875 a Miss Martin had come from Leeds to live at Nottingham Place to learn the work, and had returned to manage property there, Edinburgh had become a Training Centre, which sent workers to Perth, Dundee and Glasgow, and in 1893 a Dutch lady, Fr. Ter Meulen had come to England to train and had returned to Amsterdam to carry on the work there; nevertheless it remained true that, generally speaking, Octavia had trained professional workers only as she saw vacancies for them, and had envisaged property management in the hands of volunteers with a few more fully trained and responsible professional managers in charge. Now, however, it became necessary to revise this conception. There was no longer any need to find rich persons who would invest money in houses or Courts, these were being built in quantities, it was more than ever necessary to provide fully trained responsible workers who could take charge of them, House Property management, in fact, must acquire the status of a profession. It was one of the 'new needs which life must bring'. Octavia was quick to recognize it: 'I realized that my best plan would be not only to train such volunteers as offered, and the professional workers whom we required, but to train more professional workers than we ourselves can use, and, as occasion offers, to introduce them to owners wishing to retain small tenements in their own hands, and to be represented in them by a kind of Manager not hitherto existing. The ordinary collector is not a man of education having time to spare, nor estimating his duties as comprising much beyond a call at the doors for rent brought down to him, and a certain supervision of repairs asked for. If there existed a body of ladies, trained to more thorough work, qualified to supervise more minutely, likely to enter into such details as bear on the comfort of home life, they might be entrusted by owners with their houses. We all can remember how the training of nurses and of teachers has raised the standard of work required in both professions. The same change might be hoped for in the character of the management of dwellings let to the poor. Whether or no volunteers co-operated with them would settle itself. At any rate owners could have, as I have often told them they should have, besides their lawyer to advise them as to law, their architect as to large questions of building, their auditor to supervise their accounts, also a representative to see to their people, and to those details of repair and management on which the conduct of courts and blocks inhabited by working people depends. When people live close together, share yards, wash-houses and staircases, too often there is no one whose business it is to supervise and govern the use of what is used in common, or to see how one tenant's conduct affects others.' To this task Octavia now addressed herself with all her accustomed energy and to the end of her life it seemed to her of ever increasing importance. There was no difficulty in providing the training, she had enough fully qualified workers to train as many students as she could get, she still called for volunteers, but in addition in one Annual Letter after another she appealed for women to train professionally. 'I have had three applications for paid managers in London during the last year,' she wrote in 1903, 'which I have been unable to fill, owing to all our trained and even partially trained, helpers being absorbed by our own extended area, and there are openings in provincial areas from time to time; but it should be borne in mind that such would only be open to those capable of taking the whole responsibility of management.' The trainees came but not rapidly enough, the demand for managers increased. London estates absorbed many, presently applications came from the provinces. In 1904 Birmingham, Liverpool, Oxford, and Manchester began to consider the employment of women managers, in 1907 two ladies from Leicester came to train and in 1909 Tunbridge Wells, Torquay and Nottingham were discussing the possibility of employing such women. Nor was the work confined to England. In her last 'Letter' Octavia records: 'We continue to be able to help kindred work in foreign countries. Two more capable Dutch ladies have been over to train for house management, one of them obtained a good position on her return to Holland, she takes over charge of eighty families and of a garden for their common use and enjoyment. A Swedish lady is just beginning a course of training with us. I hope that on her return to Stockholm she may find help by associating herself with Frö Lagerstadt who came to us for training some 20 or 30 years ago and has been carrying on work there ever since.'

The number of students in training increased in a satisfactory way, Octavia felt she could never have too many of them. 'Building never was what I felt our main duty,' she wrote in 1907. 'It was always the right government of the houses which I felt the greatest need. Almost the worst house, if the household be wisely managed, is better than ever so costly a one ill managed.' The dictum has been often enough quoted with approval, it is reiterated by Royal Commissions, Advisory Councils, and all who speak with authority on Housing, but in practice it has been very generally ignored. Money has been poured out on buildings, estates have been developed with every sort of modern device and improvement, but the wise management which Octavia felt to be so essential has been very largely neglected. Houses and estates have deteriorated, those who instinctively regard the weekly wage-earner as 'that class of person' recount *ad nauseam* that they 'keep the coal in the bath' and exclaim with horror at conditions revealed by evacuation. It is still true, as Octavia so often declared, that those who endeavour to improve conditions by lavish expenditure on bricks and mortar—or concrete and steel— are doomed to disappointment. 'You cannot treat houses and tenants separately.'

In 1904 Octavia had reason to be glad that she had begun to make provision for an increased number of managers. The Ecclesiastical Commissioners were the ground landlords of much property which had been leased to others, as the leases fell in they invited Octavia to take charge of them. In some parts of Southwark the area had been leased on the old-fashioned tenure of lives, that is to say, it was held not for a specified term of years, but subject to the lives of certain persons. When the lease suddenly fell in, Octavia was confronted, at four days' notice, with as complicated a rent-collecting affair as she had ever encountered. 'The houses having been let and sub-let, I could be furnished with few particulars. I had a map, and the numbers of the houses, which were scattered in various streets over the five acres, which had reverted to the Commissioners, but I had no tenant's name, nor the rental of any tenement, nor did the tenants know or recognize the written authority, having long paid to other landlords.' Octavia tackled the situation with her usual calm confidence; she visited every tenant herself, explained the circumstances and was successful in obtaining every rent. Putting the property into repair was a slower business, and the state in which she found it gave her much food for thought for it seemed to her a very undesirable state of affairs that a body identified with the Church should have been drawing income from property over which it had no real control. 'It is curious to realize how wholly owners delegate their responsibility in a long lease.'

In the following year a still larger expansion of the work brought this question more prominently forward. In Walworth twenty-two acres containing between five and six hundred houses fell in to the Ecclesiastical Commissioners. It was an area ripe for redevelopment, and Octavia was asked to help in planning this and to take on the management of the property during the rebuilding. 'But,' she wrote, 'there remains one most important point still under the consideration of the Commissioners. It is whether this domain is to be leased to builders and managed by them and their successors for some 80 years or whether it is to remain under the direct control of the Commissioners. . . . This land is Church land, it adjoins the parish Church, it is quite near the Talbot Settlement, established by and named after the Bishop of the diocese; surely it should not pass from the control of the owners. If clauses in leases were as wisely planned and as strongly enforced as possible they could not be like the living government of wise owners, were it only that the needs and standards are for ever changing, and during the next 80 years many decisions involving changes may be desirable. . . . I can only trust that these considerations may come home to those who control Church lands and that they may find a sufficient group of trained workers to represent them faithfully and well.' Octavia's wishes prevailed, the Commissioners decided that all the working-class property in the area should remain under their direct control, and on her recommendation they appointed Miss Lumsden, who had been working with her in Lambeth, to be the manager of the houses.

The Ecclesiastical Commissioners' estates were large enough to set the standard for the district in which they were situated; the case was different when Octavia was responsible for a few houses in a difficult neighbourhood. This was a problem she had to face in Notting Hill, where, in response to an appeal from the Vicar of the Parish, she had in 1899 accepted the management of five houses. It was a very bad neighbourhood, 'corrupt, not poor, only too much money seems to reach the inhabitants from the rich people of Kensington. This district is filled with beggars and others who feed on the lavish alms of ignorant and careless donors. Vice seems rampant, whole streets are let in furnished lodgings, an extravagant form of tenure not likely to attract the steady workman, and lending itself readily to the loafer and shiftless or vicious.'

The redemption of such streets was obviously a work after Octavia's own heart. She had latterly been engaged largely with rebuilding schemes, here she came back to the problems she had first tackled, the problem of the shiftless, the pauperized, the unemployed and the almost unemployable, and these were the people she most cared to help. Once more she found herself employing her tenants in simple repairs, and educating them in the idea that they could work. 'The inhabitants are a poor lot, physically weak, old and without character or skill, just the class that are first to feel trade depression. The men need almost constantly looking after, the price must be enough to encourage them to persevere . . . and to enable them to get material and by degrees tools, yet not too high to prevent them trying for regular work under proper foremen for full hours.' The tenants responded; she noticed joyfully that they were gradually recovering their skill, many of them were becoming so useful that she no longer felt anxious when she confided tasks to them.

But she was anxious about this Notting Hill property, because though she had been able to add to her original five houses, by purchase through some of her funds, she still held too few houses; the general level was so low that it was a continual struggle to prevent deterioration. Whenever a house came into the market, unless she could buy it, it fell into the hands of those who increased the evil in the neighbourhood, the local authority more than once closed houses used for immoral purposes, but they were very soon reopened by some newcomer. Octavia was therefore confronted by a serious difficulty when, in 1910, the owner of the original five houses found himself obliged to sell them. The work done there had just begun to tell, to abandon it was not to be contemplated, but she felt no longer justified in asking people to invest in working-class dwellings, because she felt no longer certain that such an investment could be depended upon to produce a steady income. Fortunately there was a solution which secured the future of the houses. In 1886 Mrs. Scrase Dickens and Mrs. Russell Gurney had given Octavia the freehold of some houses, with Mr. Shaen's help she had made of them a Trust called the Horace Street Trust. By its terms, the Trustees were obliged to give to open spaces or any other object helpful to the people all the profit from the houses after necessary expenses had been met. The Trustees had already bought three houses in Notting Hill and now agreed to take charge of the five which were for sale. 'The result of their holding these leaseholds,' notes Octavia happily, 'even should no interest accrue from them, would be loss of money to give, not personal loss. They were clearly the people who could and should hold these houses.' The problem therefore resolved itself into the familiar and simple one of raising enough money to buy the houses, and this was easily accomplished. Octavia could leave the Notting Hill houses, happy in the knowledge that they were secure for all time.

Chapter XX

RATE AIDED BUILDING AND THE POOR LAW

'The solution depends not on machinery . . .
but on . . . men and women':
OCTAVIA in 'Letter to Fellow Workers', 1909

IT has been seen that from the very beginning of Octavia's housing work it had been a matter of principle to make her properties pay. In the early days and after the initial difficulties had been overcome, this had been easy enough, for there was a very real shortage of accommodation and no rooms ever stood empty. Gradually as it had become apparent that providing houses for the working classes was a paying proposition, a number of Societies had begun to build until there was no lack of dwellings for the more prosperous artisan. This seemed to Octavia a satisfactory state of affairs, and she confined herself more and more to those poorer families who needed help she and her workers could give. Obviously with a preponderance of poor tenants, and the rates steadily rising, it became more difficult to ensure a regular return on capital, but with care and economy, it was still possible.

Towards the end of the century, however, a new situation arose. The local authority assumed the responsibility for the housing of its citizens. It had rightly announced its intention of clearing insanitary areas, and had laid down various regulations as to new buildings. But uncertainty prevailed as to whether it proposed also itself to build, and

256

this had discouraged independent building. Furthermore, the influx of families into London, which in the last fifty years has depopulated the countryside, had begun and there was once more a shortage of working-class accommodation in many districts. In this situation the L.C.C. decided in 1898 to build tenements and enter the field as a landlord in competition with the commercial Building Societies.

To Octavia, this seemed disastrously wrong. There are some among those who hold Octavia's memory in high honour and who believe whole-heartedly in her methods, who maintain that if she were alive now, she would recognize the desirability of building by elected bodies. It is a vain and unprofitable speculation, since none can tell what an Octavia born fifty years later might have been or thought. What can be said positively is that her objection to such building was no isolated opinion, but absolutely fundamental to all her thought and work. She knew herself that all her dearest prejudices were involved. She had always thought all subsidizing wrong in principle, it was her conviction that it was the employer's business to pay his people enough to enable them to live in satisfactory conditions, and that any subsidy simply went into the pocket of the employer and encouraged the worker to feel that it was the business of the State to supply his needs.

As early as 1884, giving evidence before the Royal Commission on Housing, she had said: 'I do not think that any rate—or State—supported scheme could ever meet the requirements of the case, because if you once assume it is your duty to provide houses for the poor at a price that they assume they can pay, it will just be a rate-in-aid of wages like the old poor law system, and if the labour market is in an unsatisfactory state, wages will simply fall.' And again: 'I should object very greatly to the provision under the remunerative price of a thing, which would be simply a rate-in-aid of wages.'

She tried to look at the question dispassionately. 'I would earnestly desire not to be blinded, by interest in a form of work I know and care for, to the advantages of any fresh development which seemed to give hope of progress —but I cannot see anything but disaster in what I understand as a new departure of the L.C.C.' She stated her objections clearly enough. In the first place it was manifestly unjust that property owners should be compelled to pay rates to subsidize their competitors. 'They will erect rate-supported dwellings, let at low rents to the residents. That means that a portion of the rent of A. is to be paid by making B. pay higher rates. So that not only will the L.C.C. undersell other builders, but it will tax them higher in order to subsidize the houses owned by the L.C.C.'

Furthermore, the action of the local authority would paralyse all independent building, and thus it would be compelled to provide more and more working-class dwellings at a cost quite unwarrantable since the Building Societies and charitable Trusts left to themselves and unhampered by the threat of rate-aided competition, could rapidly meet the needs of all classes.

Octavia was indeed very clear in her mind that the function of the State and all elected bodies was to confine themselves, in housing, to 'destruction and keeping up the standard by the execution of the Sanitary law' and she deprecated a situation in which the same authority should be both supervisor and landlord.

There was yet another ground on which she protested

against the housing schemes of public authority. She thought it undesirable that voters should be the tenants of those who sought their suffrage. She had always believed that the landlord-tenant relationship should be kept distinct and on a business footing, each side recognizing and fulfilling his responsibilities punctually. Voting seemed to her, in any case, difficult for a man who was little educated; to add to the difficulty by inviting him to choose or reject a candidate who could affect his living conditions, raise or lower his rent, eject him or allow his arrears to run on, was to open the door to every sort of abuse. That the danger is a real one can hardly be denied; it is not necessary that electors or candidates should be consciously corrupt, it is difficult for the Housing Committee of a Borough Council to eject tenants who are voters, at any time, doubly so when an election is approaching; it is natural for a tenant in difficulty to count on this immunity, and once arrears of rent are permitted, they inevitably increase and the loss is borne by the solvent ratepayer. There is no way of entirely eliminating this danger; it may, however, to some extent be diminished if the property is managed by a fully trained worker, of sufficient strength of character to stand out against any sort of political pressure, but even when such a manager is in control, the last word remains with the Borough Council.

There neither was nor is, of course, any reason why a Public Authority should not employ a fully trained Manager, recently some have done so, but in Octavia's day, such a course did not commend itself to those responsible, and the rent was collected in the time honoured way by a man who 'goes round on Monday morning and stands at the door of the house and asks for the rents that are forthcoming. A certain proportion of the rents are brought down, by the honest sober steady people . . . the bad destructive tenant does not pay.' This impersonal treatment of tenants added strength to Octavia's disapproval; enough has been said of her insistence on the importance of educating the tenant, and the soundness of her view has been too often and too lately demonstrated to require underlining. Protest was useless. The L.C.C. was a comparatively new body, full of zeal for improving its domain, possessing all the energy of the new broom without the experience to direct it wisely. The power of bidding blocks of tenements arise, and then controlling them proved intoxicating, and not being hampered by the necessity of earning a return on its capital, the L.C.C. saw no reason to call a halt. Rates went up alarmingly, and increased transport facilities made it possible for many to avoid them by moving to the suburbs. It was not long before the shortage of dwellings was overtaken, and the difficulty was not to find tenements, but to find tenants. Octavia believed that money could still be usefully invested in reconditioning old houses for the worst type of tenant, but the uncertainty of letting made her refuse to accept capital except from those who had sufficient experience to judge of the risk for themselves, and sufficient wealth to be able to forgo interest on the money they offered her. In 1907 for the first time in forty-four years she had in one or two small properties to report to the owners that actually no dividend had been earned, and in one or two others that it had been diminished.

But the building went on; new blocks of flats were added in districts already overcrowded with buildings, even where letting was so difficult that 'local papers advertise for weekly tenants to whom a month or a fortnight rent free is offered.' Sadly Octavia noticed that 'Birmingham counted the empty tenements before deciding about building. This natural course does not appear to suggest itself to the London County Council.' Her protests went unheeded. Local authorities have continued to build immense blocks of flats, with a high standard of equipment and no vestige of individuality; the population of London has increased in density so that transport presents an almost insoluble problem and the workman spends all his leisure travelling to and from his work. It may be that this constitutes progress and that in an age of mass production there is no room for the small concern or for a method so personal and individual as Octavia's. Yet it is possible to regret that this is so, and to feel that something very precious to civilized human life is lost, when the individual is swallowed up in the mass and there is no room for the natural and happy relations which Octavia established with her tenants.

In 1905 Octavia was invited to become a member of the Royal Commission on the Poor Law. She was somewhat reluctant to accept, since a seat on the Commission would involve the fundamental reorganization of all her work and the abandonment of a conference on the direct payment of rates which she was just about to organize. Nevertheless she accepted. 'The questions to be dealt with are so important, the experience I have had actively in the homes of the poor for years is so great, and has been exceptional in so far as we have met one another with mutual duties, that I did not feel I could refuse.' The rearrangement of her work was managed without delay. By this time she had so many competent helpers that it was not difficult to manage and she had not the fault, so common in competent persons, of believing herself indispensable, it was part of her plan to make herself less and less so. 'The work may have gained by the interruption,' she wrote after a year of the Commission's sitting. 'The very morning I received the request to join the Commission I saw that this might be so.'

Having become a member of the Commission Octavia threw herself whole-heartedly into its work, it lasted three years, and pursued its enquiries in the provinces as well as in London. Octavia missed only one of its London meetings and was able generally to visit also the provincial towns. She found it deeply interesting 'partly by the great and important questions it suggests, partly by the large number of individuals of whose life work we got some idea;' a characteristic comment, for from her childhood she had shown an eager curiosity about ways of life other than her own. Though she disclaimed any specialist knowledge of the problems to be investigated, she had for years been dealing with the people closely affected by them, and the difficulties of the situation were familiar to her.

The work of the Royal Commission, its findings and the reforms originated by it are matter for the social historian, rather than for the biographer, but Octavia's part in its work is of very great interest. She had always in her own work refused to divide the poor into the categories of deserving and undeserving, there were those who could be helped to become self-supporting, and those who from some weakness of fibre would always require to be 'carried' by the community. She did not condemn the latter, she was fully prepared to believe that it was their misfortune rather than their fault, but she wished to ensure that none who could become independent should, through ill-considered charity or sentimental legislation, sink into their ranks. It was because the existing Poor Law authority with its workhouses, guardians, and Relieving Officers had failed to distinguish between the two classes, had treated those who were genuinely unemployed through misfortune, as if they were permanently useless, and had maintained them indefinitely instead of developing 'schemes of work or training in surroundings fit for worthy men and women', that legislators, charitable people and working classes felt the acceptance of Poor Law relief to be an indignity to which none but the most degraded could be expected to submit. Consequently, 'All round there have been growing up schemes of relief, overlapping one another, without proper enquiry, without any test . . . charitable alms are scattered wide, causing demoralization; old-age pensions are administered and decided on by a separate body from the main state relief agency, and divorced from it.'

Octavia felt that the right way to deal with this state of affairs was by a radical reform of the existing organization; the alternative, preferred by the majority of the Commission—the abolition of existing Boards of Guardians, and the substitution of statutory committees of the County Councils—did not commend itself to her. Committees 'composed mainly of those elected for other duties and already overweighted with work' seemed to her open to serious objection. 'I should have preferred an *ad hoc* authority, elected from an enlarged area with a strong nominated or co-opted element. The prospect of more hopeful work, which must open out under the fresh arrangement would probably attract the service of those interested in the poor and able to devote undivided strength and thought to them, as they would not be hindered with County Council business, nor eager for political advancement.' It is a characteristic recommendation. That the rich, the educated, the leisured should give personal service to individuals, that electors should not be invited to vote for those who must give or withhold relief, were for her fundamental principles.

Nevertheless she felt able to sign the Majority report. 'The solution depends,' she remarked, 'not on machinery which Commissioners may recommend and Parliament set up, but on the number of men and women which England can secure and inspire as faithful servants in their manifold duties.' From one recommendation of the Commission she dissociated herself, this was the recommendation to provide work for those who could not find it in the market; here her passion for facing the reality of any situation broke out: 'You will notice, however, that I break away from my colleagues in so far as I would have no unreal outside made work at all. The work should be recognized as relief or training, whenever it is not needed and carried on in the real market in the open world. . . . We seem to me to be confusing ourselves and deluding them by made work under artificial conditions.'

The Commission made its report at the end of 1908; 'I am not hopeful that my three years' work has been very helpful,' she wrote. This low estimate of her contribution to its deliberations was not, however, shared by some of her colleagues. The chairman, Lord George Hamilton, had in the course of the three years learnt to turn to her in moments of difficulty. She did not say very much, she sat, as she sits in the photograph of the Conference, square to the table, her papers before her with her arms folded over them, her whole attention on the matter in hand, her dark eyes following one speaker after another, then, 'At critical moments of discussion and controversy she would intervene with a few words of undeniable common sense and insight and solve the problem we were considering.' 'I have tried to do my best,' was Octavia's own comment on it, 'and I am glad that I did not refuse the call. I do not consider my training particularly fitted me for the post: certainly, in many ways, several of my colleagues were much better qualified for the duties; still, I had a certain amount of special experience, I have tried to render it useful as it was asked for, and now I may return to my own sphere of duty.'

Chapter XXI

LAST YEARS

'I might have given it a few more touches, but I
think it is all planned now very well':
OCTAVIA, 1912

'Now I may return to my own sphere of duty.' There was
a sigh of relief in the words; this Poor Law Commission,
however necessary and interesting, was, after all, an interruption of the work to which Octavia had given her heart;
to this she might now return, and since it had been running
so well for three years without her full attention, now that
she had time to give, it might be possible to embark on new
and satisfying developments. 'When I undertook this (Poor
Law Commission) I was able to do so because I knew that
I had in every district a faithful and wise representative
able to carry everything on, possibly really better for my
partial withdrawal, and I had been pondering what new
development my own work would take so soon as the Poor
Law Commission was over, as I could not dream of inter-
vening when all was going so well. I had visions of new developments into which I could throw my strength.'

In March, however, Octavia was taken seriously ill; she
faced with tranquillity the question of 'how my various
work would stand if I had suddenly to leave it, and the
answer was full of satisfaction and hope'; and when she recovered she still cherished her visions of some new development. These, however, were not destined to materia-
lize; a quick succession of blows hampered the organization

which had been working so well. The first of these was the death of Sir Alfred de Beck Porter, which removed a powerful ally on whom Octavia and her workers had come to depend with complete confidence. He had been responsible for all the business of the estates of the Ecclesiastical Commissioners; it was he who had recognized the importance of the Commissioners' maintaining direct control of their working-class property, and, fully endorsing the principles which underlay all Octavia's work, had supported her in all her demands of the Commissioners. Further losses followed. Matrimony in New Zealand claimed one of Octavia's colleagues, another broke down, and two more found themselves obliged for domestic reasons to relinquish their work; all were experienced and responsible workers. It was 'such an upheaval as bids fair to break up traditions and make me feel that I have to begin rebuilding . . . now it is clear that the well-known places want me once more, that I must be there, side by side with younger and new workers, to carry on government on the old lines.'

She settled down again, therefore, to the familiar round in the houses, and the daily intercourse with the tenants brought her the satisfaction she had always found in it; increasingly too she enjoyed the younger and new workers whom she was training to carry on in her tradition. Some years earlier she had taken a room in the house next to hers in Marylebone Road as an office, and here every Thursday accounts were brought to be checked and problems to be discussed. It was a formidable affair to the less competent, for though the standard of education of girls had risen to an entirely new level since the early days, there were still— as there will always be—some whose accounts showed a strange reluctance to come exactly right, who were slow to seize essential points, or apt to forget apparently unimportant details; some, perhaps, who did not reach the high level of devotion and efficiency which Octavia demanded. She had never suffered fools gladly, now at seventy she was sufficiently alarming to those who felt themselves falling short, and improvised inadequate reasons for their mistakes; there were many who sought and received comfort from Miss Yorke after one of the less happy interviews. Her sympathetic understanding, her kindness, and the sense of humour she brought to bear on the troubles of the young people who came to her, helped them to recover a sense of proportion, to face their work with renewed courage. There were some, no doubt, who abandoned the work, feeling that they could never attain the necessary standard, but those who had the strength and resolution to persevere were abundantly rewarded by gaining Octavia's confidence and friendship. She had a real affection for her pupils, would rejoice in entertaining them at Marylebone Road or at Larksfield, where she tried to spend some part of each week. There the garden never ceased to delight her, weeding remained a favourite occupation, and the country sights and sounds enchanted her, as they had always done. 'It has been a lovely summer to be in the country,' she had written in 1898. 'One gets on quite a different footing with birds and flowers and hills and sky when one lives with them day by day, from what one does in flying visits.' As she grew older, this intimacy with birds and flowers seemed ever more desirable.

There were other joys at Larksfield, too, notably the near neighbourhood of the Warren where one of her nieces, Elinor, was now living. With all her nieces Octavia had established the happiest relationship. Like most unmarried

HARRIOT YORKE.

women, she had a deep tenderness for children, and the mere fact of kinship meant so much to her, that her sister's children could not fail to call forth all her affection. From their babyhood she had delighted in them; her letters are full of references to them, when she was away she eagerly sought news of them, and as they grew old enough to care for letters she wrote them long accounts of what she was doing and seeing. She was an understanding aunt, who always treated them with that respect for their personality which is so precious to the young. As they grew up they naturally became interested in her work, in which they all took some part. Elinor was most closely associated with her, trained for Property Management, acted as her secretary, and from 1900 was one of the Horace Street Trustees; now she was married, and Octavia had the happiness of seeing her and her family in the new home.

They were happy peaceful days; the houses certainly still demanded time and energy, but there were no major problems; the National Trust, her other principal interest, went on from strength to strength acquiring new stretches of country, new headlands, new hills with wide views. If in public life there was much of which she disapproved, she did not allow it to fret her; she made her protest, but she was no longer to the forefront of the battle; a new generation must direct operations and take the responsibility for new conditions.

Yet she protested; and one protest at least requires consideration. In the last years of her life the question of extending the suffrage to women was being hotly contested. Here was a cause which claimed the enthusiasm and energy of nearly all the leading women of the day, the professional women were almost unanimous in its support. Octavia had been a pioneer in woman's work, she had indeed invented a profession for women; she had worked on equal terms with men, sitting on Royal Commissions, advising cabinet ministers and peers; she had again and again proved herself far ahead of her own generation; naturally suffragists turned to her confident that they would find in her a strong and valuable ally; had she not indeed argued that those who pay no taxes should have no vote, was she not logically bound to conclude that those who *do* pay taxes should vote? Octavia wrote to *The Times* in July, 1910; and her argument, so Victorian in tone, so incredibly contrary to all her own life had shown, must have exasperated and bewildered the suffragist party.

'I feel I must say how profoundly sorry I shall be if women's suffrage in any form is introduced into England. I believe men and women help one another because they are different, have different gifts and different spheres, one is the complement of the other: and it is because they have different powers and qualities that they become one in marriage and one also in friendship and in fellow work. In public and in private life I think one feels the various powers and in the main looks to a somewhat different help from men and from women, and that the world is made on a principle of mutual help.'

'Why,' the suffragists might well have asked, 'is making a X on a ballot paper less "womanly" than investigating drains, ordering the ejection of bad tenants, advising about the rebuilding of slums?' The answer is not easy to devise.

Yet Octavia's position was not really as inconsistent as at first sight it appears. There was a rational core to her argument, expressed in the next paragraphs.

'I think, also, that political power would militate against

270

their usefulness in the large field of public work in which
so many are now doing noble and helpful service. This
service is, to my mind, far more valuable now than any
voting power could possibly be. If you add two million
voters, unless you secure thereby better members of Parliament, you have not achieved anything, but you have
used up in achieving nothing whatever thought and time
your women voters have given to such duties. Whereas if
they have spent their time and heart and thought in the
care of the sick, the old, the young, and the erring, as guardians of the poor, as nurses, as teachers, as visitors, if they
have sought for and respected the out of sight silent work
which really achieved something, a great blessing is con-
ferred on our country.'

For her, the crux of the matter lay in her profound distrust of party politics. While as a believer in democracy,
she recognized the necessity of Parliament, at the bottom
of her heart she felt that local government was very much
more important to the ordinary citizen, whether male or
female. When her half-brother Arthur Hill refused an invitation to stand for Parliament for Reading on the grounds
that he had no time to add Parliamentary to his municipal
duties, Octavia warmly applauded his decision, being convinced that the work he did in Reading was of infinitely
more value than anything he could do at Westminster. She
continually urged the importance of getting the right men
and women on Boards of Guardians, Vestries, Parish and
Municipal Councils and all other local bodies. This, which
involved real work and daily contact with fellow citizens,
she considered really worth doing; debating in Parliament
and voting according to a Party Whip seemed by comparison waste of time. Women already had the local vote, and

made very little use of it; Octavia felt that the Parliamentary vote would still further distract them from work that lay to their hand, was waiting to be done and needed doing.

But her fiercest opposition was aroused by the tactics of the Militant Suffrage party, which reinforced her conviction that the cause in which they were used was dangerous to democracy. She had always had a horror of publicity, and for gaining anything by force rather than by reason. Since democracy depends on reasoned argument, an attempt to extract the vote by exploiting nuisance-value seemed to her a negation of every sound principle of political life. Feeling as strongly as she did about this, she could not consider the question with the detachment necessary to form a wholly rational judgment. For the moment her view prevailed, but her own achievement in education and in raising the status of woman's work made it impossible that it should continue long to do so.

Meanwhile the days slipped by with that ever-increasing speed noticed by all who have passed middle age. Each year went more quickly than the last, and each brought so much happiness that as Octavia wrote her Letter at the end of each year it was chiefly gratitude she wished to express. 'I am again writing to you to record what has been done during the past year, and as I do so, a song of thankfulness seems to be singing in my heart, as I think of the many and great mercies which have been with us, and of the joy which has been sent to us.'

But sorrow came too. In 1910 Miranda was taken ill; from the beginning of her illness, Octavia knew that there was little hope of her recovery. When the summer came she was moved to Larksfield that she might enjoy the beauty of the country. Octavia was with her for the last

weeks of her life. 'She lived all her life so near to God, so
vividly conscious of all the spiritual world that it hardly
seemed a step to the heavenly one.' Few people can have
been better loved than Miranda. She was one of those rare
souls so forgetful of self that their unselfishness is perfectly
unconscious. There are those who live for others, denying
themselves so obviously that perpetual gratitude becomes
necessary: Miranda had found a better way. She did not
need to deny herself, because all her desires were selfless,
she simply did what she wished to do and enjoyed doing,
she had, in fact, arrived at the 'perfect law of liberty' and a
radiance of happiness shone from her and made her infinitely attractive. 'It has been a chorus of love and gratitude from all whom she had known in every relation of life
—Poor Law Children, pupils, friends, servants and colleagues—all have felt something of the gracious holiness
with which she walked through life.'

Miranda's relationship with Octavia had been particularly close and happy. 'The friend, the counsellor, the companion of all my life has passed from me beyond the veil.
Life is necessarily changed for me.' Though Octavia had
always been the leading spirit, she had depended very
greatly on Miranda's judgment, recognizing that her sister
felt less passionately and therefore often more justly than
she herself did. Miranda had been happy to take the second
place, to work under her sister, to smooth the way for her,
to make her home run easily, to save and help her in every
way, and Octavia fully realized the magnitude of her debt.
'I have lived on her love for seventy years,' she wrote, 'and
have had the blessings of it daily.'

Octavia took up the burden of her work again. Her 1911
Letter, the last she was to write, was full of quiet confidence

in the work she was doing and of thankfulness at the progress of the National Trust. Two of its acquisitions particularly pleased her, because they had been given in memory of Miranda: one consisted of seven acres of Grange Fell in Cumberland, the other of part of ten and a half acres on the banks of the Wandle near Mitcham Station. 'The river here takes a wide curve and its banks are set with loosestrife and meadowsweet. It also forms a largish pond or tiny lake, surrounded by trees, and there is an island, a lovely meadow and a public path which skirts the land.'

There was another scheme she launched in this last Letter. It was for an extension of the Trust's property at Mariner's Hill. 'A fear seizes us that unless we can receive some more land, our eastern view may be spoilt by building. . . . I have already got £600 and I greatly want the rest (£900). . . . You know how much open space we have preserved by small gifts and I feel there is a great blessing in them. . . . If you know any who would *care* to hear of the opportunity . . . tell them, that if we do get this additional slope, all our view to the East will be unimpeded land and sky giving delicious sense of space; ask them to imagine the joy of that hilltop with all its view and air; ask them to leave it free for those who love it, and will find joy and peace there for years to come.'

Before the Letter was circulated Octavia knew that the time to lay down her work was at hand. She had for some time been troubled with breathlessness, and there were other symptoms which warned her that her condition was serious. When at Easter, 1912, she learned that it was incurable, she was neither surprised nor dismayed; she was simply concerned to ensure that the work she had loved so well should be effectively carried on.

There was much to do, but she had staunch friends to help her, and she had long determined the general lines on which she would dispose of her responsibilities and her possessions. In unhurried calm she arranged for the management of her houses, both her own and those she had controlled for others, for the nine banking accounts for which she was responsible, for her activities in connection with Red Cross Hall, St. Christopher's and the Settlement at Southwark. She rejoiced that Miss Yorke would continue to live in the home in Marylebone Road, responsible for much of the work and making a centre for friends and colleagues, that she could leave her own houses to her nieces who, she well knew, would regard them as a trust. It was hard work, for her weakness increased rapidly, but by the end of April she was satisfied that she had put all in order. 'I might have given it a few more touches, but I think it is all planned now very well.'

Then with Miss Yorke she went to Larksfield. It was a fine and lovely spring, and she sat hour after hour in the garden gazing at the view she had always so greatly loved, rejoicing in the poppies whose scarlet had always been her favourite colour, in the broom golden against the blue distance, in the birds who, finding nothing alarming in the human being who sat so peaceful and so still, hopped nearer and nearer to her, in the sweetness of the spring weather with its myriad sounds and scents.

In June she returned to Marylebone Road; she was losing strength rapidly and never left the house again. Miss Yorke was in devoted attendance, making the utmost of the few weeks' companionship that remained to them; her sisters, her nieces, her old friends were constantly with her, she rejoiced in their society and, as her body grew weaker, the flame of her joyous spirit burnt more steadily. She was completely at peace. Her interest in the causes she had espoused did not flag and in particular she followed with great pleasure the progress of the Fund for the purchase of the extra acres on Mariner's Hill and, to her great delight, on the day before she died, she received from a close friend a cheque for £500, which more than completed the purchase.

She was ready to go; she had had a long and vigorous life; she had experienced great sorrows and greater joys, some failures and many successes; she had accomplished far more than she had ever imagined might be possible; she had exercised great power and risen to great eminence without allowing either to spoil her; she had worked hard all her life and now she was tired. On the evening of 12th August she took leave of each member of her household, and in the course of the night her serene and untroubled spirit left the body it had so long tenanted.

Chapter XXII

THE TESTAMENT

'She, being dead, yet speaketh':
Hebrews, xi. 4

THE Dean and Chapter offered a funeral in the Abbey, but the family refused the honour, knowing that Octavia herself would have chosen to lie beside Miranda at Crockham in the churchyard with the view which had given her 'such a delicious sense of space'. She would have been puzzled to know (as in 1887) why she should be 'singled out in this kind of way', for to her it seemed that she had trod a simple enough path, doing 'just what lay before her' among 'those whom God had put near' her.

It is true that she is probably the least widely known of all the great women of the Victorian Age. 'Octavia Hill? Yes, I know the name,' a lady was heard to say at the time of the centenary celebrations. 'An open space in Kent somewhere, isn't it?' Though such complete ignorance is probably rare, there must be many who would be ashamed not to know the significance of Florence Nightingale, Dorothea Beale, Josephine Butler, or Elizabeth Garrett Anderson, who have only the haziest idea of Octavia's contribution to the national life. This ignorance is due in part to her own determined resistance to publicity, which prevented her friends, after her death, from commemorating her in any building or public memorial, and led them indeed, in their loyalty, to keep themselves and their work as much out of the public eye as possible; in part to her refusal to

277

found any organization, or to formulate her principles in any code, lest these should hamper those who should succeed her. Partly too perhaps her reputation has suffered because in the thirty years that have elapsed since her death, the values which seemed to her of paramount importance have to some extent fallen in popular estimation. The road which she indicated has certainly not been followed, and since the policies which have been pursued have not brought conspicuously successful results, it is worth while to-day, when all we have known is in the melting pot, to reconsider her principles and to see whether she has not something to contribute to the work of reconstruction which lies before us.

Octavia was the least theoretical of all reformers. She started, as she herself said, doing what lay before her as simply as possible. But because she was quick to feel for others, and because she could not see a want without trying to satisfy it, her work developed in rich variety and covered an immense field. But it all started from some concrete individual problem: her housing work had its origin in an effort to find a home for one family; the seed of the National Trust and all her work for Open Spaces was planted in a tiny playground in Marylebone, and the spirit which inspired all her efforts for the C.O.S. and the reform of the Poor Law first expressed itself in an effort to help improvident little toy-makers to save their own money to pay for their own 2*d*. dinner. If Wordsworth is right in his choice of the first characteristic of the Happy Warrior

'the generous spirit who when brought
Among the tasks of real life hath wrought
Upon the plan that pleased his boyish thought'

then Octavia must certainly be reckoned to be in the ranks of that army.

It was no doubt partly circumstance, partly temperament which first directed Octavia's attention to the needs of the individual, but Maurice's teaching confirmed her in the course on which she had embarked. From him she acquired a conviction, held with ever-deepening intensity, of the unique value of every individual, a value derived from the faith that each was the child of God and created to do His will. The importance of the individual in a democratic state is very generally conceded, and though probably most people would not be prepared to deny to him the status of a child of God, this has now come to be regarded as an academic question, irrelevant to practical policy. To Octavia it was the root of the matter. The material help she gave was merely a means to a spiritual end, and she judged any measure of reform by its effectiveness in promoting the growth of character. To any who had suggested that the material needs of the poorer citizen must be met by the State, while his spiritual condition was entirely his own private affair, she would have replied that it is not possible to separate the two, since life is sacramental and the spiritual can be expressed only through the material, and that neither the State nor any other body has the right to risk the destruction of the spirit by lavish gifts to the body.

This has seemed to many a harsh doctrine, and it has sometimes been represented as the expression of the old-fashioned attitude to the poor based on the assumption that the upper classes have some divine right to privilege and wealth. But this is to misunderstand the whole matter. Octavia recognized no superiority in the upper classes, she was as much concerned about the spiritual development of the rich as of the poor. Her objection to promiscuous charity was not merely its demoralizing effect on the recipient but also the smug self satisfaction it generated in the giver. That a wealthy man, having written a cheque, should feel himself relieved from all responsibility for unsatisfactory social conditions, from which very likely he derived part of his income, seemed to her intolerable. She was the last person in the world to minister to the complacency, or to save the pockets, of the rich.

Her view of the relation of the individual to the State was equally based on her belief in the dignity of man. Being a member of a community confers certain rights and responsibilities; it is possible to stress either. Octavia always stressed the latter, both for herself and for others. What one was able to contribute to the community always seemed to her more important than what one could get out of it, and she did not readily believe that any man would willingly take from the State what he could earn for himself. Independence was very precious to her and so far was she from regarding the poor as a class apart, that she had no doubt it was equally dear to them. It is common enough nowadays to hear those who describe themselves as 'The New Poor' complain bitterly that the working classes are better off than they, because they 'get so much done for them'. To Octavia such a state of mind would have been simply incomprehensible, for to be in a position in which it was necessary to be done for would have seemed intolerable. No man, she felt, should be forced into it. The function of the State, as she conceived it, was not to provide directly for the needs of its citizens, but so to organize society that it should be possible for every man to earn—not merely a subsistence but—a livelihood which should enable him to keep himself and his family in independence. It would appear that since Octavia's day, successive governments having found it too difficult to organize our commerce and industry in such a way as to provide the possibility of a living for all, have abandoned the effort, and turned rather to the easier business of relieving the distress which their own lack of foresight has suffered to arise. The result has not from any point of view been very satisfactory, and it may be that in the re-organization before us, we shall do well to recognize the importance of that sturdy independence which Octavia believed to be natural to the English working man.

Octavia was an idealist, but not one of those who can believe comfortably that with a little good will, all will come right. Her idealism was based on a realistic appreciation of the facts of human nature. She condemned alike the vague benevolence of the stupid and the complacency of the self-interested, knowing both to be equally dangerous and equally selfish. She distrusted improvised remedies and haphazard reforms; impulsive as she was by temperament, she had learned to curb her eagerness and to allow her reason to work on every problem presented to her before she took any action. She demanded of herself and of those who would work with her, all the intelligence and foresight that they could bring and the patience to look at every aspect of the matter in hand. If she was dealing with Open Spaces she must have a map of the whole district, and consider the rights of owners, needs of agriculture or industry, and the possibilities of recreation; if she was dealing with a poor family, she must know all its commitments and responsibilities, all sources of relief, and as far as practicable, all the possibilities open to each member. In things great or small, she demanded a plan, a really constructive effort, based on the realities of the situation.

Having decided on a course of action, she then proceeded to pursue it. Nothing could deflect her from her way; had she not learned in childhood from her mother that if a thing is right it must be done, there ceased to be any question about it? There were of course often enough obstacles and setbacks. These did not in the least daunt her. 'I am always ready for failure in preparing the hearts of people for any new thing; someone must pay the cost in disappointment, and I am quite ready to do so.'

It is tempting to speculate about the attitude Octavia would take to the vast problems we shall be called upon to face in the near future. Whether she would see any reason to modify her extreme distrust of state control, whether she would approve this or that method of national or international reconstruction, it is impossible to determine. She always recognized that no solution to any human problem is final and that each generation must find its own way through its own difficulties. But some principles she believed to be eternally true and valid for all generations. That every situation with all its difficulties and possibilities must be fairly and calmly faced, and regarded *sub specie aeternitatis*, that every individual has a contribution to make to the common life and is immeasurably the poorer if he is not enabled to make it, and that therefore the only cure of the ills of society lies in the conversion and education of individual men and women—these things it may safely be affirmed she would assert to-day. It may be that the brave new world will be built on foundations other than hers, but it can hardly be doubted that in the process of rebuilding there will be need of the shrewd judgment, the self-forgetting devotion, and above all the invincible faith in righteousness that Octavia Hill brought to the task of her generation.

INDEX

*A Novel of
the Slums of to-day!*

POOR RELIEF
by CAROLINE SLADE

RALPH STRAUS (*Sunday Times*) :
"'A very terrible but most moving
account of poor people in the slums
of a town in the United States.
Rarely has hideous poverty been set
forth in a novel so vividly or in
language so uncompromising and
direct.''

CHAUCER

THE CLERKES TALE

WITH LIFE, GRAMMAR, NOTES, AND AN
ETYMOLOGICAL GLOSSARY

LONDON : 38 Soho Square, W.
W. & R. CHAMBERS, Limited
EDINBURGH : 339 High Street
1910

Go, little booke, ...
And kisse the steps whereas thou seest pace
Of Vergil, Ovid, Homer, Lucan, Stace;
And for there is so great diuersite
In English, and in writing of our tong,
So pray I to God, that none miswrite thee,
Ne thee mis-metre, for defaut of tong :
And redd wherso thou be or eles song,
That thou be understond, I God beseech.

CHAUCER, *Troilus and Creseide*, Bk. v., 1798-1810.

PREFACE.

THE importance of the study of Chaucer depends as much upon his being the first writer of a classical English, as upon his being the earliest of our greater English poets. The language which he used became the standard of literary English and the model for succeeding writers, nor did his influence die out until the age of the Tudors brought a new era to our language and literature. The modern historical study of English has restored Chaucer to the place he held with his contemporaries and successors, and has shown that the serious study of his poetry is the threshold to an intelligent knowledge of our mother tongue.

The present volume contains the *Clerkes Tale*, one of the earliest written as well as one of the finest in the series of the *Canterbury Tales*. It is an excellent example of Chaucer's style, and of that marvellous art in constructing a story which has made him—what he is still—our greatest narrative poet. As in our preceding edition of the *Squieres Tale*, the basis of the text is the Ellesmere MS. as printed by Mr Furnivall in his magnificent Six-Text Print for the Chaucer Society; but a few readings which seemed preferable have been adopted from the other five MSS., and more particularly from the Harleian MS. as printed by Dr Morris in the Aldine edition of Chaucer's works. A few unessential changes have been made in the orthography to prevent confusion, and to make the spelling more uniform; but these are so infrequent and inconsiderable, that the present text may be accepted as substantially a transcript of the MS. of the Ellesmere scribe. A Life of Chaucer, and a sketch of his Grammar, have been given, as well as a brief account of his Versification. The Notes attempt to deal with the difficulties in the text, and the Glossary gives the signification and etymology of the words, besides serving as an Index to the lines of the poem in which these words occur. An acknowledgment of indebtedness is due to the works of Dr Morris and Professor Skeat, especially to those of the latter, who has made the whole range of Middle English so peculiarly his own, and whose great *English Etymological Dictionary* marks an epoch in the scientific study of the English tongue.

CONTENTS.

THE LIFE OF CHAUCER.

1. His Time.—CHAUCER'S LIFE AND WORKS belong to one of the greatest epochs of English History. The Elizabethan period, when England was strong both at home and abroad, and when the English drama was at its best; and the present Victorian period, when there exists everywhere unexampled activity both in literature and in science—are the only two epochs that can be compared with it. His life lay within the reigns of Edward III., Richard II., and one year of Henry IV. In the reign of Edward III. the nation—which consisted of two elements, the Norman and the Saxon—grew into one people; and the language, which had been gradually absorbing as much Norman-French as it could hold, became the ready and powerful instrument of a new literature. The year 1362 marks an important point in the history of the English Language. For in that year Edward III. passed an act of parliament authorising the use of English instead of French in courts of law, in schools, and in other public places. This is sufficient proof that the nation had become truly English. In 1380, the Bible was translated into English by Wicliffe; and this translation had a permanent effect on the character of English prose. Moreover, great events of all kinds were lifting men's minds, enlarging their ideas, and inspiring their souls: the battles of Crecy (1346) and Poitiers (1356) had been fought; the art of weaving cloth was introduced from Flanders; Windsor Castle was growing into the most splendid pile in the west of Europe; gunpowder had lately been invented; Londoners had seen two kings, the king of Scotland and the king of France, prisoners in their capital; and everywhere new powers and new ideas were stirring throughout the kingdom. And then the time was quite ready to welcome the 'ditties and songes glad,' with which Chaucer 'fulfilled the land over all'* even in the flower of his youth.

2. His Birth and Parentage.—GEOFFREY CHAUCER was born

* Everywhere.

in the year 1340 in London. And he lived most of his life in
London. Spenser, Ben Jonson, Milton, and other later writers
were also Londoners. But London in the fourteenth century
was not the vast province covered with houses—filled with smoke
and harassed by unceasing noise—that London now is. It was a
clean, quiet, almost noiseless city, full of shady gardens, every
house different in character from every other, permeated by
green lanes, and the short streets divided and refreshed by
green fields. The quiet meadows were within a few minutes'
walk of the very heart of the city. There were no cabs or
carriages, no part of the endless grind and roar that now fill
the main arteries of London; but the slow leisurely rumble of
a market-cart intensified the sweet silence. It was, indeed, as
Mr Morris says:

> London, small, and white, and clean;
> The clear Thames bordered by its gardens green.

You could hear the songs of the birds clear and thrilling in
the streets; and the citizens had the English love of the country
so thoroughly in their blood, that, on the morning of the First
of May, they rose at daybreak, with songs in their mouths and
in their hearts, to do honour to the coming summer, gathered
boughs of blossoming hawthorn, and with it decked the door-
ways of their houses—so that each street smelt from end to
end of the May, and thick bushes of green and white met the
eye on every side.

> May, with all thy floures and thy greenë,
> Welcome be thou, wel fairë fresschë May!

The streets did not swarm with people dressed in black, or in
dull and dead colours; but there were here and there groups
of persons dressed in bright red or yellow or green or blue and
white, and sometimes the one half of a man's coat was of a
different colour from that of the other side.

His father was John Chaucer, citizen and vintner of London.
His grandfather was Richard Chaucer, also a vintner; and the
name of *Chaucere* is said to be on the roll of Battle Abbey.
John Chaucer's house was in Thames Street, on a stream called
Walbrook *—because it flowed past London Wall—which rose
in Finsbury Moor, beyond the street still called Moorgate, and
flowed into the Thames near what is now Cannon Street. The

---

* There is still a street of this name.

boy went to school in the neighbourhood; and no doubt he sometimes helped his father in the wine-cellar, and filled the pots of the citizens with their daily supply of draught-wine. But Chaucer's father had a connection with the court of Edward III. He attended that king when he went with his Queen Philippa on an expedition to Flanders and Cologne; and it is to this connection that Geoffrey owed his appointment as page in the household of Elizabeth, the wife of Prince Lionel, the third son of Edward III. He was then seventeen. Young men in the time of Chaucer went either to the university, or entered the service of some nobleman as page. There they learned courtesy of manners, riding, the use of arms, and all that related to the life of a soldier, a nobleman, and a man of public affairs. There is also a tradition that Chaucer was a member of both of the universities of Oxford and Cambridge; but this is doubtful. His position in the household of Prince Lionel threw him into the society of the most distinguished men and women of the time; his imagination would be fired by the splendour of the court festivities; he would meet on frank and cordial terms the great statesmen and warriors and writers of the age.

3. His Official Life.—In the year 1359, Chaucer—then a young man of nineteen—joined the army of Edward III., which invaded France in November of that year. In this campaign Chaucer was made prisoner; but he was released under the Peace of Brétigny in 1360, when the king paid for him a ransom of £16. In the year 1367, he was appointed one of the 'valets of the king's chamber,' and is mentioned in the patent or commission as 'dilectus valettus noster.' He received, by the same patent, a pension of twenty marks* for life. John of Gaunt, Duke of Lancaster, the fourth son of Edward, a man of exactly Chaucer's age, was his great friend and patron; and he remained true to Chaucer to the end of his days. When Blanche, the wife of John of Gaunt, died at the age of twenty-nine, Chaucer wrote a beautiful poem in her honour—'The Dethe of Blaunche the Duchesse.' Between the years 1370 and 1380, the poet was employed in seven diplomatic missions—some of them of great

* A mark is 13s. 4d. But there was little or no comparison between the buying power of money in Chaucer's time and now. A sheep sold for 2s. 6d.; a horse might be bought for 18s. 4d.; a chicken cost 2d.; and the price of a day's labour at the plough was 3d. Money must have gone, then, from ten to twenty times as far as it does now.

importance. In one of these he had to treat with the Doge of Genoa regarding the choice of an English port to which Genoese vessels might trade. There is a tradition that, while on this embassy, Chaucer had an interview with the great Italian poet Petrarch at a place called Arqua near Padua ; and that Petrarch recited to him the story of the patient Griselda. But the tradition is doubtful ; and Chaucer had Petrarch's works to read the story in. Soon after his return from the embassy, on St George's day—the 23d of April 1374—the king made him a grant of a daily pitcher of wine, to be received from the king's butler at the port of London. This grant was in 1378 commuted for an annual payment of twenty marks. In the same year he was appointed comptroller of the customs of wools, skins, and leather in the port of London ; and a few days after this important appointment he received from John of Gaunt a pension of £10 a year for life as an acknowledgment of the services rendered by him and his wife Philippa to himself and his consort. Who Chaucer's wife Philippa was is not clearly made out. The ordinary tradition is that she was the daughter of a knight of Hainault, Sir Paon de Roët, king-of-arms of Guienne, and sister to Katharine, the widow of Sir Hugh Swynford, who afterwards became the wife of the Duke of Lancaster. In 1377, the last year of the reign of Edward III., Chaucer was employed along with Sir Thomas Percy (who was afterwards created Earl of Worcester) on a secret mission to Flanders ; and in the same year he was sent on a mission, in company with two other distinguished knights, to treat of peace with Charles V., king of France. In 1378, the first year of Richard II.'s reign, Chaucer was again sent to France with the Earl of Huntingdon to arrange a marriage for Richard with the daughter of the king of France. In 1382, Chaucer was appointed comptroller of the petty customs, in addition to his previous comptrollership. By the terms of his first office, he had been bound down to make every entry in the Customs books with his own hand ; but he was now allowed the privilege of employing a deputy. He would thus have more leisure for the writing of his CANTERBURY TALES, which seem to have occupied him at intervals between the years 1373 and 1400. The PROLOGUE is said to have been written while on a journey in the year 1388.

4. His Later Life.—Chaucer was in 1386 elected knight of the shire—or M.P.—for the wealthy and beautiful county of Kent. This was during the nonage of Richard II. Chaucer's friend and

patron, John of Gaunt, was abroad ; and his brother, the Duke of Gloucester, acted as regent of the kingdom. But the Duke of Gloucester hated every one who belonged to the party of his brother. Accordingly, on the 1st of December of this year, Chaucer was dismissed from both his offices. The poet was now reduced from affluence to poverty ; and he was obliged to raise money by borrowing on the security of his two pensions. His wife died in the midst of Chaucer's greatest trouble, in 1387. It was in the following year, 1388, that Chaucer made his pilgrimage to the shrine of Thomas à Becket, at Canterbury—a pilgrimage which supplied him with the frame for his great work, the Canterbury Tales. In the year 1389, Richard II., disgusted with the action of his council, suddenly dismissed them and took the reins of power into his own hands ; the party of Lancaster was restored to favour, and with this turn of affairs Chaucer again rose into prosperous circumstances. He was appointed clerk of the works at Westminster and also at St George's Chapel in Windsor Castle. He, however, lost both these posts in 1391, and was for three years out of office. In 1394, he received a grant of £20 a year for life from the king ; and it is believed that he was at this time in considerable distress from poverty and from failing health. John of Gaunt died in 1399, at the age of fifty-nine ; and Chaucer was of exactly the same age. But Henry Bolingbroke, the son of the Duke of Lancaster, deposed Richard II. No doubt, Chaucer knew Henry well, and had often dandled him upon his knee when a little boy. A day or two after his coronation the poet sent him a quaint and humorous poem—'Complaynte of Chaucer to his Purse'—every verse of which ended with the line :

Beth hevy ageyne or ellës mote I dye.

And in another stanza he calls his purse the 'queen of comfort and good company :'

Quene of comfórt and goodë companye,
Beth hevy ageyne, or ellës moote I dye.

Within four days after Henry came to the throne, though he must have been over head and ears in work with the new affairs of the crown, he doubled Chaucer's pension of twenty marks ; and the poet was again in comfort and security. On Christmas Eve 1399, he signed an agreement for the lease for fifty-three years of a house in the garden of the chapel of

St Mary, Westminster. In this house he died on the 25th of
October 1400.

5. **His Person and Works.**—Chaucer was a big stout man with
a fair face and small features. A shy and silent man, he was
given to observation of others and meditation, to hard study at
nights, and to recording in his books and poems the fruits of
'the harvest of a quiet eye.' There were two things that
Chaucer was heart-wholly fond of—study and nature. After
coming home from his hard work at the Custom-house—work,
as we have said, every part of which required his own special
attention, instead of rest and amusement, he sat over his books
till midnight, until his eyes were 'dased' with his reading
and the dull light of his lamp. Year in, year out, he was
always at his books. But, when the month of May came, and
nature was overflowing with joy and music, he shut his books
and went out into the fields to spend the day in the open air
and sunshine, among flowers and trees, and green grass and
singing birds. He says in his *Legende of Good Women:*

> Save, certeynly, whan that the monethe of May
> Is comen, and that I here the foulës syngë
> And that the flourës gynnen for to spryngë,
> Fairwel my boke, and my devocioun !

And, when he found himself there, great tides of joy and
cheerfulness swept through his heart; and such lines as these
broke from his lips with happy power :

> Herkneth these blisful briddës how they syngë,
> And seth the fresschë flourës how they spryngë ;
> Ful is myn hert of revel and solás ! *

He is one of the best story-tellers that ever lived. He knew
the weak points and the strong points of men and women ; and
he looked upon their weaknesses with a humorous and kindly
eye. He did not apportion his respect for men and women
according to their rank, but saw quite clearly that *gentilesse* or
genterye is a quality of soul and character and not of rank or
possession. And he uses one of the simplest but one of the
most beautiful similes in all literature to clench his meaning :

> Tak fuyr and ber it in[1] the derkest hous
> Bitwixë this and the mount Caukasóus,
> And lat men[2] shut the dorës and go thennë,[3]

* Nonne Prestës Tale, 380—382.

[1] Into.   [2] One.   [3] Thence or away.

Yit wol the fuyr as faire and lightë brennë
As [1] twenty thousand men might it biholde;
His [2] office naturel ay wol it holde,
Up [3] peril of my lif, til that I dye.
Her may ye se wel, how that genterye
Is nought [4] annexid to possessïoun,
Sithin [5] folk doon her operacïoun
Alway, as doth the fuyr, lo ! in his kynde !

The early literary works of Chaucer were translations from Latin, French, and Italian ; and by these translations he became widely known. One of his contemporaries speaks of him as 'grant translateur, noble Geoffroi Chaucier.' But the work of translation could not satisfy a full and original mind like Chaucer's. We find him in 1369 writing 'The Dethe of Blaunche the Duchesse ;' in 1373, the 'Lyfe of Ste. Cecile ;' in 1382, 'Troylus and Creseide ;' in 1384, his 'Hous of Fame ;' and in 1386, his 'Legende of Goode Women.' But his greatest work —and the work which gives him his high place in English Literature—is the Canterbury Tales.

6. The Canterbury Tales.—The Canterbury Tales is a kind of national epic of the fourteenth century. The framework of these tales—which is given in the Prologue—is of a quite simple and old-fashioned kind. Dickens, in his Christmas stories, imagines a set of travellers snowed up in a wayside inn, or in an open boat after shipwreck on a stormy sea; and the company, tied to each other by the bond of a common misfortune, and with a good deal of blank time on their hands, bring forgetfulness of sorrow by the recital of stories in turn. Boccaccio, in his *Decameron*, or Book of the Ten Days, presents to us a company of ladies and gentlemen who have fled from the Plague in Florence, in 1348, to a country-house, where they shut themselves up and amuse each other with stories. Mr William Morris, the poet, employs a like device in his 'Earthly Paradise.' Chaucer's are open-air tales ; and he imagines them to be told on horseback by pilgrims to the shrine of Thomas à Becket, as they amble easily along the green lanes which were then the only roads between London and Canterbury. One evening in April, nine-and-twenty pilgrims meet in Southwark, which was then a large country village on the Surrey side of London Bridge. They put up at the well-known Tabard Inn in the High Street. After dinner, when the 'reckonyngs' had been made, and the men were merry

[1] As if.   [2] Its.   [3] Upon.   [4] Not.   [5] Since.

over their wine, Harry Bailey, the host, a 'large man' with
bright eyes and frank bold speech, proposes that they should
all ride together to Canterbury; robbers were always about,
and the roads were never very safe; and that each pilgrim
should tell two tales going and two returning. There were in
all thirty-two pilgrims, for they were joined on the way by
three more; and this would have made one hundred and
twenty-eight tales in all. Only four-and-twenty remain to
us. The Prologue tells the story of their meeting, and of
Harry Bailey's proposal; and it also gives a detailed description of the appearance, dress, manners, and character of each
of the motley collection of pilgrims. The Church is numerously
represented; and no doubt Chaucer meant to seize the opportunity of exposing the vices and corruptions of the new state of
ecclesiasticism in England. The form of the drama had neither
been invented in nor imported into England in the fourteenth
century; had it been, there is little doubt that so sympathetic,
observant, and many-sided a man as Chaucer would have availed
himself of it. But, even as his poetry is, Mr Marsh is right in
saying that 'Chaucer may fairly be said to be not only the
earliest dramatic genius of modern Europe, but to have been a
dramatist before that which is technically known as the existing
drama was invented.'

CHAUCER'S GRAMMAR.

The Grammar and the Vocabulary of English.—The chief
stages of the English language are three, namely: Anglo-Saxon,
from the earliest times of which we have any records to about
1150 A.D.; Middle English, from that time to about 1500; and
Modern English, from 1500 to the present day. The vocabulary
of Anglo-Saxon is almost free from foreign admixture; the
Middle English contains a large number of Norman-French
words; while the modern English has borrowed words from
numerous sources. As regards grammar, the Anglo-Saxon is
distinguished by its full and numerous inflections, its use of
various genders for inanimate objects, its full declension of the
definite article, and the like; modern English is remarkable for
its almost total lack of inflections, and its entire disregard of
grammatical gender; while Middle English holds the inter-

mediate position, preserving many inflections in a weakened form, and retaining genders only in a very few instances, as when, for example, the *sun* is regarded as being feminine.

Of Middle English, there were three well-marked varieties or dialects : (1) Northern or Northumbrian, including what is now called Lowland Scotch ; (2) Midland, chiefly in use between the Humber and Thames ; and (3) Southern, chiefly to the south of the Thames. The Midland dialect is that which finally prevailed, and to which modern literary English is most nearly related.

The most convenient tests of difference between these three dialects are these : (*a*) The Southern dialect employs *-eth ;* the Midland, *-en ;* the Northern, *-es*, for all forms of the present plural indicative.

(*b*) The Southern and Midland dialects have *-eth* in the plural imperative ; the Northern has *-es*.

The Midland dialect between the Thames and the Humber covered a large area, and had various local varieties. The most marked of these were : (1) the Eastern Midland, spoken in Lincolnshire, Norfolk, Suffolk, and Essex, with many words and grammatical forms in common with the Northern dialect ; (2) the West Midland, spoken in Cumberland, Westmoreland, Lancashire, Cheshire, and Shropshire. Of these the more important was the East Midland, and it was this that became the standard literary English from which has come in a direct line, with but few flectional changes, the English language spoken and written at the present day. As early as the thirteenth century, it had thrown off most of the older inflections, and had fitted itself to become a national language. Among its writers were Ormin, Robert of Brunne, Wicliffe, Gower, and Chaucer. It was Chaucer's influence especially, that caused the East Midland speech to supersede the other dialects, and it is the grammar of this dialect that we must now learn.

NOUNS.

1. Number.—(*a*) The nominative plural usually ends in *ĕs :*

Fro foulës and fro bestës for to saue (line 683).

Many nouns ending in a liquid or dental letter (*l, m, n, r*, and *d, t, th*), as well as most words of more than one syllable, take *-s* only.

In the oldest English there were several plural suffixes, *-as, -an, -a, -u* (*-o*), of which the most common was *-an*. After the Norman Conquest, these were reduced (in the thirteenth century) to -*es* and -*en*, and finally the termination -*es* or -*s* became the ordinary sign of the plural. It was words of French origin that were the first to thrust out the *e*, and adopt the simple suffix -*s* or -*z*. Cf. *iugementz* (line 439), *subgetz* (line 482). Some MSS. of Chaucer give *is* and *us* for the nom. plural; but this is due, no doubt, to the dialect of the scribe who copied, as it is not likely he would be careful to note Chaucer's forms of the plural.

(*b*) Chaucer here and there retains the plural in *en*—a refined form of the old plural in *an*. Thus he has *assen*, *been* (bees), *eyen* (cf. N. E. or Scotch *een*), *flon* (arrows), *schoon*, and *ton* or *toon* (toes). This plural still survives in the Dorset dialect; and in Mr Barnes's Dorsetshire poems it is a great assistance to the rhythm and metre. Thus Mr Barnes has *housen*, *shoon*, *nesten*, and *fisten*. *En* is still the chief plural ending in West Friesic.

(*c*) We also find instances of double plurals. The only two in modern English are *brethren* and *children*. The oldest English or Anglo-Saxon plural of *brother* was *brothru*, and of *cild*, *cildru*. *Brothru* became *brothr-e*, *brethre* (*brether*), and finally *brothren*, *brethren*; while *cild-r-u* became *child-r-e* (and *childer*), and finally *child-r-en* (and *childern*). Similar double plurals in Chaucer are *doughtren* (A.S. *dohtru*, later E. *dohtre*), *sistren*, *sustren* (A.S. *sweostru*, later E. *swustre*), *fon* or *foon*, foes (A.S. *fá*), and *kine* (A.S. *cy*, pl. of *cú*). The forms *brether*, *childer*, and *kye* are still preserved in northern dialects. In *kine* the plural has been formed by vowel change, thus, A.S. *cú*, pl. *cy = ki* (-*ne*). The chief vowel changes are *a* of the sing. into *e* of the pl., *oo* into *ee*, and *ou* into *i*. Thus are formed our plurals *men*, *geese*, *feet*, *teeth*, *mice*, and *lice*, from *man*, *goose*, *foot*, *tooth*, *mouse*, and *louse*.

(*d*) Many neuter nouns had no plural ending; and we still have survivals of this in *sheep*, *deer*, *swine*, *night* (in *se'ennight* = seven nights, and *fortnight* = fourteen nights), *stone* (used as a weight), *score*, and others. So in the oldest periods of English, *year*, *winter*, and *freond* are used as plurals. See line 610, etc.

2. **Case-endings.**—(*a*) The genitive singular generally ends in *ĕs*; thus, line 291 :

> Bisyde the threshfold, in an ox*es* stalle.

Cf. also *goddes* (line 7), *emperoures* (line 168), *lordes* (line 294), etc. This was a distinct syllable in early English, and traces of this form occur in Elizabethan writers. Cf. Spenser's *Faërie Queene* I. v. 50 :

> . . . . That with stroke
> Of aspës sting herself did stoutly kill ;

and Shakspeare's *Love's Labour's Lost*, V. ii. 332 :

> To show his teeth as white as whalës bone.

It should be noticed that the ' is not the *sign* of the genitive or possessive case in modern English, but simply marks the elision of an *e*—a usage which in the eighteenth century was extended to verbs, as we find in Addison *walk'd, stretch'd*, etc. The general use of the apostrophe in the singular is not found much before the end of the seventeenth century. It was probably intended to distinguish the possessive case from the plural number. Its use may have been established from a false theory of the origin of the suffix *-s* which long prevailed, namely, that it was a contraction of *his ;* hence such expressions as, 'For Jesus Christ *his* sake' (*Prayer-Book*). This corruption occurs towards the close of the fourteenth century. Thus Trevisa has 'egle hys nest' = eagle's nest.

In the oldest English there were various declensions, as in Greek and Latin, and different genitive suffixes for the singular and plural. The oldest suffixes for the singular were *-es* (*smith-es* = smith's), *-an* (*steorr-an* = star's), *-e* (*rod-e* = rood's), *-a* (*sun-a* = son's). For the plural they were *-a* (*smitha* = smiths'), *-ena* (*steorr-ena* = stars'). In the thirteenth century the suffixes of the genitive in the singular were *-es* and *-e ;* in the plural *-ene* (*-en*), *-e*, and the modern form *-es*, which often replaced the others. In the fourteenth century *-es* (*-s*) is the ordinary suffix for both singular and plural. The suffix *-en*, *-ene* is found as late as 1387 (cf. *wycchen tongues* = tongues of witches), but is very uncommon in Chaucer.

(*b*) Some nouns have no genitive ending at all. These were feminine nouns, whose oldest genitive was *an*, which was broken down into *ë*, and then disappeared. Thus Chaucer has *lady veil*, *sonnë upriste* (the uprising of the sun), and *widow sone*. We find survivals of this genitive in *hell fire*, *Ladykirk*, and *Ladyday* (= the day of the Virgin Mary). In like manner, *fader*, *brother*, and *doughter* took no inflexion for the genitive singular ; see *doughter* (line 608), and *fader* (line 1135).

(*c*) The dative singular ends in *ë ;* but it is rare. The prepositions *for, at, on* (or *up-on*), *by, in, of, to* (or *un-to*), and *from*, govern the dative case in Anglo-Saxon, and may be considered as always governing a dative in Chaucer. Cf. lines **4, 29, 66,** **191, 398,** etc.

ADJECTIVES.

Remnants of Inflexions.—Adjectives were inflected in the oldest English (or 'Anglo-Saxon') just as German adjectives are inflected now. They had a definite form and an indefinite form (cf. *guter Mann* and *der gute Mann*). The definite form—which is preceded by the definite article, or a demonstrative pronoun, or a possessive pronoun—has an *ë* in all cases of the singular, as 'the godë man.' The plural is also denoted by a final *e*, as 'godë frendes.' The *e* is often dropped towards the end of the fourteenth century. In Chaucer it disappears in words of more than one syllable, as 'mortal batailles.'

Comparison.—The comparative degree is formed, as now, by the addition of *er*. But we find also *re*, a remnant of an older *ra*. Thus we have *derrë, nerrë, ferrë, herrë,* for *dearer, nearer, farther,* and *higher*. *Bet* and *mo* are contractions for *bettre* and *mara*. The superlative degree ends in *este*. Chaucer has *hext* (= *highest*) on the model of *next* (= *nighest*).

PRONOUNS.

1. Personal Pronouns:

FIRST PERSON.

	SINGULAR.		PLURAL.	
	Mid. Eng.	*Anglo-Saxon.*	*Mid. Eng.*	*Anglo-Saxon.*
Nom.	I, ich, ik.	ic.	we.	wé.
Gen.	min, myn.	mín.	our, oure.	úre (úser).
Dat.	me.	mé.	us.	ús.
Acc.	me.	mé (mec).	us.	ús (úsic).

SECOND PERSON.

	SINGULAR.		PLURAL.	
	Mid. Eng.	*Anglo-Saxon.*	*Mid. Eng.*	*Anglo-Saxon.*
Nom.	thou, thow.	thú.	ye.	gé.
Gen.	thin, thyn.	thín.	your, youre.	eówer.
Dat.	the, thee.	thé.	you, yow.	eów.
Acc.	the, thee.	thé (thec).	you, yhou.	eów (eówic).

THIRD PERSON.
MIDDLE ENGLISH FORMS.

	SINGULAR.			PLURAL.
	Masc.	*Fem.*	*Neut.*	
Nom.	he,	she,	hit, it.	thei, they.
Gen.	his,	hir, hire,	his.	her, here, hior.
Dat.	him,	hir, hire,	hit, it.	hem.
Acc.	him (hine),	hir, hire.	hit, it.	hem.

OLDEST ENGLISH OR ANGLO-SAXON FORMS.

	SINGULAR.			PLURAL.
	Masc.	*Fem.*	*Neut.*	
Nom.	hé.	heó,	hit.	hí, hig.
Gen.	his,	hire,	his.	hira.
Dat.	him,	hire,	him.	him.
Acc.	hine,	hí,	it.	hi, hig.

The pronoun *thow* is sometimes incorporated with the verb, as *schaltow*, *wiltow*, *seistow*. Cf. also *maystow* (line 265), *wostow* (line 325).

2. **Adjective or Possessive Pronouns.**—These were formed from the genitive case of the personal pronouns, and were declined like ordinary adjectives.

3. **Independent or Absolute Possessives.**—*Min* (plural *mine*), *our*, *oures*, ours ; *thin* (plural *thine*) ; *your*, *youres*, yours ; *hir*, *heres*, hers ; *her*, *heres*, theirs, are employed predicatively, without a following noun. The forms *hers*, *ours*, *yours*, *theirs*, are really double genitives containing a plural suffix *r* + a singular suffix *-s*. These forms were mostly confined during the thirteenth and fourteenth centuries to the northern dialects, and are probably due to Scandinavian influence.

4. **Demonstrative Pronouns.**—(*a*) The definite article *the* is used without inflexion in all cases, singular and plural. The old plural *tho* (A.S. *tha*) is still, however, occasionally used by Chaucer, but more often it is equivalent to *those*.

(*b*) The form *attë* = at the (A.S. *at tham*), occurs as in the well-known line : 'After the schole of Stratford *atte* Bow.' See also lines 130, 547, 749.

(*c*) The plural of *this* is *thise*, *thes*, *these*.

(*d*) *Thilkë* = that, the like. (A.S. *thylc*, *thylic*; from *thy*, instrumental case of *se*, *seo*, *thaet*, and *lic*, like.) See lines 197 and 892.

(*e*) *Swich* = such ; A.S. *swylc*, literally 'so-like.'

5. **Interrogative Pronouns.**—These are *who* (genitive *whos ;* dative and accusative *whom*), *which*, and *what*.

(*a*) What is often used for *why*, like the N. E. or Scotch *what for ?* Cf. line 383 :

> Of hir array *what* sholde I make a tale ?

(*b*) *Which* has often the sense of *what*, *what sort of*. It is used of either gender.

6. **Relative Pronouns.**—In our language in its oldest period,

B

who, which, and *what* were not relative but interrogative pronouns ; *whose* and *whom* were established as relatives as early as the thirteenth century ; but *who* was much later in getting a relative force, and did not come into common use before the end of the sixteenth century.

(*a*) *That* was the ordinary relative in the fourteenth century. It began during the twelfth century to take the place of the indeclinable relative *the.*

(*b*) *That* is often used with the personal pronouns ; thus, *that he* = who ; *that his* = whose ; *that him* = whom.

(*c*) *Which that* = who (line 205) ; *the whiche* = who (line 269) ; *what that* = whatsoever (line 165) ; *what man that* = whoever.

7. **Indefinite Pronouns.**—*Me* and *men* (broken down from *man*) are used for one, like the French *on.*

VERBS.

Verbs are classified, according to their mode of expressing the past tense, into **strong** and **weak** verbs. **Strong Verbs** form their past tense by change of the root vowel ; nothing is added to the root ; **Weak Verbs** form their past tense by adding -*ede* (-*de*, -*te*) to the root of the present. The final *e* often drops off, leaving the suffix -*ed* as the tense-sign.

I. REGULAR OR WEAK VERBS.

INDICATIVE MOOD.

PRESENT TENSE.

Singular.	*Plural.*
1. I lovĕ.	We loven, lovĕ.
2. Thou lovest.	Ye loven, lovĕ.
3. He loveth.	They loven, lovĕ.

PAST TENSE.

Singular	*Plural.*
1. I lovede.	We loveden, lovede.
2. Thou lovedest.	Ye loveden, lovede.
3. He lovede.	They loveden, lovede.

Properly speaking, the past tense is formed only by the suffix -*de,* the *e* in -*ede* being the connecting vowel which joins the tense-suffix to the base. In a few verbs with a long radical vowel this connecting vowel disappears, and -*de* or -*te* only is added to the base, as in *kepen, kepte ; deme, demde.* Some few weak verbs admit of a change of vowel in the past tense, as *delen, dalte ; leden, ladde ; leven, lafte.* If the root ends in *d* or *t,* preceded by another consonant, *ĕ* only is added, as in *senden, sent(e) ; wenden, went(e)*.

II. IRREGULAR OR STRONG VERBS.

Strong verbs differ from weak verbs in *not adding* any tense-suffix, the past tense being formed by vowel-change, while the past participle ends in *-en* (and by loss of *n*, in *-e*), as *holde, held, iholden, holde ; sterven, starf, storven* or *storve*.

(*a*) Some strong verbs are inflected like weak verbs, and show double forms in their past tenses, as *sleep* and *slep-te ; weep* and *wep-te*.

(*b*) Many verbs admit of a distinct vowel-change for the past-tense plural, as *sterven*, to die, past singular *starf*, past plural *storven ; binden*, to bind, past singular *band*, past plural *bunden ; write*, to write, past singular *wrat*, past plural *writen*. The second person singular had also this vowel-change, as *thou bunde*, etc.

(*c*) The first and third persons of the past indicative have no personal suffixes. That of the second person was originally *-e*, but *-est* often replaces it in verbs of the fourteenth century. Hence the conjugation of the past tense is as follows :

Singular.	*Plural.*
1. held (I held).	held-en (we held).
2. helde (thou heldest).	held-en (ye held).
3. held (he held).	held-en (they held).

Both strong and weak verbs (when the stem ends in *-t, -d, -nd, -s*) have in the third person singular present indicative *-t* for *-teth* or *-deth*, or even *-eth*, as *halt = holdeth ; rit = rideth ; sent = sendeth ; rist = riseth ; bit = biddeth ; hit = hideth*.

Subjunctive Mood.—In the present subjunctive, through all persons, the singular ends in *-e*, and the plural in *-en ;* in the past, in *-ede, -de, -te*, plural in *-eden, -den, -ten*.

Imperative Mood.—(*a*) The singular usually ends in *-e* in the case of verbs conjugated like *loven*, as *love thou*. All other verbs have no final *-e*.

(*b*) The plural terminates usually in *-eth* or *-th*, though the *-th* is often dropped.

Infinitive Mood.—(*a*) The Infinitive ends in *-en* or *-e*. The *-n* began to drop off in the Southern English dialect in the four-teenth century. See lines 13, 14, 52, 75, 99, etc.

(*b*) The gerundial infinitive, or dative case of the infinitive (preceded by *to*) is used to express purpose. In Old English this dative had the suffix *-e*, and was governed by the preposition *to* (as *tô witanne*, to know, our 'to wit'). This *e* remains in M. E., but has dropped off in modern English, which retains the construction, without the inflectional mark, as in 'I came *to tell* you,' 'this house is *to let*.' See lines 76, 81, 211, 683.

Participles.—(*a*) The present participle ends generally in *ing*. The present part. of the southern dialect ended in *inde, ende*, corresponding to the form *-ande*, which was retained in the northern dialects to a late period (Spenser has *glitterand* and *trenchand*). The modern form in *-ing* began to arise in the southern dialects in the latter part of the twelfth century. The change of *-inde* to *-ing* has caused great confusion between verbal nouns in *-ing* (O. E. *-ung*) and participles in *-ing*.

(*b*) Weak verbs had their past participle in *ed* or *d* ; strong verbs in *en* or *e* (the *n* having fallen away, as still happens in the Rhine country. Examples of the past participle in *-e* occur in lines 146, 214, 310, 1158, etc.

(*c*) The prefix *y-* or *i-* (A.S. *ge*) is frequent before the past participle. See lines 158, 213, 381, 771, etc.

DEFECTIVE VERBS.

The principal of these are *ben, been*, to be ; *conne*, to know, to be able ; *daren*, to dare ; *may ; mot ; owen*, to owe *; schal ; thar*, need ; *witen*, to know ; and *wil*. They are thus declined :

PRES. INDIC.

Sing.	*Plur.*
1. Am.	Beon, ben, aren, *or* are.
2. Art.	
3. Beth *or* is.	

Past tense, 1st and 3d, was ; 2d, were.

Beth in the imperat. pl. ; and ben (been) in the past part.

PRES. INDIC.

1. Can (I know).	Connen, conne.
2. Canst, can.	
3. Can.	

Past tense, 1st and 3d, couthe ; past part. couth, coud.

PRES. INDIC.

1. Dar (dare).	Dar *or* dorre.
2. Darst.	
3. Dar.	

Past tense, dorste, durste.

PRES. INDIC.

1. Mow *or* may.   Mowe *or* mowen.
2. Mayst *or* maist.
3. May.

Past tense, 1st and 3d, mighte, moghte.

PRES. INDIC.

1. Mot *or* moot (must).   Mooten *or* moote.
2. Must *or* moot.
3. Mot *or* moot.

Past tense, moste.

PRES. INDIC.

1. Schal.   Schullen *or* schul.
2. Schalt.
3. Schal.

Past tense, schulde and scholde.

PRES. INDIC.

1. Wat *or* wot.   Witen, wite, *or* woote.
2. Wost.
3. Wat *or* wot.

Past tense, wiste.

PRES. INDIC.

1. Wil, wol, wille.   Woln, willen *or* wille.
2. Wilt *or* wolt.
3. Wile, wol, wille.

Past tense, wolde.

The O. E. negative *ne* combines with verbs as follows :

Nam	for ne am.	Nil, Nille	for ne will.*
Nis	" ne is.	Noldë	" ne woldë.
Nas	" ne was.	Not	" ne wot.
Nere	" ne were.	Nost	" ne wost.
Nath	" ne hath.	Niste	" ne wiste.
Nadde	" ne had.	Nisten	" ne wisten.

* Cf. the phrase *Nilly willy* (= *nill he, will he*).

ADVERBS.

(*a*) These are formed from adjectives by adding -*e* to the positive degree, as *soth, sooth*, true ; *sothe, soothe*, truly.

(*b*) Adverbs that now end in -*ly* formerly ended in -*liche* (-*like*). Several have *e* before *ly*, as *boldely, softely, trewely.*

(*c*) Many adverbs are cases of nouns and adjectives—**genitive,** as *needes, whiles, twies ;* **dative,** as *hwil-um*, from *whil* = time ; *seld-um*, from *seld* = rare ; **accusative,** *alway*, from *ealne weg.*

(*d*) Adverbs occur in -*en* and -*e*, as *biforn, bifore ; withouten.*

withoute.   Many have dropped the form in -*n*, as *asondre,* *biyonde; henne, thenne.*

(*e*) Adverbs in -*es* are either *genitives,* as *needes,* &c. ; or the -*es* corresponds to -*e,* -*an,* or -*a,* as *unnethes* (A.S. *uneáthe*), *bysides* (A.S. *besidan*) ; to -*e* or -*en* as *hennes* (A.S. *heonnan*), *thennes* (A.S. *thanan*) ; or to -*st,* as in *agaynes,* ayens (A.S. *agean*).

(*f*) Many adverbs arise in prepositional forms, as, *of-newe* = newly, *on-sleep* = asleep.

Negative Adverbs.—Two negatives in Chaucer's usage do not make an affirmative.

PREPOSITIONS.—*Till* is used in M. E. as a sign of the infinitive; it formed numerous compounds, as *intil* = into.   It first made its appearance as a preposition in the northern dialect.   *Endelong* = down along (A.S. *andlang*).

CONJUNCTIONS.—*Ne* .... *ne* = neither .... nor ; *other* = or, *other* .... *other* = either .... or ; *what* .... *and* = both .... and.

CHAUCER'S VERSIFICATION.

1. **The Measure.**—Almost every poem in the *Canterbury Tales* is written in the measure called Rimed Iambic Pentameter. Each line contains five 'feet,' and in each foot there are two syllables, the first being unaccented.   When this kind of verse is unrimed, it is called blank verse; when it is rimed, heroic verse.   In either form, it is by far the most usual kind of English verse.   The *Clerkes Tale* is written in stanzas of seven lines of heroics, with three rimes, the first two alternating in a quatrain, the rime of the fourth line repeated in the fifth, and the third rime forming the sixth and seventh lines into a couplet. Chaucer borrowed this form from the French, and it became his favourite stanza.   The rime may be expressed by the formula *a b a b b c c,* by which is meant that the first and third lines rime together, as denoted by *a a ;* the second, fourth, and fifth lines rime together, as denoted by *b b b ;* and the last two, *c c.* In England, it was afterwards called *rime royal,* from its use not many years after the death of Chaucer by King James I. of Scotland, as the measure of the *King's Quhair.*

2. Trisyllabic measures sometimes occur owing to the rapid pronunciation of some syllable.   The chief syllables thus slurred

over are : final *y, -es, -er, -ie, -en, -ed,* and *-e.* In many cases *e* occurring in the middle of a word is similarly slurred over, as in eu*e*ry (line 595), nam*e*ly (line 626 and 934), reman*e*nt (line 869), reu*e*rently (line 952), etc.

3. Chaucer is fond of having eleven syllables in his line. Of course the additional syllable is unaccented. Were it accented, there would be six accents in the verse, and the line would be a hexameter. This additional unaccented syllable is generally at the end, and makes what is called a *feminine rime.* See lines 104 and 105, 182 and 183, 258 and 259, and the whole *Envoy,* lines 1177–1212, with its thirty-six consecutive rimes of this kind.

4. A final vowel is often elided or run on into a following one. The vowel with which this happens most frequently is *ë.* See lines 411, 433, etc.

5. A word adopted by Chaucer from the Norman-French may have the French accent, or it may have the English accent. (The tendency of the English accent is to go as far back—as near the beginning of a word as possible ; and it sometimes, in pursuit of this, invades a mere prefix—as in *péremptory, míscellany.*) Thus Chaucer makes no scruple about giving us *miróur* and *miróur ; róial* and *roiál ; léon* and *leóun ; hónour* and *honoúr.*

Some words of French origin are pronounced as in modern French ; thus *humble* (line 603), *stable* (line 663), *possible* (line 956), *tendre* (line 1093), are pronounced *humbl', stabl', possibl', tendr'.*

6. The final *ë,* as in French verse, may be sounded or not, as the verse demands.

(i.) In words of **Anglo-Saxon** origin it represents one of the **final vowels** a, u, e, and is thus essential. Thus *sonne,* the sun, from A.S. *sunne* (392), *knaue* from A.S. *cnafa* (444). It may represent also a **Latin** termination, as diadem*e,* from Lat. *diadema.*

(ii.) It is also a remnant of various **grammatical inflections.**

(*a*) It represents the **dative** case in **nouns** ; as stall*e* (lines 207 and 291), fest*e* (line 191), birth*e* (line 402), lapp*e* (line 585), etc.

(*b*) In **adjectives** it marks (1) the **definite form of the adjective** (that is, that form of the adjective which is preceded by *the, this, that,* or a *possessive pronoun*), as in the yong*e* (line 77), old*e* poure (line 222), new*e* (line 841), etc. ; (2) the **plural** of adjectives, as all*e* (line 38 and 188), old*e* (61),

wyse (line 116); (3) the **vocative** case of adjectives, as, O good*e*
god ! (line 852), O tendr*e*, o der*e*, o yonge children myn*e*
(line 1093).

(*c*) In **verbs**, final *e* is a sign :

(1) Of the **Infinitive** mood, as to wepe (line 13), **wyue**
(line 140), worshipe (line 166), deye (line 364), etc.

(2) Of the **Gerundial Infinitive**, as to blame (line 76), to
hauke and hunte (line 81), to speke (line 211), **to saue**
(line 683), to doone (line 99).

(3) Of the **past participles** of **strong** verbs, as bor*e*
(line 401), ybore (lines 158 and 443), swore (line 403).

(4) Of the **past tense** of **weak** verbs, as hadde (line
303), highte (line 210), *preyde* (line 548).

(5) Of the **Subjunctive** mood, as leste (105), were (line
850).

(6) Of the **Imperative** mood, as telle (line 15), keepe
(line 17), etc.

(*d*) In **adverbs**, the final *e* represents—

(1) An **older vowel** ending, as soone (line 277), A.S. *sóna*.

(2) It is the **characteristic** ending of the adverb as
distinguished from the adjective, as stille (line 293), newe
(line 3), bryghte (line 1117).

(3) It represents an **Anglo-Saxon** ending -an, as aboute,
from A.S. *ábútan ;* above, from A.S. *ábúfan.*

(4) It is a **distinct syllable** in **adverbs** ending in **ely, as**
trewely (line 53), poureliche (line 213), richely (line 267).

(iii.) It is sometimes **superfluous**, having crept into the word,
as in *bitwixe* from Anglo-Saxon *betwux ; quene,* from A.S. *cwén ;*
childe, from A.S. *cild.* Final *e* is usually written in the personal
pronouns, as oure, youre, hire, here, hise, and in this case is
silent. It is silent also where it occurs in words of more than
one syllable, and in words of Romance origin. See, however,
excellentë (*Squieres Tale,* line 145).

7. Besides, in the case of being followed by a word beginning
with a vowel, final *e* is elided before some few words beginning
with *h,* as he, his, him, hem, hir, hath, hadde, have, her, etc. In
all other cases *h* is considered as a consonant.

8. The syllables -*en,* -*er,* -*eth,* -*el,* and -*ow* are often contracted
or slurred over in pronunciation. Cf. lines 134, 376, 426, 627,
etc.

THE CLERKES TALE.

'Sir clerk of Oxenford,' our hoste sayde,
'Ye ryde as coy and stille as dooth a mayde,
Were newe spoused, sitting at the bord;
This day ne herde I of your tonge a word.
I trowe ye studie aboute som sophyme,   5
But Salomon seith, "euery thing hath tyme."
  For goddes sake, as beth of bettre chere,
It is no tyme for to studien here.
Telle vs som merie tale, by your fey;
For what man that is entred in a pley,   10
He nedes moot vnto the pley assente.
But precheth nat, as freres doon in lente,
To make vs for our olde synnes wepe,
Ne that thy tale make vs nat to slepe.
  Telle vs som merie thing of auentures;—   15
Your termes, your colours, and your figures,
Keepe hem in stoor til so be ye endite
Hy style, as whan that men to kinges write.
Speketh so pleyn at this tyme, we yow preye,
That we may vnderstonde what ye seye.'   20
  This worthy clerk benignely answerde,
'Hoste,' quod he, 'I am vnder your yerde;

Ye han of vs as now the gouernaunce,   *mostli*
And therfor wol I do yow obeisaunce,
As fer as reson axeth, hardily.   **25**
I wol yow telle a tale which that I
Lerned at Padowe of a worthy clerk,   *Padua*
As preued by his wordes and his werk.
He is now deed and nailed in his cheste,
I prey to god so yiue his soule reste !   **30**
    Fraunceys Petrark, the laureat poete,   *Francesco Pet-*
Highte this clerk, whos rethorike sweete   *language*
Enlumined al Itaille of poetrye,   *with his*
As Linian dide of philosophye   *with*
Or lawe, or other art particuler ;   **35**
But deeth, that wol nat [suffre vs] dwellen heer   *just*
But as it were a twinkling of an eye,
Hem bothe hath slayn, and alle shul we dye.
    But forth to tellen of this worthy man,
That taughte me this tale, as I bigan,   *which I have mentio*   **40**
I seye that first with hy style he enditeth,   *principal*
Er he the body of his tale writeth,   *part*
A proheme, in the which discryueth he
Pemond, and of Saluces the contree,   *Piedmont N.I.*
And speketh of Apennyn, the hilles hye,   **45**
That been the boundes of West Lumbardye,
    And of Mount Vesulus in special,
Where as the Poo out of a welle smal
Taketh his firste springing and his sours,
That Estward ay encresseth in his cours   **50**
To Emelward, to Ferrare, and Venyse ;   *Venetia*
The which a long thing were to deuyse.   *Aemelia*
And trewely, as to my iugement,
Me thinketh it a thing impertinent,
Saue that he wol conueyen his matere,   **55**
But this his tale [is], which that ye may here.'

It seems to me a thing irrelevant
excepting that he wishes to introduce his story

Heere bigynneth the tale of the Clerk of Oxenford.

Ther is, at the West syde of Itaille,
Doun at the roote of Vesulus the colde,
A lusty playne, habundant of vitaille,
Wher many a tour and toun thou mayst biholde,   60
That founded were in tyme of fadres olde,
And many another delitable sighte,
And Saluces this noble contree highte.

A markis whylom lord was of that londe,
As were his worthy eldres him bifore ;   65
And obeisant and redy to his honde
Were alle his liges, bothe lasse and more.
Thus in delyt he liueth, and hath doon yore,
Biloued and drad thurgh fauour of fortune
Bothe of his lordes and of his commune.   70

Therwith he was, to speke as of linage,
The gentilleste yborn of Lumbardye,
A fair persone, and strong, and yong of age,
And ful of honour and of curteisye ;
Discreet ynough his contree for to gye,   75
Saue in somme thinges that he was to blame,
And Walter was this yonge lordes name.

I blame him thus, that he considereth nought
In tyme coming what him myghte bityde,
But on his lust present was al his thought,   80
As for to hauke and hunte on euery syde ;
Wel ny alle othere cures leet he slyde,
And eek he nolde, and that was worst of alle,
Wedde no wyf, for ought that may bifalle.

Only that point his peple bar so sore,   85
That flokmele on a day they to him wente,
And oon of hem, that wisest was of lore,
Or elles that the lord best wolde assente
That he sholde telle him what his peple mente,
Or elles coude he shewe wel swich matere,   90
He to the markis seyde as ye shul here.

'O noble markis, your humanitee
Assureth vs, and yiueth vs hardinesse,
As ofte as tyme is of necessitee
That we to yow mowe telle our heuinesse;   95
Accepteth, lord, now for your gentillesse,
That we with pitous herte vn-to yow pleyne,
And lete your eres nat my voys disdeyne.

Al haue I nought to doone in this matere
More than another man hath in this place,   100
Yet for as muche as ye, my lord so dere,
Han alwey shewed me fauour and grace,
I dar the better aske of yow a space
Of audience to shewen our requeste,
And ye, my lord, to doon right as yow leste.   105

For certes, lord, so wel vs lyketh yow
And al your werk and euer han doon, that we
Ne coude nat vs self deuysen how
We myghte liuen in more felicitee,
Saue o thing, lord, if [it] your wille be,   110
That for to been a wedded man yow leste,
Than were your peple in souereyn hertes reste.

Boweth your nekke vnder that blisful yok
Of souereynetee, nought of seruyse,
Which that men clepeth spousail or wedlok;   115
And thenketh, lord, among your thoughtes wyse,

How that our dayes passe in sondry wyse;
For though we slepe or wake, or rome, or ryde,
Ay fleeth the tyme, it nil no man abyde.

And though your grene youthe floure as yit,   120
In crepeth age alwey, as stille as stoon,
And deeth manaceth euery age, and smit
In ech estaat, for ther escapeth noon :
And al so certein as we knowe echoon
That we shul deye, as vncerteyn we alle   125
Been of that day whan deeth shal on vs falle.

Accepteth than of vs the trewe entente,
That neuer yet refuseden your heste,
And we wol, lord, if that ye wol assente,
Chese yow a wyf in short tyme atte leste,   130
Born of the gentilleste and of the meste
Of al this lond, so that it oughte seme
Honour to god and yow, as we can deme.

Deliuer vs out of al this bisy drede,
And tak a wyf, for hye goddes sake ;   135
For if it so bifelle, as god forbede,
That thurgh your deeth your linage sholde slake,
And that a straunge successour sholde take
Your heritage, o ! wo were vs alyue !
Wherfor we pray you hastily to wyue.'   140

Her meke preyere and her pitous chere
Made the markis herte han pitee.
' Ye wol,' quod he, ' myn owen peple dere,
To that I neuer erst thoughte streyne me.
I me reioysed of my libertee,   145
That selde tyme is founde in mariage ;
Ther I was free, I moot been in seruage.

But nathelees I se your trewe entente,
And truste vpon your wit and haue doon ay;
Wherfor of my free wille I wol assente   150
To wedde me, as soone as euer I may.
But ther as ye han profred me this day
To chese me a wyf, I yow relesse
That choys, and prey yow of that profre cesse.

For god it woot, that children ofte been   155
Vnlyk her worthy eldres hem bifore;
Bountee comth al of god, nat of the streen
Of which they been engendred and ybore;
I truste in goddes bountee, and therfore
My mariage and myn estaat and reste   160
I him bitake; he may doon as him leste.

Lat me alone in chesing of my wyf,
That charge vp-on my bak I wol endure;
But I yow preye, and charge vp-on your lyf,
That what wyf that I take, ye me assure   165
To worshipe hir, whyl that hir lyf may dure,
In word and werk, bothe here and euerywhere,
As she an emperoures doughter were.

And forthermore, this shal ye swere, that ye
Agayn my choys shul neither grucche ne stryue;   170
For sith I shal forgoon my libertee
At your requeste, as euer moot I thryue,
Ther as myn herte is set, ther wol I wyue;
And but ye wole assente in swich manere,
I prey yow, speketh namore of this matere.'   175

With hertly wil they sworen, and assenten
To al this thing, ther seyde no wight nay;

Bisekinge him of grace, er that they wenten,
That he wolde graunten hem a certein day
Of his spousaille, as sone as euer he may;   180
For yet alwey the peple som-what dredde
Lest that this markis no wyf wolde wedde.

He graunted hem a day, swich as him leste,
On which he wolde be wedded sikerly,
And seyde he dide al this at her requeste;   185
And they with humble entente buxomly
Knelinge vp-on her knees ful reuerently
Him thanken alle, and thus they han an ende
Of her entente, and hoom agayn they wende.

And heer-vp-on he to his officeres   190
Comaundeth for the feste to purveye,
And to his priuee knyghtes and squieres
Swich charge yaf, as him liste on hem leye;
And they to his comandement obeye,
And ech of hem doth al his diligence   195
To doon vn-to the feste reuerence.

Explicit prima pars.
Incipit secunda pars.

Noght fer fro thilke paleys honurable
Ther as this markis shoop his mariage,
Ther stood a throp, of site delytable,
In which that poure folk of that village   200
Hadden her bestes and her herbergage,
And of her labour tooke her sustenance
After that the erthe yaf hem habundance.

Amonges this poure folk ther dwelte a man
Which that was holden pourest of hem alle;   205
But hye god som tyme senden can
His grace in-to a litel oxes stalle:

Ianicula men of that thrope him calle.
A doughter hadde he fair ynough to sighte,
And Grisildis this yonge mayden highte.   210

But for to speke of vertuous beautee,
Than was she oon the faireste vnder sonne;
For poureliche yfostred vp was she,
No likerous lust was thurgh hir herte yronne;
Wel ofter of the welle than of the tonne   215
She drank, and for she wolde vertu plese,
She knew wel labour, but noon ydel ese.

But though this mayde tendre were of age,
Yet in the brest of hir virginitee
Ther was enclosed rype and sad corage;   220
And in greet reuerence and charitee
Hir olde poure fader fostred she;
A fewe sheep spinning on feeld she kepte,
She wolde nought been ydel til she slepte.

And whan she homward cam, she wolde bringe   225
Wortes or othere herbes tymes ofte,
The whiche she shredde and seeth for hir liuinge,
And made hir bed ful harde and no thing softe;
And ay she kepte hir fadres lyf on-lofte
With euerich obeisaunce and diligence   230
That child may doon to fadres reuerence.

Vp-on Grisilde this poure creature
Ful ofte sythe this markis sette his eye
As he on hunting rood parauenture;
And whan it fil that he myghte hir espye,   235
He nought with wantoun loking of folye
His eyen caste on hir, but in sad wyse
Vp-on hir chere he wolde him ofte auyse,

Commending in his herte hir wommanhede,
And eek hir vertu, passing any wight   240
Of so yong age, as wel in chere as dede.
For though the peple haue no greet insight
In vertu, he considered ful right
Hir bountee, and disposed that he wolde
Wedde hir oonly, if euer he wedde sholde.   245

The day of wedding cam, but no wight can
Telle what womman that it sholde be;
For which merueille wondred many a man,
And seyden, whan they were in priuetee,
'Wol nat our lord yet leue his vanitee?   250
Wol he nat wedde? allas, allas the whyle!
Why wol he thus him-self and vs bigyle?'

But natheles this markis hath doon make
Of gemmes, set in gold and in asure,
Broches and ringes, for Grisildis sake,   255
And of hir clothing took he the mesure
By a mayde, lyk to hir stature,
And eek of othere ornamentes alle
That vn-to swich a wedding sholde falle.

The tyme of vndern of the same day   260
Approcheth, that this wedding sholde be;
And al the paleys put was in array,
Bothe halle and chambres, ech in his degree;
Houses of office stuffed with plentee
Ther maystow seen of deynteuous vitaille,   265
That may be founde, as fer as last Itaille.

This roial markis richely arrayed,
Lordes and ladyes in his companye,
The whiche vnto the feste were yprayed,
And of his retenue the bachelrye,   270

full musical accompaniments

With many a soun of sondry melodye,
Vn-to the village, of the which I tolde,
In this array the righte wey han holde.

Grisilde of this, god wot, ful innocent,
That for hir shapen was al this array,   275
To fecchen water at a welle is went,
And cometh hoom as soone as euer she may.
For wel she had herd seyd, that thilke day
The markis sholde wedde, and, if she myghte,
She wolde fayn han seyn som of that sighte.   280

She thoughte, 'I wol with othere maydens stonde,
That been my felawes, in our dore, and se
The markisesse, and therfor wol I fonde
To doon at hoom, as soone as it may be,
The labour which that longeth vn-to me;   285
And than I may at leyser hir biholde,
If she this wey vn-to the castel holde.'

And as she wolde ouer hir threshfold goon,
The markis cam and gan hir for to calle;
And she sette doun hir water-pot anoon   290
Bisyde the threshfold, in an oxes stalle,
And doun vp-on hir knees she gan to falle,
And with sad contenance kneleth stille
Til she had herd what was the lordes wille.

This thoughtful markis spak vn-to this mayde   295
Ful sobrely, and seyde in this manere,
'Wher is your fader, Grisildis?' he sayde,
And she with reuerence, in humble chere,
Answerde, 'lord, he is al redy here.'
And in she gooth with-outen lenger lette,   *further delay*   300
And to the markis she hir fader fette.

He by the hond than took this olde man,
And seyde thus, whan he him hadde asyde,
'Ianicula, I neither may ne can
Lenger the plesance of myn herte hyde.   305
If that thou vouche sauf, what so bityde,
Thy doughter wol I take er that I wende
As for my wyf, vn-to hir lyues ende.

Thou louest me, I wot it wel certeyn,
And art my feithful lige man ybore;   310
And al that lyketh me, I dar wel seyn,
It lyketh thee, and specially therfore
Tel me that poynt that I haue seyd bifore,
If that thou wolt vn-to that purpos drawe,
To take me as for thy sone in lawe?'   315

This sodeyn cas this man astonied so,
That reed he wex, abayst, and al quaking
He stood; vnnethes seyde he wordes mo,
But only thus: 'lord,' quod he, 'my willing
Is as ye wole, ne ayeins youre lyking   320
I wol no-thing; ye be my lord so dere;
Right as yow lust gouerneth this matere.'

'Yet wol I,' quod this markis softely,
'That in thy chambre I and thou and she
Haue a collacion, and wostow why?   325
For I wol axe if it hir wille be
To be my wyf, and reule hir after me;
And al this shal be doon in thy presence,
I wol nought speke out of thyn audience.'

And in the chambre whyl they were aboute   330
Her tretys, which as ye shal after here,

The peple cam vn-to the hous with-oute,
And wondred hem in how honeste manere
And tentifly she kepte hir fader dere.
But outerly Grisildis wondre myghte,   335
For neuer erst ne sey she swich a sighte.

No wonder is though [that] she were astoned
To seen so greet a gest come in that place ;
She neuer was to swiche gestes woned,
For which she loked with ful pale face.   340
But shortly forth this tale for to chace,
Thise arn the wordes that the markis sayde
To this benigne verray feithful mayde.

'Grisilde,' he seyde, 'ye shul wel vnderstonde
It lyketh to your fader and to me   345
That I yow wedde, and eek it may so stonde,
As I suppose, ye wol that it so be.
But thise demandes axe I first,' quod he,
'That, sith it shal be doon in hastif wyse,
Wol ye assente or elles yow auyse?   350

I seye this, be ye redy with good herte
To al my lust, and that I frely may,
As me best thinketh, do yow laughe or smerte,
And neuer ye to grucche it, nyght ne day?
And eek whan I sey "ye," ne sey nat "nay,"   355
Neither by word ne frowning contenance ;
Swer this, and here I swere our alliance.'

Wondring vp-on this word, quaking for drede,
She seyde, 'lord, vndigne and vnworthy
Am I to thilke honour that ye me bede ;   360
But as ye wol your-self, right so wol I.

And heer I swere that neuer willingly
In werk ne thought I nil yow disobeye,
For to be deed, though me were loth to deye.'

'This is ynough, Grisilde myn!' quod he. 365
And forth he goth with a ful sobre chere
Out at the dore, and after that cam she,
And to the peple he seyde in this manere,
'This is my wyf,' quod he, 'that standeth here.
Honoureth hir, and loueth hir, I preye, 370
Who so me loueth; ther is namore to seye.'

And for that no-thing of hir olde gere
She sholde bringe in-to his hous, he bad
That wommen sholde dispoilen hir right there;
Of which thise ladyes were nat right glad 375
To handle hir clothes wher-in she was clad,
But natheles this mayde bright of hewe
Fro foot to heed they clothed han al newe.

Hir heres han they kembd, that lay vntressed
Ful rudely, and with her fingres smale 380
A corone on hir heed they han ydressed,
And sette hir ful of nowches grete and smale;
Of hir array what sholde I make a tale?
Vnnethe the peple hir knew for hir fairnesse,
Whan she translated was in swich richesse. 385

This markis hath hir spoused with a ring
Brought for the same cause, and than hir sette
Vp-on an hors, snow-whyt and wel ambling,
And to his paleys, er he lenger lette,
With ioyful peple that hir ladde and mette, 390
Conueyed hir, and thus the day they spende
In reuel til the sonne gan descende.

And shortly forth this tale for to chace,
I seye that to this newe markisesse
God hath swich fauour sent hir of his grace,   395
That it ne semed nat by lyklinesse
That she was born and fed in rudenesse,
As in a cote or in an oxe-stalle,
But norished in an emperoures halle.

To euery wight she woxen is so dere   400
And worshipful, that folk ther she was bore
And from hir birthe knewe hir yeer by yere,
Vnnethe trowed they, but dorste han swore
That to Ianicle, of which I spak bifore,
She doughter nas, for, as by coniecture,   405
Hem thoughte she was another creature.

For though that euer vertuous was she,
She was encressed in swich excellence
Of thewes goode, yset in heigh bountee,
And so discreet and fair of eloquence,   410
So benigne and so digne of reuerence,
And coude so the peples herte embrace,
That ech hir louede that loked on hir face.

Nought only of Saluces in the toun
Publisshed was the bountee of hir name,   415
But eek bisyde in many a regioun,
If oon seyde wel, another seyde the same;
So spradde of hir heigh bountee the fame,
That men and wommen, as wel yonge as olde,
Gon to Saluce, vpon hir to biholde.   420

Thus Walter lowly, nay but roially,
Wedded with fortunat honestetee,
In goddes pees lyueth ful esily
At hoom, and outward grace ynough had he;

And for he sey that vnder low degree   425
Was [ofte] vertu hid, the peple him helde
A prudent man, and that is seyn ful selde.

Nat only this Grisildis thurgh hir wit
Coude al the feet of wyfly homlinesse,
But eek, whan that the cas required it,   430
The commune profit coude she redresse.
Ther nas discord, rancour, ne heuinesse
In al that lond, that she ne coude apese,
And wysly bringe hem alle in reste and ese.

Though that hir housbonde absent were anoon,   435
If gentil men, or othere of hir contree
Were wrothe, she wolde bringen hem atoon;
So wise and rype wordes hadde she,
And iugementz of so greet equitee,
That she from heuen sent was, as men wende,   440
Peple to saue and euery wrong tamende.

Nat longe tyme after that this Grisild
Was wedded, she a doughter hath ybore,
Al had hir leuer haue born a knaue child.
Glad was this markis and the folk therfore;   445
For though a mayde child come al bifore,
She may vnto a knaue child atteyne
By lyklihed, sin she nis nat bareyne.

Explicit secunda pars.
Incipit tercia pars.

Ther fil, as it bifalleth tymes mo,
Whan that this child had souked but a throwe,   450
This markis in his herte longeth so
To tempte his wyf, hir sadnesse for to knowe,

That he ne myghte out of his herte throwe
This meruellous desyr, his wyf tassaye,
Needlees, god wot, he thoughte hir for taffraye.   **455**

He hadde assayed hir ynough bifore
And fond hir euer good ; what neded it
Hir for to tempte and alwey more and more ?
Though som men preise it for a subtil wit,
But as for me, I seye that yuel it sit   **460**
Tassaye a wyf whan that it is no nede,
And putten her in anguish and in drede.

For which this markis wroughte in this manere ;
He cam alone a-nyghte, ther as she lay,
With sterne face and with ful trouble chere,   **465**
And seyde thus, ' Grisild,' quod he, ' that day
That I yow took out of your poure array,
And putte yow in estaat of heigh noblesse,
Ye haue nat that forgeten, as I gesse.

I seye, Grisild, this present dignitee,   **470**
In which that I haue put yow, as I trowe,
Maketh yow nat foryetful for to be
That I yow took in poure estaat ful lowe
For any wele ye moot your-seluen knowe.
Tak hede of euery word that I yow seye,   **475**
Ther is no wight that hereth it but we tweye.

Ye woot your-self wel, how that ye came here
In-to this hous, it is nat longe ago,
And though to me that ye be lief and dere,
Vn-to my gentils ye be no-thing so ;   **480**
They seyn, to hem it is greet shame and wo
For to be subgetz and been in seruage
To thee, that born art of a smal village.

And namely, sith thy doughter was ybore,
Thise wordes han they spoken doutelees;   485
But I desyre, as I haue doon bifore,
To liue my lyf with hem in reste and pees;
I may nat in this cas be recchelees.
I mot don with thy doughter for the beste,
Nat as I wolde, but as my peple leste.   490

And yet, god wot, this is ful looth to me;
But natheles with-oute your witing
I wol nat don, but this wol I,' quod he,
'That ye to me assente as in this thing.
Shewe now your pacience in your werking   495
That ye me hyghte and swore in your village
That day that maked was our mariage.'

Whan she had herd al this, she nought ameued
Neither in word, or chere, or countenance;
For, as it semed, she was nat agreued: 500
She seyde, 'lord, al lyth in your plesance,
My child and I with hertly obeisance
Ben youres al, and ye mowe saue or spille
Your owen thing; werketh after your wille.

Ther may no-thing, god so my soule saue,   505
Lyken to yow that may displese me;
Ne I ne desyre no-thing for to haue,
Ne drede for to lese, saue only ye;
This wil is in myn herte and ay shal be.
No lengthe of tyme or deeth may this deface,   510
Ne chaunge my corage to another place.'

Glad was this markis of hir answering,
But yet he feyned as he were nat so;

Al drery was his chere and his loking
Whan that he sholde out of the chambre go.   515
Sone after this, a furlong wey or two,
He priuely hath told al his entente
Vn-to a man, and to his wyf him sente.

A maner sergeant was this priuee man,
The which that feithful ofte he founden hadde   520
In thinges grete, and eek swich folk wel can
Doon execucion on thinges badde.
The lord knew wel that he him louede and dradde,
And whan this sergeant wiste his lordes wille,
In-to the chambre he stalked him ful stille.   525

'Madame,' he seyde, 'ye mote foryiue it me,
Though I do thing to which I am constreyned;
Ye ben so wys that ful wel knowe ye
That lordes hestes mowe nat ben yfeyned;
They mowe wel ben biwailled or compleyned,   530
But men mot nede vn-to her lust obeye,
And so wol I; ther is namore to seye.

This child I am comanded for to take'—
And spak namore, but out the child he hente
Despitously, and gan a chere make   535
As though he wolde han slayn it er he wente.
Grisildis mot al suffren and consente;
And as a lamb she sitteth meke and stille,
And leet this cruel sergeant doon his wille.

Suspecious was the diffame of this man,   540
Suspect his face, suspect his word also;
Suspect the tyme in which he this bigan.
Allas! hir doughter that she louede so

She wende he wolde han slawen it right tho, *imagined*

But natheles she neither weep ne syked, *sighed*   **545**

Consenting hir to that the markis lyked.

But atte laste speken she bigan,

And mekely she to the sergeant preyde,

So as he was a worthy gentil man,

That she moste kisse hir child er that it deyde ;   **550**

And in her barm this litel child she leyde

With ful sad face, and gan the child to kisse

And lulled it, and after gan it blisse.

And thus she seyde in hir benigne voys,

' Far wel, my child ; I shal thee neuer see ;   **555**

But, sith I thee haue marked with the croys,

Of thilke fader blessed mote thou be,

That for vs deyde vp-on a croys of tree.

Thy soule, litel child, I him bitake, *commit*

For this nyght shaltow deyen for my sake.'   **560**

I trowe that to a norice in this cas *believe*   *nurse*

It had ben hard this rewthe for to se ; *pityful sight*

Wel myghte a moder than han cryed ' allas !'

But natheles so sad stedfast was she,

That she endured all aduersitee,   **565**

And to the sergeant mekely she sayde,

' Haue heer agayn your litel yonge mayde.

Goth now,' quod she, ' and doth my lordes heste,

But o thing wol I preye yow of your grace, *favour*

That, but my lord forbad yow, atte leste   **570**

Burieth this litel body in som place

That bestes ne no briddes it to-race.' *scratch it to pieces*

But he no word wol to that purpos seye,

But took the child and wente vpon his weye. ✗

to = in pieces or apart intensifying pref.

a vatours stomen all to brake his skull

This sergeant cam vn-to his lord ageyn,   575
And of Grisildis wordes and hir chere
He tolde him point for point, in short and playn,
And him presenteth with his doughter dere.
Somwhat this lord hath rewthe in his manere;
But natheles his purpos heeld he stille,   580
As lordes doon whan they wol han hir wille;

And bad his sergeant that he priuely
Sholde this child [ful] softe wynde and wrappe
With alle circumstances tendrely,
And carie it in a cofre or in a lappe;   585
But, vp-on peyne his heed of for to swappe,
That no man sholde knowe of his entente,
Ne whenne he cam, ne whider that he wente;

But at Boloigne to his suster deere,
That thilke tyme of Panik was countesse,   590
He sholde it take and shewe hir this matere,
Bisekinge hir to don hir bisinesse
This child to fostre in alle gentilesse;
And whos child that it was he bad hir hyde
From euery wight, for ought that may bityde.   595

The sergeant goth, and hath fulfild this thing;
But to this markis now retourne we;
For now goth he ful faste ymagining
If by his wyues chere he myghte se,
Or by hir word aperceyue that she   600
Were chaunged; but he neuer hir coude fynde
But euer in oon ylyke sad and kynde.

As glad, as humble, as bisy in seruyse,
And eek in loue as she was wont to be,

Was she to him in euery maner wyse;   605
Ne of hir doughter nought a word spak she.
Noon accident for noon aduersitee   *no accidental sign*
Was seyn in hir, ne neuer hir doughter name *of any calamity*
Ne nempned she, in ernest nor in game.   *was seen in her*

Explicit tercia pars.
Sequitur pars quarta.

In this estaat ther passed ben four yeer   610
Er she with childe was; but, as god wolde,
A knaue child she bar by this Walter,
Ful gracious and fair for to biholde.
And whan that folk it to his fader tolde,
Nat only he, but al his contree, merie   615
Was for this child, and god they thanke and herie.

Whan it was two yeer old, and fro the brest
Departed of his norice, on a day
This markis caughte yet another lest
To tempte his wyf yet ofter, if he may.   620
O needles was she tempted in assay!
But wedded men ne knowe no mesure,   } *Chaucerian humour.*
Whan that they fynde a pacient creature. }

'Wyf,' quod this markis, 'ye han herd er this,
My peple sikly berth our mariage,   625
And namely sith my sone yboren is,
Now is it worse than euer in al our age.   *mind disposition*
The murmur sleeth myn herte and my corage;
For to myne eres comth the voys so smerte,
That it wel ny destroyed hath myn herte.   630

Now sey they thus, "whan Walter is agoon,
Than shal the blood of Ianicle succede

And been our lord, for other haue we noon;"
Swiche wordes seith my peple, out of drede.
Wel oughte I of swich murmur taken hede;   635
For certeinly I drede swich sentence,
Though they nat pleyn speke in myn audience.

I wolde liue in pees, if that I myghte;
Wherfor I am disposed outerly,
As I his suster seruede by nyghte,   640
Right so thenke I to serue him pryuely;
This warne I yow, that ye nat sodeynly
Out of your-self for no wo sholde outraye;
Beth pacient, and ther-of I yow preye.'

'I haue,' quod she, 'seyd thus, and euer shal,   645
I wol no thing, ne nil no thing certayn
But as yow list; nought greueth me at al,
Though that my doughter and my sone be slayn,
At your comandement, this is to sayn.
I haue nought had no part of children tweyne   650
But first siknesse, and after wo and peyne.

Ye ben our lord, doth with your owen thing
Right as yow list; axeth no reed at me.
For, as I lefte at hoom al my clothing,
Whan I first cam to yow, right so,' quod she,   655
'Lefte I my wil and al my libertee,
And took your clothing; wherfor I yow preye,
Doth your plesance, I wol your lust obeye.

And certes, if I hadde prescience
Your wil to knowe er ye your lust me tolde,   660
I wolde it doon with-outen necligence;
But now I wot your lust and what ye wolde,

Al your plesance ferme and stable I holde ;
For wiste I that my deeth wolde do yow ese,
Right gladly wolde I deyen, yow to plese.   665

Deth may nought make no comparisoun
Vn-to your loue :' and, whan this markis sey
The constance of his wyf, he caste adoun
His eyen two, and wondreth that she may
In pacience suffre al this array.   670
And forth he goth with drery contenance,
But to his herte it was ful greet plesance.

This vgly sergeant in the same wyse
That he hir doughter caughte, right so he,
Or worse, if men worse can deuyse,   675
Hath hent hir sone, that ful was of beautee.
And euer in oon so pacient was she,
That she no chere made of heuinesse,
But kiste hir sone, and after gan it blesse ;

Saue this ; she preyede him that, if he myghte,   680
Hir litel sone he wolde in erthe graue,
His tendre lymes, delicat to sighte,
Fro foules and fro bestes for to saue.
But she non answer of him myghte haue.
He wente his wey, as him no thing ne roughte ;   685
But to Boloigne he tendrely it broughte.

This markis wondred euer lenger the more
Vp-on hir pacience, and if that he
Ne hadde soothly knowen ther-bifore,
That parfitly hir children louede she,   690
He wolde haue wend that of som subtiltee,
And of malice or for cruel corage,
That she had suffred this with sad visage.

But wel he knew that next him-self certayn
She louede hir children best in euery wyse.   695
But now of wommen wolde I axen fayn,
If thise assayes myghte nat suffyse?
What coude a sturdy housbond more deuyse
To preue hir wyfhod and hir stedfastnesse,
And he continuing euer in sturdinesse?   700

But ther ben folk of swich condicion,
That, whan they haue a certein purpos take,
They can nat stinte of hir entencion,
But, right as they were bounden to a stake,
They wol nat of that firste purpos slake.   705
Right so this markis fulliche hath purposed
To tempte his wyf, as he was first disposed.

He waiteth, if by word or contenance
That she to him was changed of corage;
But neuer coude he fynde variance;   710
She was ay oon in herte and in visage;
And ay the ferther that she was in age,
The more trewe, if that it were possible,
She was to him in loue, and more penible.

For which it semed thus, that of hem two   715
Ther nas but o wil; for, as Walter leste,
The same lust was hir plesance also,
And, god be thanked, al fil for the beste.
She shewed wel, for no worldly vnreste
A wyf as of hir-self no thing ne sholde   720
Wille in effect, but as hir housbond wolde.

The sclaundre of Walter ofte and wyde spradde,
That of a cruel herte he wikkedly,

For he a poure womman wedded hadde,
Hath mordred bothe his children priuely.   725
Swich murmur was among hem comunly.
No wonder is, for to the peples ere
Ther cam no word but that they mordred were.

For which, wher as his peple ther-bifore
Had loued him wel, the sclaundre of his diffame   730
Made hem that they him hatede therfore,
To ben a mordrer is an hateful name.
But natheles, for ernest ne for game
He of his cruel purpos nolde stente;
To tempte his wyf was set al his entente.   735

Whan that his doughter twelf yeer was of age,
He to the court of Rome, in subtil wyse
Enformed of his wil, sente his message,
Comaunding hem swiche bulles to deuyse
As to his cruel purpos may suffyse,   740
How that the pope, as for his peples reste,
Bad him to wedde another, if him leste.

I seye, he bad they sholde countrefete
The popes bulles, making mencion
That he hath leue his firste wyf to lete,   745
As by the popes dispensacion,
To stinte rancour and dissencion
Bitwixe his peple and him; thus seyde the bulle,
The which they han publisshed atte fulle.

The rude peple, as it no wonder is,   750
Wenden ful wel that it had ben right so;
But whan thise tydinges cam to Grisildis,
I deme that hir herte was ful wo.

D

But she, ylyke sad for euermo,
Disposed was, this humble creature,   755
Thaduersitee of fortune al tendure.

Abyding euer his lust and his plesance,
To whom that she was yeuen, herte and al,
As to hir verray worldly suffisance ;
But shortly if this storie I tellen shal,   760
This markis writen hath in special
A lettre in which he sheweth his entente,
And secrely he to Boloigne it sente.

To the erl of Panik, which that hadde tho
Wedded his suster, preyde he specially   765
To bringen hoom agayn his children two
In honurable estaat al openly.
But o thing he him preyede outerly,
That he to no wight, though men wolde enquere,
Sholde nat telle, whos children they were,   77c

But seye, the mayden sholde ywedded be
Vn-to the markis of Saluce anon.
And as this erl was preyed, so dide he ;
For at day set he on his wey is goon
Toward Saluce, and lordes many oon,   775
In riche array, this mayden for to gyde ;
Hir yonge brother ryding hir bisyde.

Arrayed was toward his mariage
This fresshe mayde, ful of gemmes clere ;
Hir brother, which that seuen yeer was of age,   780
Arrayed eek ful fresh in his manere.
And thus in greet noblesse and with glad chere,
Toward Saluces shaping her iourney,
Fro day to day they ryden in her wey.

Explicit quarta pars.
Sequitur pars quinta.

Among al this, after his wikke vsage,   785
This markis, yet his wyf to tempte more
To the vttereste preue of hir corage,
Fully to han experience and lore
If that she were as stedfast as bifore,
He on a day in open audience   790
Ful boistously hath seyd hir this sentence:

'Certes, Grisild, I hadde ynough plesance
To han yow to my wyf for your goodnesse,
As for your trewthe and for your obeisance,
Nought for your linage ne for your richesse;   795
But now knowe I in verray soothfastnesse
That in greet lordshipe, if I wel auyse,
Ther is greet seruitute in sondry wyse.

I may nat don as euery plowman may;
My peple me constreyneth for to take   800
Another wyf, and cryen day by day;
And eek the pope, rancour for to slake,
Consenteth it, that dar I vndertake;
And treweliche thus muche I wol yow seye,
My newe wyf is coming by the weye.   805

Be strong of herte, and voyde anon hir place,
And thilke dower that ye broughten me
Tak it agayn, I graunte it of my grace;
Retourneth to your fadres hous,' quod he;
'No man may alwey han prosperitee;   810
With euene herte I rede yow tendure
The strook of fortune or of auenture.'

And she answerde agayn in pacience,
'My lord,' quod she, ' I wot, and wiste alway
How that bitwixen your magnificence   815
And my pouerte no wight can ne may
Maken comparison ; it is no nay.
I ne heeld me neuer digne in no manere
To be your wyf, no, ne your chamberere.

And in this hous, ther ye me lady made—   820
The heighe god take I for my witnesse,
And also wisly he my soule glade—
I neuer heeld me lady ne maistresse,
But humble seruant to your worthinesse,
And euer shal, whyl that my lyf may dure,   825
Abouen euery worldly creature.

That ye so longe of your benignitee
Han holden me in honour and nobleye,
Wher as I was nought worthy for to be,
That thonke I god and yow, to whom I preye   830
Foryelde it yow; there is namore to seye.
Vn-to my fader gladly wol I wende,
And with him dwelle vn-to my lyues ende.

.   .   .   .

And of your newe wyf, god of his grace   841
So graunte yow wele and prosperitee :
For I wol gladly yelden hir my place,
In which that I was blisful wont to be.
For sith it lyketh yow, my lord,' quod she,   845
' That whylom weren al myn hertes reste,
That I shal goon, I wol goon whan yow leste.

But ther as ye me profre swich dowaire
As I first broughte, it is wel in my mynde

It were my wrecched clothes, no-thing faire,   850
The which to me were hard now for to fynde.
O goode god! how gentil and how kynde
Ye semed by your speche and your visage
The day that maked was our mariage!

But sooth is seyd, algate I fynde it trewe—   855
For in effect it preued is on me—
Loue is nought old as whan that it is newe.
But certes, lord, for noon aduersitee,
To deyen in the cas, it shal nat be
That euer in word or werk I shal repente   860
That I yow yaf myn herte in hool entente.

.   .   .   .

The remenant of your Iewels redy be
In-with youre chambre, dar I saufly sayn;   870
Naked out of my fadres hous,' quod she,
'I cam, and naked mot I turne agayn.
Al your plesance wol I folwen fayn;
But yet I hope it be nat your entente
That I smokles out of your paleys wente.'   875

.   .   .   .

'The smok,' quod he, 'that thou hast on thy bak,   890
Lat it be stille, and ber it forth with thee.'
But wel vnnethes thilke word he spak,
But wente his wey for rewthe and for pitee.
Biforn the folk hir-seluen strepeth she,
And in hir smok, with heed and foot al bare,   895
Toward hir fader hous forth is she fare.

The folk hir folwe wepinge in hir weye,
And fortune ay they cursen as they goon;

But she fro weping kepte hir eyen dreye,
Ne in this tyme word ne spak she noon.   900
Hir fader, that this tyding herde anoon,
Curseth the day and tyme that nature
Shoop him to ben a lyues creature.

For out of doute this olde poure man
Was euer in suspect of hir mariage ;   905
For euer he demed, sith that it bigan,
That whan the lord fulfild had his corage,
Him wolde thinke it were a disparage
To his estaat so lowe for talighte,
And voyden hir as sone as euer he myghte.   910

Agayns his doughter hastilich goth he,
For he by noyse of folk knew hir cominge,
And with hir olde cote, as it myghte be,
He couered hir, ful sorwefully wepinge ;
But on hir body myghte he it nat bringe.   915
For rude was the cloth, and more of age
By dayes fele than at hir mariage.

Thus with hir fader for a certeyn space
Dwelleth this flour of wyfly pacience,
That neither by hir wordes ne hir face   920
Biforn the folk, ne eek in her absence,
Ne shewed she that hir was doon offence ;
Ne of hir heigh estaat no remembrance
Ne hadde she, as by hir contenance.

No wonder is, for in hir grete estaat   925
Hir goost was euer in pleyn humylitee ;
No tendre mouth, non herte delicat,
No pompe, no semblant of roialtee,
But ful of pacient benignitee,

Discreet and prydeles, ay honurable,   930
And to hir housbonde euer meke and stable.

Men speke of Iob and most for his humblesse,
As clerkes, whan hem list, can wel endite,
Namely of men, but as in soothfastnesse,
Though clerkes preise wommen but a lyte,   935
Ther can no man in humblesse him acquyte
As womman can, ne can ben half so trewe
As wommen ben, but it be falle of-newe.

[Pars Sexta.]

Fro Boloigne is this erl of Panik come,
Of which the fame vp sprang to more and lesse,   940
And in the peples eres alle and some
Was couth eek, that a newe markisesse
He with him broughte, in swich pompe and richesse,
That neuer was ther seyn with mannes eye
So noble array in al West Lumbardye.   945

The markis, which that shoop and knew al this,
Er that this erl was come, sente his message
For thilke sely poure Grisildis;
And she with humble herte and glad visage,
Nat with no swollen thought in hir corage,   950
Cam at his heste, and on hir knees hir sette,
And reuerently and wysly she him grette.

'Grisild,' quod he, 'my wille is outerly,
This mayden, that shal wedded ben to me,
Receiued be to-morwe as roially   955
As it possible is in myn hous to be.
And eek that euery wight in his degree
Haue his estaat in sitting and seruyse
And heigh plesance, as I can best deuyse.

I haue no wommen suffisant certayn   960
The chambres for tarraye in ordinance
After my lust, and therfor wolde I fayn
That thyn were al swich maner gouernance;
Thou knowest eek of old al my plesance;
Though thyn array be badde and yuel biseye,   965
Do thou thy deuoir at the leste weye.'

'Nat only, lord, that I am glad,' quod she,
'To doon your lust, but I desyre also
Yow for to serue and plese in my degree
With-outen feynting, and shal euermo.   970
Ne neuer, for no wele ne no wo,
Ne shal the gost with-in myn herte stente
To loue yow best with al my trewe entente.'

And with that word she gan the hous to dyghte,
And tables for to sette and beddes make;   975
And peyned hir to don al that she myghte,
Preying the chambereres, for goddes sake,
To hasten hem and faste swepe and shake;
And she, the moste seruisable of alle,
Hath euery chambre arrayed and his halle.   980

Abouten vndern gan this erl alyghte,
That with him broughte these noble children tweye,
For which the peple ran to seen the sighte
Of hir array, so richely biseye;
And than at erst amonges hem they seye,   985
That Walter was no fool, though that him leste
To chaunge his wyf, for it was for the beste.

For she is fairer, as they demen alle,
Than is Grisild, and more tendre of age,

And fairer fruyt bitwene hem sholde falle,   990
And more plesant, for hir heigh lynage ;
Hir brother eek so fair was of visage,
That hem to seen the peple hath caught plesance,
Commending now the markis gouernance.—

Auctor. 'O stormy peple ! vnsad and euer vntrewe !   995
Ay vndiscreet and chaunging as a vane,
Delyting euer in rombel that is newe,
For lyk the mone ay wexe ye and wane ;
Ay ful of clapping, dere ynough a Iane ;
Your doom is fals, your constance yuel preueth,   1000
A ful greet fool is he that on yow leueth !'

Thus seyden sadde folk in that citee,
Whan that the peple gazed vp and doun,
For they were glad, right for the noueltee,
To han a newe lady of her toun.   1005
Namore of this make I now mencioun ;
But to Grisild agayn wol I me dresse,
And telle hir constance and hir bisinesse.—

Ful bisy was Grisild in euery thing
That to the feste was apertinent ;   1010
Right nought was she abayst of hir clothing,
Though it were rude and somdel eek to-rent.
But with glad chere to the yate is went
With other folk to grete the markisesse,
And after that doth forth hir bisinesse.   1015

With so glad chere his gestes she receyueth,
And conningly, euerich in his degree,
That no defaute no man aperceyueth ;
But ay they wondren what she myghte be

That in so poure array was for to see,   1020
And coude swich honour and reuerence;
And worthily they preisen hir prudence.

In al this mene whyle she ne stente
This mayde and eek hir brother to commende
With al hir herte, in ful benigne entente,   1025
So wel that no man coude hir prys amende.
But atte laste, whan that thise lordes wende
To sitten doun to mete, he gan to calle
Grisild, as she was bisy in his halle.

'Grisild,' quod he, as it were in his pley,   1030
'How lyketh thee my wyf and hir beautee?'
'Right wel,' quod she, 'my lord; for, in good fey,
A fairer sey I neuer non than she.
I prey to god yiue hir prosperitee;
And so hope I that he wol to yow sende   1035
Plesance ynough vn-to your lyues ende.

O thing biseke I yow and warne also,
That ye ne prikke with no tormentinge
This tendre mayden, as ye han doon mo;
For she is fostred in hir norishinge   1040
More tendrely and, to my supposinge,
She coude nat aduersitee endure,
As coude a poure fostred creature.'

And whan this Walter sey hir pacience,
Hir glade chere and no malice at al,   1045
And he so ofte had doon to hir offence,
And she ay sad and constant as a wal,
Continuing euer hir innocence oueral,
This sturdy markis gan his herte dresse
To rewen vp-on hir wyfly stedfastnesse.   1050

'This is ynough, Grisilde myn,' quod he,
' Be now namore agast ne yuel apayed ;
I haue thy feith and thy benignitee,
As wel as euer womman was, assayed,
In greet estaat and poureliche arrayed.   1055
Now knowe I, goode wyf, thy stedfastnesse,'—
And hir in armes took and gan hir kesse.

And she for wonder took of it no kepe ;
She herde nat what thing he to hir seyde ;
She ferde as she had stert out of a slepe,   1060
Til she out of hir masednesse abreyde.
'Grisild,' quod he, ' by god that for vs deyde,
Thou art my wyf, [ne] non other I haue,
Ne neuer hadde, as god my soule saue !

This is thy doughter which thou hast supposed   1065
To be my wyf ; that other feithfully
Shal be myn heir, as I haue ay purposed ;
Thou bare him in thy body trewely.
At Boloigne haue I kept hem priuely,
Tak hem agayn, for now maystow nat seye   1070
That thou hast lorn non of thy children tweye.

And folk that otherweyes han seyd of me,
I warne hem wel that I haue doon this dede
For no malice ne for no crueltee,
But for tassaye in thee thy wommanhede,   1075
And nat to sleen my children, god forbede !
But for to kepe hem priuely and stille,
Til I thy purpos knew and al thy wille.'

Whan she this herde, aswowne doun she falleth
For pitous joye, and after hir swowning   1080

She bothe hir yonge children vn-to hir calleth,
And in hir armes, pitously weping,
Embraceth hem, and tendrely kissing
Ful lyk a mooder, with hir salte teres
She batheth bothe hir visage and hir heres. 1085

O, which a pitous thing it was to se
Hir swowning, and hir humble voys to here !
'Graunt mercy, lord, that thanke I yow,' quod she,
'That ye han saued me my children dere !
Now rekke I neuer to ben deed right here ; 1090
Sith I stonde in your loue and in your grace,
No fors of deeth, ne whan my spirit pace !

O tendre, o dere, o yonge children myne,
Your woful mooder wende stedfastly
That cruel houndes or som foul vermyne 1095
Hadde eten yow ; but god, of his mercy,
And your benigne fader tendrely
Hath doon yow kept ;' and in that same stounde
Al sodeynly she swapte adoun to grounde.

And in hir swough so sadly holdeth she 1100
Hir children two, whan she gan hem tembrace,
That with greet sleighte and greet difficultee
The children from hir arm they gonne arace.
O many a teer on many a pitous face
Doun ran of hem that stoden hir bisyde ; 1105
Vnnethe abouten hir myghte they abyde.

Walter hir gladeth and hir sorwe slaketh ;
She ryseth vp abaysed from hir trance,
And euery wight hir ioye and feste maketh,
Til she hath caught agayn hir contenance. 1110

Walter hir dooth so feithfully plesance, *treated her so kindly*
That it was deyntee for to seen the chere
Bitwixe hem two, now they ben met yfere. *together*

Thise ladyes whan that they her tyme sey,
Han taken hir, and in-to chambre gon,   **1115**
And strepen hir out of hir rude array,
And in a cloth of gold that bryghte shoon,
With a coroune of many a riche stoon
Vp-on hir heed, they in-to halle hir broughte,
And ther she was honoured as hir oughte.   **1120**

Thus hath this pitous day a blisful ende,
For euery man and womman doth his myght
This day in murthe and reuel to dispende *revelry*
Til on the welkne shoon the sterres lyght. *sky*
For more solempne in euery mannes sight *magnificent*   **1125**
This feste was, and gretter of costage,
Than was the reuel of hir mariage.

Ful many a yeer in heigh prosperitee
Liuen this two in concord and in reste,
And richely his doughter maried he   **1130**
Vn-to a lord, oon of the worthieste
Of al Itaille; and than in pees and reste
His wyues fader in his court he kepeth,   *Simple pathos.*
Til that the soule out of his body crepeth. —

should have been mentioned at beginning of verse.

His sone succedeth in his heritage   **1135**
In reste and pees, after his fader day;
And fortunat was eek in mariage,
Al putte he nat his wyf in greet assay.
This world is nat so strong, it is no nay,
As it hath ben of olde tymes yore,   **1140**
And herkneth what this auctour seith therfore.

This storie is seyd nat for that wyues sholde
Folwen Grisild as in humilitee,
For it were importable, though they wolde;
But for that euery wight in his degree   1145
Sholde be constant in aduersitee
As was Grisild, therfor this Petrark writeth
This storie, which with hy style he enditeth.

For, sith a womman was so pacient
Vn-to a mortal man, wel more vs oughte   1150
Receyuen al in gree that god vs sent;
For greet skile is, he preue that he wroughte.
But he ne tempteth no man that he boughte,
As seith seint Iame, if ye his pistil rede;
He preueth folk al day, it is no drede,   1155

And suffreth vs, as for our excercise,
With sharpe scourges of aduersitee
Ful ofte to be bete in sondry wyse;
Nat for to knowe our wil, for certes he,
Er we were born, knew [al] our freletee;   1160
And for our beste is al his gouernance;
Lat vs than liue in vertuous suffrance.

But o word, lordinges, herkneth er I go:—
It were ful hard to fynde now a dayes
In al a toun Grisildes thre or two;   1165
For, if that they were put to swiche assayes,
The gold of hem hath now so badde alayes
With bras, that though the coyne be fair at eye,
It wolde rather breste atwo than plye.

For which heer, for the wyues loue of Bathe,   1170
Whos lyf and al hir secte god mayntene

In heigh maistrie, and elles were it scathe, *harmful*

thynne it were a great pity

I wol with lusty herte fresshe and grene
Seyn yow a song to glade yow, I wene,
And lat vs stinte of ernestful matere :—   1175
Herkneth my song that seith in this manere.

parting word of Chaucer
i.e. epilogue

Lenuoy de Chaucer.   *A masterpiece of Rhyme.*

Grisilde is deed, and eek hir pacience,
And bothe atones buried in Itaille ;   *at once*
For which I crye in open audience,   *public*
No wedded man so hardy be tassaille   1180   *so bold as to assail*
His wyues pacience, in hope to fynde
Grisildes, for in certein he shal faille ! ✗

O noble wyues, ful of heigh prudence,
Lat non humilitee your tonge naille,   *restrain*
Ne lat no clerk haue cause or diligence   *inclination*   1185
To write of yow a storie of swich meruaille
As of Grisildis pacient and kynde ;
Lest Chicheuache yow swelwe in hir entraille !   *lean cow. By some brought in mediaeval romance that fed on patient wives*

Folweth Ekko, that holdeth no silence,   *imitate*
But euere answereth at the countretaille ;   *in return*   1190
Beth nat bidaffed for your innocence,   *be not befooled*
But sharply tak on yow the gouernaille.   *management*
Emprinteth wel this lesson in your mynde
For commune profit, sith it may auaille.

Ye archewyues, stondeth at defence,   1195   *ruling wives*
Sin ye be stronge as is a greet camaille ;   *lion - camel*
Ne suffreth nat that men yow don offence.
And sklendre wyues, fieble as in bataille,   *slender*
Beth egre as is a tygre yond in Ynde ;
Ay clappeth as a mille, I yow consaille.   1200

Always chatter was a mill

Ne dreed hem nat, do hem no reuerence;
For though thyn housbonde armed be in maille,
The arwes of thy crabbed eloquence
Shal perce his brest, and eek his auentaille;
In jalousye I rede eek thou him bynde,   1205
And thou shalt make him couche as doth a quaille.

If thou be fair, ther folk ben in presence
Shew thou thy visage and thyn apparaille;
If thou be foul, be fre of thy dispence,
To gete thee frendes ay do thy trauaille;   1210
Be ay of chere as lyght as leef on lynde,
And lat him care, and wepe, and wringe, and waille!

NOTES.

INTRODUCTORY NOTE.

The principal part of the *Clerkes Tale* is a translation of Petrarch's *De obedientia et fide uxoria mythologia* ('A Myth upon Wifely Obedience and Faith'). (The chief passages that are Chaucer's own are lines 103-105, 147, 215-217, 375-376, 382-383, 932-938, 995-1008, and 1163-1212.) The story, however, was not Petrarch's own, but was borrowed by him from Boccaccio, in whose *Decamerone* it appears as the last tale—the tenth tale of the tenth day. Boccaccio's tale was written about 1348, and Petrarch's Latin version appears to have been written in 1373. It is accompanied by a letter to Boccaccio, in which Petrarch says that the story had always pleased him when he heard it many years before. The story would thus appear to have been older than Boccaccio, and certainly we soon find it widely diffused and highly popular. It was the subject of a mystery in French verse in 1393, and its heroine Griselda is painted among the celebrated lovers on the walls of the Temple in Lydgate's poem, *The Temple of Glass*, together with Dido, Penelope, Alcestis, and Lucretia. The beauty of the story, as well as its allegorical value as a lesson teaching the duty of submission to the will of God, seems to have touched the popular imagination, and we find it to have been the subject of numerous plays and ballads, and to have held its place in literature down to Miss Edgeworth's domestic novel, *The Modern Griselda*. Chaucer makes the Clerk say that he had learned the tale at Padua from the lips of Petrarch himself, and in all probability he identifies himself here with the Clerk, and speaks out his own personal experience, as he was absent from Italy on the king's business from the December of 1372 to the November of 1373. During his embassy, he visited Genoa and Florence, and it is very probable that on this journey he may have met Petrarch at Padua, as that poet's residence was hard by at Arqua. Of course, there is no direct evidence of this beyond the inherent probability of his having been likely to make such a visit from his admiration for Petrarch, and the persistency of the tradition. The really noteworthy point is this: that while neither the *Romaunt of the Rose* nor the *Book of the Duchess* exhibits any trace of Italian influence, the same assertion cannot be made of any poem produced by Chaucer after the date of this Italian journey. Although he may have first heard the story from the lips of Petrarch, it is certain that he had the Latin version of the latter before him when he wrote. This is shown as well by the closeness of Chaucer's version as by the fact that, in the margins of the Ellesmere and Hengwrt MSS., numerous quotations from that version are actually written on the margins, each in its proper place. The test of metre, as Mr Skeat points out, gives the same result, as it shows that it was one of his early works. It is most probable that the main part of the poem was written soon after 1373, and that it was afterwards fitted, with some changes and additions, into the series of the *Canterbury Tales*. The Prologue must, of course, have been written subsequently to Petrarch's death in 1374, and the mention of the wife of Bath in line 1170 shows that the conclusion also was a late addition. But though

our poem is distinctly founded, as we have seen, on Petrarch's moralised version,
the poetical treatment of the story is so individual, that it all comes afresh from
the mind of Chaucer. 'Its pathos is heightened by the humanising touch with
which the English poet reconciles the most matter-of-fact reader to its question-
able aspects. He feels that the incidents of the myth are against nature, and
at every difficult turn of the story, he disarms the realist with a light passage
of fence, and wins to his own side the host of readers who have the common
English turn for ridicule of an ideal that conflicts with reason.'

The Clerk is one of the most finished portraits in Chaucer's famous group
of pilgrims. His description in the Prologue to the *Canterbury Tales* is as
follows (lines 285–308) :

'A Clerk there was of Oxenford also,
    That unto logic hadde long i-go.
    As lene was his hors as is a rake,
    And he was not right fat, I undertake ;
    But lokede holwe, and therto soberly.
    Ful thredbare was his overeste courtepy (*upper cloak*),
    For he hadde geten him yit no benefice,
    Ne was so worldly for to have office.
    For him was levere have at his beddes heed,
    Twenty bookes, clad in blak or reed,
    Of Aristotle and his philosophie,
    Then robes riche, or fithele, or gay sawtrie.
    But al be that he was a philosophre,
    Yet hadde he but litel gold in cofre ;
    But al that he mighte of his frendes hente (*get*),
    On bookes and his lernyng he it spente,
    And busily gan for the soules preye
    Of hem that gaf him wherwith to scoleye (*study*).
    Of studie took he most cure and most heede,
    Noght o word spak he more than was neede,
    And that was seyd in forme and reverence,
    And short and quyk, and ful of hy sentence.
    Sownynge in moral vertu was his speche,
    And gladly wolde he lerne, and gladly teche.'

LINE

3. **Were newe spoused**, who should
be newly married.

5. **Sophyme**, a sophism or trick of
logic. One of the principal branches
of study in the middle ages was the
Aristotelian philosophy.

6. See Ecclesiastes, iii. 1, where
Solomon, the reputed author of this
book, says : 'To everything there is a
season, and a time to every purpose
under the heaven.'

7. **As beth**, I pray you be. *As* is
often used thus with the imperative
mood. Cf. *Squieres Tale*, 458 : '*As
doth* your-seluen grace ;' *Knightes*

Tale, 1444 : '*As keep me fro thi
vengeaunce*,' &c.

12. **Lent**, the fast of forty days,
beginning with Ash Wednesday and
continuing until Easter, observed by
many Christian churches in commemo-
ration of the fast of our Saviour. It
occurs in spring-time, and the old
sense is simply 'spring.' The A.S.
lencten, spring, is supposed to be
derived from *lang*, long, because in
spring the days lengthen.

16. **Colours** and **figures** are accented *coloúrs* and *figúres*. Many
French words carried their French
accent with them into English usage.

Cf. *manère* (174), *matère* (99 and 175), *fauòur* (102), *malice* (692), *coràge* (220), *visàge* (693), *mesùre* (256), *statùre* (257), &c. There is another allusion here to logic, the principal study of the Clerk, who was the representative of learning among Chaucer's pilgrims.

18. Hy style, learned, pedantic style.

19-20. The *Canterbury Tales* are above all popular, and the host is, so to speak, charged with the constant injunction of the cardinal principle of popularity as to both theme and style. The Clerk follows the injunction of the Host by omitting, as 'impertinent' (54), the long geographical and descriptive proem of his original, Petrarch, as well as by adding a facetious moral to the 'ernestful matere' (1175) of his story.

22. Yerde, rod, guidance. Cf. our modern expression, 'under the rod.' The word appears also in the phrase, 'to gird at,' to gibe or sneer at; the M. E. *girden*, to strike as with a rod, being derived from *gerde*, a rod, softened to *yerde*, English *yard*. Milton has 'griding' (*Paradise Lost*, vi. 329) from the same root. See also Spenser's *Faerie Queene*, II. viii. 36.

27. Padowe, Padua, in the north of Italy. Petrarch lived at Arqua, in the immediate vicinity of Padua. See note on page 66.

29. Petrarch died July 18, 1374.

31. Frauncëys Petrark, Francesco Petrarca, the first and greatest lyric poet of Italy, was born at Arezzo, in Tuscany, in 1304. His father was a native of Florence, but had been obliged to go into exile with his party in 1302. The boy was brought up at Avignon, where the papal court was then held, and hither, after seven years spent in the study of law at Montpellier and Bologna, he returned at the age of twenty-two. For some time he gave himself with equal devotion to the pursuit of pleasure and the study of the Latin classics. He became widely known for his scholar-ship, and he soon numbered among his friends the most illustrious men of his time. A chance meeting with Laura de Noves in a church early in 1327, transformed the dandy and scholar into a great poet. For ten years he lived near her in Avignon, meeting her at church, at festivities, and in society, and he sung her beauty and his love in those imperishable sonnets which ravished the ears of his contemporaries, and have not yet ceased to charm. Laura, who had been married for two years before Petrarch saw her, though not insensible to a worship which spread her name over the civilised world, and made an emperor (Charles IV.) beg to be introduced to her and to be allowed to kiss her forehead, gave no encouragement to the too passionate poet's love, which thus became refined into a dream or ideal romance. So impersonal did it become, that many, even among his contemporaries, have doubted whether Laura was a real personage at all, or anything other than an imaginary ideal of womanhood in a dream of the poet's mind. Petrarch lived for some years in the romantic valley of Vaucluse, devoting himself entirely to literary pursuits. At Rome, on Easter-day, 1341, he was publicly crowned with the laurel of the poet—an honour which tradition told had also been bestowed on Virgil, Horace, and Statius. From 1353, Petrarch lived in Italy, mostly at Milan, and in 1370 he removed to Arqua, where he died peacefully, July 18, 1374. In scholarship, Petrarch takes his place almost as the father of modern learning. He was a most devoted student of Latin literature, and he lavished his time and money in copying and collecting manuscripts. He foresaw a new phase of European culture, and it is as the apostle of humanism, as well as the greatest master of Italian lyrical verse, that his name is still remembered.

33. Of, with.

34. **Linian.** Tyrwhitt points out that this is the once illustrious canonist Giovanni di Lignano. He was made Professor of Canon Law at Bologna in 1363, and here he died in 1383. He was as distinguished in philosophy as in canon law, and his epitaph describes him as 'a second Aristotle, Hippocrates and Ptolemy.'

36. **Suffre.** The *-re* is slurred over in reading.

37. **Eye.** This word is pronounced as long *e*, followed by an indistinctly sounded *e*.

38. As Linian died in 1383, this Prologue must have been written after that date. For the date of Petrarch's death, see note to line 31.

43. **Proheme.** This is the somewhat tedious descriptive introduction already spoken of in note to lines 19–20.

44. **Pemond,** Piedmont, a province in Northern Italy.——**Saluces,** Saluzzo, south of Turin.

45. **Apennyn,** the Apennines, the ridge of mountains running throughout Italy, separating in their northern part the plain of **Lombardy** from Piedmont.

47. **Mount Vesulus,** Monte Viso.

48. **Poo,** the river Po, which rises on the east side of Monte Viso in the Cottian Alps near the French frontier, flows mainly eastwards, and empties into the Adriatic, after a course of 360 miles.

51. **To Emelward,** towards Æmilia. Tyrwhitt notes that this region was called Æmilia from the *Via Æmilia,* which crossed it from Placentia (Piacenza) to Rimini. Placentia stood upon the Po. Petrarch's description of this part of the course of the Po is a little different. He speaks of it as 'dividing the Æmilian and Flaminian regions from Venice.'——**Ferrare,** Ferrara, near the mouth of the Po. ——**Venyse,** the province of Venetia.

57–63. This passage is highly praised by Mr Lowell in his fine essay on Chaucer, in *My Study Windows.* He

says: 'The first stanza of the *Clerkes Tale* gives us a landscape whose stately choice of objects shows a skill in composition worthy of Claude, the last artist who painted nature epically. The Pre-Raphaelite style of landscape entangles the eye among the obtrusive weeds and grass-blades of the foreground, which, in looking at a real bit of scenery, we overlook ; but what a sweep of vision is here ! and what happy generalisation in the sixth verse, as the poet turns away to the business of his story ! The whole is full of open air.'

73. This line contains in 'strong' and 'yong' an instance of *sectional rime,* or rime existing between syllables contained in the same section of a verse. This was well known to all our early dialects, not as a substitute for alliteration, but merely an addition to it. See Guest's *History of English Rhythms,* Book I., chap. vi.

76. **To blame.** This is the gerundial infinitive. See Chaucer's Grammar, page 19—Infinitive Mood (*b*).

77. **Yonge,** the definite form of the adjective.

82. **Leet he slyde,** he let go, unattended to. Cf. Shakspeare, *The Taming of the Shrew,* Induction vi., where Sly says, 'Let the world slide,' and in Induction ii. 146, 'Let the world slip.'

83–84. **Nolde** = would not . . . **No.** Two negatives in Chaucer's usage do not make an affirmative.

85. **Bar so sore,** bore so ill, were so much grieved at.

86. **Flokmele,** in a troop. Petrarch has *catervatim.* The word is formed from M. E. *floc* (A.S. *flocc*), a flock, and the M. E. termination, *-mele, -melum* = A.S. *mælum,* dat. pl. of *mæl,* a portion. Cf. *lim-mele,* limb from limb (literally, 'in limb-pieces'), which occurs in Layamon, and our *piece-meal,* by portions, at a time (literally, 'by piece-pieces').

93. **And yiveth.** The Ellesmere MS. has 'to yeue.'

93-94. 'As often as **it** is necessary for us to tell our griefs to you.'

99-100. 'Although I have nothing to do with this matter more than any other man who is here present.'—— **Matere.** This word is accented on the second syllable, *matére*. See note to line 16.

101. Ye. The marquis is addressed throughout as **ye**, not thou, such being more respectful.

106. So wel vs lyketh yow = it pleases us so well with regard to you. Here we have a construction with two datives. **Ye** is the nominative case of the pronoun, **yow** the dative and accusative.

107. 'And all your actions at all times have brought it about that,' etc.

111. Yow leste, it may please you. **Yow** is in the dative case.

116-117. We often find rhymes in Chaucer formed merely by repeating the syllable. Words repeated as here must be used in different senses. Cf. *Squieres Tale*, 105-106:

'Al be it that I can nat sowne his *style*,
Ne can nat clymben ouer so hy a *style*.'

120. Scan :

'And thóugh | your gréen | e yoúth | e flóur' | as ýit.'

127. Accepteth. The plural form of the imperative is used in agreement with 'ye,' the pronoun of address to a superior.

128. Refuseden. The full forms of the past tenses of weak verbs, or such as add *-ede* to the stem to form the past tense, are seldom found written as here in full without elision of the final *e* before a vowel following, or abridgement of the medial *e*. Other instances in this poem are *seruede* (line 640), and *hatede* (line 731).——For **your** the Ellesmere MS. has 'thyn.'

130. Chese yow, choose for you (yourself).

134. Scán thus :

'Deliúer | us oút | of ál | this bís | y drédë.'

The final syllable is here slurred over. The final syllables slurred in this way are *-en*, *-er*, *-eth*, *-el*, and *-ow*. See Chaucer's Versification, page 24, section 8.

137. Linage. The Ellesmere MS. has 'lyne.'

142. Markis, in the genitive case.

145. I me reioysed of, I rejoiced in.

147. Ther, where.

154. Prey. Chaucer often omits the final *e* in the first person singular indicative of verbs.——**Yow.** This the Ellesmere MS. omits.

157. Bountee, goodness.——**Streen,** stock, breed.

160. Mariage, pronounced as a tri-syllable.

163. Endure, I will take upon myself to bear.

165. That what = whatsoever. The Ellesmere MS. omits 'what.'

168. As, as if.

172. As euer moot I thryue, as ever I hope to prosper.

174. But = unless.——For **swich** the Ellesmere MS. has 'this.'

180. Of = for.

194. Comandement, pronounced as a word of four syllables.

198. There as = there where.

205. Which that = who.

208. Thrope. This is the dative case.

210. Highte. This is the only English verb with a passive sense; thus *he hight* = he was named.

211. For **beautee** the Ellesmere MS. has 'bountee.'

214. Likerous. The medial *e* is dropped here in reading.

215. 'Very much more often she drank from the well than the wine cask.'

220. Rype and sad corage, a mature and staid disposition.—— Coráge, with the French accent, see note to line 16.

223. Spinning, spinning the while.

227. Shredde, cut into slices.—— Seeth, boiled, seethed.

229. On-lofte = aloft. 'And always she kept up (sustained) her father's life.'

230. Scan:

'With eúer | ich ób | eisaúnce | and
díl | igénce.'

232. Grisilde, with the accent thus,
Grisílde. In line 210 again, this is the
unaccented syllable. Again, in line
255 it is Grisíldis. The accent of
many words is thus variable for the
convenience of rhythm. Cf. in
Chaucer, *hónour* and *honoúr*, *mírour*
and *miroúr*, *róial* and *roiál*, *sólempne*
and *solémpne*, &c.

233. Scan:

' Ful óft | e sýthe | this márk | is sétte
| his éye.'

——For setto the Ellesmere MS. has
'caste.'

237. In sad wyse, in a sober or
staid manner.

238. The Ellesmere MS. has 'gan'
instead of wolde.

239. Wommanhede, womanhood.
The A.S. word is *wífhád*, wifehood.
Woman is a corruption of A.S. *wífman*,
wife-man, the word *man* being formerly
applied like Lat. *homo* to both sexes.
The word became *wimman* (pl.
wimmen) in the 10th century, and
this plural is preserved in the spoken
language to the present day. In the
12th century, it became *wumman*
(just as A.S. *widu* became *wudu*,
wood), whence provincial English
wumman; and lastly, *woman*. Cf.
leman, from A.S. *leófman* and *Lam-
mas* from A.S. *hláfmæsse*. See Skeat's
Etymological English Dictionary,
under this word.

242. For haue the Ellesmere MS.
has 'hadde.'

243. Note that *he* is emphatic, perhaps in contrast to 'peple' in the
preceding line.

253. Hath doon make, hath caused
to be made. Cf. 1098: 'hath *doon*
yow kept.'

254. Asure. Blue was the colour
of truth, whence the common expression, 'true blue.' Cf. *Squieres
Tale*, 644:

'And by hir beddes heed she made a
    mewe,
And couered it with veluettes *blewe*,
In signe of trewthe that is in wommen
    sene.'

The earliest connection of the colour
blue with truth is perhaps to be traced
back to one of the typical garments of
the Jewish High Priest, which was a
robe all blue. The phrase 'true blue'
was first assumed by the Scottish
Covenanters in opposition to the scarlet
badge of Charles I., and hence it was
taken by the troops of Leslie in 1639.
The adoption of the colour was one
of those religious pedantries in which
the Covenanters affected a Pharisaical
observance of the letter of Scripture
and the usages of the Hebrews; and
thus, as they named their children
Habakkuk and Zerubbabel, and their
chapels Zion and Ebenezer, they
decorated themselves with blue ribbons
because the following sumptuary precept was given in the law of Moses:
'Speak unto the children of Israel, and
bid them that . . . . they put upon
the fringe of the borders a riband of
blue' (Numbers, xv. 38). See *Notes
and Queries*, First Series, vol. iii.
pp. 116 and 194.

257. Scan:

'Bý | a maýd | e, lýk | to hír | statúrě.'

This license of making the first foot
consist of a single accented syllable
was first pointed out by Professor
Skeat, who quotes as examples of
nine-syllable lines from Mr Tennyson's
Vision of Sin:

'*Thén* | methought I heard a hollow
    sound
Gáth | ering up from all the lower
    ground.'

260. Vndern (literally 'the interven-
ing period'), mid-forenoon, about 9
A.M. The A.S. *undern* meant, as here,
the third hour, about 9 A.M.; later, it
meant about 11 A.M.; and, still later,
mid-afternoon, about 3 P.M.

265. Maystow, for *mayst thou*. Cf.

wostow (line 325), and also *shaltow*, *artow, wiltow*.

266. **Last** = lasteth, extends. Other instances of a similar contraction of the third person singular of the present tense from stems ending in *d* or *t*, are *sit* for *sitteth*, *bit* for *biddeth*, *stant* for *standeth*, *writ* for *writeth*, *sent* for *sendeth* (line 1151).

276. **Went**, gone. *Went* is now used only as the past tense of *go*. M. E. *wenden* from A.S. *wendan*, to turn, a causal form of *windan*, to turn. The past tense was *wende*, which became *wente*, and finally, *went*.

293. Scan:

'And wíth | sad cón | tenán | ce knél | eth stílle.'

Many French nouns retained in this way their final *e* after being introduced into our language.

299. Scan:

Answér | de, lórd | he ís | al réd | y hére.'

Cf. *Squieres Tale*, 599:

'What he *answérdë* it nedeth nat reherce.'

315. **Sone** pronounced as a dissyllable, *sonë*. The *e* here corresponds to the A.S. final vowel *u*, *sunu*, a son. Cf. *stedë* from A.S. *stéda*, *banë* from A.S. *bana*, *cuppë* from A.S. *cuppe*.

321, 322. **Gouerneth.** Janicula addresses his lord as 'ye' and 'yow,' and uses the plural of the imperative as more respectful.

325. **Wostow** = wost thou, knowest thou. See line 265, and note thereon.

327. **Reule hir,** 'rule herself,' 'guide her conduct.'

339. **Woned.** For the double participial ending in this word, see the Glossary. With it compare the modern forms *hoist-ed* and *graft-ed*, as if from verbs *hoist*, *graft*, in place of the older and more correct forms *hoist* for *hoised*, from *hoise*; and *graft* for *graffed*, from *graff*. So also our *interest-ed*, from *interest* for *interessed*, from the older verb *interess*.

342. **Arn, are.** This is a northern form, Old Northumbrian *aron*, as distinguished from A.S. (Wessex) *sindon*. See Glossary, under **Arn**. Before the Norman Conquest, there were two principal dialects in our language, a northern and a southern. The southern was the literary language, and in it are written almost all our oldest books. Its grammar is very uniform, and its vocabulary free from Scandinavian terms. The northern dialect has a very scanty literature. It has a considerable admixture of Scandinavian words, and a number of grammatical inflections unknown to the southern. Some of the principal points in which the northern dialect differs from the southern are these:

(*a*) The loss of *n* in the infinitive ending of verbs; as N. *drinc-a* = S. *drinc-an*, to drink.

(*b*) The first person singular indicative ending in *u* or *o* instead of *e*; as N. *drinc-o* = S. *drinc-e*, I drink.

(*c*) The second person singular present indicative, and the second person singular perfect indicative of weak verbs, ending in *-s* rather than *-st*; as N. *thu ge plantad-es* = S. *ge plantod-est*, thou hast planted.

(*d*) The third person singular, the third person plural present indicative, and the second person plural imperative, frequently ending in *s* instead of *th*; as N. *he gewyrces* = S. *gewyrcath*, he works; and N. *hia onfoas* = S. *hi onfoath*, they receive.

(*e*) The occasional omission of *ge* before the passive participle; as N. *hered* = S. *geherod*, praised; N. *bledsed* = S. *gebletsod*, blessed.

(*f*) The occasional use of the active participle in *-and* instead of *-end*; as N. *drincande* = S. *drincende*, drinking. (We find this surviving even in Spenser.)

(*g*) Plurals ending in *a, u, o*, or *e*, instead of *-an*; as N. *heorta* =

S. *heortan*, hearts; N. *witegu =*
S. *witegan*, prophets; N. *ego =*
S. *eagan*, eyes; N. *nome =*
S. *naman*, names.

(*h*) -*es* used instead of -*e* as the
genitive suffix of feminine nouns.

(*i*) *The* and *thio* found for *se* (masculine) and *seo* (feminine) = the.

(*j*) The plural article *tha* occurring
for the demonstrative pronoun
hi = they.

After the Norman Conquest, the dialects
became more marked; and in the 13th
and 14th centuries, we can distinguish
three great varieties of English—the
northern, midland, and southern. For
the chief points of difference between
these, see Chaucer's Grammar, page 13;
and Dr Morris's *Historical Outlines
of English Accidence*, chapter iv.

346. Stonde, be fixed.

350. Auyse, take the matter into
consideration. Skeat quotes the legal
formula, *le roy s'avisera*, for expressing
the royal refusal to a proposed measure.

353. Do, 'cause you to laugh or feel
grieved.'

357. For our the Ellesmere MS.
reads 'yow.'

364. 'Even if I were to die for it,
though it would be very hard to me to
die.' Me is dative, the construction
being impersonal.

375. Ladyes, pronounce as a trisyllable, *ladyes*.

376. Scan:

'To hándle | hir clóth | es whér | in
shé | was clád.'

The last syllable is sometimes slurred
over in this way.   See note to line 134,
and Chaucer's Versification, page 24,
section 8.

379. Kembd. The final -*ed* of the
past participle in weak verbs is usually
a distinct syllable, but we find a
tendency to change the -*ed* into -*d*; and
even when it is written as -*ed*, it is often
sounded as -*d*, as *undressed* in this
line, and *ydressed* in line 381.

381. Corone, a nuptial garland.
Among our ancestors, after the bene-

diction in the church, both the bride
and bridegroom were crowned with
chaplets of flowers.

384. Scan:

'Unnéthe | the péple | hir knew | for
hir | fairnéssé.'

389. Lette, delayed, used intransi-
tively.

392. In *sonne*, the sun, the final *e*
corresponds to the A.S. final vowel in
sunne, and is therefore essential. See
Chaucer's Versification, page 23, 6, i.
The most frequent vowel endings of
A.S. nouns were *a, e, u*. All three
were, in the 14th century, represented
by the *e* final. A.S. nouns in *a* are
masculine, as *nama*, a name; *tíma*,
time; *móna*, the moon. Nouns in *e*
belong to various genders. Many are
feminines and neuters with inflections
like *nama*, *tíma*, and *móna*. Such
are *sunne*, the sun; *heorte*, the heart;
róse, the rose, feminines; *eáre*, the
ear, is neuter. Nouns in *u* are
generally feminine, as *scólu*, school;
lufu, love; *sceamu*, shame; *lagu*,
law; but there are some masculine,
as *sunu*, a son; *wudu*, a wood.

397. Rudenesse, pronounced in four
syllables.

403. Scan:

'Vnnéth | e trów | ed they, | but
dórst' | han swórë.'

405. For nas the Ellesmere and
Harleian MSS. read 'were.'

409. Thewes, qualities of mind.
This is the invariable meaning of the
word in M. E., and indeed down to
the 16th century. It is so used by
Spenser, who of course is affectedly
archaic in his use of words. Cf.
Faerie Queene, I. x. 4:

'The mother of three daughters, well
          upbrought
In goodly *thewes*, and godly exercise.'

In Shakspeare, the word always
means *sinews, strength*, and to this
sense the word is now confined. Cf.
Henry IV., Part II., III. ii. 276:
'Care I for the limb, the *thewes*, the

stature, bulk, and big assemblance of a man;' also *Julius Cæsar*, I. iii. 81; and *Hamlet*, I. iii. 12.

412. Embrace, take hold of, make impression upon.

415. For bountee, the Ellesmere MS. has 'beautee.'

418. For fame, the Ellesmere MS. reads 'name.'

421. Roially, because the virtues of Griselda were royal.

425. For low, the Ellesmere MS. reads 'heigh.'

436. Scan :

' If gén | til mén, | or óther' | of hír | contrée.'

The last syllable of 'othere' is slurred over in reading. See note to line 134.

439. Iugementz, a trisyllable. The plural in -*ĕs* is used where the stem is monosyllabic. When the stem has two or more syllables, the plural ending is written -*s* (or -*z*), and sometimes -*es*, in which case the ending does not make an additional syllable. Another plural in -*z* is subgetz, line 482.

444. ' Although it would have been liefer (she would rather have) to her to have borne a male child.'——Knaue, A.S. *cnafa*, *cnapa*, a boy. Cf. Dutch *knaap*, a lad, Icelandic *knapi*, a servant-boy, German *knabe*, a boy. According to Skeat, these words are all of Celtic origin, as the Celtic boys were *servants* to the Teutons. Cf. Gaelic *cnapach*, a youngster.——For knaue, the Ellesmere MS. reads 'man.' So also in lines 447 and 612.

449. Tymes mo = at more times, at other times.

452. To knowe, the gerund.

469. Gesse means simply ' to think,' as still in New England.

480. Gentils. Adjectives of one syllable usually form the plural by adding -*ĕ*. In words of two or more syllables, the -*ĕ* drops off. The word *gentils* is considered as a noun, and follows the ordinary rule of nouns. So subgetz in line 482.

482. Subgetz. See note to line 480.

483. Thee is much less respectful than *ye*. In lines 484 and 489 we have *thy*, but *your* again in line 492 and in 496. Griselda addresses her lord with *your*, lines 501 and 504; *yow*, 506; and *ye*, 508. The sergeant again addresses Griselda as *ye*, 526 and 528.

496. Hyghte, promised. A.S. *hâtan*, to promise, past tense *hêht*, past participle *hêton*. The word still survives in Scotch. It occurs in the Scotch ballad, *Willy drowned in Yarrow* :

' And Willy *hecht* to marry me
  Gin e'er he married ony.'

504. Thing, possession.

508. Dredĕ, a dissyllable.

516. 'Soon after this, about as long as one would take to go the length of a furlong or two.'

519. A maner sergeant, a kind of sergeant. Cf. 'maner wyse,' 605; 'maner wyght,' *Squieres Tale*, 138 and 329; 'maner doctrine,' *Prioresses Tale*, 1689; and 'maner thing,' *Monkes Tale*, 3951.

523. Louede and dradde. Read ' lov'd' and draddĕ.'

525. Stalked him, marched himself.

533. His cruel purpose is indicated with great skill by his abruptly breaking off.

535. Chere, 'and began to make a face (to look) as though,' &c.

547. Atte laste, at the last. So also ' atte leste,' 130, 570; 'atte fulle,' 749.

548. Preyde, pronounced 'preydĕ.' In line 680, 'preyede him,' pronounced 'preyĕd' him.'

559. Him, to him, dative case.

570-571. That should have been followed by ' ye burie' in next line, instead of the imperative ' burieth.'

572. To-race, may scratch or tear to pieces. This prefix *to-*, A.S. *tó-*, meaning 'in twain,' 'asunder,' is cognate with German *zer-*; Gothic *dis-* (*d* standing for *t* as in Gothic *du* = English to), Latin *dis-*, Greek *di-* (only used in the sense of ' double '). It occurs in about fifty

A.S. verbs, as *tó-beran*, to bear apart, remove, *tó-berstan*, to burst asunder, *tó-brecan*, to break asunder, &c. *All* was often added as a kind of intensive, meaning 'wholly,' not only before the prefix *to-* only, but before the prefixes *for-* and *bi-* also, and ultimately the *all* came to be considered as belonging to the *to-* (as if *all-to* were short for *altogether*), and consequently *all-to* appeared as a sort of adverb, and was considered as such by Surrey and Latimer. No instance of this later use occurs before 1500. Most verbal prefixes (such as *for-* and *be-*) were written in old MSS. apart from the verb, and this rendered the error more easy. It is still retained in our English Bible, Judges ix. 53, where 'all to-brake' is often incorrectly printed 'all-to brake.' See the thorough discussion of the question in Skeat's *Etymological Dictionary*.

583. Sholdë, a dissyllable. It is seldom pronounced as a monosyllable.

585. Scan:

'And cárie | it ín | a cófre | or ín | a láppë.'

586. 'But on the penalty of having his head cut off.'

589. Boloigne, a trisyllable. This is Bologna.

591. Scan:

'He shóld |' it táke | and shéw |' hir thís | matére.'

See line 583, and the note thereon.

602. Euer in oon, always in one and the same state. See also 677.

603. Humble, pronounced 'humbl'.'

607. 'No accidental or unusual appearance, as if in consequence of some calamity, was seen in her.'

608. Hir doughter name, her daughter's name. *Doughter* here is in the genitive case. See note to line 1136.

610. Yeer. Many nouns in the oldest English, originally neuter and flectionless in the plural, have the same form for the singular and the plural,

as *winter, night, deer, folk, thing, horse, foot,* &c. We still say a *fort-night* (= fourteen nights), *se'nnight* (= seven nights), 'six *foot* high,' 'ten *score*,' 'twelve *stone* weight.' *Deer, sheep, swine*, and *neat* still admit of no plural sign whatever, but these words have acquired a kind of collective sense; cf. the use of *fish, fowl, fruit, gross, fathom,* &c.

615. Merïë, a trisyllable.

625. Sikly berth, 'bear hardly,' 'dislike.'

626. In 'namely,' the *e* is slurred over; in 'sone,' the *e* is elided before *y*.

634. Out of drede, out of doubt, certainly.

640. Scan:

'As I' | his sús | ter sér | uedé | by níghtë.'

648. The final *-er* in 'doughter' is slurred over in reading; *sone* is a dissyllable, the *e* corresponds to the A.S. termination *u*. See note to line 392.

653. At = for, after *axe*. 'To ask at anyone' is still used in Scotch.

663. Scan:

'Al yoúr | plesánc | ë   férm | 'and stábl | ' I hóldë.'

666. 'The pain of death is not to be compared to the pleasure of your love.'

675. Worsë, a dissyllable.

680. Scan:

'Saue thís ; | she préy | ed' hím | that íf | he mýghtë.'

687. Euer lenger, 'ever the more the longer he thinks of it.' *The* here is the old instrumental case of the demonstrative pronoun *the*. It is the A.S. *thý*, as in *thý mare* = Latin *eo magis*. This use of *the* before comparatives is the only remnant in modern English of the old instrumental case.——**Wondred**, all the other MSS. but the Ellesmere read 'wondreth.'

690. Louede, pronounced 'lov'dë.'

695. Scan:

She lóu'd |`' hir chíld | ren bést | in éu | ery wýsë.

699. Wyfhod, womanhood. This is the usual word, not 'wommanhede,' as in 239 and 1075.

704. For a the Ellesmere MS. reads 'that.'

706-707. Purposed, purpos'd; **disposed,** dispos'd.

711. Ay oon, ever the same.

713-714. Possible, pronounced 'possibl';' **penible,** 'penibl'.' **Penible,** painstaking.

718. Thanked, pronounced 'thankëd.'

719-721. 'She showed clearly that for no worldly trouble should a wife of herself have in practice any will different from that of her husband.'

722. Sclaundre of; slander (bad report) about.

724. For = because that.

730. Scan:

'Had loú'd | him wéll, | the sclaúndre | of his | diffámë.'

731. Hatede, a trisyllable. Cf. 'seruede' (singular) in line 640.

733. Ernest. We still use the word in the noun form in the phrase 'in earnest.'

738. Message for messenger.

748 and **750. Peple.** The final syllable elided in both cases.

771-772. Girls were frequently married at twelve years of age. Cf. the *Preamble of the Wyves Tale of Bathe,* 4:

'For, lordynges, sith I twelf yeer was of age,

Housbondes at chirche dore I have had fyve.'

780. Seuen. The *-en* is slurred over in reading.

785. In after, the *-er* is slurred over.

793. Note that the marquis uses **yow** and **your** in this speech to Griselda. See note to line 483.

797. If I wel auyse, if I am well advised.

818. I ne heeld, a trisyllabic measure.

820. Lady means literally 'loaf-kneader.' A.S. *hláfdige—hláf,* a loaf; and probably *dæege,* a kneader, from the root seen in Gothic *digan,* to knead; and in English *dike* and *dairy.* ——**Lord** means literally 'loaf-keeper.' A.S. *hláford,* probably for a supposed form, *hláfweard,* a loaf-ward—*hláf,* a loaf, and the root of *ward.*

828. Honour, pronounced here 'hónour,' but 'honoúr' in line 1021. See note to line 232.

846. Whylom, *whílum* is the instrumental or dative plural of *hwíl,* meaning 'at times.' Other adverbs from datives are *ever* (A.S. *æfre*), *never* (A.S. *næfre*) (from *piece, piece-meal,* of French origin, and A.S. *mælum,* in pieces). *The while, ay, some deal, alway, otherwise,* etc., are due to the accusative. Many, as *needs,* are due to genitives.

850. Were, in agreement with 'clothes.'

855. Algate, in all respects, formed from 'all' and 'gate,' a way. Cf. *alway,* A.S. *ealne weg,* where both words are in the accusative singular. Later forms are: *alne way, al way,* and *alway.* The occasional use of the genitive singular, and the common habit of using the genitive singular suffix *-es* as an adverbial suffix, have produced the second form *always.* Other old accusatives that now have a genitive form are: *sideways, sometimes, the whilst, straightways,* &c.

857. 'Love when it is old is not what it was when it was new.' These fine lines (851-861) are Chaucer's own. Cf. the lines in the beautiful and anonymous Scottish ballad (first published in Allan Ramsay's *Tea Table Miscellany,* in 1724):

'O waly, waly, but love be bonny,

A little time while it is new,

But when 'tis auld, it waxeth cauld,

And fades away like the morning-dew.'

871. Doubtless suggested by Job i. 21.

873. Plesance, a trisyllable, as in line 663.

892. Wel vnnethes, 'very uneasily,' 'with great difficulty.'——**Thilke,** that, the same. The A.S. *thylc*, *thýlíc* is formed from *thý*, the instrumental case of *seo, seo, thæt*, and *ílc*, like; thus corresponding to Latin *ta-lis*, Sanskrit *ta-drisha*; Greek *tēlikos*. *Ilk* is still used in Scotland in the phrase 'of that *ilk*' (as 'Buchanan of that *ilk*' = of that *same*), when the name of a property is the same as the family name.

902. See Job iii. 3.

903. A lyues creature, a living creature. **Lyues** is used here as an adverb. It is the genitive singular of the noun *lyf*; A.S. *líf*, genitive *lífes*, dative *lífe*, plural *lífas*. Other adverbs formed from genitives are: *needes, whiles, twies*, &c. The preposition *of* has taken the place of the genitive adverbial suffix, as *of necessity, of course, of purpose, of a truth*, &c. In some cases we have *of* (or *in, at, a, on*) with the old genitive, as *anights, of mornings, on Sundays, now-a-days* (= *now-on dayes*), *indoors*.

905. Euer, pronounced *eu'r*, also in line 926.——**Suspect,** accented *súspect*.

911. Agayns, towards. The word is formed from A.S. *ongeân* by adding the genitive adverbial suffix *-es*. The *on-* is the A.S. and modern English *on-*, generally used in the sense of *in*; *geân*, again, related to the noun *gang*, 'a going,' 'a way,' or at least to the verb *gán*, to go.

916–917. 'For the cloth was rough and many days older than it was at the time of her marriage.'

934. Namely of men, 'especially of men.'

935. 'Though clerks give but little praise to women.' Many of the monkish stories, as in the *Disciplina Clericalis* and *Gesta Romanorum*, turn on the faults and weaknesses of women. These monkish inmates of the cloister had no opportunity of learning the real nature of women at its best amid the sweetness and purity of domestic life, and their pages teem with the foolish imaginations of a prurient and childish ignorance. How sweet and wholesome are the words of Chaucer contrasted with the prevailing tone of the tales, in prose and verse, of his own as well as former times !

'Ther can no man in humblesse him
      acquite
As womman can, ne can ben half so
      trewe
As wommen ben.'

And with what fine raillery the *Wife of Bath* asserts her plea for the other side !

. . . 'If women had but written stories
As clerkes have within their oratories,
They would have writ of men more
      wickednesse
Than all the race of Adam may re-
      dresse.'

No doubt Chaucer's poetry contains many hard hits at the foibles of women, but most of these show that curiously intimate acquaintance with their ways, which implies a close and kindly observation, and an interest reminding us of the delicate touch of Addison in the *Spectator*. As a youth, Chaucer saw the true glory of love in a devoted wife when he sang of Alcestis ; and in his maturest years, his ideal of love is still the devoted wife, when he sings of the perfect meekness of Griselda, 'the flour of wyfly pacience.' The two most effective of his *Canterbury Tales* are tributes to the most distinctly feminine and wifely virtue of fidelity, and these come as well from the wide and grave experience of the world of the Man of Law, as from the cloistered solitude of the Clerk of Oxenford.

938. But it be falle of-newe, 'unless it has happened very recently.'

940. To more and lesse, 'to greater and smaller,' 'to everybody.'

941. Alle and some, 'one and all.'

948. Sely, simple, innocent. This word meant originally 'timely,' then 'lucky,' 'happy,' 'innocent,' and lastly, 'foolish.' In some parts of Scotland it still means 'weak in health or strength.' Other instances of words that have suffered a similar degradation of meaning are *knave, villain, boor, varlet, menial, paramour, minion, wench,* &c.

963. The marquis addresses Griselda here with 'thyn' and 'thou,' and she replies with 'yow' (969 and 973). See note to line 483.

965. Yuel biseye, 'ill beseen,' 'evil to look on.' Scan :

'Though thýn | arráy | be bádd' | and yu'l | biséyĕ.'

981. See note to line 260.

984. Richely biseye, 'rich to look at,' the opposite of 'yuel biseye' in line 965.

993. Scan :

'That hém | to séen | the pepl' | hath caught | plesáncĕ.'

995-1008. These lines are not in Petrarch. Chaucer, as an adherent of the court, had little knowledge of the poor or sympathy with their political aspirations. He was not a man of the people like his contemporary William of Langland, with his heart full of hopeless bitterness at the misery of the poor man's life, and the extortions of the rich and powerful.

995. Vnsad, unsettled.

999. 'Ever full of idle talk, dear enough at a farthing.'——**Iane,** a very small coin, properly of Genoa.

1002. Sadde folk, 'more serious folk.'

1011. Abayst, abashed. The *-ed* ending before a vowel or *h* is sounded as *-d.* It has here become *-t.*

1012. To-rent, rent or torn in pieces. See note to line 572.

1021. Honour, pronounced here 'honoúr;' see, however, *hónour* in line 828, and note to line 232.

1031. How lyketh thee, how pleases thee.

1039. Mo, 'more,' 'others'= another. Tyrwhitt suggests that Chaucer wrote 'mo' instead of 'me' for the sake of rime, and notes this as one of the 'most licentious corruptions' that he has observed in Chaucer; but Professor Skeat, in his edition of the *Clerkes Tale,* observes that this use of *mo,* though not common, occurs in some other instances, and that it is an intentional expression of a hint of extreme delicacy. 'The use of *me* would have been a *direct* charge of unkindness, spoiling the whole story.'

1037-1043. The perfect patience of Griselda reaches its highest point in these beautiful and touching lines.

1049. Gan his herte dresse, 'began to prepare his heart.'

1052. Agast, terrified. *Agast* is short for *agasted,* past participle of M. E. *agasten,* to terrify, from A.S. prefix *ā-* and *gæstan,* allied to Gothic *us-gais-jan,* to terrify. *Ghost* is from the same root. Shakspeare has *gasted* (*King Lear,* II. i. 57), and *gastness* (*Othello,* V. i. 106).

1053. The Marquis once more uses the more respectful 'thy.'

1056. For goode, all the other MSS. save the Ellesmere read 'dere.'

1066. That other, referring to the boy.

1067. Purposed occurs in three of the MSS. ; the reading of three (including the Ellesmere and Harleian) is 'supposed,' one (the Petworth) has 'disposed.'

1068. Bare. The final *e* in the second person singular of strong verbs is often omitted. In this case, of course, it is not sounded, coming before *him.*

1071. Non, either.

1079. Skeat quotes the following fine passage from Morley's *English Writers* (Vol. II., Part I., p. 324) : 'And when Chaucer has told all, and dwelt with an exquisite pathos of natural emotion, all his own, upon the patient mother's piteous and tender kissing of her recovered children—for there is nothing in Boccaccio, and but half a sentence in Petrarch, answering to those four beautiful stanzas (1079-1106) —he rounds all, as Petrarch had done, with simple sense, which gives religious meaning to the tale, then closes with a lighter strain of satire, which protects Griselda herself from the mocker.

1090-1092. 'Now I care not to be dead (to die) just now, since I stand in your love and favour, it is no matter for death nor when my spirit may pass away.'

1098. Hath doon yow kept = hath caused you to be kept.

1100. Swough, swoon. The M. E. *swowen, swoghen* is from the A.S. *swôgan,* to resound. *Sigh* and *swoon* seem to be allied words as well as *sough.*

1103. Arace, to remove forcibly. The Old French *aracer* is from Latin *eradicare,* from *e,* out of, and *radicem,* accusative of *radix,* a root.

1117. Bryghte. The adverb was usually formed thus, by adding *e* to the adjective. This *e* has now vanished, and where another adverbial suffix (commonly -*ly*) has not taken its place, the word robbed of its syllable is considered as the adjective used adverbially. It is, however, the legitimate though corrupt descendant of the old adverb. The superlative of the adjective ends in *ste,* that of the adverb in *st.*

1125. Solempne, pronounced *solémpne.* The word is accented variously. Cf. *sólempne (Squieres Tale,* 61), and *solémpne (ib.* 111).

1133 and **1134.** These are lines of eleven syllables, as also 1109. The final -*eth* in each of these lines is redundant.

1136. Fader day, father's day. *Fader* here is in the genitive case, like *doughter* in line 608. *Fader, brother,* and *doughter* took no inflection for the genitive singular. This was also the case with feminine nouns whose oldest genitive was *an,* which was broken down into *ě,* and then disappeared. In Chaucer, we find *ladyveil* and *widow sone.* This still survives in *hell-fire, Lady-day,* etc.

1141. Auctour, Petrarch. See note to line 31.

1148. Hy style. Cf. line 41.

1151. In gree, with submission.—**Sent,** for *sendeth.* Cf. *last* = lasteth, in line 266, and the note thereon.

1152. 'For there is great reason that he should prove what he has created.'

1153. Boughte, redeemed.

1154. See James i. 13. 'This epistle gives,' says Morley (p. 325), 'the spiritual doctrine to which Petrarch, and after him Chaucer, would apply the tale of Griselda's patience. Having pointed to this moral, the Clerk of Oxford ends cheerily. Nowadays, Griselds are very hard to find ; wherefore, and for love of the wife of Bath, he will say them a song, and so he ends with a playful touch of satire in the *Envoy.*'

1155. It is no drede, 'there is no fear,' 'beyond doubt.' Cf. 'out of drede' = certainly, 636.

1162. At this point Petrarch concludes, and from this point to the end the lines are Chaucer's own.

1177. The metre changes here from the ordinary seven-line stanza to a six-line stanza. All the stanzas are connected together by a sequence of the same rimes, there being but three rimes throughout, -*ence* in the first and third line of every stanza, -*aille* in the second, fourth, and sixth, and -*ynde* in the fifth line. There are thus thirty-six consecutive rimes. These are all *feminine* rimes, or rimes that are more than monosyllabic rimes like *fire, tire,* &c. The rime of these stanzas may be expressed in a formula similar to that given for the ordinary seven-line stanza on page 22, thus : *a b a b c b.*

1178. Atones, at once. A.S. *æt.*

at, and *ánes*, once, the genitive of *án*, one.

1188. **Chicheuache** (literally, 'lean cow'), a beast in mediæval romance that fed on patient wives. Tyrwhitt notes that the allusion is to the subject of an old ballad still preserved. It is an ancient kind of Pageant, in which two beasts are introduced, called *Bycorne* and *Chichevache*. The first is supposed to feed upon *obedient husbands*, and the other upon *patient wives*; and the humour of the piece consists in representing *Bycorne* as pampered with a superfluity of food, and Chichevache as half starved. *Chiche* is of French origin. It appears in Chaucer's *Tale of Melibeus*: 'scarsetee and *chyngerie*' (*Canterbury Tales*, line 7912), and in *The Romaunt of the Rose* (line 5591):

'For he that hath mycches (*loaves*)
    tweyne,
Ne value in his demeigne
Lyveth more at ese, and more is riche,
Than doth he that is *chiche*.'

1189. **Folweth**, imitate Echo, who always gives back her answer.

1190. **At the countretaille**, at the counter-tally, in return.

1200. 'Always chatter on like a mill.'

1204. **Auentail.** Skeat notes that this was the lower half in the movable part of a helmet which admitted air, called by Spenser the *ventayle*, *Faerie Queene*, III. ii. 24; IV. vi. 19; V. viii. 12; and by Shakspeare the *beaver*, *Hamlet*, I. ii. 230. He quotes further from Douce's *Illustrations of Shakespeare*, that the movable part of the helmet in front was made in two parts, which turned on hinges at the sides of the head. The upper part is the *visor*, to admit of vision; the lower the *ventail*, to admit of breathing. Both parts could be removed from the face, but only by lifting them *upwards*, and throwing them *back*. If the visor alone were lifted, only the upper part of the face was exposed; but if the *ventail* were lifted, the visor also went with it.

1207. **Ther**, where.

1211. 'As light as a leaf on a linden-tree' was formerly a common proverb. See *Piers Plowman*, Passus i. 154:

'Was neuere leef vpon lynde lighter
    ther-after.'

ETYMOLOGICAL GLOSSARY AND INDEX.

The following abbreviations are used : A. S. = Anglo-Saxon (English down to about 1150); M. E. = Middle English (from that time to about 1500); O. Fr. = Old French; Fr. = French (modern); Ger. = German; Dut. = Dutch; Scand. = Scandinavian; Icel. = Icelandic; L. = Latin; Gr. = Greek; *art.* = article; *n.* = noun; *v.* = verb; *pron.* = pronoun; *adj.* = adjective; *adv.* = adverb; *prep.* = preposition; *conj.* = conjunction; *interj.* = interjection; *part.* = participle; *pp.* = past participle; *pr.* = present; *pt.* = past; *p.* = person; *t.* = tense; *s.* = singular; *pl.* = plural; *comp.* = comparative; *superl.* = superlative; *subj.* = subjunctive; *imp.* = imperative; *impers.* = impersonal; *masc.* = masculine; *fem.* = feminine; *neut.* = neuter; *interrog.* = interrogative; cf. (Lat. *confer*) = compare; *gen.* = genitive; *dat.* = dative; *acc.* = accusative; *def.* = definite form of the adjective; cog. = cognate; the symbol — means 'directly derived from.' The numbers refer to the line of the *Clerkes Tale* in which the word occurs. A knowledge of the principal prefixes and suffixes in use in the English language is assumed.

A

A, *art.* 2, 4, etc., a ; al a = the whole of a, 1165. A.S. *án.*

A, *prep.* on, in, by ; now a dayes = now in these days, 1164. A.S *on.*

Abayst, *pp.* abashed, 317, 1011 ; abaysed, amazed, 1011. O. Fr. *esbahir* (Fr. *ébahir*), made up of O. Fr. *es-* (= L. *ex*, out, very much), and *bahir*, to express wonder, a word of imitative origin from the interj. *bah!* of astonishment.

Abouen, *prep.* above, 826. A.S. *âbúfan*, short for *an-be-ufan*, literally 'on-by-upward.'

Abouten, *prep.* about, near, 1106. A.S. *âbútan, onbútan*, short for *on-be-útan*, literally ' on-by-outward.'

Abreyde, *v. pt. s.* started, 1061. A.S. *abregdan*, to twist out ; *bregdan*, to weave. From the same root is *-braid* in up*braid.*

Abyde, *v.* to remain, 1106 ; *pres. part.* abyding, awaiting, 757. A.S. *âbídan*, *â* (= Ger. *er-*), *bídan*, to wait.

Accepteth, *v. imp. pl.* accept, 96, 127.

Fr. *accepter*—L. *acceptare*, a frequentative of *accipere*, to receive, *ac-* (= *ad-*) and *capere.*

Accident, *n.* an unusual appearance, 607. Fr.—L. *accident-*, stem of pr. part. of *accidere*, to happen, *ac-* (for *ad-*) and *cadere*, to fall.

Acquyte, *v.* to acquit one's self, 936. O. Fr. *aquiter*—Low L. *acquietare*—L. *ac-* (for *ad-*), to, *quietare*, formed from *quietus*, discharged, originally 'quiet.'

After, *prep.* according to, 327. A.S. *æfter*, a comp. form, meaning ' more off,' ' further off,' made up of root *af* (= Gr. *apo*, E. *of*) and the comp. suffix *-ter.*

After that, *conj.* according as, 203.

Agast, *pp.* terrified, 1052. Short for *agast-ed*, pp. of M. E. *agasten*, to terrify—A.S. *â-*, prefix, and *gæstan*, to frighten.

Agayn, *adv.* again, 1070 ; ageyn, 575. More commonly *ayein* — A.S. *ongegn, ongeán.*

Agayns, *prep.* towards, 911. The modern form is *against*, extended from the M. E. form with *adv.*

suffix -es. A.S. ongeán, made up of on and geán, again, which is perhaps connected with gán, to go.

Age, n. life, 627. O. Fr. edage—Low L. ætaticum—L. aetat-, stem of ætas, age.

Agoon, pp. departed, dead, 631. A.S. ágán, pp. of v. ágán, to pass by.

Agreued, pp. aggrieved, 500. O. Fr. agrever, to overwhelm—L. gravari, to burden, gravis, heavy.

Al, adv. completely, as in 'all to-brake' in Judges, ix. 53; and Knightes Tale, 1899: 'al is to-brosten thilke regioun;' conj. although, 99.

Al, pl. alle, adj. all, 1165; alle and some, one and all, 941. A.S. eal, pl. ealle, cog. with Icel. allr, Gothic alls, pl. allai, &c.

Alayes, n. pl. alloy, 1167. O. Fr. a lai, according to rule—L. ad legem, 'according to law,' the phrase used with reference to the mixing of metals in coinage.

Algate, adv. in all respects, 855. Literally 'all gates,' made up of all and gate = way. Cf. always, which is compounded in the same way. Gate in this sense is Scand., and is still used in the north of England and in Scotland. Cf. Icel. gata, a way.

Alliance, n. alliance, marriage, 357. O. Fr. alier, to bind up—L. al- (= ad-) and ligare, to bind.

Alwey, adv. always, 458, 810. The M. E. alles weis, in every way, is a gen. case—A.S. ealne weg, every way, an acc. case. See also Algate.

Alyghte, v. to alight, 981. M. E. alihten stands for of-lihten, the prefix a- being = A.S. on. The simple form lihtan occurs in A.S. from leóht, light.

Alyue, adv. alive, 139. Not originally an adj. but for a liue—A.S. on life, in life, hence 'alive.' Life is the dat. case of lif, life.

Ambling, pr. part. ambling, 388. O. Fr. ambler, to go at an easy pace—L. ambulare, to walk.

Ameued, v. pt. s. moved, 498. Through

O. Fr. from L. amovere, to move away.

And, conj. if, 16, 29, etc. A.S. and.

Anoon, adv. immediately, 435; **anon**, 772, 806. A.S. on án, literally 'in one (moment).'

Answerde, v. pt. s. answered, 21. A.S. andswerian—and-, against, in reply, and swerian, to swear, to speak.

A-nyghte, adv. in the night, 464. A.S. on nihte, in the night.

Apayed, pp. pleased, 1052. O. Fr. apaisier, to pacify—a pais, to a peace—L. ad pacem, to a peace.

Apennyn, the Apennines, 45.

Aperceyue, v. to perceive, 600; pr. s. aperceyueth, 1018. Fr. apercevoir—L. ad-, and percipere.

Apertinent, adj. suitable, 1010. O. Fr. apartenir—L. ad- and pertinere—per, thoroughly, and tenere, to hold.

Apese, v. to appease, 433. See Apayed.

Apparaille, n. dress, 1208. O. Fr. aparailler, to dress—a-, to, and pareiller, to put like things with like—Low L. pariculus, similar, formed from L. par, equal.

Arace, v. to tear away, 1103. O. Fr. aracer (Fr. arracher)—L. eradicare, to tear up from the root—radic-, stem of radix, a root.

Archewyues, n. pl. archwives, ruling wives, 1195. Arch- is a Gr. prefix, though it comes to us through A.S. arce-, which we find in very early use in arce-bisceop. This form was borrowed from L. archi-, Gr. archi-, from Gr. archein, to be first.

Arn, v. pr. pl. are, 342. This is the old Northumbrian aron, aren, a form of Scand. origin corresponding to the A.S. (Wessex) form sindon. Aren is put for all persons in the plural. Cf. Icel. er-u, they are. Both forms are due to the same ultimate root, ar-on = as-on and s-ind-on = as-ind-on being alike from the primitive Aryan root as-anti, they are, from which also come Sanscrit s-anti, Gr. eis-in, L. sunt, Ger. s-ind, Icel. er-u (for es-u).

Array, n. order, arrangement, 262, 670.

F

O. Fr. *arrai*, *arroi*, of Scand. origin; cf. Danish *rede*, Icel. *reidha*, *reidhi*, implements.

Arwes, *n. pl.* arrows, 1203. A.S. *arewe*, *earh*; cog. with Icel. *ör*, an arrow.

As, *conj.* like, as, 2, 7, etc.; **As** now, at this time, 23. A contraction of *also*.

Assay, *n.* trial, 621, 1138; *pl.* assayes, 697, 1166. O. Fr. *essai*—L. *exagium*, a trial of weight—Gr. *exagion*, a weighing.

Assayed, *pp.* tried, 1054.

Assenten, *v. pr.* 3 *pl.* agree, 176. O. Fr. *assentir*—L. *assentire*, to approve.

Astoned, *pp.* astonished, 337.

Astonied, *v. pt. s.* astonished, 316. A.S. *ástunian*, to stun completely, from which comes *astony*, afterwards lengthened to *astonish*, also *astound*, by addition of excrescent *d* after *n*, as in *sound*, from Fr. *son*.

Asure, *n.* azure, blue, 254. O. Fr. *azur* for *lazur*, mistaken for *l'azur* —Low L. *lazur*—Arabic *lájward*, a blue colour.

Aswowne, *adv.* in a swoon, 1079. M. E. *a* for A.S. *on*, in, and in M.E. *swounen*, *swoghenen*, formed from M. E. *swowen*, *swoghen*, which is a weak verb, closely allied to A.S. *swógan*, to sough, sigh as the wind, a strong verb, of which the pp. *geswógen* occurs with the actual sense of 'in a swoon.'

Asyde, *adv.* aside, 303. For *on side*. A.S. *side*, side, allied to *síd*, wide.

At, *prep.* at, 27, 57, etc.; from, 653. A.S. *æt*; cog. with Icel. *at*, Gothic *at*, L. *ad*.

Atones, *adv.* at once, 1178. A.S. *æt*, at, and *ánes*, gen. of *án*, one.

Atoon, *adv.* at one, 437. A.S. *æt*, at, and *án*, one.

Atte, for *at the*; **atte laste**, at the last, 547, 1027; **atte leste**, at the least, 130; **atte fulle**, fully, 749.

Atteyne, *v.* to attain, 447. O. Fr. *ateindre*—L. *attingere*, from *at-* (for *ad-*) and *tangere*, to touch.

Atwo, in two, 1169. For *on two*.

Auaille, *v.* to avail, 1194. O. Fr. *a-*

(L. *ad-*) and *valoir*, *valer*—L. *valere*, to be strong.

Auctour, *n.* author, 1141. L. *auctor*, from *augere* (*auctus*), to increase.

Audience, *n.* hearing, 329, 637, 1179. Through Fr. from L. *audientia*, a hearing, *audire*, to hear.

Auentaille, *n.* aventail, 1204. See note to line 1204. O. Fr. *ventaille*, breathing piece of a helmet—L. *ventus*, wind.

Auenture, *n.* chance, 812; *pl.* auentures, adventures, 15. Through Fr. from L. *adventura*, feminine of *adventurus*, about to happen—*ad* and *venire*, to come.

Auyse, *v.* to deliberate, 238, 350, 797. Through Fr. from L. *visum* from *videri*, to seem.

Axen, *v.* to ask, 696; **axe**, 326; *1 p. s. pr.* **axe**, 348; *pr. s.* axeth, 25; *imp. pl.* axeth, 653. A.S. *ácsian*; cf. Dut. *eischen*, Ger. *heischen*.

Ayeins, *prep.* against, 320. See **Agayns**, 911.

B

Bachelrye, *n.* the company of young men, 270. O. Fr. *bacheler*—Low L. *baccalarius*, a boy attending a baccalaria or cow-farm, according to Brachet from Low L. *bacca*—L. *vacca*, a cow.

Bad, *v. pt. s.* bade, 373. A.S. *beódan*, to command.

Badde, *adj. pl.* 522. A Celtic word; cf. Cornish and Breton *bad*, Gaelic *baodh*.

Bar, *v. pt. s.* bore, 85, 612; *2 p. s. pt.* bare, barest, 1068. See **Bere**.

Bareyne, *adj.* barren, 448. O. Fr. *baraigne* (*brehaigne*), of doubtful origin. According to Diez from a Low L. *barus*.

Barm, *n. dat.* 551; usually in this case barme. A.S. *bearm*—*beran*, to bear.

Bathe, Bath, 1170.

Beautee, *n.* beauty, 211. O. Fr. *beltet*, *belteit*—Low L. acc. *bellitat-em*—L. *bellus*, fine.

Bede, *v. 2 p. pl. pr.* offer, 360. A.S. *beódan*, to bid.

Ben, *v.* to be, 937; *pr. s. subj.* be, 17; *imp. pl.* beth, 7. A.S. *beón,* to be, from the same ultimate root as L. *fui,* I was.

Benignely, *adv.* benignly, 21. O. Fr. *benigne* (Fr. *bénin*)—L. *benignus,* kind.

Bere, *v.* to bear; *pr. s.* berth, 625. A.S. *beran;* cf. L. *ferre.*

Bestes, *n. pl.* beasts, 201, 572, 683. O. Fr. *beste* (Fr. *bête*)—L. *bestia.*

Bete, *pp.* beaten, 1158. A.S. *beátan,* to beat.

Beth, see Ben.

Bidaffed, *pp.* befooled, 1191. Intensive prefix *be-, bi-* (A.S. *be- bi-*), and *daffe,* a foolish person, connected with *deaf.* A.S. *deáf.*

Bifalleth, *v. pr. s.* happens, 449; *pt. s. subj.* bifelle, were to befall, 136. A.S. *befeallan,* from *be-,* prefix, and *feallan,* to fall.

Bigyle, *v.* to beguile, 252. M. E. prefix *be-, bi-* (A.S. *be-, bi-*) and *gylen, gilen,* to deceive—O. Fr. *guile,* deceit, from an old Teutonic root, represented by A.S. *wil,* Icel. *vel, væl,* a trick.

Birthe, *n.* birth (*dat.*), 402. A.S. *beorth,* from *beran,* to bear.

Biseke, *v.* to beseech; *1 p. s. pr.* biseke, I beseech, 1037; *pr. part.* bisekinge, beseeching, 178, 592. Prefix *be-* and *seken*—A.S. *sécan,* to seek.

Biseye, *pp.* displayed; *yuel biseye,* ill looking, 965; *richely biseye,* splendid looking, 984. A.S. *besegen,* pp. of *beseón,* from *seón,* to see.

Bisinesse, *n.* diligence, 1008. A.S. *bysig,* active.

Bisyde, *prep.* beside, 777, 1105. A.S. *be sídan,* by the side of, the first word being the prep., the latter the dat. case of *síd,* a side.

Bitake, *v. 1 p. s. pr.* I commit, 161, 559. M. E. *betaken* is formed from M. E. *taken,* to take, to deliver, with prefix *be-* (= A.S. *be-, bi-*). M. E. *taken* is Scand., as in Icel. *taka,* Swedish *taga,* Danish *tage.*

Bitwixen, *prep.* between, 815. A.S. *betweox,* from *twá,* two.

Bityde, *v.* to befall, 79; *pr. s. subj.* bityde, may betide, 306. A.S. *tídan,* to happen, from *tíd,* time.

Biwailled, *pp.* bewailed, 530. Prefix *be-, bi-* (A.S. *bi-*) and *wailen,* a Scand. word, seen in Icel. *væla,* to wail, cry woe.

Blame, to, *gerund,* to blame, 76. O. Fr. *blasmer*—L. *blasphemare*—Gr. *blasphēmein,* to speak ill.

Blesse, blisse, *v.* to bless, 553, 679. A.S. *bletsian, bledsian — blód,* blood, therefore originally 'to consecrate by blood' either by sacrifice or by sprinkling.

Blisful, *adj.* happy, 844, 1121.

Blisse, *v.* to bliss, 553. See Blesse.

Blood, *n.* offspring, 632. A.S. *blód,* from *blówan,* to bloom, as *blood* is the symbol of 'blooming' or 'flourishing' life.

Body, *n.* the chief subject, the substance, 42. A.S. *bodig,* a bondage, the body, considered as *confining* the soul.

Boistously, *adv.* loudly, 791. A Celtic word, seen in Welsh *bwystus,* ferocious, from *bwyst,* ferocity.

Boloigne, Bologna, 686, 763, 939.

Bord, *n.* board, table, 3. A.S. *bord,* the side of a ship; cog. with Icel. Dut. and Ger. *bord.*

Bore, *pp.* born, 401; **born,** borne, 444. A.S. *beran,* to bear, pp. *boren.*

Boughte, *v. pt. s.* redeemed, 1153. A.S. *bóhte,* I bought, *pt.* of *bycgan,* to buy.

Bounden, *pp.* bound, 704. A.S. *bunden,* pp. of *bindan,* to bind.

Bountee, *n.* bounty, 157, 415. O. Fr. *bonteit*—L. *bonitat-,* stem of *bonitas,* goodness, from *bonus,* good.

Boweth, *v. imp. pl.* bow, 113. A.S. *búgan,* to bend.

Brest, *n.* breast, 617. A.S. *breóst;* cog. with Ger. *brust,* Dut. *borst.*

Breste, *v.* to burst, 1169. A.S. *berstan;* cog. with Dut. and Ger. *bersten.*

Briddes, *n. pl.* birds, 572. A.S. *bridd,* a bird, especially the young of birds.

Broches, *n. pl.* brooches, 255. Named from the pin that fastens a brooch,

M. E. *broche*, a pin—Fr. *broche*—
Low L. *brocca*—L. *broccus*, a point.

Bryghte, *adv.* brightly, 1117. A.S.
beorht, bright ; cog. with Icel. *bjartr.*

Bulles, *n. pl.* bulls (papal), 739, 744.
So called from the *bulla*, the leaden
ball or seal affixed to an edict.

Burieth, *v. imp. pl.* bury, 571. A.S.
byrigan, *byrgan*, formed by the
change of *o* to *y* from *borg-en*, pp. of
beorgan, to hide, protect.

But, *conj.* unless, 174, 938. A.S. *bútan*,
conj. except ; *prep.* besides ; originally an adv. meaning 'outside ;' contracted from *be-útan*, which is
compounded of *be*, by, and *útan*,
adv. without.

Buxomly, *adv.* obediently, 186. M. E.
boxom, *buhsum*—A.S. *búg-an*, to
bend, obey, and -*sum*, suffix, as in
'win-*some*.'

Bynde, *v.* 2 *p. s. pr. subj.* bind, 1205.
A.S. *bindan*, to bind.

C

Camaille, *n.* a camel, 1196. O. Fr.
camel—L. *camelus*—Gr. *kamēlos*—
Hebrew *gāmál*. Cf. Arabic *jamal.*

Can, *v.* 1 *p. s. pr.* I am able,
304. A.S. *cunnan*, to know, pr. *ic
can*, pt. *ic cúdhe.*

Care, *v.* to feel anxiety for, 1212.
A.S. *caru*, *cearu*, anxiety ; cog.
with Gothic *kara*, sorrow, Icel. *kæri*,
complaint.

Carie, *v.* to carry, 585. O. Fr. *carier*,
to carry, *car* (Fr. *char*), a car—L.
carrus, a word of Celtic origin,
perhaps derived from Gaul as it
occurs first in Cæsar ; cf. Breton
karr, a chariot, Welsh *car*, Irish
carr.

Cas, *n.* case, occasion, 430, 561 ; chance,
316. Through Fr. from L. *cas-*,
stem of *casus*, from *cadere*, to fall.

Caughte, *v. pt. s.* took, 619 ; *pp.* caught,
1110. *Catch* is from O. Fr. *cachier*,
chacier, through a Low L. form from
L. *captare*, to catch, from *capere*, to
take.

Certayn, *adv.* certainly, 694. O. Fr.
certein—L. *cert-us*, sure.

Certes, *adv.* certainly, 106, 659.
Through Fr. from L. *certe*, surely.

Cesse, *v.* to cease, 154. Through Fr.
from L. *cessare*, frequentative of
cedere, to yield, go.

Chace, *v.* to pursue, 393. See **Caughte.**

Chambres, *n. pl.* sleeping-rooms, 263.
O. Fr. *cambre*—L. *camera*, *camara*,
a vault.

Charge, *v.* 1 *p. s. pr.* I charge, 164.
Through Fr. from Low L. *carricare*,
to load a car—L. *carrus.* See **Carie.**

Charge, *n.* responsibility, 163, 193. See
above.

Charitee, *n.* love, 221. O. Fr. *charitet*
—L. *caritat-*, stem of *caritas*, from
carus, dear.

Chaunged, *pp.* changed, 601. O. Fr.
changier (Fr. *changer*)—Low L.
cambiare—L. *cambire*, to exchange.

Chere, *n.* demeanour, 238, 241, 535, 782;
show, 678 ; kindly expression, 1112.
O. Fr. *chere* (Fr. *chère*)—Low L.
cara, the face.

Chese, *v.* to choose, 130, 153. A.S.
ceósan, pt. *ceás ;* cog. with Ger.
kiesen and Gothic *kiusan.*

Chesing, *n.* a choice, 162.

Cheste, *n.* a chest, coffin, 29. A.S.
cyste—L. *cista*—Gr. *kistē*, a chest.

Chicheuache, *n.* 'the lean cow,' 1188.
From Fr. *chiche*, lean—L. *ciccus*, a
trifle, and *vache*—L. *vacca*, a cow.
See note to line 1188.

Choys, *n.* choice, 154, 170. O. Fr.
chois (Fr. *choix*), *choisir*, to choose,
of Teutonic origin ; cf. Gothic *kiusan*,
to choose.

Clad, *pp.* clothed, 376. M. E. *clothen*,
clathen, pt. *clothede*, *cladde*, pp.
clothed, *clad.* Formed from A.S.
cládh, cog. with Dut. *kleeden* from
kleed, Scotch *kleid*, Ger. *kleiden.*

Clappeth, *v. imp. pl.* keep up a constant
clatter, 1200. From a supposed but
unverified A.S. form, *clappan*, to
clap ; cog. with Icel. *klappa*, Dut.
klappen.

Clapping, *n.* foolish talk, 999.

Clepen, *v.* to call ; men clepeth, people
call, 115. A.S. *cleopian*, *clypian*,
to call.

Clere, *adj. pl.* clear, 779. O. Fr. *cler*, *clair*—L. *clarus*.

Clerk, *n.* a clerk, student, 1; *pl.* **clerkes**, writers, 933. A.S. and O. Fr. *clerc*, —L. *clericus*—Gr. *klĕrikos*, one of the clergy—*klēros*, a lot.

Cofre, *n.* a coffer, box, 585. O. Fr. *cofre*, also *cofin*—L. *cophinus*—Gr. *kophinos*, a basket.

Collacion, *n.* a conversation, 325. O. Fr. *collation*—L. *collation-*, stem of *collatio*, a bringing together, *collatum*, supine of *conferre*.

Coloures, *n. pl.* ornaments of style, 16. O. Fr. *colour* (Fr. *couleur*)—L. *color*.

Comandement, *n.* a commandment, 649. O. Fr. *commander*—L. *commendare*.

Commune, *adj.* common, 431; *pl.* the common people, 70. O. Fr. *commun*—L. *communis*.

Comparisoun, *n.* comparison, 666, 817. Through Fr. from L. *comparatio*—*comparare*, to adjust.

Comuuly, *adv.* commonly, 726.

Conninngly, *adv.* skilfully, 1017. *Cunning* was originally pr. part. of M. E. *cunnen*, to know—A.S. *cunnan*, to know. See **Can**.

Constance, *n.* constancy, 668, 1000, 1008. Through Fr. from L. *constantia*, from *constare*, to stand together.

Constreyneth, *v. pr. s.* constrains, 800. O. Fr. *constraindre*—L. *constringere*, to bind together.

Contenance, *n.* demeanour, 924, 1110. O. Fr. *contenance*—L. *continentia*, which in later L. meant ' gesture,' from *continere*, to hold together.

Contree, *n.* country, 436. O. Fr. *contree*—Low L. *contrada*, a region, literally ' what lies opposite,' from L. *contra*, opposite.

Conueyen, *v.* to convey, 55; *pt. pl.* **conueyed**, went as convoy, 391. O. Fr. *conveier*—Low L. *conviare*—L. *con-* (*cum*), with, and *via*, a way.

Corage, *n.* courage, mind, 511, 950; disposition, 220, 692, 787; will, 907. O. Fr. *corage*—L. *cor*, the heart.

Corone, *n.* a crown, garland, 381;

coroune, 1118. O. Fr. *corone* (Fr. *couronne*)—L. *corona*.

Costage, *n.* cost, 1126. O. Fr. *coster* (Fr. *coûter*)—L. *constare*.

Cote, *n.* a cot, 398. A.S. *cote*, cog. with Dut. *kot*.

Cote, *n.* a coat, a woman's outer garment, 913. O. Fr. *cote* (Fr. *cotte*)—Low L. *cota*, of Teutonic origin. Ultimately cog. with the foregoing word, which originally meant a ' covering.'

Couche, *v.* to cower down, 1206. O. Fr. *coucher*—L. *collocare*, to put together.

Coude, *v. pt. s.* knew, 1021. See **Can**.

Couered, *v. pt. s.* covered, 914. O. Fr. *covrir* (Fr. *couvrir*)—L. *co-operire*.

Countesse, *n.* a countess, 590. From O. Fr. *conte*, *comte*, a count—L. *comit-*, stem of *comes*, a companion.

Countretaille, *n.* correspondence; at the countretaille, correspondingly, in return, 1190. Fr. *contre*, against, and *taille*, a notch, a tally or score kept on a piece of stick by *notches*—L. *talea*, a slip of wood.

Couth, *pp.* known, 942. A.S. *cúdh*, known, *pp.* of *cunnan*. See **Can**.

Coy, *adj.* still, 2. O. Fr. *coi*, *coit*—L. *quietus*.

Coyn, *n.* coin, 1168. O. Fr. *coin*—L. *cuneus*, a wedge.

Crabbed, *adj.* cross, 1203. Literally ' crab-like,' from the noun *crab*, A.S. *crabba*; cog. with Danish and Ger. *krabbe*.

Crepeth, *v.* 3 *p. s. pr.* creeps, 1134. A.S. *créopan*, cog. with Dut. *kruipen*.

Croys, *n.* cross, 556. O. Fr. *crois* (Fr. *croix*)—L. *cruc-*, stem of *crux*.

Cures, *n. pl.* cares, 82. Through Fr. from L. *cura*.

Curteisye, *n.* courtesy, 74. O. Fr. *corteisie*, *corteis*, courteous, *cort*, a court—Low L. *cortis*, a court-yard —L. *cors*, *cohors*, an inclosure.

D

Dar, *v.* 1 *p. s. pr.* I dare, 803. A.S. *ic dear*, *pt. ic dorste*.

Day, *n.* day, 152, 183, 391, etc.; *pl.* dayes, now a dayes, now-a-days, 1164. A.S. *dæg*, *pl.* *dagas*; cf. Dut., Danish, and Swedish *dag*, Ger. *tag*.

Dede, *n.* a deed (*dat.*) 241. A.S. *dǽd*.

Deeth, *n.* death, 36, 510. A.S. *deádh*; cog. with Ger. *tod*.

Deface, *v.* to obliterate, 510. O. Fr. *desfacer*—O. Fr. *des-* (= L. *dis*), apart, and *face*—L. *facies*.

Defaute, *n.* defect, 1018. O. Fr. *deffaute*, *defaut*, *default*—O. Fr. *def-* (= L. *dif-* for *dis-*), apart, and *falte*, *faute*, a fault—Low L. *fallita*, a deficiency, pp. of Low L. *fallire*, to fail—L. *fallere*, to fail.

Delyt, *n.* delight, 68. O. Fr. *deliter*—L. *delectare*, to delight.

Delytable, *adj.* delightful, 62, 199.

Delyting, *pr. part.* delighting, 997.

Demandes, *n. pl.* questions, 348. Through Fr. from L. *de-mandare*, to intrust.

Deme, *v.* to judge, 133; 1 *p. s. pr.* deme, 753; *pr. pl.* demen, 988. A.S. *déman*, to judge, from *dóm*, doom.

Dere, *adj.* (*voc.*) 101, 1056; *pl.* 999, 1089, 1093. A.S. *deóre*, *dýre*; cog. with Ger. *theuer*.

Despitously, *adv.* despitefully, cruelly, 535. O. Fr. *despit*—L. *despectus*, contempt.

Deuoir, *n.* duty, 966. O. Fr. *devoir*, *dever*, to owe—L. *debere*.

Deuyse, *v.* to narrate, 52; to contrive, 698, 739; deuysen, to imagine, 108. O. Fr. *deviser*, *devise*, a plan, through Low L. forms from L. *dividere*, to divide.

Deyen, *v.* to die, 665, 859; deye, 364; *pt. s.* deyde, 550, 1062. A Scand. word; cf. Icel. *deyja*.

Deyntee, *adj.* dainty, 1112. O. Fr. *daintie*—L. *dignitat-*, stem of *dignitas*, worthiness, *dignus*, worthy.

Deyntenous, *adj.* dainty, 265.

Dide, *v. pt. s.* did, 185. A.S. *dón*, pt. *dyde*, pp. *gedón*. The *pt. t.* is formed by reduplication.

Diffame, *n.* a bad report, 540, 730. O. Fr. *defamer*—L. *diffamare*, to spread a bad report, from *dif-* (for *dis-*), apart, and *fama*, a report.

Digne, *adj.* worthy, 818. Through Fr. from L. *dignus*.

Dignitee, *n.* dignity, 470.

Discryue, *v.* to describe; *pr. s.* discryueth, 43. O. Fr. *descrive*, short form of *descrivre*—L. *describere*.

Disdeyne, *v.* to disdain, 98. O. Fr. *desdein*, *desdegner*, from O. Fr. *des-* (L. *dis-*), apart, and *degner* (L. *dignari*), to think worthy, from L. *dignus*, worthy.

Disparage, *n.* disgrace, 908. O. Fr. *desparager*, through a Low L. *paraticum* from L. *par*, equal.

Dispence, *n.* expense, 1209. O. Fr. *despense* (Fr. *dépense*)—L. *dispensare*, to weigh out.

Dispensacion, *n.* a dispensation, 746.

Displese, *v.* to displease, 506. Through Fr. from L. *dis*, and *placere*, to please.

Dispoilen, *v.* to despoil, 374. O. Fr. *despoiller* (Fr. *dépouiller*)—L. *despoliare*, to plunder.

Do, don, *v.* to do, to cause, 353; *pr. s.* doth forth = continues, 1015; gerund, to doone, 99; *imp. pl.* doth, 568, 652; *pp.* doon, 253, 1098. A.S. *dón*, pt. *dyde*, pp. *gedón*; cog. with Dut. *doen*, Ger. *thun*, Gr. *ti-thē-mi*.

Doom, *n.* judgment, opinion, 1000.

Dore, *n.* a door, 282. A.S. *duru*; cog. with Dut. *deur*, Ger. *thür*, *thor*.

Dorste, *v. pt. s.* durst, 403. See Dar.

Doughter, *n.* a daughter; *gen.* doughter, daughter's, 608.

Doutelees, *adv.* without doubt, 485. O. Fr. *douter*, later *doubter*—L. *dubitare*, to doubt.

Dowaire, Dower, *n.* dower, 807, 848. O. Fr. *doaire*—Low L. *dotarium*—L. *dotare*, to endow.

Dradde, *v. pt. s.* dreaded, 523; *pp.* drad, dreaded, 69. See Drede.

Drank, *v. pt. s.* drank, 216. A.S. *drincan*, pt. t. *dranc*, pp. *druncen*. Cf. Ger. *trinken*, Dut. *drinken*.

Drawe, *v.* to draw, 314. A.S. *dragan* (by change of *g* to *w*). Cf. Dut. *dragen*, Ger. *tragen*.

Drede, *v.* 1 *p. s. pr.* I fear, 636; *imp. s.* dreed, fear, 1201; *pt. s.* dredde, feared, 181. A.S. *drædan,* found only in compounds, as *ondrædan,* to dread.

Drede, *n.* dread, fear, 358, 462, 634, 1155.

Drery, *adj.* sad, 514. A.S. *dreórig,* sad, originally 'gory,' and formed with suffix-*ig* from A.S. *dreór,* gore —*dreósan,* to drip.

Dresse, *v.* to address one's self, 1007, 1049. O. Fr. *dresser,* through Low L. forms from L. *directus,* pp. of *dirigere,* to direct.

Dreye, *adj. pl.* dry, 899. A.S. *dryge;* cog. with Dut. *droog,* dry, Ger. *trocken,* dry.

Dure, *v.* to endure, 166, 825. L. *durare*—*durus,* hard.

Dye, *v.* to die, 38. See **Deyen**.

Dyghte, *v.* to prepare, 974. A.S. *dihtan,* to arrange—L. *dictare,* to dictate.

E

Echoon, *adj.* each one, 124.

Eek, *conj.* also, 521. A.S. *eác;* cog. with Dut. *ook,* Ger. *auch.*

Effect, *n.* effect, 721. Through Fr. from L. *effectum,* acc. of *effectus,* pp. of *efficere,* to work out.

Egre, *adj.* eager, 1199. O. Fr. *egre* (Fr. *aigre*)—L. *acrem,* acc. of *acer,* sharp.

Ekko, *n.* echo, 1189. L. *echo*—Gr. *ēchō.*

Eldres, *n. pl.* elders, forefathers, 65, 156. A.S. *yldra,* comparative of *eald,* old.

Emelward, towards the Æmilian Way, 51.

Emprinteth, *imp. pl.* imprint, 1193. O. Fr. *empreinte*—L. *imprimere,* to press upon.

Encresen, *v.* to increase; *pr. s.* encreseth, 50; *pp.* encressed, 408. Fr. *en* (L. *in*), and O. Fr. *creisser*—L. *crescere,* to increase.

Endite, *v.* to write; *pr. pl.* 2 *p.* endite, 17; *pr. s.* enditeth, 41, 1148. O. Fr. *indicter, inditer*—Low L. *indic-*

tare, a frequentative, from L. *indicare,* to point out.

Endure, *v.* to take upon, 163. Fr. from *en* (L. *in*), and *durer*—L. *durare,* to last.

Enformed, *pp.* informed, 738. Through Fr. from L. *informare,* to put into form.

Engendred, *pp.* begotten, 158. O. Fr. *engendrer*—L. *ingenerare.*

Enlumined, *v. pt. s.* illumined, 33. Through Fr. from L. *illuminare.*

Enquere, *v.* to ask, 769. O. Fr. *enquerre, enquerir*—L. *inquirere,* to search into.

Entencion, *n.* intention, 703. Through Fr. from L. *intentionem,* acc. of *intentio.*

Entente, *n.* intention, 189, 735, 874.

Entraille, *n.* entrails, 1188. O. Fr. *entrailles*—Low L. *intralia, in-tranea* — L. *interanea,* inward things, from *inter,* within.

Equitee, *n.* equity, justice, 439. O. Fr. *equite* — L. *æquitatem,* acc. of *æquitas*—*æquus,* just.

Er, *conj.* before, 178. A.S. *ær;* cog. with Gothic *air,* Dut. *eer,* Icel. *ár.*

Ere, the ear; *pl.* eres, 629. A.S. *eáre;* cog. with Dut. *oor,* Ger. *ohr.*

Ernest, *n.* earnest, seriousness, 733. A.S. *eornest* (*n.*); cog. with Dut. and Ger. *ernst.*

Ernestful, *adj.* full of earnestness, serious, 1175.

Erst, *adv.* before, 336; at erst = at first, 985. A.S. *ærest,* superl. of *ær,* soon.

Erthe, *n.* the earth, 203. A.S. *eordhe;* cog. with Icel. *jördh,* Gothic *airtha,* Ger. *erde.*

Ese, *n.* ease, 217, 434. O. Fr. *aise,* the same word as Italian *agio.* Perhaps Celtic, as in Gaelic *adhais,* ease.

Estaat, state, 160, 767; way, 610. O. Fr. *estat*—L. *statum,* acc. of *status,* pp. of *stare,* to stand.

Estward, *adv.* eastwards, 50. A.S. *eást* (adv.) in the east, and adv. suffix signifying direction, -*weard,* gen. -*weardes.*

Ete, *v.* to eat; *pp.* eten, 1096. A.S. *etan*; cog. with Icel. *eta*, Ger. *essen*, L. *edere*.

Euel, *adv.* ill, 1052. A.S. *yfel* (adj. and n.); cog. with Dut. *euvel*, Ger. *übel*, &c.

Euer, *adv.* ever, 107, &c. A.S. *æfre*, ever.

Euene, *adj.* even, 811. A.S. *efen, efn*; cog. with Dut. *even*, Gothic *ibns*, Ger. *eben*.

Euerich, *adj.* every one, 1017. A.S. *æfre*, ever, and *ælc*, each (Scotch *ilk*).

Euermo, *adv.* continually, 754. A.S. *æfre*, ever.

F

Fader, *n.* father; *gen. s.* fader, 1136, fadres, 809; *pl.* fadres, fathers, ancestors, 61. A.S. *fæder*, cog. with L. *pater*, Gr. *patēr*, Gothic *fadar*, Icel. *fadhir*, Ger. *vater*.

Fairnesse, *n.* fairness, beauty, 384. A.S. *fæger*, cog. with Gothic *fagrs*.

Falle, *v.* to fall, happen, 126; belong, suit, 259. A.S. *feallan*; cf. Ger. *fallen*.

Fame, *n.* good report, 418. Through Fr. from L. *fama*.

Fare, *v.* to fare, get on; *pp.* fare, fared, gone, 896; *imp. s.* far, 555. A.S. *faran*, cog. with Icel. *fara*, Ger. *fahren*.

Faste, *adv.* fast, 598. A.S. *fæst*, fast, firm.

Fayn, *adv.* gladly; wolde fayn = would fain, would be glad to, 696. A.S. *fægen*, fain, glad.

Fecchen, *v.* to fetch, 276. See Fette.

Feet, *n.* a performance, 429. O. Fr. *fait*—L. *factum*.

Felaw, *n.* a fellow; *pl.* felawes, companions, 282. A Scand. word; Icel. *félagi*, *félag*, companionship—*fé*, property, and *lag*, a laying together, a law.

Fele, *adj. pl.* many, 917. A.S. *fela*; cog. with Ger. *viel*, &c.

Ferde, *v. pt. s.* fared, behaved, 1060. See Fare.

Ferme, *adj.* firm, 663. Through **Fr.** from L. *firmus.*

Ferrare, Ferrara, 51.

Ferther, *adv.* further, 712.

Feste, *n.* a feast, 191. O. Fr. *feste* (Fr. *fête*)—L. *festa*, pl. of *festum.*

Fette, *v. pt. s.* fetched, 301. A.S. *feccan*, *pt. feahte*, pp. *gefetod.*

Fey, *n.* faith, 9, 1032. O. Fr. *feid*, *fei*—L. *fidem*, acc. of *fides*, faith.

Feynting, *n.* fainting, 970. O. Fr. *feint*, weak, pretended, pp. of *feindre*, to feign—L. *fingere.*

Fieble, *adj.* feeble, 1198. O. Fr. *foible* for a supposed form *floible*—L. *flebilis*, doleful, hence 'weak'—*flere*, to weep.

Figures, *n. pl.* figures of speech, 16. Through Fr. from L. *figura.*

Fil, *pt. s.* occurred, 449, 718. A.S. *feallan*, to fall; cog. with Icel. *falla*, Ger. *fallen*, etc.

Fingres, *n. pl.* fingers, 380. A.S. *finger*; cog. with Dut. *vinger*, Icel. *fingr.*

Fleeth, *v. pr. s.* flies, 119. Scand.; cf. Icel. *flúja*, *flæja*, to flee.

Flokmele, *adv.* in a great number, 86. A.S. *flocc*, a flock (perhaps a variant of *folk*), and *mæl*, a time, portion of time, hence 'portion of food eaten at stated times.' The dat. pl. *mælum*, in parts, is thus used adverbially.

Flour, *n.* flower, choice, 919. Fr.—L. *flor-em*, acc. of *flos.*

Folwen, *v.* to follow, 1143; *imp. pl.* folweth, 1189. A.S. *fylgan, fyligan*, to follow. Cog. with Ger. *folgen.*

Folye, *n.* folly, 236. O. Fr. *folie*—*fol*, a fool—L. *follis*, a wind-bag, pl. *folles*, puffed cheeks, as of the jester.

Fond, *v. pt. s.* found, 457. A.S. *findan*, cog. with Ger. *finden.*

Fonde, *v.* to try, 283. A.S. *fandian*, to try, connected with *findan*, to find.

Forbede, *v.* 3 *p. s. imp.* may be forbid: **God forbede** = God forbid, 136, 1076; *pt. s.* forbad, forbade, 570. A.S. *forbeódan*; cf. Ger. *verbieten.*

Forgeten, pp. forgotten, 469. A.S. *forgitan;* cf. Ger. *vergessen,* Dut. *vergeten.*

Forgoon, v. to forego, 171. A.S. *forgán,* to pass over.

Fors, n. force, importance ; **no fors** = no matter, 1092. O. Fr. *force*—Low L. *fortia,* strength—L. *forti-,* stem of *fortis,* strong.

Forthermore, adv. furthermore, 169. *Further* is the comp. of *fore,* not of *forth.* A.S. *furthur,* from *for-e* (adv.), before, with comp. suffix. Cf. Dut. *vorders,* comp. of *vor,* before, with comp. suffix *-der-s,* and Gr. *proteros,* comp. of *pro,* before.

Foryelde, v. to yield in return for, 831. A.S. *forgyldan,* to recompense, *gyldan,* to pay, yield.

Foryetful, adj. forgetful, 472. A.S. *forgitol.* See Forgeten.

Foryiue, v. to forgive, 526. A.S. *forgifan;* cf. Ger. *vergeben,* Dut. *vergeven.*

Fostred, pp. nurtured, 1043. A.S. *fóstrian*—*fostor,* nourishment, allied to *fóda,* food.

Foul, adj. foul, ugly, 1209. A.S. *fúl;* cf. Ger. *faul,* Dut. *vuil.*

Founde, pp. found, 146 ; **founden,** 520. See Fond.

Fraunceys, Francis, 31.

Fre, adj. free, bounteous, 1209. A.S. *freó;* cog. with Icel. *frí,* Ger. *frei.*

Frely, adv. freely, 352.

Freletee, n. frailty, 1160. O. Fr. *fraile*—L. *fragilis,* easily broken.

Freres, n. pl. friars, 12. O. Fr. *frere, freire*—L. *fratrem,* acc. of *frater,* a brother.

Fulfild, pp. fulfilled, 596. A.S. *fulfyllan*—*ful,* full, and *fyllan,* to fill.

Fulliche, adv. fully, 706.

Furlong, n. a furlong ; **furlong wey** = a distance of a furlong, a short time, originally 'a furrow-long,' 516. A.S. *furh,* a furrow, and *lang,* long.

G

Game, n. sport, 609, 733. A.S. *gamen,* sport ; cog. with Icel. *gaman.*

Gan, v. pt. s. began. Used as an auxiliary = did, 392, 679; in pl. **gonne** = did, 1103. A.S. *ginnan,* to begin, commonly *on-ginnan,* pt. *ongann,* pp. *ongunnen.*

Gazed, v. pt. s. gazed, 1003. A Scand. word; allied to *aghast.*

Gemmes, n. pl. gems, precious stones, 254, 779. Through Fr. from L. *gemma,* a bud, also a jewel.

Gentilesse, n. nobility, excellence, 96; delicate nurture, 593.

Gentilleste, adv. noblest, 72.

Gentils, n. pl. gentry, people of rank, 480. O. Fr. *gentil*—L. *gentilis,* belonging to the same clan—*gens,* a clan.

Gere, n. gear, clothing, 372. A.S. *gearwe, fem. pl.* preparation, dresses—*gearo,* ready, whence also *yare.*

Gesse, v. 1 p. s. pr. I suppose, 469. Scand.; cf. Danish *gisse,* Swedish *gissa,* to guess.

Gest, n. a guest, 338; pl. **gestes,** 339. A.S. *gæst, gest, gast;* cog. with Dut. and Ger. *gast,* L. *hostis,* &c.

Gete, v. to get (gerund), 1210. A.S. *gitan, gæt, giten.*

Glade, v. to make glad, 1174; pr. s. **gladeth,** cheers, 1107; imp. s. 3 p. **glade,** may he comfort, 822. Formed from A.S. *glæd,* shining, bright, glad ; cog. with Dut. *glad,* smooth, bright, Ger. *glat,* smooth.

Gon, goon, v. to go, 288, 847; pr. pl. **goon,** 898; pp. **goon,** 774. A.S. *gán,* a contracted form of *gangan,* to go.

Gonne, v. pt. pl. did, 1103. See Gan.

Goode, adj. (voc.) good, 852. A.S. *gód;* cog. with Gothic *gods,* Ger. *gut,* &c.

Goost, n. a spirit, 926, 972. A.S. *gást;* cog. with Dut. *geest,* Ger. *geist.*

Goth, v. imp. pl. go, 568 ; 3 p. s. pr. **gooth,** 300. See Gon.

Gouernaille, n. management, 1192. Literally 'the steering of the helm.' Fr. *gouvernail*—L. *gubernaculum,* the helm of a ship.

Gouernance, n. control, arrangement, 23, 994, 1161.

Gouerneth, v. imp. pl. arrange, 322.

O. Fr. *governer*—L. *gubernare*—Gr. *kybernaein*, to steer.

Grace, *n.* favour, 424. O. Fr. *grace*—L. *gratia.*

Graue, *v.* to bury, 681. A.S. *grafan*, to dig; cog. with Ger. *graben*, &c.

Graunten, *v.* to grant, 179; *pt. s.* graunted, 183; *imp. s.* 3 *p.* graunte = may he grant, 842. O. Fr. *graanter*, a later spelling of *craanter*, to caution—Low L. *creantare*, put for *credentare*—L. *credent—credere*, to believe.

Graunt mercy for Fr. *grand merci*, many thanks, 1088.

Gree, *n.* gratitude, 1151. Through Fr. from L. *gratus*, pleasing.

Greene, *adj.* (*def.*) green, 120. A.S. *grēne;* cog. with Ger. *grün*, Dut. *groen*, etc.

Grete, *adj.* (*voc.*) great, 382. A.S. *grēat;* cog. with Dut. *groot*, Ger. *gross.*

Grette, *v. pt. s.* greeted, 952. A.S. *grētan*, to visit; cog. with Dut. *groeten*, Ger. *grüssen.*

Gretter, *adj.* (comp.) greater, 1126.

Greueth, *v. pr. s.* (used impersonally) it vexes, 647. Through Fr. from L. *gravare*, to weigh down.

Grisildis, Griselda, 210; Grisild, 232; Grisilde, 365.

Grucche, *v.* to murmur at, 170, 354. O. Fr. *groucher*, *grocer*, to murmur; a Teutonic origin, but ultimately imitative.

Gyde, *v.* to guide, 776. O. Fr. *guider*, of Teutonic origin; from a source allied to Gothic *witan*, to watch, and A.S. *witan*, to know.

Gye, *v.* to guide, rule, 75.

H

Habundance, *n.* abundance, 203. Through O. Fr. *abondance*, from L. *abundantia*, *abundare*, to overflow.

Habundant, *adj.* abundant, 59.

Hadde, *v. pt. s.* had, took, 303, 438; *pt. pl.* hadden, 201.

Han, *v. pr. pl.* have, 107, 188, 381.

Handle, *v.* to handle, touch, 376. A.S. *handlian* formed from *hand.*

Hardily, *adv.* boldly, 25. O. Fr. *hardi*, brave, of Teutonic origin.

Hardinesse, *n.* boldness, 93.

Hastif, *adj.* hasty, 349. O. Fr. *hastif—haste* (Fr. *hâte*), haste, of Scand. origin.

Hastilich, *adv.* quickly, 911.

Hatede, *v. pt. s.* hated, 731. A.S. *hatian*, to hate, *hete*, hatred; cog. with Dut. *haat*, Ger. *hass.*

Haue, *v.* to have, 242; *imp. s.* haue, take, 567. A.S. *habban*, pt. *hæfde*, pp. *gehæfd.*

Hauke, *v.* to hawk, 81. The M. E. forms of the noun are *hauk*, *hauek* (= *havek*)—A.S. *hafoc*, *heafoc.* Cf. Dut. *havic*, Ger. *habicht.*

Heeld, *v.* 1 *p. s. pt.* I held, considered, 818; *pt. pl.* helde, 426. A.S. *healdan*, pt. *heōld;* cog. with Dut. *houden*, Ger. *halten.*

Heer, *adv.* here, 36. A.S. *hér*, adv.; from the base of *hé*, he.

Heer-vp-on, *adv.* hereupon, 190.

Hem, *pron. pl. acc.* them, 17, 38, etc.; (*dat.*) 481, etc. A.S. *him*, dat. s. and pl. of *hé.*

Hente, *v. pt. s.* seized, 534; *pp.* hent, seized, 676. A.S. *hentan*, to seize.

Her, *pron.* (possessive) their, 185, 187, etc. A.S. *heora*, gen. pl. of *hé.*

Herbergage, *n.* harbourage, abode, 201. Of Scand. origin. Icel. *herbergi*, a harbour, literally 'army shelter,' from Icel. *herr*, an army, and *barg*, pt. t. of *bjarga*, to shelter. Cf. the Old High Ger. *hereberga*, a camp, from Old High Ger. *heri* (Ger. *heer*), an army, and *bergan*, to shelter (whence Fr. *auberge*, and Italian *albergo*).

Herbes, *n. pl.* herbs, 226. Through Fr. from L. *herba.*

Here, *v.* to hear, 56. A.S. *hýran*, *héran*, pt. t. *hýrde*, pp. *gehýred;* cog. with Dut. *hooren*, Ger. *hören.*

Heres, *n. pl.* hair, 379, 1085. A.S. *hær;* cog. with Dut. *haar.*

Herie, *v. pr. pl.* praise, 616. A.S. *herian*, to praise, *here*, fame.

Herkneth, *v. imp. pl.* listen, 1141, 1163.

A.S. *hyrcnian*, extended from *hyran*, to hear.

Herte, *n.* heart, 412; *gen. s.* or *pl.* **hertes**, 112. A.S. *heorte.* Cf. Dut. *hart*, Ger. *herz.*

Hertly, *adj.* hearty, 176, 502.

Heste, *n.* command, 128, 568; *pl.* **hestes**, 529. The final *t* is excrescent, as in *whils-t*, *amongs-t*, &c. A.S. *hæs*, a command—*hátan*, to command.

Heuinesse, *n.* heaviness, grief, 432, 678. M. E. *heui* (= *hevi*)—A.S. *hefig*, heavy—A.S. *hef-*, stem formed from *hebban* (pt. t. *hóf*), to heave.

Hewe, *n.* hue, appearance, 377. A.S. *hiw*, colour.

Highte, *v. pt. s.* was called, was named, 32, 210. A.S. *hátte*, I am called, I was called, *pt. t.* of A.S. *hátan*, to call, to be called or named.

Him, *pron. dat. s.* and *pl.* to them, 65, 79, etc. A.S. *him*, dat. s. and pl. of *hé*, he.

His, *pron.* (possessive neut.) its, 263, etc. A.S. *his*, gen. s., neuter of *hé*.

Holde, *v.* to hold; *pr. s. subj.* 287; *pp.* **holde**, 273, **holden**, 205, 828. A.S. *healdan*; cog. with Dut. *houden*, Ger. *halten.*

Homlinesse, *n.* homeliness, domestic duty, 429. The M. E. *hoom*, home, is from A.S. *hám*; cog. with Dut. and Ger. *heim.*

Honest, *adj.* honest, honourable, 333. O. Fr. *honeste* (Fr. *honnête*)—L. *honestus*, honourable.

Honestetee, *n.* honour, 422.

Honoureth, *v. imp. pl.* honour ye, 370. Through Fr. from L. *honorare.*

Honurable, *adj.* honourable, 767.

Hool, *adj.* whole, 861. A.S. *hál*, whole; cog. with *hale*, M. E. *heil*, of Scand. origin.

Hors, *n.* a horse, 388. A.S. *hors* (neut.) *pl. hors.* Cf. Icel. *hross*, Ger. *ross.*

Hoste, *n.* host, 1. O. Fr. *host* (Fr. *hôte*)—L. *hostem*, acc. of *hostis*, an enemy, originally 'a stranger,' 'a guest.'

Houndes, *n. pl.* hounds, dogs, 1095. A.S. *hund*; cog. with Dut. *hond*, Ger. *hund.*

Housbond, *n.* a husband, 698. A.S. *husbonda*, of Scand. origin. Icel. *húsbôndi*—Icel. *hús*, a house, and *búandi*, dwelling in, pr. part. of *búa*, to dwell.

Humanitee, *n.* kindness, 92. L. *humanitas—humanus—homo*, a man.

Humilitee, *n.* humility, 1143. O. Fr. *humiliteit*—L. *humilitatem*, acc. of *humilitas—humilis*, low.

Hunte, *v.* to hunt, 81. A.S. *huntian*, to capture.

Hunting, *n.* hunting, **on hunting** = on hunting, 234.

Hy, *adj.* high, elevated, 18; (*dat.*) **hye**, 135; *pl.* **hye**, 45. A.S. *heáh*, *héh*; cf. Dut. *hoog*, Ger. *hoch.*

Hyghte, *v. pt. pl.* 2 *p.* promised, 496. A.S. *hatan*, to promise, pt. t. *ic héht.*

I

Ialousye, *n.* jealousy, 1205. O. Fr. *jalous* (Fr. *jaloux*), jealous—Low L. *zelosus*—L. *zelus*—Gr. *zêlos*, ardour.

Iame, James, 1154.

Iane, *n.* a small coin, properly of Genoa, 999. L. *Janua*, Genoa.

Ianicle, Janicola, 404, 632; **Ianicula**, 208, 304.

Impertinent, *adj.* not pertinent or relevant, 54. Fr. *im-* = L. *im-* (for *in-*), not, and L. *pertinent-*, stem of pr. part. of *pertinere*, to pertain to.

Importable, *adj.* not to be endured, 1144. L. *importabilis—in*, not, and *portare*, to carry.

Inwith, *prep.* within, 870.

Iob, Job, 932.

Itaille, Italy, 33, 266.

Iugement, *n.* judgment, opinion, 53; *pl.* **iugementz**, 439. Fr. *juge*, a judge —L. *judicem*, acc. of *judex—jus*, law.

K

Kembd, *pp.* combed, 379. A.S. *cemban*, to comb, pt. *cembde.*

Kepe, *n.* heed, care, 1058. A.S. *cépan*, to traffic, also to store up—*céáp*,

barter, price, from L. *caupo*, a
huckster.

Kepeth, *v. pr. s.* keeps, 1133; *pt. s.*
kepte, kept, 223; *pp.* kept, 1098.

Kesse, *v.* to kiss 1057; *pt. s.* kiste, 679.
M. E. *coss*, a kiss (whence the verb
kissen)—A.S. *coss*, whence *cyssan*,
verb. Cf. Dut. *kus*, Ger. *kuss*, a
kiss.

Knaue, *n.* a boy, 444, 447; **knaue child**
= a man-child or boy, 612. A.S.
cnafa, *cnapa*, of Celtic origin. See
note to line 444.

Knowen, *pp.* known, 689. A.S.
cnáwan, pt. *cneów*, pp. *cnáwen*.

L

Ladde, *v. pt. pl.* led, 390. A.S. *lædan*,
pt. *lædde*. Cf. Dut. *leiden*, Ger.
leiten.

Lappe, *n.* a wrapper, 585. The M. E.
lappen, also *wlappen*, is another form
of *wrappen*, which is a derivative of
warp.

Lasse, *adj. pl.* smaller; **lasse and more**
= smaller and greater, all, 67. A.S.
læssa (adj.) less, *læs* (adv.).

Last, *v. pr. s.* lasts, extends, 266. A.S.
læstan, to observe, to last, originally
'to follow in the track of,' from *lást*,
a foot-track.

Lat, *v. imp. s.* let, 162. See Lete.

Laughe, *v.* to laugh, 353. A.S. *hlehhan*,
hlihan (pt. t. *hlóh*). Cf. Dut.
lagchen, Ger. *lachen*.

Laureat, *adj.* laureate, crowned with
laurel, 31. L. *laureatus*—*laurea*.

Leef, *n.* a leaf, 1211. A.S. *leáf*; cog.
with Dut. *loof*, Ger. *laub*.

Leet, *v. pt. s.* let, 82. See Lete.

Lenger, *adj.* longer, 300; **euer lenger
the more** = the longer, the more,
687. A.S. *lengra*, comparative of
lang.

Lente, *n.* Lent, the forty-days' fast,
beginning with Ash Wednesday.
The fast is in spring-time, and the
old sense is simply spring, 12. A.S.
lencten, the spring.

Lenuoy, *n.* l'envoy, the epilogue spoken
at the close, 1177. Fr. *l'envoi*—
envoyer, to send.

Lese, *v.* to lose, 508. A.S. *leósan*, pt.
leás, pp. *loren*; cog. with Dut.
liezen (seen only in compound *ver-
liezen*), and with Ger. *lieren* (seen in
ver-lieren).

Lest, *n.* desire, 619. See Lust.

Leste, *v. pr. s. subj.* it may please
(impers.), 105; *pt. s.* it pleased, 716,
986. A.S. *lystan*, to choose, generally used impersonally.

Leste, *adj.* (superl.) least, 966, *pl.* leste,
67. A.S. *læsast*, whence *læst* by contraction.

Lete, *v.* to let, 745; *imp. pl.* lete, let,
98. A.S. *lætan*, to let, pt. *leót*, pp.
læten; cog. with Dut. *laten*, Ger.
lassen.

Lette, *v. pt. s.* delayed, 389. Used in-
transitively. A.S. *lettan*, to hinder
—*læt*, late.

Lette, *n.* let, hindrance, 300.

Leue, *v.* to leave, 250. A.S. *læfan*, to
leave a heritage—*láf*, a heritage—
lifian, to remain, from which comes
live.

Leuer, *adv.* liefer, rather, 444. A.S.
leóf; cf. Dut. *lief*, Ger. *lieb*.

Leueth, *v. pr. s.* believes, 1001. In the
M. E. *beleuen* (*beleven*), the prefix
be- (by) is substituted for the older
prefix *ge-*. A.S. *gelýfan*, to believe,
hold dear—*ge-*, prefix, and *leóf*,
dear.

Leye, *v.* to lay, 193. A.S. *lecgan*, pt.
legde, pp. *gelegd*; causal of *licgan*, to
lie.

Leyser, *n.* leisure, 286. O. Fr. *leisir*
(Fr. *loisir*), leisure, originally an infinitive—L. *licere*, to be permitted.

Lief, *adj.* dear, 479. A.S. *leóf*.

Lige, *adj.* liege, 310; *pl.* liges, subjects,
67. O. Fr. *lige*, of Teutonic origin.
Cf. Ger. *ledig*.

Likerous, *adj.* lustful, sinful, 214.
M. E. *lechur*, *lechour*—O. Fr.
lecheor, one addicted to gluttony
and lewdness, literally 'one who
licks up'—O. Fr. *lecher* (Fr. *lécher*),
to lick—Old High Ger. *lechon* (Ger.
lecken), to lick.

Linage, *n.* lineage, 71, 137, 795.
Through Fr. from L. *linea*, a line.

Linian, the canonist Giovanni di Lignano, 34. See note to line 34.

List, *v. pr. s.* (impersonally) it pleases, 647, 933. A.S. *lystan*, to desire, *lust*, pleasure.

Liuen, *v.* to live, 109. A.S. *lifian*, to live, to remain; cf. Dut. *leven*, Ger. *leben*.

Loked, *v. pt. s.* looked, 340. A.S. *lócian*, to look.

Loking, *n.* looking, appearance, 514.

Longeth, *v. pr. s.* belongs, 285. A.S. *langian*, to lengthen—*lang*, long. The original sense is to become long, hence to stretch the mind after, to crave, also to apply, belong.

Lordshipe, *n.* lordship, 797. A.S. *hláford*, a lord (probably for *hláf-weard*, a loaf ward), *hláf*, a loaf, and *weard*, a guard.

Lore, *n.* lore, learning, 87, 788. A.S. *lár*, lore; cog. with Dut. *leer*, Ger. *lehre*.

Lorn, *pp.* lost, 1071. A.S. *leósan*, to lose, pt. *leás*, pp. *loren*.

Louede, *v. pt. s.* loved, 413, 690. The A.S. *lufu*, love, is closely allied to lief.

Loueth, *v. imp. pl.* love ye, 370.

Loth, *adj.* loth, unwilling, 364. A.S. *láдh*, from the pt. t. of *lidhan*, to travel.

Low, *adj.* low, humble, 425. Scand.; Icel. *lágr*, low, Danish *lav*.

Lulled, *v. pt. s.* soothed, 553. A Scand. word, ultimately of imitative origin.

Lumbardye, Lombardy, 72; **West Lumbardye**, 46, 945.

Lust, *v. pr. s.* (impersonally) it pleases, 322. See **List**.

Lust, *n.* pleasure, 80, 968; wish, 658. See **List**.

Lusty, *adj.* pleasant, 59.

Lyght, *n.* light, 1124. A.S. *leóht*, cog. with Dut. and Ger. *licht*.

Lyk, *adj.* like, 257, etc. A.S. *líc*, *ge-líc*; cog. with Ger. *g-leich*, Dut. *ge-lijk*.

Lyken, *v.* to please, 506; *pr. s.* lyketh, it pleases, 106, 311, 845, 1031. A.S. *lícian*, to delight, literally 'to be like,' from *líc*, *ge-líc*, like.

Lyklinesse, *n.* probability, 396.

Lymes, *n. pl.* limbs, 682. A.S. *lim.*

Lynage, *n.* lineage, 991. See **Linage**.

Lynde, *n.* a linden-tree, 1211. A.S. *lind*, the tree; cog. with Dut. *linde*, Ger. *linde*.

Lyte, *adv.* a little, 935. A.S. *lyt*, *lytel*, little; cog. with Dut. *luttel*.

Lyues, *n. gen. s.* life's, 308. A.S. *líf*, gen. *lifes*, dat. *lífe*. This gen. is also used adverbially = living, 903.

M

Maille, *n.* mail, armour, 1202. O. Fr. *maille*—L. *macula*, a spot, a hole, mesh of a net.

Manaceth, *v. pr. s.* menaces, 122. O. Fr. *menace*—L. *minacia*, a threat—*minaci-*, stem of *minax*—*minæ*, things threatening to fall.

Maner, *n.* manner, kind of; **maner sergeant** = kind of sergeant, 519; **maner wyse** = kind of way, 605.

Manere, *n.* manner, way, 781, 1176. O. Fr. *maniere*, manner—*manier* (adj.), habitual, allied to *manier*, to handle, *main*, the hand—L. *manus*.

Maried, *v. pt. s.* (transitively) he caused to be married, 1130. Through Fr. from L. *maritare*, to marry—*maritus*, a husband.

Markis, *n.* a marquis, 64; *gen. s.* marquis', 994. O. Fr. *markis*—Low L. *marchensis*, a prefect of the marches—Old Ger. *marcha*, a march or boundary. A *march* in Scotland is a boundary.

Markisesse, *n.* a marchioness, 283, 394, 942, 1014.

Masednesse, *n.* amazement, 1061. M. E. *masen*, to confuse, is of Scand. origin; cf. Icel. *masa*, to prate.

Matere, *n.* matter, subject, 90, 1175. O. Fr. *matere*, *matiere*—L. *materia*.

May, *v.* 1 *p. s. pr.* I may, 304. M. E. *mowen* (infinitive), pr. *may*, pt. *mighte*—A.S. *mugan*, to be able, pr. *mæg*, pt. *mihte*.

Mayde, *n.* a maid, maiden, 257, 377, 446, 779. A.S. *mægden*, *mægedh*, a maiden.

Mayntene. *v. pr. s. imp.* may he maintain, 1171. Fr. *maintenir*—L. *manu tenere*, to hold in the hand.

Maystow = mayst thou, 265, 1070.

Meke, *adj.* meek, 141. Scand.; cf. Icel. *mjúkr*, soft, Swedish *mjuk*.

Melodye, *n.* melody, 271. Fr. *melodie*—L. *melodia*—Gr. *melōdia*, a singing, from *mel-os*, a song, and *ōdē*, an ode.

Merie, *adj.* glad, 615. A.S. *merg*, merry, perhaps of Celtic origin. Cf. Irish and Gaelic *mear*, merry.

Meruaille, **merueille**, *n.* marvel, 248, 1186. Fr. *merveille*—L. *mirabilia*, wonderful things, from *mirari*, to wonder.

Meste, *adj.* (superl.) most, 131. A.S. *mæst*.

Mesure, *n.* measure, 256; moderation, 622. O. Fr. *mesure*—L. *mensura*, from *metiri*, to measure.

Mette, *v. pt. pl.* met, 390. A.S. *mētan*, to find, meet, formed (with the usual vowel change from *ō* to *ē*) from A.S. *mōt*, a meeting.

Mille, *n.* a mill, 1200. A.S. *myln*, *mylen*—L. *molina*, extended from *mola*, a mill.

Mo, *adj. pl.* (comp.) more, 318; tymes mo = at more times, at other times, 449; mo = more than her, others besides, 1039. A.S. *má*, more in number, perhaps originally an adverbial form like L. *magis*, Ger. *mehr*.

Mordred, *pp.* murdered, 725, 728. A.S. *morthor*, murder, *morth*, death. Cf. Icel. *morth*, Ger. *mord*, and the cog. L. *mors*.

Mordrer, *n.* a murderer, 732.

More, *adj.* (comp.) greater, **more** and **lesse**, greater and lesser, 940. A.S. *mára*, a double comp. form, cog. with Icel. *meiri*, Gothic *maiza*.

Mot, 1 *p. s. pr.* I must, 872; **moot**, 172; 2 *p. s. pr. subj.* mot thou = mayst thou, 557; *pr. pl.* 2 *p.* mote, ye must, 526; *pt. s. subj.* moste, might, 550. M. E. *mot*, *moot*, I am able, *pt.* moste, muste—A.S. *ic mót*, pt. *ic móste*, I must; as if from an infinitive *motan.* Cf. Ger. *müssen*, pr. t. *ich muss*, pt. t. *ich musste.*

Mowe, *v. pr. pl.* may, 530. See May.

Murthe, *n.* mirth, 1123. A.S. *myradh*, *mirhth*, *mirigth*, mirth—*merg*, merry. See Merie.

Myghte, *v. pt. subj.* 1 *p. s.* I could, 638. See May.

Myn, *pron.* (possessive) my, 143, 365. A.S. *mín*, gen. of *ic*, I.

N

Naille, *v. imp.* 3 *p. s.* let it nail or fasten, 1184; *pp.* nailed, fastened, 29. A.S. *nægel*; cog. with Dut. and Ger. *nagel.*

Namely, *adv.* especially, 484, 626. A.S. *nama*, a name; cog. with Dut. *naam*, Ger. *name*, L. *nomen* or *gnomen*, Gr. *onoma*, Sanskrit *náman.*

Nas = ne was, was not, 405, 432. A.S. *næs*, was not.

Nat, *adv.* not, 12, 36, 98, etc. A.S. *náwiht*, also *náht*—*ná*, not and *wiht*, a whit.

Nay, *adv.* no, 177; as opposed to yea, 355; it is no nay = there is no denying it, 817, 1139. Scand., cf. Icel. *nei*. *Nay* is the negative of *aye*.

Ne, *adv.* not, 4; nor, 363, 1092. A.S. *ne*, not, nor. Cf. Gothic *ni*, Russian *ne*, Irish, Gaelic, and Welsh *ni*, L. *ne* (in *non-ne*), and Sanskrit *na*, not.

Necligence, *n.* negligence, 661. Through Fr. from L. *negligentia.*

Nede, *adv.* (dat. form) needs, 531; (gen. form) nedes, 11. A.S. *nýd*; cog. with Ger. *noth*, Dut. *nood.*

Neded, *v. pt. s.* it needed, 457.

Needles, *adv.* needlessly, 621; needlees, 455.

Nekke, *n.* neck, 113. A.S. *hnecca*; cog. with Dut. *nek*, Ger. *nacken.*

Nempned, *v. pt. s.* named, 609. A.S. *nemnan*, to name.

Neuer, *adv.* never, 1090, etc. A.S. *næfre*, from *ne*, not, and *æfre*, ever.

Newe, *adj. def.* new, 841; *adv.* newly, 3, 378. A.S. *niwe*, *neowe*; cog. with Dut. *nieuw*, Ger. *neu*, etc.

Nil, *v.* 1 *p. s. pr.* I desire not, 646; I will not, 363; *pr. s.* will not, 119.

A.S. *nillan*, short for *ne willan*, not to wish. Cf. L. *nolle*.

Nis = ne is, is not, 448.

Noblesse, *n.* nobility, 782. Through Fr. and Low L. forms from L. *nobilis*.

Noght, *adv.* not, 197, &c. See Nat.

Non, *adj.* none, 1071. A.S. *nân—ne*, not, and *ân*, one.

Norice, *n.* a nurse, 561, 618. O. Fr. *norrice* (Fr. *nourrice*)—L. *nutricem*, acc. of *nutrix*, a nurse, *nutrire*, to nourish.

Norished, *pp.* nourished, brought up, 399.

Norishinge, *n.* nourishing, nurture, 1040.

No thing, *adv.* in no respect, 228, 480.

Noueltee, *n.* novelty, 1004. O. Fr. *noveliteit*—L. *novelitatem*, acc. of *novelitas—novus*, new.

Nowches, *n. pl.* jewels, 382. O. Fr. *nouche*—Low L. *nusca*, a brooch, of Teutonic origin.

Ny, *adv.* nearly; wel ny = almost, 82. A.S. *neáh; adj. adv.* and *prep.*

Nyght, *n.* night, 354. A.S. *niht*, *neaht; cog.* with Dut. and Ger. *nacht*, Icel. *nâtt*, L. *nox* (stem *noct-*), Gr. *nux* (stem *nukt-*).

O

Obeisaunce, *n.* obedience, 24, 230, 502. O. Fr. *obeisance* (Fr. *obéïssance*)—L. *obedientia*, *obedire*, to obey.

Obeisant, *adj.* obedient, 66.

Of, *prep.* by, 70; with, 33; for, 180; of grace = by his favour, 178. A.S. *of*; cog. with Gr. *apo*, L. *ab*, Icel. Dut. and Gothic *af*, Ger. *ab*.

Office, *n.* duty; houses of office = servants' offices, 264. Through Fr. from L. *officium*.

Of-newe, *adv.* anew, 938.

Ofte, *adj. pl.* many, 226; *adv.* often, 722; *adv.* (comparative) ofter, oftener, 215, 620. A.S. *oft*; whence M. E. *ofte*, with added *-e*, and lastly, *ofte-n*, with added *-n*; cog. with Icel. *oft*, Gothic *ufta*, Ger. *oft*.

On, *prep.* on, in, at, 80, 81, etc. A.S.

on; cog. with Dut. *aan*, Icel. *á*, Danish *ân*, Ger. *an*, &c.

Onlofte, *adv.* aloft, 229. Scand., cf. Icel. *á lopt* (pronounced *loft*). The prefix *a* = Icel. *á* = A.S. *on*, in.

Oon, *adj.* one, the same, 711; oon the fairest = one who was the fairest, 212; euer in oon = continually alike, 602, 677; many oon, many a one, 775. A.S. *ân;* cog. with L. *un-us*, Icel. *einn*, Dut. *een*, Ger. *ein*.

Otherweyes, *adv.* otherwise, 1072. A.S. *ôther*, other, second, is for *anther;* cog. with Dut. and Ger. *ander*, L. *alter* (for *anter*), Sanskrit *antara*, other.

Oueral, *adv.* in all respects, 1048. A.S. *ofer* is cog. with Dut. *over*, Ger. *über*, Gothic *ufar*, Gr. *hyper*, L. *s-uper*.

Oughte, *v. pt. s. subj.* it should behove us, 1150; *pt. s. indic.* it was fit, it was due, 1120. A.S. *âgan*, to owe, the pr. t. is *ic ah*, really an old pt. t.: hence the pt. t. *ic âhte*, from which M. E. *ahte*, *aughte*, *oughte*, the modern *ought*.

Our, *adj.* our, 357. A.S. *ûre*, of us, gen. pl. of *wé*, we.

Outerly, *adv.* utterly, 335, 639. A.S. *ûtor*, utter, a compar. of *ût*, out.

Outraye, *v.* to become outrageous, 643. O. Fr. *ontrage*, *oultrage* (Fr. *outrage*)—*oltre* (Fr. *outre*), beyond, with suffix *-age* (= L. *-aticum*)—L. *ultra*, beyond.

Owen, *adj.* own, 504, 652. The M. E. forms are *ayen*, *awen*, *owen*—A.S. *âgen*, own, originally pp. of *âgan*, to possess.

Oxenford, Oxford, 1.

Oxes, *n. gen. s.* ox's, 207, 291. A.S. *oxa*, pl. *oxan*, cf. Ger. *ochse*, Dut. *os*.

Oxe-stalle, *n.* ox-stall, 398. A.S. *oxan steal*, *oxan* being *gen.* of *oxa*, and *steal*, *stæl*, a station, a stall.

P

Pace, *v. pr. s. subj.* may pass away, 1092. Through Fr. and Low L. from L. *passus*, a step.

Padowe, Padua, 27.

Paleys, *n.* palace, 197. Through Fr. from L. *palatium*, a building on the Palatine hill at Rome.

Panik, a district in Italy, 764, 939.

Parauenture, *adv.* peradventure, 234. Fr. *par*, by, and *aventure*, adventure. See **Auenture**.

Parfitly, *adv.* perfectly, 690. O. Fr. *parfit, parfeit* (Fr. *parfait*)—L. *perfectus*, pp. of *perficere*, to complete.

Passed, *pp.* passed, spent, 610; *pr. part.* passing, surpassing, 240. See **Pace**.

Pemond, Piedmont, 44.

Penible, *adj.* painstaking, 714. Through Fr. *penible* and *peine*, from L. *pœna*.

Peples, *n. gen. s.* people's, 412. O. Fr. *pueple* (Fr. *peuple*)—L. *populum*, acc. of *populus*, people.

Perce, *v.* to pierce, 1204. Fr. *percer*, through Low L. forms from L. *pertundere*, to thrust through.

Persone, *n.* a person, 73. O. Fr. *persone* (Fr. *personne*)—L. *persōna*, a mask used by an actor, hence a character assumed, from *per*, through, and *sonare*, to sound.

Petrark, Petrarch, 31, 1147.

Peyne, *n.* pain; **vpon peyne** = under a penalty, 586. Fr.—L. *pœna*.

Peyned hir, *pt. s.* (reflexive) took pains, 976.

Pistil, *n.* epistle, 1154. O. Fr. *epistle*, also *epistre*—L. *epistola*—Gr. *epistolē*.

Pitous, *adj.* sad, 1121. O. Fr. *piteus*—Low L. *pietosus*—L. *pietas*.

Playn, *adj.* plain; in short and **playn** = in brief, plain terms, 577. Through Fr. from L. *planus*, flat, evident.

Playne, *n.* a plain, 59. Through Fr. from L. *plānus*, plain, flat.

Plentee, *n.* plenty, 264. O. Fr. *plente, plentet*—L. *plenitatem*, acc. of *plenitas*, from *plenus*, full.

Plesance, *n.* pleasure, 501, 658, 663, 672, 873, 959, 964; kindness, 1111. Through Fr. from L. *placere*.

Pley, *n.* play, sport, 10, 11, 1030. A.S. *plega*, a game.

Pleyn, *adv.* plainly, openly, 19, 637.

Pleyne, *v.* 1 *p. pl. pr. subj.* we may complain, 97. Fr. from L. *plangere*, to complain.

Plowman, *n.* a ploughman, 799. M. E. *plouh, plow*, also A.S. *ploh*, is a borrowed word, probably Scand. The A.S. word for *plough* is *sulh*. Cf. Icel. *plógr*. Grimm has doubts as to its being really a Teutonic word, and Skeat suspects it to be Celtic; Gaelic *bloc*, a block of wood.

Plye, *v.* to bend, 1169. Through Fr. from L. *plicare*.

Poetrye, *n.* poetry, 33. O. Fr. *poëterie*—L. *poeta*—Gr. *poiētēs*.

Point, *n.* point; **point for point** = in every point, 577. Fr. from L. *punctum*.

Poo, the river Po, 48.

Pope, *n.* the Pope, 741; *gen.* **popes**, 746. L. *papa*, pope, father.

Pouerliche, *adj.* poorly, 213, 1055.

Pouerte, *n.* poverty, 816. O. Fr. *poverte* (Fr. *pauvreté*)—L. *paupertatem*, acc. of *paupertas*, from *pauper*, poor.

Poure, *adv.* poorly, 1043. O. Fr. *povre*—L. *pauperem*, acc. of *pauper*.

Pourest, *adj.* (superl.) poorest, 205.

Prescience, *n.* foreknowledge, 659. Through Fr. from L. *præscientia*, knowledge beforehand.

Presence, *n.* presence, 1207. O. Fr. *presence*—L. *presentia*.

Preue, *n.* proof, 787. Fr. *preuve*—Low L. *proba*, a proof—L. *probare*, to test.

Preue, *v.* to test, 699; *pr. s. subj.* he **preue** = that he test, 1152; *pr. s.* **preueth**, proves, 1000, 1155; *pp.* **preued**, approved, 28, 856. O. Fr. *prover*—L. *probare*, to test, try the goodness of.

Preyde, *v. pt. s.* prayed, besought, 548, 765; *pp.* **preyed**, 773. O. Fr. *preier*—L. *precari*, to pray.

Preyers, *n.* prayer, 141. O. Fr. *preiere*—L. *precaria*, fem. of adj. *precarius*, obtained by prayer, from *precari*.

Prikke, *v.* 2 *p. s. subj.* prick, torture, 1038. A.S. *pricu, prica,* a point.

Priuee, *adj.* privy, secret, 192, 519. O. Fr. *prive*—L. *privatus,* apart.

Priuitee, *n.* privity, secrecy, 249.

Profred, *pp.* proffered, 152. O. Fr. *proferer,* to produce—L. *pro-ferre,* to bring forward.

Proheme, *n.* a proem, prologue, 43. O. Fr. *proëme*—L. *proœmium*—Gr. *prooimion,* an introduction.

Prydeles, *adj.* free from pride, 930. A.S. *prýte,* regularly formed (by the usual change from *ú* to *ý*) from *prút,* proud.

Prys, pryse, *n.* price, estimation, 1026. O. Fr. *pris, preis*—L. *pretium,* price.

Pryuely, *adv.* secretly, 641. See Priuee.

Publisshed, *pp.* published, spread abroad, 415, 749. The M. E. *publisshen* is formed irregularly from Fr. *publier*—L. *publicare.*

Purposed, *pp.* purposed, 1067. M. E. *purpos*—O. Fr. *pourpos, propos,* a purpose—L. *propositum,* neuter of pp. of *pro-ponere,* to propose.

Purveye, *v.* to purvey, to provide, 191. O. Fr. *porvoir* (Fr. *pourvoir*)—L. *pro-videre,* to foresee, to provide.

Put, *pp.* put, 471. A.S. *potian;* according to Skeat, of Celtic origin; cf. Gaelic *put,* to push, thrust, Welsh *pwtio,* to push, Cornish *poot,* to push.

Q

Quaille, *n.* a quail, 1206. O. Fr. *quaille* (Fr. *caille*)—Low L. *quaquila,* a quail; of Teutonic origin, but ultimately imitative. Cf. Dut. *kwaken,* to croak, to quack.

Quaking, *pr. part.* quaking, 317, 358. A.S. *cwacian,* to quake; allied to *quick,* alive.

Quod, *v. pt. s.* quoth, said, 319, 624, etc. A.S. *cwædh,* pt. t. of *cwedhan,* to say.

R

Rancour, *n.* rancour, malice, 432, 747.

Fr. from L. *rancorem,* acc. of *rancor,* spite.

Rather, *adj.* (compar.) sooner, 1169. M. E. *rather* is compar. of *rath,* early—A.S. *hradhe* (*adv.*), quickly, *hrædh* (*adj.*), quick.

Recchelees, *adj.* reckless, 488. A.S. *réce-leás*—*récan,* to care; cf. Dut. *roekeloos.*

Receyuen, *v.* to receive, 1151. O. Fr. *recever*—L. *recipere.*

Rede, *v.* 1 *p. s. pr.* I advise, 811, 1205. A.S. *rædan*—*ræd,* counsel.

Redresse, *v.* to set right, 431. Through Fr. *re-* and *dresser* from L. *re-* and *directus,* pp. of *dirigere,* to direct.

Redy, *adj.* ready, 299. A.S. *ræde,* ready—*ræd-on,* pt. pl. of *ridan,* to ride.

Reed, *adj.* red, 317. A.S. *reáð;* cog. with Ger. *roth,* Dut. *rood,* &c.

Reed, *n.* counsel, 653. A.S. *ræd,* counsel.

Refuseden, *v. pt. pl.* refused, 128. O. Fr. *refuser,* through a Low L. form from L. *refundere,* to pour back, restore.

Reioysed, *v. pt. s.* 1 *p.* (reflexive), I rejoiced, 145. O. Fr. *resjoïs-,* stem of pr. part. of *resjoïr* (Fr. *réjouir*), from *re-,* again, and O. Fr. *esjoïr,* to rejoice—L. *ex-,* very, and *gaudere,* to rejoice.

Rekke, *v.* 1 *p. s. pr.* I care, 1090. A.S. *récan,* to care.

Relesse, *v.* 1 *p. s. pr.* I release, 153. O. Fr. *relessier* (Fr. *relaisser*)—L. *relaxare.*

Remenant, *n.* a remnant, 869. O. Fr. *remenant*—L. *remanent-,* stem of pr. part. of *remanere,* to remain.

Retenue, *n.* retinue, suit, 270. O. Fr. *retenue,* a body of retainers, fem. of *retenu,* pp. of *retenir*—L. *retinere.*

Rethorike, *n.* rhetoric, 32. Fr. *rhetorique*—L. *rhetorica* (*ars*)—Gr. *hrétorika, hrétór,* an orator.

Retourneth, *v. imp. pl.* return, 809. Through Fr. from L. *re-* and *tornare,* to turn in a lathe.

Reuel, *n.* revelry, 392, 1123. O. Fr.

revel, reveler—L. *re-bellare*, to rebel.

Reuerence, *n.* reverence, respect, 196. Through Fr. from L. *reverentia.*

Reule, *v.* to rule; reule **hir** = guide her conduct, 327. O. Fr. *riule, reule* (Fr. *règle*)—L. *regula*—*regere*, to rule.

Rewen, *v.* to rue, pity, 1050. A.S. *hreówan*; cf. Ger. *reuen.*

Rewthe, *n.* ruth, pity, 579, 893; a pitiful sight, 562. Of Scand. origin. Cf. Icel. *hrygdh*, ruth; allied to A.S. *hreówan.*

Ringes, *n. pl.* rings, 255. A.S. *hring*; cog. with Dut. and Ger. *ring*, Icel. *hringr.*

Roially, *adv.* royally, 955. O. Fr. *real, roial* (Fr. *royal*)—L. *regalis*, royal.

Roialtee, *n.* royalty, 928. O. Fr. *realte, reialte*—L. *regalitatem*, acc. of *regalitas*—*regalis.*

Rombel, *n.* rumour, 997. There is a provincial English *rommle* in use = to speak low. Cf. Dut. *rommelen*, to buzz, Danish *rumle.*

Rome, *v. pr.* 1 *p. pl.* we roam, 118. Also *ramen*, allied to A.S. *á-ræman*, to spread out. Cf. provincial *rame, raim*, to stretch, roam.

Rome, Rome, 737.

Rood, *v. pt. s.* rode, 234. See **Ryden.**

Roote, *n.* root, source, base, 58. Scand. Cf. Icel. *rót*, Danish *rod.* Put for *vrót* = *vbrt*, allied to Gothic *waurts*, a root, A.S. *wyrt*, a wort, a root.

Roughte, *v. pt. s.* (impersonal) it recked; him roughte = he recked, 685. A.S. *récan*, pt. *ic róhte.*

Route, *n.* a company, 382. Through Fr. from L. *rupta*—*rumpere*, to break.

Rude, *adj.* rude, rough, 916. Through Fr. from L. *rudem*, acc. of *rudis.*

Rudely, *adv.* rudely, 380.

Rudenesse, *n.* rudeness, 397.

Ryden, *v. pr. pl.* ride, 784; *pt. s.* rood, 234. A.S. *ridan*, pt. *rád*, pp. *riden*; cf. Dut. *rijden*, Ger. *reiten.*

Rype, *adj.* ripe, seasonable, 220; *pl.*

rype, 438. A.S. *rípe*, fit for reaping, *ríp*, harvest—*rípan*, to reap; cf. Dut. *rijp*, Ger. *reif*, ripe.

Ryse, *v.* to rise; 3 *p. s. pr.* **ryseth,** 1108. A.S. *rísan*, pt. *rás*, pp. *risen.*

S

Sad, *adj.* firm, fixed, constant, 693, 754; sober, 220, 237; *pl.* **sadde,** grave, serious, 1002; original sense, 'sated,' hence 'tired,' 'grieved.' A.S. *sæd*, sated. Cf. Ger. *satt.*

Sadly, *adv.* firmly, 1100.

Sadnesse, *n.* constancy, patience, 452.

Salomon, Solomon, 6.

Salte, *adj. pl.* salt, 1084. A.S. *sealt*, originally an *adj.* as in *sealt wæter*, salt (salted) water. Cf. Icel. *saltr*, Danish and Swedish *salt*, Dut. *zout.*

Saluces, Saluzzo, 44, 63, 414; **Saluce,** 420.

Saue, *prep.* save, except, 76, 508. Fr. *sauf*—L. *salvus.*

Saue, *v.* to save, to keep, 683; 3 *p. s. imp.* may he save, 505, 1064. Fr. *sauver*—L. *salvare, salvus*, safe.

Saufly, *adv.* safely, 870.

Sayde, Seyde, *v. pt. s.* said, 501, 526, 554, etc. See **Seye.**

Scathe, *n.* scathe, harm, 1172. A.S. *sceadhan*, pt. *scód*; cf. Dut. and Ger. *schaden.* The n. *skaith* is still used in Scotland.

Sclaundre, *n.* slander, ill fame, 722. O. Fr. *esclandre*, earlier form *scandele*, whence *escandle, escandre*, and finally, *esclandre*, with inserted *l.* *Slander* is thus a doublet of *scandal.*

Scourges, *n. pl.* scourges, plagues, 1157. O. Fr. *escorgie* (Fr. *écourgée*), a scourge—L. *excoriata*, 'flayed off,' fem. of the pp. of *excoriare*, to strip the skin off.

Se, *v.* to see, 599, etc.; *pt. s.* sey, 1044: *pp.* seyn, 280. A.S. *seón*, pt. *seáh*, pp. *gesegen*; cf. Dut. *zien*, Ger. *sehen.*

Secrely, *adv.* secretly, 763. Through Fr. from L. *secret-us*, pp. of *se-cer-nere*, to put separate.

Secte, *n.* suite, company, **1171.** Through Fr. from Low L. *secta*, a

set of people—L. *sec-* (as in *sec-undus*), base of *sequi*, to follow.

Seeth, *v. pt. s.* seethed, boiled, 227. A.S. *seódhan*, pt. *seádh*, pp. *soden*. Cf. Ger. *sieden*.

Selde, *adj. pl.* few; **selde tyme** = few times, 146; *adv.* seldom, 427. A.S. *seld*, rare; cog. with Dut. *zelden*, Ger. *selten* (*adv.*).

Sely, *adj.* simple, innocent, 948. A.S. *sælig*, *gesælig*, timely—A.S. *sæl*, time, season; cf. Dut. *zalig*, Ger. *selig*. The original meaning was 'timely,' then 'happy,' 'lucky,' 'innocent,' lastly, 'simple.'

Semblant, *n.* semblance, outward appearance, 928. Through Fr. from L. *simulare*.

Seme, *v.* to seem, appear, 132; *pt. s.* (impers.) **semed**, it seemed, 396. A.S. *séman*.

Sent, *v. pr. s.* sends, 1151. A.S. *sendan*, to send, 3 *p. s. pr.*, *he sent* or *sendeth*; cog. with Dut. *zenden*, Ger. *senden*.

Sergeant, *n.* a sergeant, an officer, 519, 524, 575, 596, etc. O. Fr. *sergant*, *serjant*—Low L. *servientem*, acc. of *serviens*, an officer—pr. part. of L. *servire*, to serve. **Sergeant** is thus a doublet of *servant*.

Seruage, *n.* service, 147, 482. Through Fr. from L. *servus*.

Seruede, *v.* 1 *p. s. pt.* I served, 640. Through Fr. from L. *servare*.

Seruisable, *adj.* serviceable, 979.

Seruitute, *n.* servitude, 798. Through Fr. from L. *servitudo*.

Seruyse, *n.* service, 603, 958. Through Fr. from L. *servitium*.

Sette, *v.* to place, 975; *pt. s.* **sette**, cast, 233; put, 382; *pp.* **set**, appointed, 774. A.S. *settan*, causal of *sittan*, to sit.

Sey, *v. pt. s.* saw, 1044. See **Se**.

Seye, *v.* to say; 3 *p. pl. pr.* **sey**, 631; 1 *p. s. pr.* **seyɵ**, 351; 3 *p. pl. pr.* **seyn**, 481. A.S. *secgan*, pt. *ic sægde*, pp. *gesæd*.

Seyn, *pp.* seen, 280, 608; 3 *p. pl. pr.* 481. See **Se**.

Shake, *v.* to shake, 978. A.S. *scacan*, pt. *scôc*, pp. *scacen*.

Shal, *v.* 1 *p. s. pr.* I shall (do so); 1 *p. pl.* **shul**, we must, 38. A.S. *ic sceal*.

Shaltow for shalt thou, 560.

Shapen, *pp.* planned, 275. A.S. *sceapan*, *scapan*, pt. *scôp*, pp. *scapen*; cf. Ger. *schaffen*.

Sholde, *v. pt. s.* ought to, 247, 261; was obliged to, 515. A.S. *sceolde*, pt. of *sceal*.

Shoon, *v. pt. s.* shone, 1124. A.S. *scínan*, pt. *scán*, pp. *scinen*; cf. Ger. *scheinen*.

Shoop, *v. pt. s.* laid plans for, 198; created, 903; contrived, 946. See **Shapen**.

Shredde, *v. pt. s.* shred, cut, 227. A.S. *screádian*, to shred, *screáde*, a piece.

Shul, 38. See **Shal**.

Sikerly, *adv.* surely, 184. M.E. *siker*—L. *securus*, secure; whence also Dut. *zeker*, Ger. *sicher*, &c.

Sikly, *adv.* ill, 625. A.S. *seóc*, sick: cf. Dut. *ziek*, Ger. *siech*.

Siknesse, *n.* sickness, 651.

Sin, *conj.* since, 448. Contracted from A.S. *síth-thám*, written also *síth-than*, after that, from *síth*, late (Ger. *seit*) and *thám*, dat. case of the definite article or demonstrative pron., *the*.

Sit, *v. pr. s.* (impers.) it setteth or suits; **yuel it sit** = it suits ill, 460. A.S. *sittan*, pr. *sit*, pt. t. *sæt*, pp. *seten*.

Site, *n.* site, situation, 199. Through Fr. from L. *situm*, acc. of *situs*, a place.

Skile, *n.* reason, 1152. Scand., cf. Icel. *skil*, a distinction.

Sklendre, *adj. pl.* slender, 1198. Old Dut. *slinder*, thin.

Slake, *v.* to slacken, leave off, 705; to cease, 137; to end, 802; *pr. s.* **slaketh**, assuages, 1107. A.S. *sleacian*, to grow slack—*sleac*, slack.

Slawen, **slayn**, *pp.* slain, 544, 536.

Sleen, *v.* to slay; gerund, 1076; *pr. s.* **sleeth**, slays, 628. A.S. *sleán*, contracted form of *slahan*, pt. *slôh*, pp. *slegen*. Cf. Dut. *slaan*, Ger. *schlagen*.

Sleighte, *n.* a contrivance, 1102. Put for *sleighth*—Scand., as in Icel. *slægdh*, slyness, *slægr*, sly.

Slepte, *v. pt. s.* slept, 224. A.S. *slæpan*, *slêpan*, pt. *slép*; cf. Dut. *slapen*, Ger. *schlafen*.

Slyde, *v.* to slide, 82. A.S. *slídan*, pt. *slád*, pp. *sliden*.

Smale, *adj. pl.* small, 380, 382. A.S. *smel*; cf. Ger. *schmal*.

Smerte, *adv.* smartly, 629.

Smerte, *v.* to smart, feel grieved, 353. A.S. *smeortan*; cog. with Dut. *smarten*, Ger. *schmerzen*.

Smit, *v. pr. s.* smites, 122. A.S. *smitan*, pt. *smát*, pp. *smiten*. Cf. Dut. *smijten*, Ger. *schmeissen*.

Smok, *n.* a smock, 890. A.S. *smoc*—A.S. *smog-en*, pp. of *smeógan*, *smúgan*, 'to creep into,' so called because 'crept into,' or put on over the head.

Smokles, *adj.* without a smock, 875.

Snow-whyt, *adj.* snow-white, 388. A.S. *snáw*, snow, and *whít*, white.

Sodeyn, *adj.* sudden, 316. O. Fr. *sodain*, *sudain*—L. *subitaneus*—*subitus*, sudden.

Softe, *adv.* softly, 583. A.S. *sôfte*; cf. Ger. *sanft*, soft.

Solempne, *adj.* grand, 1125. O. Fr. *solempne*—L. *solemnem*, acc. of *solemnis*, occurring yearly like a religious rite, from *sollus*, entire, and *annus*, a year.

Somdel, *adv.* partially, 1012.

Somme, *pron. indefinite, pl.* 76. A.S. *sum*, pl. *sume*.

Somwhat, *adv.* in some degree, 579. A.S. *sum hwæt*.

Sendry, *adj.* sundry, 271. A.S. *syn-drig*, formed with suffix -*ig* (modern English -*y*), from *sundor* (adv.), asunder.

Sone, *n.* a son, 626, 676, &c. A.S. *sunu*. Cf. Dut. *zoon*, Ger. *sohn*.

Sooth, *n.* truth, 855. A.S. *sôth*, true.

Soothfastnesse, *n.* truth, 796. A.S. *sôthfest*, where the suffix is the same as in *stead-fast* and *shame-fast*.

Soothly, *adv.* verily, 689. A.S. *sôthlice*, verily.

Sophyme, *n.* sophism, 5. L. *sophisma*—Gr. *sophisma*.

Sore, *adv.* sorely, 85. A.S. *sâr*, painful; cog. with Dut. *zeer*.

Soueraynetee, *n.* sovereignty, 114.

Souereyn, *adj.* sovereign, 112. O. Fr. *soverain*—Low L. *superanus*, chief—L. *super*, above.

Souked, *pp.* sucked, 450. A.S. *súcan*, pt. *seác*, pp. *socen*.

Soun, *n.* sound, 271. Fr. *son*—L. *sonum*, acc. of *sonus*, sound.

Sours, *n.* source, origin, 49. O. Fr. *sors*, *surse*, from the fem. of the pp. of O. Fr. *sordre* (Fr. *sourdre*—L. *surgere*, to rise.

Space, *n.* an opportunity, 103. Fr. *espace*—L. *spatium*.

Spak, *v. pt. s.* spake, 295. See Speken.

Specially, *adv.* especially, 312. Short for *especial*. O. Fr. *especial*—L. *specialis*—*species*, a kind.

Speken, *v.* to speak, 547; *pt. s.* spak, 295; *imp. pl.* speketh, 175. Late A.S. *specan*, A.S. *sprecan*, pt. *spræc*, pp. *sprecen*.

Spille, *v.* to destroy, 503. A.S. *spillan*, *spildan*, to destroy, *spild*, destruction.

Spousaille, *n.* espousal, wedding, 180; spousail, 115. Through Fr. from L. *sponsalia*, nuptials.

Spoused, *pp.* espoused, 3, 386. O. Fr. *espouser*—L. *sponsa*, fem. of pp. of *spondere*, to promise.

Spradde, *v. pt. s.* spread, 418, 722. A.S. *sprædan*; cf. Ger. *spreiten*.

Springing, *n.* beginning, 49. A.S. *springan*, to spring up, pt. *sprang*, pp. *sprungen*; cog. with Dut. and Ger. *springen*.

Squieres, *n. pl.* squires, 192. O. Fr. *escuyer*—Low L. *scutarius*, a shield-bearer—L. *scutum*, a shield.

Stable, *adj.* stable, fixed, 663, 931. Through Fr. from L. *stabilis*.

Stake, *n.* a stake, 704. A.S. *staca*, a stake.

Stalle, *n. dat.* a stall, 207, 291. A.S. *steal*, *stæl*, gen. *stealles*, dat. *stealle*.

Stalked, *v. pt. s.* walked, 525. A.S.

stælcan, to walk warily, allied to *stealc*, high.

Stedfastly, *adv*. assuredly, 1094.

Stedfastnesse, *n*. steadfastness, 699. A.S. *stedefæst*, firm in its place—*stede*, place, *fæst*, firm.

Stente, *v*. to cease, leave off, 734, 972; *pt. s.* **stente**, 1023. See **Stinte**.

Sterres, *n. gen. pl.* of the stars, 1124. A.S. *steorra*, a star.

Stert, *pp*. started, 1060. Allied to Dut. *storten*, to rush, Ger. *stürzen*, also to Old Dut. *steerten*, to flee, perhaps originally 'to turn tail,' and thus allied to A.S. *steort*, a tail, which appears in *stark-naked*, a corruption of M. E. *start-naked*, literally 'tail-naked.'

Stille, *adv*. stilly, quietly, 1077. A.S. *stille*, still—*steal*, *stæl*, a stall.

Stinte, *v*. to stint, cease, 1175; to end, 747. The M.E. forms are *stintan*, *stentan*—A.S. *styntan* in *for-styntan—stunt*, stupid.

Stonde, *v*. to stand, to be fixed, 346; *imp. pl.* **stondeth**, stand, 1195; *pt. s.* **stood**, 318; *pt. pl.* **stoden**, 1105. A.S. *standen*, p.t. *stôd*, pp. *standen*; cog. with Dut. *staan* (pt. *stond*), Ger. *stehen* (pt. *stand*).

Stoon, *n*. a stone, a gem, 121, 1118. A.S. *stân*. Cf. Dut. *steen*, Ger. *stein*.

Stoor, *n*. a store, 17. O. Fr. *estor*, *estoire*, store, provisions—L. *instaurare*, to construct.

Stormy, *adj*. violent, boisterous, 995. A.S. *storm*; cog. with Ger. *sturm*.

Stounde, *n*. hour, time, 1098. A.S. *stund*, *stond*, a space of time. Cf. Ger. *stunde*, an hour.

Streen, *n*. strain, stock, breed, 157. A.S. *strŷnd—strŷnan*, to beget.

Strepeth, *v. pr. s.* strips, 894; *pr. pl.* **strepen**, 1116. A.S. *strŷpan*, to strip; cog. with Dut. *stroopen*, to plunder.

Streyne, *v*. to constrain, 144. O. Fr. *estraindre*, to wring hard—L. *stringere*.

Strook, *n*. a stroke, 812. A.S. *strác*, pt. t. of *strícan*, to strike.

Stryue, *v*. to strive, 170. O. Fr.

estriver, to strive, *estrif*, strife; of Scand. origin, as in Icel. *strídh*, strife.

Studien, *v*. to study, 8; 2 *p. pl. pr.* **studie**, 5. O. Fr. *estudie* (Fr. *étude*) —L. *studium*, zeal, study.

Sturdinesse, *n*. sternness, 700.

Sturdy, *adj*. cruel, 698, 1049. O. Fr. *estourdi*, amazed, also rash, pp. of *estourdir*, to amaze; of doubtful origin.

Style, *n*. mode of writing, 18, 41. Through Fr. from L. *stylus*, a way of writing.

Subgetz, *n. pl.* subjects, 482. O. Fr. *suiet*, *suiect* (Fr. *sujet*)—L. *subjectus*, pp. of *subjicere*.

Subtiltee, *n*. a device, 691. Through Fr. from L. *subtilitatem*, acc. of *subtilitas—subtilis*.

Suffisance, *n*. sufficiency, 759. Fr. *suffisance*—L. *sufficere*.

Suffisant, *adj*. sufficient, 960.

Suffrance, *n*. endurance, 1162. O. Fr. *sofrance—soffrir*—L. *sufferre*.

Suffreth, *v. imp. pl.* suffer, 1197.

Suffyse, *v*. to suffice, 740. Through Fr. *suffis-*, base of *suffis-ant*, pr. part. of *suffire*, to suffice—L. *sufficere*.

Supposinge, *n*. a supposition, 1041. Fr. *supposer*—L. *sub* and Fr. *poser*, to place. See note to line 1041.

Suspecious, *adj*. suspicious, 540. O. Fr. *suspezion* (Fr. *soupçon*)—L. *suspicionem*, acc. of *suspicio—suspicere*.

Suspect, *n*. suspicion, 905. Through Fr. from L. *suspectus*, pp. of *suspicere*, to suspect.

Sustenance, *n*. sustenance, support, 202. Through Fr. from L. *sustinentia—sustinere*.

Suster, *n*. sister, 589, 640. Skeat refers it to Scand., as in Icel. *systir*, Swedish *syster*; cog. with A.S. *sweostor* and Ger. *schwester*.

Swappe, *v*. to strike, 586; *pt. s.* (intransitive) **swapte**, fell down suddenly, 1099. Closely allied to *sweep* and *swoop*. The A.S. *swâpan*, to sweep along, pt. t. *sweôp*, pp. *swâpen*; is cog. with Icel. *sveipa*, Ger. *schweifen*, etc.

Swelwe, *v. pr. s. subj.* swallow, 1188.

Formed from A.S. *swolg-en*, pp. of *swelgan*, to swallow; cf. Dut. *zwelgen*, Ger. *schwelgen*.

Swepe, *v.* to sweep, 978. This verb corresponds to the causal form of A.S. *swápan*, to swoop.

Swere, *v.* to swear; *pt. pl.* sworen, 176, 2 *p.* **swore**, 496; *pp.* **swore**, sworn, 403. A.S. *swerian*, pt. *swór*, pp. *sworen*; cog. with Dut. *zweren*, Ger. *schwören*.

Swich, *pron.* such, 174, 183, 336, etc. Other M. E. forms, *swulc*, *swilc*— A.S. *swylc*. Cf. Dut. *zulk*, Ger. *solch*.

Swollen, *pp.* swollen with pride, 950.

Sworen, *v. pt. pl.* swore, 176. See **Swere**.

Swough, *n.* a swoon, 1100. M. E. *swowen*, *swoghen*, to swoon, a weak verb, closely allied to the strong verb, A.S. *swógan*, to move noisily, the pp. of which (*ge-swógen*) actually occurs with the sense 'in a swoon.' Allied to *sough*.

Swowning, *n.* a swooning, a swoon, 1080. See foregoing word.

Syked, *v. pt. s.* sighed, 545. Both forms, *syken* and *sighen*, occur in M. E. A.S. *sícan*, to sigh, pt. *sác*, pp. *sicen*.

Sythe, *n. pl.* times; *ful ofte sythe* = full oftentimes, 233. A.S. *síth* (for *sinth*), a journey, time, whence *síthian*, to travel; cf. Icel. *sinni* (for *sinthi*), a walk, a time, and Gothic *sinth*, a time.

T

Taffraye, for *to affraye*, to frighten, 455. O. Fr. *effraier*—Low L. *exfrediare*, to break the peace—L. *ex* and Old High Ger. *fridu* (Ger. *friede*), peace.

Take, *pp.* taken, 702. M. E. *taken*, pt. *tok*, pp. *taken*, from Scand. Cf. Icel. *taka*, pt. *tók*, pp. *tekinn*, to seize.

Tale, *n.* a long story, 383. A.S. *talu*, a number, also a narrative. Cf. Dut. *taal*, Icel. *tal*, speech, Ger. *zahl*, number.

Talyghte, for *to alyghte*, to alight, 909. See **Alyghte**.

Tamende, for *to amende*, to redress, 441. Through Fr. from L. *emendare*, to free from faults—*e*, out of, and *mendum*, a fault.

Tarraye, for *to arraye*, to arrange, 961. See **Array**.

Tassaille, for *to assaille*, to assail, 1180. O. Fr. *assailler*, to attack—L. *ad*, to, and *salire*, to leap, rush forth.

Tassaye, for *to assaye*, to test, 454, 1075. See **Assay**.

Teer, *n.* a tear, 1104; *pl.* teres, 1084. A.S. *teár*, *tær*; cog. with Icel. *tár*, Ger. *zähre*, etc.

Tellen, *v.* to tell, 26; *imper. s.* telle, 9, 15, etc. A.S. *tellan*, pt. *tealde*, pp. *teald—talu*. See **Tale**.

Tembrace, for *to embrace*, to embrace, 1101. O. Fr. *embracer*, to grasp in the arms—O. Fr. *em-* for *en-* (= L. *in*) and *brace*, the grasp of the arms —L. *brachia*, the arms.

Tendrely, *adv.* tenderly, 686. Through Fr. from L. *tener*, tender, originally thin, allied to *tenuis*, thin.

Tendure, for *to endure*, to endure, bear, 756, 811. See **Endure**.

Tentifly, *adv.* attentively, 334. Formed from the base of *tend*, derived through Fr. from L. *tendere*, to stretch, a word allied to *tenere*, to hold.

Thaduersitee, *n.* the adversity, 756. O. Fr. *advers*, often *avers* (Fr. *averse*)—L. *adversus*, pp. of *advertere*, to turn to.

Than, *adv.* then, 127, 212, etc. A.S. *thonne*, closely allied to *thone*, acc. s. masc. of the demonstrative pron. *the*; cf. Ger. *denn*.

Thanke, *v.* 1 *p. s. pr.* I thank, 1088. A.S. *thanc*, *thonc*, favour; cog. with Dut. *dank*.

Thenke, *v.* 1 *p. s. pr.* I think, 641; *imp. pl.* thenketh, 116. M. E. *thenken*, to think, was originally distinct from the impersonal v. *thinken*, to seem. The pt. t. of *thenken* should have been *thoghte*, and of *thinken*, *thughte*; but both were merged in the form *thoughte*, modern English *thought* (Skeat). *Thenken* is from A.S. *thencan*, pt. *thohte*.

Ther, *adv.* there, 147, 152, 173, etc.; where, 1207; **there as,** there where, 198. A.S. *thær, ther*; cog. with Dut. *daar*.

Therbifore, *adv.* beforehand, 689, 729.

Therefore, *adv.* on that account, 445, 1141. *Therefore* = A.S. *fore thære* = because of the (thing), some fem. *n.* being understood.

Ther-of, *adv.* with respect to that, 644.

Thewes, *n. pl.* qualities, 409. A.S. *theáwas*, pl. of *theáw*, habit. In Shakspeare and modern English, *thews* means sinews or strength. The Scotch *thowless* means 'wanting strength.'

Thilke, *pron.* (demons.) that, 278, 360, 892, 948, etc. A.S. *thylc, thýlíc*, from *thý*, instrumental case of *se, séo, thæt*; and *líc*, like.

Tho, *adv.* then, 544.

Thonke, *v.* 1 *p. s. pr.* I thank, 830. See **Thanke.**

Thought, *n.* thought, anxiety, 80. A.S. *thoht, ge-thoht—thoht*, pp. of *thencan*, to think.

Thoughte, *v. pt. s* (impersonal) seemed, 406. See **Thenke.**

Threshfold, *n.* threshold, 288, 291. *Thresh-old = thresh-wold*, literally 'the piece of wood threshed or beaten by the tread of the foot'—A.S. *therscwald—thersc-an*, to thresh; and *wald*, wood.

Throp, *n.* a thorp or village, 199; *dat.* **Thrope,** 208. A.S. *thorp*; cog. with Ger. *dorf*, Dut. *dorp*, etc.

Throwe, *n.* a short period, 450. A.S. *thrág, thráh*, a short time.

Thryue, *v.* to thrive, 172. Scand.; as in Icel. *thrífa*, to grasp, hence *thrífask* (with suffix -*sk* = -*sik*, self), to seize for one's self, to thrive.

Thurgh, *prep.* through, 69, 137. A.S. *thurh*; cog. with Dut. *door*, Ger. *durch*.

Tonge, *n.* the tongue, 1184. A.S. *tunge*; cf. Icel. *tunga*, Dut. *tong*, Ger. *zunge*.

Tonne, *n.* a tun, 215. A.S. *tunne*; cf. Dut. *ton*, Ger. *tonne*.

To-race, *v. pr. pl. subj.* may scratch to pieces, 572. For prefix *to-*, see **Torent**, and note to line 572. *Race* comes through Fr. from L. *radere*, to scrape.

Torent, *pp.* rent in pieces, 1012. Prefix *to-* (= Ger. *zer-*, Gothic and L. *dis-*), meaning 'in twain,' 'apart,' is common in M. E. *Rent*, from A.S. *hrendan*. See note to line 572.

Tormentinge, *n.* a tormenting, 1038. O. Fr. *torment*—L. *tormentum*, an engine for throwing stones.

Trance, *n.* a trance, 1108. Through Fr. from L. acc. *transitum*, a passing away.

Translated, *pp.* changed, 385. Through Fr. from Low L. *translatare*—L. *translatus*, pp. of *transferre*.

Trauaille, *n.* travail, toil, 1210. Fr. *travail*, through provincial and Low L. forms from L. *trabes*, a beam pierced with holes to confine the feet.

Tree, *n.* tree, wood, 558. A.S. *treó, treów*; cog. with Icel. *tré*, etc.

Tretys, *n.* a treaty, 331. O. Fr. *tretis, traitis*, a thing well handled, *traiter*—L. *tractare*, to handle.

Trewely, treweliche, *adv.* truly, 53, 804. A.S. *treówe, trýwe*, true; cf. Ger. *treu*, Dut. *treow*.

Trouble, *adj.* troubled, 465. O. Fr. *trubler* (Fr. *troubler*)—L. *turbula*, diminutive of *turba*, a crowd.

Trowe, *v.* 1 *p. s. pr.* I trow, believe, 471. A.S. *treówian* formed from n. *treówa*, trust; cog. with Icel. *trúa*, to trow, *trúr*, true.

Twelf, *adj.* numeral, twelve, 736. A.S. *twelf, twelfe*; cog. with Dut. *twaalf*, Ger. *zwölf*.

Tweye, *adj.* two, 476; **Tweyne,** 650. A.S. *twegen* (masc.), *twá* (fem.), *twá* or *tu* (neut.), two; cog. with Dut. *twee*, Ger. *zwei*.

Twinkling, *n.* a twinkling, 37. A.S. *twinclian*, to twinkle, a frequentative of *twink*, which appears in M. E. *twinken*, to wink.

Tyding, *n.* tidings; *pl.* **tydinge**, 752.
M. E. *tidinde*, later *tidinge*, afterwards *tidings*—Scand.; as in Icel.
tíðhindi, neut. pl., things that
happen—*tíðh*, time; cf. Danish
tidende, Dut. *tijding*, Ger. *zeitung*.

Tymes, *n. pl.* times, 226. A.S. *tíma;*
cog. with Icel. *tími*, Danish *time*,
etc. From the same ultimate root
as Tide.

V

Vane, *n.* a vane, 996. A.S. *fana*, a
small flag; cog. with Dut. *vaan*,
Ger. *fahne*.

Vanitee, *n.* vanity, 250. Through Fr.
from L. acc. *vanitatem—vanus*,
empty.

Venyse, Venice, 51.

Vermyne, *n.* vermin, 1095. Through
Fr. from L. *vermis*, a worm.

Verray, *adj.* very, true, 343. O. Fr.
verai (Fr. *vrai*)—L. *verac-*, stem
of *verax—verus*, true.

Vertu, *n.* virtue, 216. Through Fr.
from L. acc. *virtutem—vir*, a man.

Vesulus, Monte Viso, 47, 58.

Vgly, *adj.* ugly, 673. Scand.; cf. Icel.
uggligr, fearful—*ugg-r*, fear, and
ligr = A.S. *-líc*, like.

Visage, *n.* face, 693. Through Fr.
from L. acc. *visum—videre*, to
see.

Vitaille, *n.* victuals, 59, 265. O. Fr.
vitaille—L. neut. pl. *victualia—
victus*, pp. of *vivere*, to live.

Vncerteyn, *adj.* uncertain, 125. Negative *un-* and *certain*—O. Fr. *certein*
—L. *certus*.

Vnder, *prep.* under, 22, 113, etc.

Vndern, *n.* the time from 9 A.M. to
mid-day, 260, 981. Derived from
A.S. *under*, among, between.

Vnderstonde, *v.* to understand, 20.
A.S. *understandan*, to stand under
or among, hence to comprehend—
A.S. *under*, under, and *standan*, to
stand.

Vndertake, *v.* to undertake to say, 803.
Compounded of *under* and M. E.
taken. See Take.

Vndigne, *adj.* unworthy, 359. Negative

un- and *digne*, through Fr. from L.
dignus.

Vndiscreet, *adj.* indiscreet, 996. Negative *un-* and O. Fr. *discret*—L.
discretus, pp. of *dis-cernere*.

Vnlyk, *adj.* unlike, 156. Negative *un-*
and *líc*, commonly *ge-líc*.

Vnnethe, *adv.* uneasily, with difficulty,
384, 403. Negative *un-* and A.S.
eáðh, easy.

Vnnethes, *adv.* with difficulty, 318, 892.

Vnreste, *n.* unrest, 719. Negative *un-*
and A.S. *rest*, *rest;* cog. with Dut.
rust, Danish and Swedish *rast*.

Vnsad, *adj.* unsettled, 995. See Sad.

Vnto, *prep.* unto, 11, 97, etc. *Unto*
is not found in A.S.

Vntressed, *pp.* unarranged, 379. Fr.
tresser, to plait—Low L. *tricia*,
variant of *trica*, a plait—Gr.
tricha, threefold, a common way of
plaiting hair.

Vouche, *v.* to vouch, 2 *p. s. pr. subj.*
vouche, 306. O. Fr. *voucher*—L.
vocare—voc-, stem of *vox*, voice.

Voyden, *v.* to get rid of, 910; *imp. s.*
voyde, depart from, 806. O. Fr.
voide, empty (Fr. *vide*)—L. *viduum*,
acc. of *viduus*, empty.

Voys, *n.* voice, report, 98, 629, 1087.
O. Fr. *vois* (Fr. *voix*)—L. *vocem*,
acc. of *vox*, voice.

Vpon, *prep.* upon, 163. A.S. *uppon—
upp*, up, and *on*, on.

Vs, *pron.* us, 9, 13, 14, etc. A.S. *ús*,
dat. pl. of *wé*, we ; the acc. pl. is *ús*,
úsic.

Vs self, *pron.* ourselves, 108.

Vsage, *n.* usage, 693, 785. Through
Fr. from L. *usus*, use—*uti*, to use.

Vttereste, *adj.* (superl.) utterest, 787.
Formed from A.S. *út*, out; comp.,
útor, *uttor*, outer, hence superl.,
vtterest = outerest.

W

Waille, *v.* to wail, 1212. Scand.; as in
Icel. *væla* (formerly *wæla*), literally
'to cry woe'—*væ, vei* (interj.), woe !

Waiteth, *v. pr. s.* watches, 708. O. Fr.
waiter, to watch, *waite*, a watchman—Old High Ger. *wahta*, a

watchman, *wahhen* (Ger. *wachen*), to be awake.

Wal, *n.* a wall, 1047. A.S. *weall*—L. *vallum*.

Walter, Walter, 421, 631, etc.

Wane, *v.* 2 *p. pl. pr.* wane, 998. A.S. *wanian*, to wane—*wan, won*, deficient.

Wantoun, *adj.* wanton, 236. M. E. forms, *wantoun* and *wantowen*—M. E. *wan-*, prefix, 'lacking'—A.S. prefix *wan-*, and *towen*—A. S. *togen*, pp. of *teón*, to draw.

Waterpot, *n.* a waterpot, 290. A.S. *wæter*; cog. with Dut. *water*, Ger. *wasser*; and M. E. *pot*, from Celtic, as Welsh *pot*.

Wedlok, *n.* wedlock, 115. A.S. *wedlác—wed*, a pledge, and *lác*, a sport, also a gift to a bride.

Weep, *v. pt. s.* wept, 545. M. E. *wepen*, pt. *weep, wep*—A.S. *wépan*, to cry aloud, *wóp*, a clamour.

Wel, *adv.* well, certainly, 215, 635, 892. A.S. *wel*; allied to Will.

Wele, *n.* wealth, 474, 842, 971. A.S. *wela*, weal—*wel* (adv.), well.

Welkne, *n.* the welkin, the sky, 1124. Other M. E. forms are *welkin, welkene, welken, wolken*—A.S. *wolcnu*, pl. of *wolcen*, a cloud.

Welle, *n.* a well, 215, 276. A.S. *wella* —*weallan*, to well up.

Wende, *v.* to wend, go; *pr. pl.* wende, go, 189; 1 *p. s. pr. subj.* wende, 307; *pp.* went, 276. A.S. *wendan*. See note to line 276.

Wene, *v.* 1 *p. s. pr.* I ween, 1174; *pt. pl.* wenden, 751; *pp.* wend, 691. A.S. *wénan*, to imagine—*wén*, expectation.

Were, *v. pt. s. subj.* were, should, 850; 2 *p. pl. pr.* weren, were, 846. A.S. *wæs*, I was; *wære*, thou wast; pl. *wæron*, were; subj. s. *wære*, pl. *wæron*.

Werk, *n.* work, 107. A.S. *weorc, werc*.

Werketh, *v. imp. pl.* act, 504. A.S. *weorc, werc*; cog. with Dut. and Ger. *werk*.

Werking, *n.* deeds, actions, 495.

Wexe, *v.* 2 *p. pr. pl.* wax, increase,

998; *pt. s.* wex, 317. A.S. *weaxan*, pt. *weóx*, pp. *geweaxen*; cog. with Dut. *wassen*, Ger. *wachsen*.

Wey, *n.* way, 273. A.S. *weg*; cog. with Dut. and Ger. *weg*, Icel. *vegr*.

Whan, *adv.* when, 1092, etc. A.S. *hwænne*.

What, *pron.*, 79; (interrog.), why, 383; what that = whatever, 165; what = who, 1019. A.S. *hwæt*, neut. of *hwá*, who.

Whenne, *adv.* whence, 588. A.S. *hwanan*, whence.

Wher, *adv.* where, whether, 60, etc.; wher as = where that, 829. In M. E. *wher* is very common for *whether*. A.S. *hwær, hwar*, where; allied to *hwá*, who. *Whether* is from A.S. *hwæðher*, which of two.

Wherein, *adv.* in which, 376.

Which, *pron.* 52, 217; which that = who, 205. A.S. *hwilc, hwelc*, short for *hwi-lác—hwi*, instrumental case of *hwá*, who, and *líc*, like.

Whider, *adv.* whither, 588. A.S. *hwider, hwæder*.

Whos, *pron. relative, gen.* whose, 770. A.S. *hwæs*, gen. of *hwá*, who.

Whyl, *adv.* while, 166, etc.

Whylom, *adv.* once, formerly, 64, 846. A.S. *hwílum*, at times, dat. pl. of *hwíl*, a time.

Wight, *n.* a wight or person, 240, 400, 769, 1109. A.S. *wiht*, a creature. Cf. Dut. *wicht*, a child; Ger. *wicht*, Gothic *waihts* (fem.), *waiht* (neut.), a whit.

Wikke, *adj.* wicked, 785. Originally a pp. with the sense 'rendered evil,' from the obsolete adj. *wikke*, which is connected by Grimm with A.S. *wicca*, a wizard, the fem. of which is *wicche*, a witch. *Wicked* would thus mean literally 'bewitched.'

Wikkedly, *adv.* wickedly, 723.

Wille, *n.* will, desire, 326, 953; **Wil**, 176. A.S. *willa*—A.S. *willan*, to will. Cf. Dut. *wil*, Icel. *vili*, Ger. *wille*.

Wille, *v.* to will, 721. A.S. *willan*, pt. t. *wolde*; cog. with Dut. *willen*, Icel. *vilja*, Ger. *willen*, etc.

Willing, *n.* desire, 319. Originally pr. part. of the above verb.

Willingly, *adv.* willingly, 362.

Wisly, *adv.* certainly, 822. A.S. (adj., ultimately used as adv.) *gewis,* certain, from prefix *ge-* and adj. *wis,* certain; allied to *wise* and *wit,* from the root of *witan,* to know; cf. Dut. *gewis* (adj. and adv.), Ger. *gewiss,* certainly.

Wiste, *v.* 1 *p. s. pt.* I knew, 814. M. E. (infinitive) *witen,* pr. t. *I wot,* with 3 *s. he wot* (later *wotteth*), and 2 *p. thou wost* (later *wottest*), pl. *witen;* *pt. t.* wiste, *pp.* wist. A.S. *witan,* pr. t. *ic wát, thú wást, he wát,* pl. *witon;* pt. t. *wiste,* also *wisse,* pl. *wiston,* pp. *wist.* Gerund *tó witanne* (modern English, *to wit*).

Wit, *n.* intelligence, 459. A.S. *wit—witan,* to know.

With, *prep.* with, 186, 230, 489, etc. A.S. *widh;* cf. Icel. *vidh,* etc.

With-outen, *prep.* without, 661; **withoute,** *adv.* outside, 332. A.S. *with-útan,* prep. and adv.

Witing, *n.* knowledge, 492.

Wo, *adj.* sad, 753.

Wo, *n.* woe, 139. A.S. *wá,* interj. and adv.; cf. Icel. *vei,* Dut. *vee,* Ger. *weh.*

Wol, *v.* 1 *p. s. pr.* I desire, 646; 2 *p.* **wolt,** wilt, 314; 1 *p. s. pt.* **wolde,** I should like, 238, 638; *pt. pl.* wolde, wished, 1144. M. E. *willen,* pt. *wolde*—A.S. *willan,* pr. *wile* (2 *p. wilt*), pt. *wolde.*

Wommanhede, *n.* womanhood, 239, 1075. The corresponding A.S. word is *wífhád.* See note to line 239.

Woned, wont, *pp.* wont, accustomed, 339, 844. This is the proper use of wont, as *pp.* of *won,* to dwell, to become used to. It afterwards became used as an adj. and then as a n., and its origin being forgotten, the pp. suffix *-ed* was again added, producing the modern form *wont-ed,* in which the suffix occurs twice over = *won-ed-ed* (Skeat). *Woned* is pp. of M. E. *wonien*—A.S. *wunian,* to dwell. See note to line 339.

Worse, *adv.* (compar.) worse, **675.** A.S. *wyrs* (adv.), *wyrsa* (adj.).

Worshipe, *v.* to respect, 166. **A.S.** *weorthscipe,* honour—*weorth* (adj.), honourable, with suffix *-scipe* (English *-ship*), allied to *shape.*

Worshipful, *adj.* worthy of worship **or** honour, 401.

Wortes, *n. pl.* worts, roots, 226. **A.S.** *wyrt;* cf. Ger. *wurz.*

Wostow, for *wost thou,* knowest thou, 325. See **Wiste.**

Wot, *v.* 1 *p. s. pr.* I know, 814; *pr. s.* wot, knows, 274. See **Wiste.**

Woxen, *pp.* waxed, grown, 400. See **Wexe.** M. E. *waxen,* pt. *wox, wex,* pp. *woxen, wexen*—A.S. *weaxan,* pt. *weóx,* pp. *geweaxen;* cog. with Dut. *wassen,* Ger. *wachsen.*

Wrappe, *v.* to wrap, 583. M. E. *wrappen* is also written *wlappen* (whence our **lap**); allied to **warp,** from A.S. *wearp,* a warp in weaving—*wearp,* pt. of *weorpan,* to cast, throw.

Writen, *pp.* written, 761. M. E. *writen,* pt. *wroot,* pp. *writen*—A.S. *writan,* pt. *wrát,* pp. *writen.* Cf. Dut. *rijten,* Ger. *reissen,* to cut.

Wrothe, *adj. pl.* angry, 437. A.S. *wrádh* (adj.), wroth; allied to **writhe,** A.S. *wridhan,* to twist about, pt. *wrádh,* pp. *widhen.*

Wroughte, *v. pt. s.* contrived, made, 463, 1152. M. E. *werchen, wirchen,* pt. *wroughte,* pp. *wrought*—A.S. *wyrcan,* also *wircan, wercan,* pt. *worhte,* pp. *geworht.*

Wyde, *adv.* widely, 722. A.S. *wíd;* cog. with Dut. *wijd,* Ger. *weit.*

Wyfly, *adj.* wifelike, 429, 919, 1050. A.S. *wíflíc.* A.S. *wíf* (neut. n.), a woman, pl. *wíf;* cog. with Dut. *wijf,* Ger. *weib.*

Wynde, *v.* to wind, 583. M. E. *winden,* pt. *wand, wond,* pp. *wunden*—A.S. *windan,* pt. *wand,* pp. *wunden.* Cf. Dut. and Ger. *winden.*

Wyse, *n. dat.* wise, way, 673. A.S. *wíse,* way; originally 'wiseness,' from *wíse* (adj.), wise; cf. Dut. *wijs,* Ger. *weise* (n.).

Wyue, to wive, take a wife, 140, 173. A.S. *wífian,* to take a wife—*wíf,* a wife. Cf. Dut. *wijf,* Ger. *weib.*

Wyues, *n. gen. s.* wife's, 599.

Y

Yaf, *v.* 1 *p. s. pt.* I gave, 861; *pt. s.* yaf, 193, 203. See **Yiue.**

Yate, *n.* gate, 1013. M. E. forms, *gate, yate*—A.S. *geat,* a gate, opening; cog. with Dut. *gat,* a hole, gap. Originally 'a way to *get* in,' from A.S. *gæt,* pt. t. of *gitan,* to get.

Ybore, *pp.* born, 158, 310, 484, also borne, 443; **yborn,** 72; **yboren,** 626. A.S. *beran,* pp. *geboren.*

Ydel, *adj.* idle, 217. A.S. *ídel,* vain; cog. with Dut. *ijdel,* Ger. *eitel.*

Ydressed, *pp.* dressed, 381. See **Dresse.**

Ye, *adv.* yea, 355. The simple affirmative; *yes* is a strengthened form often accompanied by an oath in our early writers. A.S. *geá;* cog. with Dut. Swedish and Ger. *ja,* Icel. *já.*

Ye, *n.* eye, 37; **at yë** = to sight, 1168; *pl.* yen, 669. M. E. *eye, eighe,* pl. *eyes, eyen* (whence *eyne*)—A.S. *eáge,* pl. *eágan.* Cf. Dut. *oog,* Icel. *auga,* Ger. *auge.*

Ye, *pron.* ye, 508. A.S. *ge,* nominative; *eówer,* gen. ; *eów,* dat. and acc.

Yeer, *n.* a year, 402; *pl.* yeer, years, 610. A.S. *geár, gér,* pl. *geár;* cog. with Dut. *jaar,* Ger. *jahr.*

Yelden, *v.* to yield, 843. A.S. *gieldan, gildan,* pt. t. *geald,* pp. *golden,* to pay, give up ; cog. with Dut. *gelden,* to pay, Ger. *gelten,* to be worth.

Yerde, *n.* yard, rod, 22. A.S. *gyrd, gierd,* a rod ; cog. with Dut. *garde,* Ger. *gerte.*

Yeuen, *pp.* given, 758. See **Yiue.**

Yfere, *adv.* together, 1113.

Yfeyned, *pp.* feigned, 529. O. Fr. *feindre*—L. *fingere,* to form, feign.

Yfostred, *pp.* fostered, 213. A.S. *fóstrian*—*fóstor,* food.

Yit, *adv.* yet ; **as yit** = hitherto, 120. A.S. *git, get, giet,* moreover.

Yiue, *v.* to give, 1034 ; *pr. s.* yiueth, gives, 93 ; *pr. s. imp.* yiue, may he give, 30. M. E. *geuen, yeuen,* pt. *yaf* or *gaf,* pp. *yiuen, gifen, youen*—A.S. *gifan,* pt. *geaf,* pp. *gifen.*

Ylyke, *adv.* alike, 602, 754. A.S. *gelíce.*

Ymagining, *pr. part.* imagining, 598. Through Fr. from L. *imaginari.*

Ynde, India, 1199.

Ynough, *adv.* enough, 75, 365. The *y* or *ge-* here is a mere prefix. A.S. *genóh, genóg,* pl. *genoge*—*geneáh,* it suffices ; cog. with Dut. *genoeg,* Ger. *genug.*

Yond, *adv.* yonder, 1199. A.S. *geon,* yon.

Yonge, *adj. def.* young, 777 ; *voc.* 1093. A.S. *geong;* cog. with Dut. *jong,* Ger. *jung,* etc.

Yore, *adv.* formerly, 1140 ; for a long time, 68. A.S. *geára* (adv.), formerly, literally 'of years,' originally gen. pl. of *geár,* a year.

Your, *pron.* your, 128, 567, etc. A.S. *eówer,* your, originally gen. of *ge,* ye.

Yow, *pron.* you, 105, 154, etc. A.S. *eów,* dat. and acc. of pronoun *ge.*

Yprayed, *pp.* asked to come, 269. M. E. *preyen*—O. Fr. *preier* (Fr. *prier*)—*precari,* to pray.

Yronne, *pp.* run, 214. A.S. *rinnan,* pt. *rann,* pp. *gerunnen;* cog. with Ger. and Dut. *rennen.*

Yset, *pp.* set, 409. A.S. *settan,* to set, to make to sit, causal of *sittan,* to sit. Cf. Icel. *setja,* Ger. *setzen,* Dut. *zetten.*

Yuel, *adv.* ill, 460, 965. A.S. *yfel,* (adj. and n.); cog. with Dut. *euvel,* Ger. *übel,* Icel. *illr.*

Ywedded, *pp.* wedded, 771. A.S. *weddian,* to pledge, betroth--A.S. *wed,* a pledge ; cog. with Icel. *vedh,* Ger. *wette,* etc.

EXAMINATION QUESTIONS.

1. Write a short account of the life of Chaucer, with the names and supposed dates of his principal poems.

2. What do you understand by Middle English, and what are its characteristics as distinguished from earlier and later English?

3. What were the principal varieties of English in Chaucer's time, and what are the chief distinguishing marks of each?

4. What were the case-endings of Chaucer's nouns?

5. Give the etymology of the following: *Abayst, acquyte, agast, alayes, algate, alwey, array, assay, astonied, aswowne, asure, bachelrye, blesse, carie, cote* (a coat), *entraille, felaw, hest, housbond, kepe, lent, lordshipe, markis, outraye, owen, persone, plowman, quaille, rewthe, sclaundre, scourge, sely, sergeant, sikerly, sklendre, sleighte, solempne, sooth, souereyn, spousaille, swelwe, swough, therefore, threshfold, throp, tyding, vnnethe, voyden, waille, wantoun, wight, wikke,* and *ynough.*

6. Explain fully the following words and phrases: *In euery maner wyse; al had hir leuer haue born a knaue child; ful ofte sythe; hath doon yow kepe; it is no drede; as beth of bettre chere; vndern; a furlong wey or two; flokmele; herbergage; threshfold; tretys; nowches; barm; a lyues creature; dayes fele; after his fader day; more and lesse; yuel biseye; gan his herte dresse; auentaille; four yeer; but it be falle of newe; dere ynough a Iane; mo; Chicheuache.*

7. Name the various significations of the final *e* in Chaucer with regard to nouns and adjectives, both as marking derivation and inflection.

8. Give some account of the sources from which Chaucer derived the story of the *Clerkes Tale.*

9. Give some account of the measure of the *Clerkes Tale,* and of the *Envoy.*

10. What is the history of the words: *Wonted,* the *to-* in 'all to-brake,' *arn, knaue, thewes, thilke,* and *sely?*

11. Discuss the adverbs in Middle English; what are their terminations, and what is the origin of these?

12. What is Chaucer's place among English poets, and to what qualities as a poet does he owe it?

Edinburgh: Printed by W. & R. Chambers, Limited.

The Clerkes Tale.

The main part of this tale is a rather close translation of Petrarch who himself learned the story from Boccaccio. It is the very last tale — the tenth tale of the tenth day in the Decamerone written shortly after the year 1348. (vide English note)

Chaucer follows Petrarch almost word for word in many passages though Petrarch by no means closely follows Boccaccio. We may conclude therefore that Chaucer & Petrarch met at Padua early in 1373; that Petrarch told Chaucer the story by word of mouth either in French or Italian; & that Chaucer shortly after obtained a copy of P's Latin version which he kept constantly before him whilst making his own translation